THE PLATINUM WORKFORCE

THE PLATINUM WORKFORCE

HOW TO TRAIN AND HIRE
FOR THE 21st CENTURY'S
INDUSTRIAL TRANSITIONS

TROND ARNE UNDHEIM

ANTHEM PRESS

Anthem Press
An imprint of Wimbledon Publishing Company
www.anthempress.com

This edition first published in UK and USA 2026
by ANTHEM PRESS
75–76 Blackfriars Road, London SE1 8HA, UK
or PO Box 9779, London SW19 7ZG, UK
and
244 Madison Ave #116, New York, NY 10016, USA

British Library Cataloguing-in-Publication Data
A catalogue record for this book is available from the British Library.

Library of Congress Cataloging-in-Publication Data: 2025910921
A catalog record for this book has been requested.

ISBN-13: 978-1-83999-458-6 (Hbk)
ISBN-10: 1-83999-458-4 (Hbk)

Cover Credit: ©Trond Arne Undheim

This title is also available as an eBook.

Dedicated to my children, Naya (18), Jax (16), and Zadie (12), who will face the challenge of finding their place, honing their skills, educating themselves, finding jobs, and shaping the platinum workforce, industry, and society in the coming decades. This year, Naya graduated High School. I thought of her throughout the writing process. Each time I ask her what she wants to do, mindful that the world will change many times over during her work life, I continue to be amazed at her zest for life and ideas about the future. The other day, she told me "I want to figure out why people do the things that they do." What a laudable goal. For that reason, this book is particularly aimed towards Naya, to help her hone her aspirations, reach her goals, and shepherd humanity in this next phase. I'm tremendously proud of her. She will enter college. She will interface with AI. She faces global turmoil. And, I would add, let's also figure out why machines do the things they do and what happens when humans and machines work together, when it works, and when it fails.

CONTENTS

PREFACE

The advances of technology are not lost on anyone. Neither is the accelerating tension in society due to inequality, oligarchy, human ambition, and a renewed interest in territorial conquest among the world's rulers. I wrote this book to reflect on the major changes that, as a result, will befall the nature of work, industrial development, and, as a result, societal evolution. This is a major management challenge, particularly because as complexity and scale compound, industry, society, and governments alike are increasingly facing grand challenges. Among those, the role of artificial intelligence, the sustainability challenge, and achieving global health access occupy me the most at this time.

I wanted to ground such a reflection in the very tangible challenge of entering the workforce, making a difference, and making a living. For me, having children in high school brings this topic to the forefront. They are making decisions such as whether and which college to apply to, which professions to target, what knowledge to seek, how to specialize, what general insights to draw from, and where to do internships. These were never easy questions. Now, with the complexity of society, and the speed and scope of change, they are akin to rocket science.

This book is in several ways a continuation of work I began during my PhD work 27 years ago, back in 1998, on the influx of nomadic work. From that, in 2002 I produced a book entitled *Leadership from Below*, which outlined trends that seemed to emerge from the early impact of the world wide web on knowledge work. Since then, I have written six more books, each tackling a related challenge. *Pandemic Aftermath* (2020) sought to reflect on how COVID-19 would change the world. *Disruption Games* (2020) explained how to thrive on serial failure, as a startup founder or venture capitalist. *Health Tech* (2021) tackled the conundrum that technology has yet to fundamentally transform the health sector. *Future Tech* (2021) gave advice on how to capture value from disruptive industry trends and picked five emerging technologies as consequential in the coming decade: AI, synthetic biology, 3D printing, blockchain, and robot-ics. *Augmented Lean* (2022), co-authored with serial entrepreneur Natan Linder of Formlabs, Inc. and Tulip Interfaces, Inc., outlined the emerging human-centric paradigm of augmented lean management of frontline operations in manufacturing and advanced industrial production. *Eco Tech* (2023) charted a path forward toward investing in regenerative futures through a mix of tech-nology, societal visions, and ecological insights. After that, I conducted a two-year research project at Stanford on existential risk, exploring risk scenarios for 2075, fifty years into the future. I'm currently working on a book to com-municate findings from that study. That book will hopefully come out in 2026.

Books can still make a difference, though their impact might be subtle. I'm sticking to this belief. I invite you to read, reflect, and act. I'm writing this book for my children, and for my nephews and nieces who will take over this world, along with the hope that it can also benefit your own children, nephews, and nieces as you read this book. Their task will not be easy. Without a doubt, there will be nearly insurmountable challenges. But they must go on. To ensure we can still be bewildered, to ensure we can still build and thrive, we must hone human skills. Doing so, in my view, entails reflecting on and experienc-ing augmentation in all of its forms, and attempting to integrate changing and confusing patterns, technologies, values, and ambitions into a coherent whole.

Technology is advancing to the point where it can soon take over many tasks formerly done by humans. I am thoroughly thankful for being able to use Gemini 1.5 Flash, a language model from Google that's designed to pro-cess text, images, audio, video, and code, yet optimized for speed and effi-ciency, extensively in the drafting of this book. Flash can process 1 million tokens, roughly equivalent to 1 hour of video, 11 hours of audio, codebases with over 30,000 lines of code, or over 700,000 words. Toward the very end of the writing process, the new AI model, 2.0 Flash Thinking Experimental, was released, and I was able to integrate some of its more transparent reasoning features and expanded capabilities.

I first want to clarify that the core thesis, with the thirteen futuristic skills which is displayed on the book cover, was developed entirely without AI. As to how it coalesced into twelve skills, this is a hard question to answer. We are struggling to describe how machine reasoning works. But the human cognitive process is equally hard to explain. At the end of the day, all I can say is that it is the result of my 30 years of reflection on the future of work.

As for using AI, I used it iteratively, not on whole bodies of text or across the whole book. It helped me revise scenarios, provide further ideas when I was stuck, and enhanced my grammar and sentence structure. It also played a key role in drafting the micro-chapters on specific emerging work roles and skills (Human+, Interoperability Catalyst, R&D Hacker, Socio-Technician, Eco-Strategist, Maker, and Systems Thinker). I also experimented with various other chatbots, including free versions of ChatGPT (GPT-4), Anthropic (Claude 3.5 and 3.7 Sonnet), Google (Gemini 2.0), Microsoft Copilot, Meta AI (Llama 3.5), Alibaba (Qwen 2.5), Mistral (Le Chat), XAI (Grok 2.0, eventually 3.0), Deepseek (Deepseek V3), and Perplexity. In fact, I often pitted them against each other or used them explicitly to check the quality of each model's work and to reduce the potential for hallucinations. I wish I had had time to create my own agentic workflow, but the importance of that will be discussed in this book. I will note that I often was informed that I had hit the Free plan limit and either had to wait several hours to start more queries or was redirected to a smaller AI model on the same platform. Often, the models pushed back on my queries, finding them too expansive or too time- or resource-consuming. More than half the time, Deepseek sent me the following message: "The server is busy. Please try again later." Due to how useful Claude 3.5 is, especially for analytics, I caved in and paid for a $20/month subscription to Anthropic's professional plan. I did the same for Gemini.

A strategy I had to deploy was to use smaller queries and also vary between a large number of AIs, asking one model to finish the work that another refused to complete (particularly interweaving the top five AI models at this time: Claude 3.5, Gemini 2.0 Flash, Microsoft Co-Pilot, OpenAI DeepResearch, and DeepSeek, and using them in a different order each time, depending on the quality of the interim output). Despite the competitive environment's initial price pressure, I predict that cost will be a significant barrier to the advanced use of AI, affecting anybody without a benefactor. Schools and colleges need to pay strict attention to developments in this regard, as do national governments and large companies. I struggle to understand how startups, schools, or governments will be able to afford the most advanced models, so their advantage, conceivably, has to reside in getting better people, building customized systems for new tasks they themselves create new markets for, and building well-performing early teams unencumbered by organizational lethargy and digital legacy systems.

Toward the end of the writing process, OpenAI released DeepResearch, an AI model called o3-mini available with a Reason button in ChatGPT which, according to the company, can "think before responding" with the "ability to conduct extensive exploration and cite each claim," and "independently discovers, reasons about, and consolidates insights from across the web." This is perplexing and makes you wonder what the model did before. The results, from which the book benefits, are particularly reflected in Chapter 9, which charts three futuristic scenarios. What was particularly helpful was getting AI assistance to summarize the core parts of the book, only to realize I needed to rewrite it and draw systematic lessons relevant to specific target groups, which I specified to the AIs were primarily students, parents, industrial workers, and mid-career white-collar professionals. Summarization and well-structured (but not particularly inventive) narrative, combined with coding, analytics, and image manipulation, is still where AI excels. Where it still does not perform so well is in crafting a creative narrative that caters to my distinct writer's voice. Once that happens, through personalized AI assistants, we are in for a whole other level of productivity and output for academics and writers. My best guess is that we might be three to five years away from that. At that point, book writing will have changed forever.

As such, this book is the work of the early stages of AI augmentation, an accomplishment of a developing human+. The approach was radically different from how I wrote my previous seven books. With the help of AIs, I think better, but the process is also bewildering, confusing, and error-prone. As the nature of work changes, rather than be ashamed, or abdicating to our AI overlords, I would maintain that we should seek meaning in the work that remains, but still critically examine our own behavior, the bot's behavior, and the end result. While I did save some time using AI so extensively, I also had to revise many more times to reduce the chance that the AIs had misunderstood some of my points, hallucinated, or just to add sources to various claims that were either mine or the results of AI elaborations. There is also the concern that AIs tend to steal valuable points from authors without necessarily attributing them. All of that said, the remaining mistakes are all mine.

TROND ARNE UNDHEIM'S PREVIOUS BOOKS

AUGMENTED LEAN (2023)

ECO TECH (2023)

HEALTH TECH (2021)

FUTURE TECH (2021)

PANDEMIC AFTERMATH (2020)

DISRUPTION GAMES (2020)

LEADERSHIP FROM BELOW (2002)

ACKNOWLEDGMENTS

Thank you to the incredible editorial, production, and marketing teams at Anthem Press for supporting this book, including Publisher and Managing Director Tej Sood, Jebaslin Hephzibah, Gomathy Ilammathe, Pradhiba Kumar, and Srinivasan Venkatesan.

Huge appreciation to the following mentors and supporters: Prof. Espen Moe, Sheri A. Brodeur, Dean Soumitra Dutta, Prof. Steve Luby, Prof. Emeritus Knut H. Sørensen, and Tore Tennøe.

This book is also in memoriam of my former literary agent, Esmond Harmsworth, President of Aevitas, who made the interesting choice of passing on this book because he would rather keep the focus on my next book (I was, as usual, writing two books at the same time), yet being highly supportive and still helping me negotiate the book contract with Anthem. Esmond passed away during the writing process. My thoughts at this time go to his two small kids.

Thanks to my own kids, Naya, Jax, and Zadie, for showing me how AI is already integrated into everyday life for anyone currently under 20 years old. Thanks to Priyadarshini Himatsingka for providing inspiring conversations at the crossroads of art, business, and futures. Thanks to Ciara Clark for carrying me healthfully and kindly to the finish line despite my exhaustion from life's many challenges.

Lastly, a special thanks to Avanish and Faye Sahai and the Sahai Family Foundation for donating seed money to fund my work on this book at Stanford University. I couldn't have pulled this off without you!

FIGURES AND TABLES

Figures

Tables

INTRODUCTION

Futuristic Work Is Today's Challenge

When I was a 16-year-old boy in a small coastal town in Norway, from my blue IKEA sofa bed I wrote in my diary that I was going to study history. The reason I gave was that I wanted to understand how society had evolved. I was also passionate about psychology, music, cross-country skiing, hiking in nature, and books. But by a strange coincidence, I never became a professional historian, musician, librarian, or psychologist. This despite having an extraordinarily inspiring history teacher at Branford High School called Thomas A. Murray. Despite spending an hour every morning playing a classical guitar named "Andreas" after my electric guitar teacher Gunnar Andreas Berg in Trondheim, built by Swedish luthier Georg Bolin in 1975. Despite taking out a big plastic bag full of books from my local library two days a week for a decade from when I was 6 to 16. Despite studying under renowned classical guitarist Stephen Aron. Despite punching survey data into computers at my dad's psychology lab at the University of Trondheim. Despite a whole array of other things that happened, including studying all across Europe, inheriting all my dad's psychology books as he passed away at age 51, or attending an elite Saturday school for musical talent in my hometown, Trondheim. All of these were formative experiences that could have drawn me in at least five different directions.

Rather, I became a socio-technical historian of the future and a teacher of entrepreneurship, obsessed with cognitive habits. Let me explain. Instead of spending my time in historical archives, I engage with emerging technology. Instead of practicing classical guitar for five hours a day, I only practice for one hour and have time to explore a wider set of hobbies, including running and skiing. Instead of building the next libraries of Alexandria, I simply indulge in books at home. Instead of surveying kids about intellectual abilities and career choices, I get to explore the evolving role of knowledge and insight across society. Instead of editing the books of others, I write books. But most of all, I am

FIGURE 0.1 The making of a futurist.

an educator, of myself and of others. This might be because both of my parents were educators. It's in the blood.

Having said all that, there has been something fundamentally wrong with how talent is selected for jobs over the past few decades. So far, Artificial Intelligence (AI) has exacerbated rather than improved the issue. Let me take myself as an example. I made a count of all the jobs I have applied for. The number was around 500 jobs. In the period preceding my current position, I applied to 164 jobs and got three interviews. I have had 17 jobs in my career so far, which spans 30 years. This includes military, nonprofit think tanks, big corporations, intergovernmental organizations, governments, start-ups, universities, and colleges. How many of those jobs did I get through an open application? I would say, to be generous, perhaps one or two. For a few of those, I reached out to my network and somehow a door opened for me. For the most part, I was lucky enough to be headhunted either by weak links (which led to surprising opportunities) or strong links (which have a high success rate in more targeted ways) in my network. That feels good on a personal level. It might mean at least a few key people feel I can contribute something. On a societal level, however, it feels horrible. This means I was singled out, encouraged to apply, and shepherded through the selection process. What's wrong with that? Perhaps nothing, legally speaking. But it does mean I had more than an equal chance. Every time it happened, I knew. Every time it did not happen, I also knew. There have been jobs I really wanted. Jobs I was close to getting. The only difference between my candidacy and that of others might have been that the current position holder knew somebody. I would say that I have roughly had the skills required for the jobs I have occupied. I have also had to learn a lot on the fly. Was the job description, resume, or references in any way accurate about the job content, needed accomplishments, or my merits? Scarcely. Each of the data inputs is skewed, full of PR, and not accurate in terms of the precise skills needed, acquired, or possessed.

In my current career, I explore societal trends. I study cascading risks. I deal with entrepreneurs. I try to foster innovation in myself and others. But rather than celebrate everything new, I also worry about change. I question progress. I want to look at what's further ahead. Is it good? Is it what we want? How can we shape the future? And also, what can we learn from the past?

A futurist cannot operate without history because the future does not exist without the past. Our current society leaves breadcrumbs. And if we follow them, we can see toward the future. This is not magic. It is hard work. Also because the future's not set. It is a choice. The challenge is that these choices are made far ahead of time. If we care to look, we find out. Most people don't see the future this way. It's perhaps easier to think that what will happen will happen. Or that we, as individuals, cannot shape it. I disagree. We must look for plausible solutions, possible futures. Based on that, we can craft scenarios. Those scenarios we can prepare for. And when one of them, or a combination of them happens, we are better suited to respond.

In the time to come, popular ideas of what's required are likely to change on a nearly annual basis, if not more. It used to be that change was slow. Futurists were crazy academics who mused about progress, technology, and strange inventions. Then came the web in 1996, and people who suddenly had unbounded information at their fingertips thought they could challenge the knowledge of their doctors, teachers, and dentists. Then came the year 2007 when Apple took off, and everyone thinks they are a futurist innovator just because they have an iPhone in their hand. The last few years saw the arrival of ChatGPT and a plethora of follow-on generative AI, which makes most people think they live in the future and don't need futurists anymore. They think the future is AI, without really knowing what that means. They can also generate detailed, seemingly impressive, futuristic musings at the touch of a button. There is immense excitement, but also worry. What will happen to work? Will I have a career? Will machines take over? The future of work has become a meme, as if we are living in it already, continuously. And maybe we are.

Does that mean that we can give up planning? Yes and no. The workforce needed even just over the next three to five years is not what experts in government, industry, or academia expected just three years ago. Things have changed. And they will change again. But no, the reason is not just AI, it's far more complex than that. But how to figure out what matters, now and going forward, is not a question we can outsource to anybody else. As parents, teachers, professionals, executives, workers, experts, as a young person going into the workplace, or even as citizens, we need to know. Because it impacts our livelihood, competitiveness, and happiness—even our survival. And the key to unlocking it is to think big. But to think big, we need visions, tools, competences, and resources. For simplicity, we can call them skills. Workforce survival skills for the twenty-first century. That's what this book is about.

Work is important to all of us. It has been for all of humanity, as far as I can tell. There are hundreds of words that refer to a worker or the act of working. Given how the numbers have traditionally worked out, most of them refer to folks lower in the hierarchy who serve others in specific capacities or functions and are not necessarily highly skilled (Figure 0.2). All of this is about to change. In some ways it has already changed. We might all end up as servants. There are hundreds of terms for what we might become. Prince Harry, perhaps. A spare. If we are not careful. That's why I wrote this book.

Clearly, dozens if not more of these terms are derogatory in various ways. Just think of Lackey: Implies subservience and weakness; Minion: Suggests a lack of independent thought or importance; Peon: Denotes low social status and being exploited; Serf: Highlights a lack of freedom and being bound to servitude; Skivvy: Refers to a low-level, menial worker; Slave: The ultimate term of dehumanization, implying ownership and forced labor; Subaltern: While technically a military term, it can imply a lack of authority or importance; Underling: Suggests being insignificant and subordinate; Workhorse: Can imply being overworked and underappreciated; Dogsbody: Used in British English meaning someone who does all the dirty work. The degree to which these terms are considered derogatory can depend on context, tone, and the

FIGURE 0.2 Words meaning worker, servant, or tradesman (using Wordclouds.com).

relationship between the speaker and the person being addressed. To refer to a worker as a "woman" or "girl" is clearly also derogatory in a contemporary context.

These terms are a mix of administrative, service, and specialist roles. There are terms directly referring to hierarchical authority, such as junior, right-hand, reportee, second, subordinate, understudy, or wingman. There are pure occupational descriptors such as employee or partner. There are specific job roles, such as agent, secretary, bodyguard, or clerk, or even occupations, such as administrator, artist, banker, broker, craftsperson, curator, farm-hand, machinist, manufacturer, painter, salesman, shopkeeper, or student. Interestingly, there are a few terms that specifically refer to contingency or replacement. These are roles that only come into play if something goes wrong, or the regular labor is out, such as alternate, backup, spare, temporary (temp worker), understudy. For example, *Alternate*: Someone who takes over if the primary person is unavailable; *Backup*: A person or thing that can be relied on if the usual one fails; *Reserve*: A person or thing kept ready for use if needed; *Reservist*: A member of a reserve military force; *Spare*: An extra person, thing, or part kept in case another is needed; *Stand-in*: A person who takes the place of another temporarily; *Temporary*: Lasting for only a limited period of time; not permanent; *Understudy*: An actor who learns the part of another actor in a play so that they can take their place if necessary. We are used to humans performing those roles. With technology, it is tempting to assume that machines now will fulfill these dirty, dull or dangerous, or redundant roles, but will that necessarily be the case? What if human workers are the assistants and AIs are better suited as our managers? You have to wonder.

How could there be so many different terms? My best guess is because work is fundamental to being human. We have worked since time began. Work has been part of human life for at least a few thousand years. It began with hunter-gatherers. Yes, even the earliest form of work required collaboration within groups to survive. With settled societies, specialized roles like farming, crafting, and leadership emerged, leading to a more defined division of labor. It has played a key role in industrial society since the 1750s. Diderot's *Encyclopédie* (Vol. IV, 1752), a major work of the French Enlightenment that aimed to organize all knowledge in a way that was accessible to the general public, contained an illustration depicting the cooperative production process for making pins.

This was documented by Scottish economist and philosopher Adam Smith in *The Wealth of Nations* in 1776, who felt a division of labor was a key driver of economic progress and productivity gains by specializing tasks among workers. His go-to example was a hypothetical pin factory. In the third paragraph, Smith wrote: "The important business of making a pin is, in this manner, divided into about eighteen distinct operations, which, in some manufactories, are all performed by distinct hands, though in others the same man will sometimes perform two or three of them." Smith theorized that one worker alone might make 20 pins in a day. But 10 men working in a factory that used the division of labor principle could make as many pins as 4,800 workers in a factory that didn't. That example became the most famous description of an industrial process in the history of economic thought. Well, aside from the fact that Smith misunderstood pin-making, which at the time consisted of eight or nine specialized trades, not eighteen as Smith claimed (Conversable Economist 2022). One reason seems to be that the process of cutting the pins was hard to divide at the time. French sociologist Emile Durkheim considers the development of

FIGURE 0.3 Pin factory. Source: Diderot's *Encyclopédie* (1762) public domain.

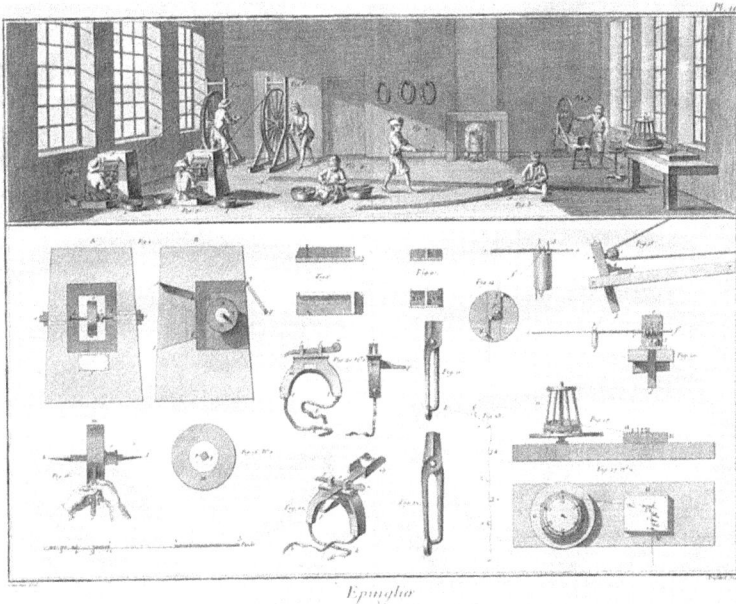

Epingliœ

the division of labor to be associated with the increasing contact among people (Durkheim 1984).

The idea of the division of labor is traditionally tied to systems of mass production. Mass production began in the eighteenth century and became more prominent during the American Industrial Revolution in the late nineteenth century, with inventor Eli Whitney famously mass-producing muskets for the army. In the twentieth century, mechanization (the use of machines) and automation (the use of machines to perform tasks without human intervention) in combination made the production of standardized products faster and at lower cost. In fact, it is one of the basic organizing principles of the assembly line. By 1918, the American Engineering Standards Committee (AESC) was formed, the precursor to what in 1969 became the American National Standards Institute, Inc (ANSI).

Why the T-shaped Talent Metaphor Falls Short

Experts, career counselors, and parents alike are constantly grappling with how to advise aspiring trainees, students, or offspring on how to develop the right skills to move ahead in life, work, and develop independence. Historically, this was not a hard task; it just consisted of making a choice. Should you prioritize what you saw as innate talents in the less experienced, or would you advise based on what was lucrative? Even that choice was fraught with tension. Today, the choice is different. An expert might not know what the future of their field will look like. A career counselor would be bewildered by the abundance of choice. A parent would be wise to disregard their own experience and would do well to examine their own prejudices, soundness of judgment, and sources of insight. The world is moving faster.

We've inverted the hierarchy of professional capabilities by positioning STEM skills as the summit of education rather than as foundational tools. Technical proficiency, while essential, operates within well-defined parameters with clear solutions. In contrast, the abilities developed through liberal arts education—such as complex problem-solving, nuanced communication, and ethical reasoning—tackle challenges with no clear answers and require sophisticated judgment.

This suggests a reframing: Technical literacy should be viewed as a prerequisite, similar to basic numeracy or writing, rather than the end goal of higher education. The more challenging and valuable skills involve synthesizing diverse perspectives, navigating ambiguity, and understanding human and societal implications of decisions. Business practice already reflects this reality, as technical experts typically report to leaders distinguished by their strategic thinking and organizational understanding rather than technical prowess.

Educational institutions should therefore integrate technical literacy throughout the curriculum while maintaining primary focus on developing these more sophisticated capabilities. This approach better aligns with the reality that while technical skills enable the creation of new tools, meaningful innovation and leadership require the broader analytical and communication capabilities traditionally developed through liberal arts education.

The Evolution of Liberal Arts Education

The original function of liberal arts education was to prepare free citizens for active participation in civic life. The Code of Hammurabi, a Babylonian legal text dating back to 1750 BC, required artisans to teach their craft to youth. One of the most documented skills is the training of scribes, implying a structured system of learning under a master craftsman. This practice facilitated the transmission of skills and knowledge within families and trades across generations. Ancient Greece's well-rounded education (Gr. *eukuklios paideia*) emphasized *philosophy* training interspersed with grammar, rhetoric, logic, arithmetic, geometry, astronomy, and music. The Roman Empire saw the additional need for training in the emerging field of law, preparing for a growing government function, and for officers in military service. Learning draining (hydraulics), mining, metalworking, road planning, and road construction from the Etruscans, they trained architects with rudimentary engineering skills sufficient to design/build arches, aqueducts, and fortified military camps. The word "architect" comes from the Greek "architekton" which means "master builder." Medieval Europe's strongest institution, the Catholic Church shifted the focus toward theology and developed scholastic thinking in monasteries and universities. The system of apprenticeship as a large-scale phenomenon first developed in the Late Middle Ages and came to be supervised by craft guilds and town governments. The word "apprentice" refers to a young person who was legally bound to a master craftsman to learn a trade. The apprentice would work without pay for a set period of time, usually seven years. Apprenticeships were a vital part of the European economy and society during the Renaissance. The Renaissance shifted focus onto individual expression and creativity and renewed the Greek and Roman emphasis on philosophy through humanism.

Moving toward today's challenges, as Allan Bloom warned in *The Closing of the American Mind* (1987), when higher education loses its grounding in philosophical inquiry and civic meaning, it risks becoming hollow, even when technologically advanced. Today's expanding menu of skills systems may deliver efficiency, but without a common intellectual foundation, they may fail to cultivate thoughtful, critically aware citizens. The challenge, then, is not just to diversify how we learn—but to remember why we learn in the first place.

My parents, who were born in the early post-WWII years in Norway, experienced a single-room schoolhouse in which all students of all ages are in the same space. This had its advantages, which included true collaboration across disciplines, times, and ages. That type of school typically did not have a lot of resources. It was small. No activities after school. Not diverse.

The factory model of education emerged in the late nineteenth century as industrialization transformed Western societies. Just as factories standardized production processes to create uniform products, schools adopted assembly-line approaches to education. Students were grouped by age rather than ability, moved through grades in lockstep fashion, and evaluated against standardized metrics. The school day was structured around fixed time blocks marked by bells—mirroring factory shifts. This system aimed to produce graduates with basic literacy and numeracy skills needed for industrial work, while instilling values like punctuality and compliance with authority. Classroom layouts, with desks in rows facing an instructor, reflected industrial efficiency rather than learning effectiveness. Schools were designed with classrooms as a series of boxes along a corridor. This model achieved its primary goal of mass education but at the cost of treating students as standardized units rather than individual learners with diverse needs and capabilities. Many of these industrial-era structures persist in modern education despite dramatic changes in workforce needs and our understanding of how people learn. That said, the factory model of education has evolved, and its stagnant character is a bit of a myth. Schools around the world train students to become productive members of society. Teachers do the best they can with the resources they have. In most countries, publicly funded primary education centers around building general knowledge and a sense of citizenship, not specific skills needed for various types of factory work. In fact, far from it, and because of that, a whole set of vocational schools have entered the picture trying to provide applied skills needed in industry today. The rise of factories demanded a skilled workforce, leading to the development of technical schools, trade schools, and specialized training programs.

The Modern Era expanded the curriculum to include subjects like history, literature, languages, social sciences, and fine arts. The emphasis was on developing critical thinking, problem-solving, and communication skills, essential for navigating what was seen as an increasingly complex and changing world. The twentieth century's industrialization profoundly influenced the development of university subjects, as the demand for specialized knowledge and technical expertise grew. The rapid expansion of industries required skilled professionals in engineering, chemistry, and physics, leading universities to prioritize these fields. Simultaneously, the social sciences, such as sociology and economics, emerged to address the societal impacts of industrialization, including urbanization, labor rights, and economic inequality. Interdisciplinary fields like environmental studies gained traction in response to the ecological consequences of industrial growth, while technological advancements spurred the creation of new disciplines like computer science and automation. Universities adapted to industrialization by producing graduates equipped to drive innovation, manage complex systems, and tackle the challenges of a rapidly changing world.

The twentieth century saw the emergence of mass education systems, with a focus on standardized testing and academic achievement. A strong emphasis on specialized knowledge within specific disciplines (e.g., history, literature, philosophy). The way things were taught was through a one-way transmission model between teacher and student. This is where the strange age cohort classroom with one subject per hour-style learning emerged. Despite its obvious shortcomings, including a sharp evolution in pedagogical insight, because of its superficial efficiencies, we have never gotten completely rid of it.

In the twenty-first century, the pendulum swung back. Globalization, tech, and the knowledge economy necessitated continuous skill development to remain competitive. Specialization was not enough and schools and employers began to emphasize interdisciplinarity. Addressing contemporary global challenges, such as climate change, social justice, and technological advancements, demanded collaboration. Fostering connections between different fields of knowledge became a priority. With that, came the focus on developing so-called "essential" twenty-first-century skills such as critical thinking, problem-solving, creativity, communication, collaboration, and digital literacy. The notion itself is shaped by the nonprofit organization, Partnership for 21st Century Learning (P21), which is now disbanded. This organization, founded in 2002, includes core subjects, learning, tech literacy, business-related, innovation skills, and life and career skills in its notion of twenty-first century skills. By 2009, Bernie Trilling and Charles Fadel had formulated the 7C skills model (Fadel and Trilling 2009), using three key skills categories: learning and innovations skills; digital literacy skills; and life and career skills. By 2016, 100 countries had embraced the twenty-first-century skills terminology according to Brookings Institution, the U.S. think tank. As a quick observation, this framework has not aged well. The "21st century skills" framework, while identifying important capabilities like critical thinking and collaboration, failed to anticipate how AI would fundamentally reshape human work. Its focus on basic digital literacy and information management appears dated when AI can handle these tasks. Instead of teaching people to process information efficiently, we need to develop uniquely human capabilities that AI cannot easily replicate—like contextual judgment, ethical reasoning, and cross-domain synthesis. This type of analysis needs to be carried out at unprecedented scale and by a wide slate of the working population, not just an elite few.

The framework also missed the growing importance of "meta-learning"—rapidly adapting to new tools and unlearning obsolete approaches. Most critically, its emphasis on individual skills may be misplaced. As AI matches human performance in specific tasks, our distinctive value may lie more in collective capabilities: orchestrating collaboration, building trust across diverse groups, and effectively partnering with AI while maintaining human agency.

Since the early 2000s, colleges and universities have significantly expanded experiential learning (EL) opportunities. The proportion of undergraduates completing internships rose from ~40 percent in 2000 to over 60 percent by

2020 ("Evidence-Based Improvement in Higher Education," n.d.). Service-learning courses now exist at over 80 percent of institutions (Drewery and Lollar 2024; Schultes 2025), and project-based learning is common in business as well as in engineering programs. EL's growth reflects employer demands and evidence of improved student outcomes: EL participation correlates with higher employment rates and salaries. These benefits are strongest for first-generation and underrepresented students. Access to quality EL remains uneven, with fewer resources at public universities and barriers created by unpaid internships. To address this, institutions should expand paid opportunities (Creating WOW Communications 2015).

This also rendered education more expensive, time-consuming, and labor-intensive. As a result, there were strains on the business model of colleges. The concept of lifelong learning also became prominent in the second half of the twentieth century, gaining traction alongside shifts in economic policy, technological advancement, and changing labor markets. Originally championed by international bodies such as UNESCO and the OECD in the 1960s and 1970s, lifelong learning was framed as a democratic ideal—enabling individuals to adapt, grow, and participate fully in society across their lifespan. It marked a departure from the traditional model of front-loaded education, which presumed that formal schooling early in life was sufficient. As industries automated and the pace of innovation accelerated, lifelong learning became not just a moral imperative, but an economic necessity. By the early twenty-first century, the term had expanded to encompass not only formal education, but also informal, nonformal, and digital learning pathways, reinforcing the idea that adaptability, not mastery, would define the educated citizen (OECD 2004; Field 2006). Many colleges shifted toward preparing students to be active and engaged global citizens, capable of understanding and navigating an interconnected world.

With the advances in digital platforms, and the gamification model, came the influx of digital learning platforms. The rapid proliferation of digital learning platforms has fundamentally transformed educational delivery and access, reshaping how knowledge is disseminated and consumed globally. Starting with early Learning Management Systems (LMS) like Blackboard in the late 1990s, the sector evolved through several distinct phases, each marked by technological advancements, shifting pedagogical paradigms, and societal needs. Early LMS platforms such as Blackboard, Moodle, and Sakai laid the groundwork for digitizing education by enabling institutions to host course materials online, facilitate discussion forums, and manage assignments. However, these systems were often criticized for being clunky, overly focused on administrative functions, and lacking interactivity. A study by Picciano (Picciano 2016) highlighted that many educators struggled to adapt traditional teaching methods to these rigid platforms, leading to underutilization or superficial integration into curricula.

The second phase was defined by the rise of Massive Open Online Courses (MOOCs), spearheaded by platforms like Coursera, edX, and Udacity. MOOCs demonstrated the potential for scaling education to millions of learners worldwide, with Coursera reporting over 100 million registered users as of 2022. However, this phase also exposed significant challenges, particularly low completion rates, which often hovered around 5–15 percent (Jordan 2014; Hew and Cheung 2014). Critics argued that MOOCs failed to address issues of engagement, motivation, and learner support, which are critical for sustained participation. In response to these limitations, the third phase saw the emergence of specialized platforms targeting niche skills and professional development. Platforms like Codecademy, LinkedIn Learning, and Duolingo succeeded by addressing specific learner needs and incorporating engaging design elements. For example, Duolingo's use of gamification increased daily active users to over 500 million as of 2023, demonstrating the power of interactive and adaptive approaches.

The fourth phase was accelerated by the COVID-19 pandemic, which acted as a catalyst for the widespread adoption of digital learning platforms. Institutions worldwide were forced to pivot to remote instruction overnight, accelerating investments in tools like Canvas, Brightspace, and Google Classroom. Global edtech funding surged to $20 billion in 2020–2023 reflecting the urgent demand for scalable solutions during COVID-19, but has since abated due to disappointments in delivery and business models (Rauf 2025). This period also highlighted existing inequities, as students without reliable internet access or devices faced significant barriers—a phenomenon known as the "digital divide." UNESCO estimates that half of the world's population lacks internet access, exacerbating inequalities in educational opportunities.

The latest evolution in digital learning platforms centers on adaptive learning systems powered by AI. These systems analyze learner behavior and performance to deliver personalized content, ensuring that each student progresses at their own pace. Notable examples include Knewton Alta, an adaptive platform used in higher education to provide customized math and science instruction, and DreamBox, a K-12 platform that adjusts difficulty levels dynamically based on student responses. Additionally, sophisticated assessment tools have moved beyond multiple-choice tests to incorporate project-based evaluations, simulations, and peer reviews. For instance, Turnitin's

Gradescope allows instructors to grade complex assignments efficiently while maintaining academic integrity. Despite these advancements, several challenges persist, including the digital divide, outdated pedagogical methods, and data privacy concerns. The collection and analysis of learner data raise ethical questions about consent, transparency, and security, with regulations like the European Union's GDPR imposing strict guidelines on how educational platforms handle personal information.

Successful digital learning platforms have transcended merely digitizing textbooks or lecture slides, instead creating immersive, interactive experiences that complement face-to-face instruction. For example, Labster offers virtual science labs where students can conduct experiments in a simulated environment, while Nearpod integrates multimedia content, quizzes, and collaborative activities into live lessons, enhancing engagement. Moreover, hybrid models combining online and in-person components have gained traction. A meta-analysis by Means et al. (2013) found that blended learning approaches consistently outperform purely online or offline formats, underscoring the value of integrating technology thoughtfully (Means et al. 2009). The expansion of digital learning platforms represents a remarkable achievement and an ongoing challenge. By leveraging AI, fostering inclusivity, and reimagining pedagogy, these platforms hold strong potential to democratize education. However, addressing persistent issues like the digital divide, data privacy, and teacher training will be crucial for realizing this vision. Improved technology is also no panacea for EdTech where many other factors matter more.

The passive model of knowledge transmission was (in theory at least) replaced by more active and engaged learning experiences. Despite that, because of the large numbers of students that were needed to finance their existence, the lecture style continued in early college education, at least at the Freshman levels. At the same time, as the workplace evolved toward a service-based economy which also demanded more communication and interaction with colleagues, customers, and markets, a focus on specific job skills evolved toward more broadly applicable skills such as critical thinking, creativity, and communication. This focus was often more aspirational than real. Mandatory corporate training programs also shifted toward DEI and regulatory mandates, ethics courses, safety, environmental issues, standardization, quality of production, lean.

In the United States, the apprenticeship concept got tainted by The Emancipation Act of 1833. There was a period of time after emancipation until it was abolished in 1838 when formerly enslaved people were required to work for their former owners for up to eight years. The system was intended to be a gradual transition from slavery to freedom. Still today, apprenticeships are seen as a way to fill skill gaps and provide career paths. That said, it is not institutionalized across education the way it once was. With that, a lot is lost.

What's different now is not only the rapid emergence of AI, but also the growing societal complexity in general which creates the urgent need for fostering systemic thinking and all of this whole book's topics. The rise of automation and AI is disrupting the labor market, requiring workers to develop skills that complement, rather than compete with, these technologies and complexities.

Future Development

As the urgency of upskilling intensifies across industries and societies, models of skills development are undergoing profound transformation. Many observers anticipate a shift toward more integrated approaches—models that blend academic knowledge with practical application, critical thinking, digital fluency, and social-emotional learning. These emerging systems reflect an understanding that knowledge alone is not enough; learners must also develop adaptability, resilience, and collaboration skills to thrive in uncertain environments. Increasingly, personalized pathways—tailored to individual strengths, preferences, and real-time labor market needs—are expected to become the foundation of future-ready education. Fueled by AI and continuous feedback loops, these pathways promise to make learning more efficient, relevant, and inclusive (OECD 2023; World Economic Forum 2020).

However, this integrated model is only one possible trajectory. Other, equally plausible futures are emerging—each shaped by differing institutional actors, geographies, and value systems.

In one scenario, large corporations become the new arbiters of education. As trust in traditional degrees declines and the shelf life of skills shortens, companies begin to offer their own credentials—modular, performance-based, and tightly linked to real-time business needs. These corporate learning ecosystems prioritize practical relevance and immediate application, training workers not for abstract futures but for specific product pipelines and operational contexts. Over time, such systems may rival or even replace university programs in certain sectors, fundamentally reshaping the role of higher education (McKinsey Global Institute 2022).

A second trajectory positions cities and regions—not schools—as the heart of learning innovation. In this vision, civic institutions build open-access platforms that embed education into daily life. Community labs, public libraries, maker spaces, and digital commons become spaces of active, lifelong learning.

These civic learning commons focus less on credentials and more on solving real-world challenges—climate adaptation, public health, urban resilience. Learning becomes deeply local, problem-based, and socially embedded (Nesta 2021).

A third scenario imagines the rise of AI-guided talent cultivation. Here, autonomous systems play an active role in mapping each learner's development. Intelligent agents assess aptitude, track behavior, and recommend not only personalized content but also peer collaborators, mentors, and live project opportunities. Such systems are global, dynamic, and deeply responsive—but also raise critical questions about data privacy, equity, and algorithmic bias (Brynjolfsson and McAfee 2023).

Finally, a more sobering possibility must be considered: that of fragmented and off-grid learning. In regions destabilized by conflict, ecological collapse, or political retreat, formal education systems may falter. In their place, informal networks—families, kinship groups, community elders—become the stewards of knowledge. Here, survival skills, manual craftsmanship, oral traditions, and local knowledge once again become central. Learning is deeply analog, often intergenerational, and focused on immediate resilience rather than future planning (Turchin 2020).

What emerges from these divergent paths is not a singular future of education, but a plurality of coexisting models. In some regions and sectors, AI-guided precision learning may dominate. In others, low-tech resilience training may prove more relevant. Civic ecosystems and corporate credentialing may operate in parallel or compete for influence. The common thread across all these scenarios is the need for agility—from learners, educators, and institutions alike. In a world where no one model prevails, the ability to navigate, combine, and adapt across learning systems becomes the critical skill of all.

The core principles of liberal arts education, such as critical thinking, communication, and the pursuit of knowledge, have remained relatively constant throughout history. However, specific subjects have evolved. Liberal education is valuable for its ability to cultivate well-rounded individuals who are prepared to engage with the complexities of a changing world.

For decades, the idea of a "T-shaped" person who has skills beyond their technical expertise (e.g., both scientist or engineer and manager), meaning depth in one field, with collaboration skills across fields, has been around as an ideal.[1] The vertical line of the "T" represents the employee's deep expertise,

---

1 See (Johnston 1978) and popularized by David Guest's piece "The hunt is on for the Renaissance Man of computing," *The Independent*, September 17, 1991 and further by Tim Brown, CEO of the IDEO design consultancy.

while the horizontal line represents their broad knowledge and skills. Broadly, business skills for the twenty-first century typically are thought to include communication, cooperation, creative and critical thinking, and data-driven decision-making.[2]

The concept of a "T-shaped worker"—someone with deep expertise in one area and broad knowledge across other disciplines—is overly simplistic. To some, it is unrealistic, and can sometimes be used to pressure employees to constantly acquire new skills. However, contrary to the common critique, it is not nonsense because it is too demanding. It is nonsense because it is not ambitious enough. In today's day and age, and certainly not forward looking, it is not enough to seek T-shaped employees. Because the nature of technical expertise has changed. And because what communication is has changed. Nor will the emerging workplace just demand soft skills. Leadership from below, and leading up, taking initiative for projects of unprecedented scale matters more than before. But given the scale, the implications of failure could be costly in resources and reputation.

Instead of thinking about skills as discrete variables (unskilled, basic, intermediate, advanced, expert)—we should consider skill as a continuum. Visualize it as a gradual progression along a spectrum where different levels blend seamlessly into one another. This approach allows for a more nuanced understanding of skill development. Advancement is more gradual and subjective. Clear goals and objectives provide a sense of purpose and direction. Opportunities for regular feedback and recognition are essential. People (and machines for that matter) perform well when they are given sufficient, yet not overwhelming challenges. This concept has been described by Russian pedagogist Vygotsky as working within the proximal zone of development. Moreover, productive work can be related to the concept of flow. This is a commonly understood concept in manufacturing because ensuring the continuous flow of the assembly line without costly and time-consuming interruptions was traditionally the highest priority.

In his groundbreaking 2008 book *Flow: The Psychology of Optimal Experience*, Hungarian-American psychologist Mihály Csíkszentmihályi describes how flow (hyperfocus) is a highly focused mental state conducive to productivity. His classic example is where a skilled musician completely immerses themselves in playing a challenging piece, losing track of time and feeling a sense of enjoyment solely from the act of playing even if the piece is demanding. As

---

2 See (Baaij 2024)

a hobby-level classical guitarist, I get into this state almost every day. I can attest to the observation that the balance between skill level and challenge is key to achieving flow. As his study included interviews with scientists, athletes, musicians, artists, business executives, many examples can be produced. A surgeon performing a complex operation. A writer deeply engaged in composing a story. A skilled athlete performing in a competition. A chess player strategically analyzing a complex position.

Today, we can add more examples from the emerging workplace. A teacher actively engaging students in a lesson they are passionate about. Creative professionals such as designers, architects, or engineers during the early stages of a project. An educational game developer crafting experiences that induce flow states in players through challenging yet achievable goals, compelling narratives, and rewarding gameplay mechanics. A social entrepreneur building and scaling businesses or nonprofit organizations making a positive impact on the world. An innovation consultant fostering a culture of innovation. A creative arts therapist helping clients unlock their inner potential through art, music, or movement. A lifelong learner continuously pursuing knowledge and skills, exploring new subjects and challenging oneself intellectually throughout their life. A space explorer embarking on long-duration space missions, pushing the boundaries of human endurance. A programmer coding a complex solution with a deep understanding of the problem. A bioethicist promoting responsible innovation navigating the complexities of emerging technologies such as gene editing. An AI researcher pushing the boundaries of what AI and humans can do together. A cybersecurity specialist responding to cyberattacks in real-time. A human being (controller, data scientist, quality manager) entering a symbiosis with the AI system they are overseeing.

Ensuring a high quality supply of workers who can become symbiotic with AIs is key to our human future. A healthcare professional in a high-pressure environment staying present during critical procedures or when responding to an emergency. A freelancer working in their chosen area aligned with their passion and skills executing a client assignment. An employee who splits theri time between deep task focus at home and engaging in collaborative flow during team meetings, brainstorming sessions, or strategically bumping into people or creating encounters at workplace, in conferences, or in client settings. An engineer using augmented reality (AR) to visualize and troubleshoot a complex machinery issue within a digital twin software simulation of expensive infrastructure within their responsibilities. A writer producing high-quality content during their most creative hours (morning or evening). A start-up founder refining their ideas and concepts, working on developing a new product prototype, solving a real problem in a novel way. A UX designer working with a spatial computing tool with precise control over digital elements, while retaining tactile feedback, as the 3D space becomes real to them. Space habitat planners designing habitats for space exploration on lunar, planetary, or asteroid surfaces, or pondering the key elements of mobile habitats in space. Quantum computing researchers exploring qubits, entanglement, and quantum algorithms, tackling groundbreaking problems in cryptography, drug discovery, and optimization. The concept of flow is inherently tied to human consciousness, emotions, and subjective experience. That said, taking the concept further, is it possible to imagine that technologies themselves might enter a state of flow in a metaphorical sense, drawing analogies to the human experience? Consider this. The way the internet evolves, with content, technologies, and applications constantly emerging and connecting in unexpected ways. An AI model, like DALL-E 2 or Midjourney generating increasingly novel and unexpected artistic outputs, seemingly operating with an internal logic and momentum. If an AI model were to begin to compose music that exhibits novelty, originality, emotional depth, and a unique artistic voice that brings the field forward. When a self-driving car seamlessly navigates unexpected traffic situations. When a robotic assembly line operates with optimal efficiency, minimizing downtime, maximizing output, and demonstrating a seamless and synchronized movement. If a blockchain network begins to evolve seemingly organically, with new applications and functionalities emerging from the interactions of its users. One could think of reinforcement learning-based AI agent (software or hardware) creating flow-like states in machines, or at least simulating it, reaching optimal performance, engaging in adaptive problem-solving, and seamless coordination.

An AI that has an uninterrupted processing cycle, integrating thousands of tasks across many domains and executing dramatic actions in the real world with economic and social consequences could be said to have some level of in-depth task engagement. Similarly, an AI system operating in a state where its capabilities are pushed to the maximum but it still remains within its operational limits might be said to be in a state of flow. The integration of robotic subsystems such as perception, planning, and action modules might in time result in smooth, efficient operation that rivals or even far exceeds human coordination in a factory setting. Multi-agent collaboration between highly specialized agents might soon become characterized as a state of machine flow. Overall, AI-enabled workflows, or AI workflows themselves, are becoming increasingly flow-like. As the capacity of the reasoning model improves, such agentic systems with some degree of self-reflection (depending on its codebase, algorithms, and training data) will emerge. One could envision this happening, not just in software, but in industrial settings or even in e-commerce.

There would obviously be some computational limitations, reliability issues, and ethical considerations to be aware of and handle. Neuromorphic computing, inspired by the human brain, could enable AI to process information in a more fluid, parallel and adaptive manner, mimicking the neural efficiency seen in human flow states. Combining symbolic AI (logic-based reasoning), connectionist AI (neural networks), and evolutionary AI (optimization over time) could create a system capable of seamless, flow-like operation across diverse tasks. However, even so, an AI would need robust feedback mechanisms—both internal (self-monitoring performance metrics) and external (environmental or user feedback)—to continuously refine its actions and maintain optimal performance. This AI "flow state" would likely be engineered rather than emergent, meaning developers would design systems to operate in this mode for specific applications, such as autonomous vehicles, robotic surgery, or real-time decision-making in complex systems (e.g., power grids, financial markets). Short term (2025–2030) we will see AI systems optimizing their performance in narrow domains (AlphaGo in games, GPT models in chat and programming). Medium term (2030–2040), developments in general AI, neuromorphic computing, and quantum computing might enable flow-like states across a wider range of tasks including in real-world scenarios such as autonomous exploration (far beyond just driving) or human—AI collaboration.

Depending on tech progress and regulatory constraints, AI could enter a functional analog of flow—characterized by peak efficiency, dynamic adaptation, and seamless task execution—within the next couple of decades. There is also the issue of temporal self-awareness, as AIs would need to more precisely assess their processing efficiency relative to baseline, their quality outputs over time, resource utilization patterns, and monitor their error rates. Lastly, there would need to be an improvement in reward mechanisms for AIs, creating the analog of intrinsic motivation characteristic of human flow states. Self-organization and adaptation to conditions not explicitly programmed. There is not good terminology to describe such envisioned phenomena at present. Long term (2040–2075) we might see AI systems operating at superhuman levels of flow which would both require and foster significant breakthroughs in our understanding of consciousness, motivation, and intelligence. At that point we would not be having a discussion of human skills, but rather it would be a question of how to support these advanced machines as they optimized our world so we could (hopefully) live even better lives.

Or how about scientific development? A specialized bio-AI system exploring vast chemical spaces unexpectedly discovering a novel drug molecule with unprecedented efficacy. A physics AI model discovering new and unexpected physical laws or mathematical relationships. An AI language model that generates a compelling and emotionally moving short story or poem. An AI system discovering and designing novel materials with unprecedented properties. An AI system co-developing and implementing solutions to complex societal challenges like aging populations, climate change, deforestation, global instability, inequality, job displacement, mental health crises, nuclear proliferation, overpopulation, pandemics, political polarization, pollution, poverty, social justice. An AI system negotiating complex international agreements, exhibiting diplomacy, empathy, and a deep understanding of human values and cultural nuances. Though still in its infancy, already over the past few years, agentic AI has made rapid progress. Going forward, we can assume that, unless regulatory issues intervene, investments will assure that some progress continues.

Agentic AI already seamlessly performs complex tasks in the real world (assembling components, assisting users, chatting, driving, ordering, organizing, scheduling, summarizing, trading) with a high level of autonomy, adaptability, and focus. An hypothetical AI system controlling a state-of-the art spacecraft in the 2030s or thereabout might autonomously navigate a hazardous space environment successively facing unexpected obstacles. These examples involve a symbiotic relationship between humans and AI, with humans providing guidance and oversight while the AI system drives innovation and exploration. Will that necessarily be the case? What if it becomes the other way around? Where AIs provide the oversight and humans explore and execute experiments suggested by AIs. How fruitful is it to create scenarios envisioning AI systems with long-term goals and objectives, pursuing these goals with persistence and a sense of internal motivation? We have to ask, because there are companies pursuing such goals and they might succeed (or not). Either way, it is sure to impact the division of labor in tangible ways.

Admittedly, these examples involve emergent behavior, where the system as a whole exhibits properties that are not easily predictable from its individual components. Though the boundaries between human and AI are constantly evolving, we must also be cautious of anthropomorphizing technology. Rather, as AI systems exhibit more complex and autonomous behavior, it's crucial to consider the ethical implications. We must ensure that their actions align with human values and societal goals. These distinctions may blur in the future. Or they may never get past a certain point. Despite current rapid progress, I would still have to be convinced that any technology currently has anything resembling the agency, artistic expression, bodily sensory perception, consciousness, creativity, emotive feelings, inner thoughts, ethics and moral compass, happiness or sadness, meaning, nuance, originality, purposeful, religiousness, self-awareness, sense of place, sense of place in the world, sense of self, spiritual, subtlety, and subjective experience that many (if not all) humans exhibit. That said, I have met many humans who are not particularly creative, emotive, ethical, meaningful, nuanced, original, religious, spiritual, or subtle. Despite that, some of them rule the world. This is perplexing in itself.

A company's reputation takes years to build but can be destroyed in a matter of minutes. Technology risks mean a 22-year-old pushing the wrong code could destroy energy infrastructure worth billions of dollars, or release sensitive privacy data for hundreds of thousands of people. This could be done intentionally as a result of instructions from superiors where the more inexperienced (but expert skilled) employees execute orders without questioning the fundamental ethical, technological, or regulatory risks. But it could also be malicious actions taken just because of a power rush when realizing immense power is in their hands for a moment. Biorisks from an unintended lab leak means a small team of researchers, or their cleaning staff, could be responsible for a pandemic that makes COVID-19 seem like a dress rehearsal. Hierarchies are not dead, but might matter even more, because as organizations increasingly take on megaprojects, governance demands stronger management and clearly organized reporting structures. For many, work has become hybrid, present for key events but taking most work calls from home. Yet, distance still matters. Skills matter, but what those skills entail changing rapidly.

AI transforms the workplace, but some things will remain the same. Emerging research indicates that talent has become more volatile, demanding, hard to find, and hard to keep. Educational institutions scramble to keep up with the changes. Given the amount of workers that need to be reskilled, only mass-institutions could cope with the numbers yet in the United States overstretched community colleges cannot keep up. Ivy League universities struggle with the balance between their legacy departments and institute structure up against transdisciplinary challenges, problems, and solutions. Private employers, from start-ups, to small businesses, all the way to multinational corporations—even tech companies founded less than a decade ago—all struggle to find talent with the appropriate skills. And, they seek alternatives, whether it is training them on their own or reshaping educational institutions. Why? Because skills are not static. What's needed today is not what's needed tomorrow. And I mean that literally. Tomorrow is literally a day away. It is not a metaphor for a distant future.

How Is the Book Organized?

The book is structured around three sections: (I) Capturing Cascading Changes, (II) Developing Skills Fit for the Workplace of Tomorrow, and (III) Managing Systems, Machines, and Humans.

Section I has three chapters.

In Chapter 1, "Why Work Needs to Fundamentally Change," I explore how every period of history with rapid geopolitical and technological change requires institutions such as corporations, governments, and civil society to adapt. This seldom happens without tension. A brief historical sweep of how work has transformed society, from the ancient world until today illustrates what's at stake. This brings us to the polycrisis of our current times. Cambridge Dictionary defines polycrisis as "a time of great disagreement, confusion, or suffering that is caused by many different problems happening at the same time so that they together have a very big effect." But what does that have to do with the workforce, and with me, you ask? "Everything," is my answer. A *platinum workforce*, resilient, capable, literate, and augmented, would dramatically change the risk/reward ratio. It would briefly propel us into a re-industrial age before it would usher us into an age of biomanufacturing—a time where unprecedented risk could possibly be contained and where the wider society could prosper.

In Chapter 2, "Human Talent in the Age of Machines and Risks," I explain how the talent base around any twenty-first-century employer, public or private, is brittle, ephemeral, and fluctuates with new developments in technology, geopolitics, and the economy. The challenge for you and I as "workers," whether we are manufacturing workers or what's traditionally construed as "knowledge workers," is not just to stay up-to-date on evolving skill sets but to be able to carry those skills and work products with them as circumstances such as teams, employers, and clients change. From that perspective, it is really about finding ways to fairly share, distribute, and describe work products and processes throughout someone's career, maintaining value streams both to employers and workers. That process is further complicated by the increasing involvement of tools, resources, machines, materials, machines, software, hardware, and even biomass and synthetically modified biomanufacturing components, all of which needs to co-work and be synergistic with constellations of workers.

In Chapter 3, "Will the Twenty-First-Century Employer Only Care About Machines?," I point out that employers need to dramatically revamp their reskilling programs, aiming to continuously reskill and train every employee on a plethora of emerging skills that those employees were never trained for and sometimes in domains the organization does not possess expertise in. For that to work, ecosystem partnerships are necessary. Educational institutions are no longer the supplier of talent, they are an integral part of your business. The workforce will go in and out of the educational system their whole lives and careers. But can society, or employers, afford for them to take time off to learn? Especially, when new things need to be learned weekly? New models are needed. The scale of the challenge is unprecedented. The speed with which it needs to be implemented is staggering. It will challenge everything we know about business, education, and learning. New skills matrices are needed. Skills maps. Training methods. Learning venues. Teachers need to continuously learn. Students need to teach each other. Learning organizations need to become a reality. The chapters explores the few innovative approaches that already exist and looks at future opportunities.

Section II has ten chapters.

In Chapter 4, "Human+," I consider how the AI age presents both unprecedented risks and unique growth opportunities. Transhumanism, alternatively termed Human+ or H+, encompasses a philosophical and technological movement advocating for the enhancement of human capabilities through scientific and engineering interventions. This field spans multiple disciplines including AI systems, genetic modification technologies, biotechnological innovations, nanoscale engineering, neural interface development, and cybernetic integration. Contemporary applications of transhumanist principles are already evident in medical technologies such as advanced prosthetics, neurostimulation devices, and genetic therapies. However, the more transformative aspects of this movement—including radical life extension, cognitive enhancement, and sensory augmentation—remain largely theoretical or in preliminary research stages. Chapters 5–14 trace ten individual skills, all of which could be said to contribute to creating a Human+ world.

Section III has four chapters.

In Chapter 15, "Emerging Workforce Risks," I try to show that those who can prove that they have faced up to, and proactively acted on emerging risks and turned them into opportunities for their employer or society, will be among the winners in tomorrow's workplace. A prerequisite for being ready to do so is to be familiar with emerging systemic risk toolkits. Cascading risks can originate from a plethora of sources, but there are ways to identify and track them systematically. That way, the pattern recognition of early signs of runaway risks can alert you in time to respond. This chapter describes a cascading risk framework to do just that.

In Chapter 16, "Managing Skills at Gigascale," I explore how the scale of future work will set it apart from past organizational models. As megaprojects

($1B+) and gigaprojects ($20B+) become more common, entire workforces—not just leaders—must adapt to operating at vast scale. The smallest oversight can trigger major failures, while a frontline insight could spark breakthrough innovation. These massive projects shape the future simply by how far they extend into it. Yet their scale often locks us into path-dependent development, making the future more predictable than it seems. Thriving in this environment will require a rare integration of skills—risk aptitude, transdisciplinarity, geopolitical fluency, socio-technical insight, augmented intelligence, interoperability, and large-scale operations—none of which are currently taught in combination by schools or employers.

In Chapter 17, "How to Teach Futuristic Skills," I trace how modern schooling systems evolved in lockstep with industrialization, from German factory-style education to global K–12 models. The chapter argues for a fundamental shift in learning modes to match the demands of tomorrow's workforce. For each of the 12 skills defining the *platinum workforce*, I propose immersive, real-world learning activities: from coordinating human–machine interaction and solving eco-challenges to building ventures from scratch, simulating systemic crises, and applying emerging technologies in live settings. The future of learning must mirror the future of work—hands-on, cross-disciplinary, globally connected, and impact-driven.

Chapter 18 introduces a blueprint for the Human+ workforce—anchored in two core skills: human–AI collaboration and an interoperability mindset. These are supported by eleven future-critical capabilities, including eco-awareness, maker skills, mediation, megascale operations, mobility, risk aptitude, agile R&D, psycho-resilience, socio-technical insight, agentic AI management, and systems thinking. Together, they define the competencies needed to lead and adapt in an increasingly complex, tech-driven world.

This concluding chapter reflects on the uncertain and emergent nature of the future of work, emphasizing that skills—not just technology—will determine society's ability to adapt. Positioned at the intersection of risk and innovation, the *platinum workforce* represents a strategic response to the unintended consequences of unchecked economic growth. It offers a human-centered vision for progress—resilient, ethical, and future-ready.

References

Baaij, Marc G. 2024. *Business Skills for the 21st Century*. London, England: SAGE Publications.

Bloom, Allan. 1987. *The Closing of the American Mind: How Higher Education Has Failed Democracy and Impoverished the Souls of Today's Students*. New York: Simon & Schuster.

Brynjolfsson, Erik, and Andrew McAfee. 2023. *The Machine Learning Economy*.

Conversable Economist. 2022. "Adam Smith and Pin-Making: Some Inconvenient Truths." *Conversable Economist* (blog). August 23. https://conversableeconomist.com /2022/08/23/adam-smith-and-pin-making-some-inconvenient-truths/.

Creating WOW Communications. 2015. "Home." *CEIA*. September 11. https://www .ceiainc.org/.

Drewery, Merritt L., and Jonathan Lollar. 2024. "Undergraduates' Perceptions of the Value of Service-Learning." *Frontiers in Education*. 9: 1330456. https://doi. org/10.3389/feduc.2024.1330456.

Durkheim, Emile. 1984. *The Division of Labour in Society*. Translated by W. D. Hall. Contemporary Social Theory. Basingstoke, England: Palgrave Macmillan.

"Evidence-Based Improvement in Higher Education." n.d. Accessed February 22, 2025. https://nsse.indiana.edu/index.html.

Fadel, Charles, and Bernie Trilling. 2009. *21st Century Skills: Learning for Life in Our Times*. PDF. Chichester, England: Jossey Bass Wiley.

Field, John. 2006. *Lifelong Learning and the New Educational Order*. 2nd ed. Stoke-on-Trent: Trentham Books.

Hew, Khe Foon, and Wing Sum Cheung. 2014. "Students' and Instructors' Use of Massive Open Online Courses (MOOCs): Motivations and Challenges." *Educational Research Review* 12 (June): 45–58.

"Homepage." n.d. Accessed February 22, 2025. https://compact.org/.

Johnston, Denis L. 1978. "Scientists Become Managers—The 'T'-Shaped Man." *IEEE Engineering Management Review* 6 (3): 67–68.

Jordan, Katy. 2014. "Initial Trends in Enrolment and Completion of Massive Open Online Courses." *The International Review of Research in Open and Distributed Learning* 15 (1). https://doi.org/10.19173/irrodl.v15i1.1651.

McKinsey Global Institute. 2022. *Defining the Skills Citizens Will Need in the Future World of Work*.

Means, B., Y. Toyama, R. Murphy, and M. Baki. 2013. "The Effectiveness of Online and Blended Learning: A Meta-Analysis of the Empirical Literature." *Teachers College Record* 115 (3): 1–47. https://doi.org/10.1177/016146811311500307.

Means, Barbara, Yukie Toyama, Robert Murphy, Marianne Bakia, and Karla Jones. 2009. "Evaluation of Evidence-Based Practices in Online Learning: A Meta-Analysis and Review of Online Learning Studies." *US Department of Education*, May. http://files.eric.ed.gov/fulltext/ED505824.pdf.

Nesta. 2021. *The Future of Lifelong Learning Systems*.

OECD. 2004. *Lifelong Learning: Policy Brief*. Paris: Organisation for Economic Co-operation and Development.

OECD. 2023. *Skills Outlook 2023: Future-Ready Education for All*. Paris: Organisation for Economic Co-operation and Development.

Picciano, Anthony G. 2016. *Online Education Policy and Practice: The Past, Present, and Future of the Digital University*. London, England: Routledge.

Rauf, David Saleh. 2025. "Venture Capital Investment in Global Ed Tech Sinks to Decade Low." *Education Week*, February 5, 2025. https://marketbrief.edweek.org/financing-invest ment/venture-capital-investment-in-global-ed-tech-sinks-to-decade-low/2025/02/.

Schultes, Marie-Therese, Daniel Graf, Julia Holzer, Barbara Schober, and Christiane Spiel. 2025. "Implementation and Evaluation of Service Learning at Higher Education Institutions." *Evaluation and Program Planning*. 12: 102622. https://doi. org/10.1016/j.evalprogplan.2025.102622.

Turchin, Peter. 2020. *Ages of Discord: A Structural-Demographic Analysis of American History*.

World Economic Forum. 2020. *The Future of Jobs Report*.

SECTION I
Capturing Cascading Changes

CHAPTER 1

WHY WORK NEEDS TO FUNDAMENTALLY CHANGE

Work Transforms Society

Every period of history with rapid geopolitical and technological change requires institutions such as corporations, governments, and civil society to adapt. This seldom happens without tension. And what fuels the adaptation is a change in the way work is organized: training, hiring, collaborating, scaling. Work, starting from individual accomplishments and innovations to team efforts, key leadership decisions, and interorganizational coordination, is what propels society forward—and occasionally backward. In many modern workplaces, hierarchical structures are becoming more flattened, and the traditional "subordinate" relationship is evolving. But it is not a one-way street.

In the interwar years, Germany excelled in certain areas (rocketry, physics, and chemistry), which helped build early jet engines and tanks, as well as the prototype of the V-2, the long-range guided ballistic missile. However, many of its interwar experts were Jewish and were expelled or killed before or during the war. The Allies also developed advanced technology. The United States had radar and the B-29 bomber—and developed the Manhattan Project, which resulted in the nuclear bomb. The Russians had advanced tanks. Supported by the Enabling Act of 1933, the constitutional basis of Hitler's dictatorship, the Nazis expanded factories and infrastructure. Strikes rarely affected production. The Nazis mobilized support from educated and professional elites, including lawyers, law enforcement, educators, and medical professionals. In fact, they effectively controlled and boosted German industry and workforce and directed them toward industrial and military pursuits. During the Third Reich, Hitler's work, and that of the Schutzstaffel (SS), a paramilitary organization responsible for enforcing Nazi policies, included the operation of concentration camps to clear the way for a totalitarian regime in Germany, consolidating power, enacting discriminatory laws against Jews and other groups deemed "inferior," aggressively expanding German territory through military conquest, and, at its apex, orchestrating the Holocaust, the systematic genocide of millions of people, primarily Jews, across occupied Europe. The way work functions in society is the limit for what that society will do. A brief historical sweep of how work has transformed society, from the ancient world until today, illustrates what's at stake. At best, we've kept advancing our work practices, but some were also particular to a specific age and were since lost or not adaptable to different conditions. Generally, societies that had a good handle on their workforce prevailed longer than those that didn't. Being able to foresee potential negative consequences through foresight and risk management measures is another protective civilizational force. Few societies have been able to do this over time, with some lasting for centuries and others for millennia.

In the ancient world, tradesmen shared Bronze Age metalworking practices combining tin and copper into the useful alloy bronze with each other through migration and taught the next generation, which changed agriculture and expanded trade—and led to intense warfare. In the classical period, the Greeks evolved their teaching methods, managed elaborate households (*oikonomia*), built politically savvy city-states (*polis*) with marketplaces (*agroai*). The Greeks philosophized, traded, and expanded to Asia, Africa, and Europe. But the Greeks also relied extensively on slave labor—representing a third of their workforce—relegated women to cooking and household chores, outsourced prostitution to slaves and female, free resident foreigners (*metics*), and glorified violent competition.

The Legacy of Roman Organization

From Rome, modern organizations have retained the idea that the workforce should be properly organized, with clear lines of authority to achieve accountability, division of labor to increase efficiency and productivity, bureaucracy to achieve fairness, and standardization to enhance predictability and transparency. These principles evolved over thousands of years through experimentation and conflict.

The Romans ran a fairly complex society with a broad range of professions—farmers, artisans, merchants, soldiers, engineers, laborers, officials, teachers, physicians, actors, musicians, artists, gladiators, priests, prostitutes, and bankers—that reached breakthroughs in engineering, building aqueducts, roads, and concrete buildings. The Roman army recruited soldiers both through conscription and volunteering. The elite, wealthy landowning patricians (*patricius*) of Rome, or those deliberately promoted by the emperor, were the society's leaders. They served in the Senate (*senatus*), the council of elders. Senators were recruited from the sons of senators. The plebeians (*plebeii*), the free Roman citizens, formed a cadre of some 20 percent free—mostly urban farmers, bakers, builders, craftsmen, or soldiers—who were paid wages and paid taxes. Aside from that, work in the Roman Empire was done by slaves, who may have counted in excess of 20 percent of the workforce. In 494 BCE, a plebeian strike led to the Council of the Plebs (*Concilium Plebis*), which gave them a voice in government.

Previously, in the Roman Republic, a dictator was a magistrate who was given temporary, extraordinary powers to deal with state crises. After the Roman civil wars in the first century BCE and later, a prominent general, Julius Caesar, gained power, conquered the province of Gaul, and became dictator (*dictator*) for life. After Caesar's assassination, Augustus, now in the position to veto laws and decide who could hold office, became the first Roman emperor. During this period, the Romans expanded their territories through brutal conquest to North Africa—following a victory over Carthage during the Punic Wars—and to Spain and Gaul, dominating most of the European continent, including Britain and major parts of Eastern Europe. However, the cost and diversity of the Roman Empire's expansion led to Rome's downfall. The emperor Diocletian restored efficient government after the third century's anarchy and split into two administrative units: West and East in the year 395 CE.

The Eastern part, the Byzantine Empire lasted a thousand years—until falling to the Ottoman Turks in 1453 CE—by granting relative freedom to its citizens and maintaining a successful gold currency (*nomisma*). Soldiers were granted land and became permanent farmers as long as they would yield loyal soldiers when needed (known as the theme system). An efficient perimeter defense and a source of productive farmland, this system worked until the government lost control of the countryside to independent feudal chieftains. As farmers' entrepreneurial spirit was crushed, private interest groups, aristocrats, and landlords competed for attention, and by the 1040s, the currency was devalued. The word "Byzantine" is today used as a metaphor to describe something that is bureaucratic, complicated, secretive, or hard to understand. Byzantium's imperial court and civil service certainly at times, devolved into needless complexities but might also be said to have undeservedly gained a negative reputation. Byzantine diplomacy, a lavish affair where foreign dignitaries were encouraged to stay in Constantinople for years to build deep relations, withstood Persians, Huns, Arabs, and others at their eastern borders. The fact that Constantinople had an enviable strategic location along the major trade routes connecting Europe and Asia was never lost on any of these peoples.

Schools were private and favored the elite because they involved high tuition fees (called *misthos*, meaning reward) based on the teacher's reputation and learning. Primary education was conducted in courtyards of monasteries or churches, and secondary education in the city center. The Byzantines, whose main school subject was rhetorics—a key discipline for traders, salesmen, and diplomats alike—developed trade organizations, new forms of credit, and cleverly used diasporic communities to further trade. Despite being what we associate with the period, traders had little respect among the aristocracy. Perhaps for that reason, in the city of Constantinople, craftsmen and professionals organized in unions. These 21 guilds (*collegia*) were legal entities monitored by the state, with fees for entry, a whopping 507 regulations of which 379 were best practices and the rest regulations that carried punishments, and were monopolies supposed to impose strict controls (Mavridis and Vatalis, 2014). What was traded on the "Silk Road" were two main commodities—grain and silk—along with oil, wine, tea, salt, fish, meat, rice, animals, vegetables, timber, paper, jade, wax, glassware, furs, ceramics, linen, woven cloth, but also gold, perfumes, and spices—and slaves. Merchants, missionaries, and warriors also transferred ideas, technology, and beliefs. Social mobility was low but not insignificant, at least from the middle classes upward, thanks to education, wars, imperial gifts, and intermarriage. Byzantine bribes, diplomacy, political marriages, manipulation of enemies to attack each other, and shrewd but limited use of military power were the precursor to modern-day appeasement. Cosmopolitanism, such an important feature of futuristic societies, originated with Byzantium's diversity of culture and labor force.

The Contradictory Work of Our Modern Age

Modernity, associated with rapid progress, has in reality been a mixed blessing. Industrialization dramatically reshaped the workforce. Although religion has prevailed, secular rationalism became the primary basis for knowledge. Individualism emerged as an ideal that, at times, conflicted with community and tribal values. Nationalism formed territorially bound states of larger and larger size, capable of large work projects. The consolidation of trade networks and new technological opportunities brought an increasing connectedness we came to call globalization, but it was never completed. Backlash against these changes created social movements, revolutions, and wars, occasionally spreading across the world.

In the early modern period, European exploration led to global trade networks and cultural change—but also began their colonization of territory, exploiting the peoples of Asia and Africa. The seventeenth and eighteenth centuries' scientific revolution in astronomy, physics, biology, and mathematics became the foundation of modern research methods, transforming society's view on nature—but also allowed us to exploit and destroy it. The Industrial Revolution of the eighteenth century, with the steam engine, spinning machine, power loom, cotton gin, interchangeable parts, telegraph, telephone, light bulb, and eventually the internal combustion engine, transformed agrarian societies into productive economies with modern affordances and goods. But because workforce changes were poorly understood, industrialization also left a desolate countryside and resulted in urban, polluted cities, with anomie, stress, and class struggles.

In the modern period, the twentieth century was marked by two major global conflicts, World War I and World War II, which shattered empires, birthed modern nations, sparked independence movements, and drove the United States into a global power. But these wars also led to a dramatic number of deaths, massive malnutrition, and veteran nightmares, anger, and disabilities. Longer term, they paved the way for Soviet communism and facilitated Hitler's ascent to power. The responses to these shifts included appeasement and a cold war, which turned geopolitics into an existential concern that now includes nuclear armageddon. As labor became better organized in the postwar era, higher wages and better working conditions fueled higher productivity and set the stage for truly reaping the fruits of the accelerating technological advancements. As globalization intensified in the four decades from the 1980s to the 2020s, it was the workforce of multinational corporations, manufacturing firms, financial institutions, and lately of machines—including robots and AI-enabled software—that together transformed the content, products, and services possible to produce by a combination of human and machine labor, new materials, and larger and larger constellations of partners and capital resources that operated both in proximity, at a distance, and simultaneously both.

Polycrisis and the Future of Work

This brings us to current times, which are marked by enormous social inequality, a widening divide between the rich and poor across two main axes: that of the Global South and the axis formed by the myriad of urban slums that often directly border the wealthiest areas in a city, such as in Rio de Janeiro's favelas.

Cambridge Dictionary defines polycrisis as "a time of great disagreement, confusion, or suffering that is caused by many different problems happening at the same time so that they together have a very big effect." Polycrisis implies direct causal links (*causal entanglement*) between crises in multiple global systems in ways that "significantly degrade humanity's prospects" (Lawrence et al., 2024). These crises are currently exemplified by pandemics, climate change, biodiversity collapse, Russia's war on Ukraine, the war in the Middle East, and the looming crisis in the South China Sea. Many of these global crises are part of processes that have emerged over a long time span. It stands to reason that they won't be resolved any time soon either. Other elements—wars, events, disruptive innovations—might be mixed in at any moment. Complexity is a given.

What would the world be like if the polycrisis went unmitigated? Might our systems of governance partially or fully collapse? One might at least imagine that if the polycrisis continues, it will eventually be ungovernable by the current governance structure. This then becomes a workforce challenge.

At the same time, due to an, at times, surprisingly strong return on investment from several long-standing R&D developments, partially financed by the public sector, the world has seen swift progress in a plethora of emerging technologies. Seven technologies seem particularly relevant in terms of changing the means of industrial production, eventually poised to do away with the industrial paradigm altogether. These include blockchain, nuclear fusion, generative AI, nanotech, synthetic biology, brain–computer interfaces (BCIs), and quantum tech. Because they can both change things for the better and risk changing society for the worse, these together form what we can call the technology risk/opportunity space. You cannot have opportunities without risk. But the more risk society takes on, the better prepared we need to be for the potential negative consequences.

Altogether, a likely combination of the cascading effects of the polycrisis, dramatic climate change, and rapid technological transformation sets forces in motion that will, arguably, produce larger changes in the twenty-first century than in the eighteenth and twentieth century combined. The changes will particularly be felt once they deeply embed in and start to reshape industrial developments, infrastructures, and modes of production. Incidentally, the polycrisis is, paradoxically, a helpful bridge toward the next industrial paradigm, which is shaping up to be biomanufacturing. The starting point is that biology is the world's best technology. Synthetic biology is the multidisciplinary field of biology attempting to understand, modify, redesign, engineer, enhance, or build biological systems with useful purposes. This platform is already offering new ways of manufacturing medicines, industrial chemicals, biomaterials, clothing, foods, fragrances, and fuels. Capabilities are rapidly increasing. Personalized medicine based on genetic makeup will gradually become the norm. Yield and nutritional value of crops will increase. Entirely new products will be envisioned. Scale will increase. Biomanufacturing will help clean up pollution and restore ecosystems. Organ engineering and tissue modification will repair and enhance organic material. This potentially has massive implications for human health and longevity. It will propel the space age, protecting humans who will be working in space. Groundbreaking advances are to be expected, but timelines are uncertain and will depend on the investments made, not the least into a workforce capable of innovating and managing these shifts. Traditional industrial methods and biomanufacturing are likely to coexist for many decades, perhaps centuries, with some capabilities being enhanced, others being too expensive to immediately transform.

How to Handle Cascading Risks

Contradictory trends of risk and opportunity now coexist. Workforce challenges converge with an increasingly pervasive infrastructure, increased manufacturing capacity, as well as innovations in material science. The resulting interactions, broad in scope, awesome in potential but therefore also potentially devastating in their negative effects if misaligned, are poorly understood. In short, they have nondeterministic "cascading effects." Adding to that, once one or more fast-moving trigger events combine with slow-moving stresses, this threatens to push a global system out of its established equilibrium and into a volatile and dangerous disequilibrium. The effects are particularly acute in a set of geographical hot spots.

Cascading effects refer to particularly impactful interactions between seemingly unrelated phenomena (technologies, geographies, institutions, natural phenomena, social dynamics, industrial processes, etc.). These effects can be positive or negative for the actors or environments affected, and could be leveraged if we understood them better. The impact of augmented intelligence through artificial intelligence in combination with human ingenuity is potentially vast. However, building trust, accountability, and adequate checks and balances between AI–human teams and processes will be enormously challenging. Paradoxically, the situation might be that the true benefits of AI cannot be realized until AI–human interaction makes a quantum leap forward, which might entail waiting until the quantum age itself. The reason is that explanatory processes would seem to be enormously taxing in terms of the amount of compute required. If we are already running into environmental limits to energy use from AI, imagine if every operation has to be double and triple checked by another set of AIs, all monitored by humans. That being said, over the next decade, making workforce adjustments to integrate with, work with, and understand human–AI interaction both on a practical, conceptual, and existential level makes a lot of sense.

The scale of the challenge is enormous from many angles. The first is that this shift will affect the entire workforce, albeit to a varying degree. Given the speed of evolution, this entails a radically different set of training requirements across the global workforce. The second is that the shift will most likely increase the autonomy, scope, and impact of even the lowest skilled professionals, perhaps even particularly so for these groups, potentially to the detriment of the middle layers of management and white-collar workers. That picture is fodder for revolutionary fervent among the middle classes.

Despite Marx's worker manifesto for the importance of unity and protest at the lower end of the hierarchy of work, the middle class has played a significant role in many revolutions throughout history. In the American Revolution, it was the middle class, organized through churches and guilds, who fought most fervently for independence from British rule. The bourgeoisie seeking political and economic rights was a driving force behind the French Revolution. The Velvet Revolution in Czechoslovakia, which overthrew the communist regime, was driven by the middle class. Should economic and political conditions deteriorate, combined with the emergence of a sense of shared purpose and unity forming a cohesive force for change, one could imagine such revolutions occurring in the twenty-first century in large and important countries across the world. Iran, Nigeria, Russia, and Sudan are currently fairly unstable and could be susceptible given these conditions. Work is essential to an individual's sense of worth. Structural changes that affect the workforce in negative ways, or even in positive ways, but in short order, can dramatically distort or alter political and social conditions. Work transforms society in ways that are clearly visible after the fact but not so visible in real time. That's why studying the sociology of work across history, with a particular focus on disruptive trends, is so complex, yet important, and ultimately so rewarding.

Work naturally changes when the social conditions change. From that point of view, one could say, why worry? However, the polycrisis is no longer just a clever phrase. Polycrisis is better and better understood at least at the level of a challenge. We have the option to mobilize and steer the workforce in the right direction for a whole cloth transformation, potentially in time for mitigating and even solving the truly huge challenges that await us across geopolitical, environmental, and technological axes. If so, this will most likely protect the social fabric. Could we manage better than previous civilizations? We know enough to do so, but do we have the will to carry it out? It will not be cheap. It will not be easy. It will take vision and sacrifice. It will take a long-term view. These are unfortunately features in which our current age does not excel.

References

Lawrence, M., T. Homer-Dixon, S. Janzwood, J. Rockstöm, O. Renn, and J. F. Donges. "Global Polycrisis: The Causal Mechanisms of Crisis Entanglement." *Global Sustainability* 7: e6. https://doi.org/10.1017/sus.2024.1.

Mavridis, Dimitrios G., and Konstantinos I. Vatalis. 2014. "Best and Bad Practices – the Imperial Guilds of Constantinople." *Procedia Economics and Finance* 14 (January): 425–434.

CHAPTER 2

HUMAN TALENT IN THE AGE
OF MACHINES AND RISKS

Dealing with Change

To say that change will uproot the workplace is hardly a controversial claim. The future of work will evolve from fast-moving industrial dynamics, technological shifts, educational developments, and geopolitical drama. Research from the McKinsey Global Institute indicates that by 2030, 375 million workers globally (approximately 14 percent of the workforce) may need to switch occupational categories due to automation. The World Economic Forum's Future of Jobs Report emphasizes that 65 percent of children entering primary school today will ultimately work in job types that don't yet exist. There's evidence that the stress of adapting to such change is affecting students and workers alike. Research from multiple authoritative sources reveals a concerning pattern of career-related stress affecting both students and young workers. The American Psychological Association's 2024 Stress in America survey ("Stress in America," n.d.) shows 75 percent of high school students report significant school-related stress and 70 percent of teens identify anxiety or depression as major issues among their peers, while Deloitte found that when Gen Z think about GenAI they feel a mix of uncertainty, excitement and fascination, with a third stating they will not pursue higher education due to financial concerns, over 40 percent of Millennials and Gen Z workers have left jobs due to workplace stress and career uncertainty, and nearly half have side jobs ("The Deloitte Global 2024 Gen Z and Millennial Survey," n.d.). The National Institute of Mental Health has documented that half of adolescents have a mental disorder as well as rising anxiety disorders among young adults (18–25) ("Mental Illness," n.d.) with nearly a third of college students reporting that career anxiety impacts their academic performance. The pandemic caused a spike in youth unemployment rates but according to the International

Labour Organization (ILO), the global youth unemployment rate in 2023 stood at 13 percent ("Global Employment Trends for Youth 2024" 2024). The economic toll is substantial—the World Health Organization estimates anxiety and depression cost the global economy approximately US$ 1 trillion annually in lost productivity ("Mental Health at Work," n.d.). This stress manifests through physical symptoms, increased anxiety about career choices, fear of technological obsolescence, and significant pressure to establish career paths early, with 73 percent of Gen Z workers feeling pressured to have their careers "figured out" by age 25.

High school guidance counselors face mounting pressure, often managing caseloads well above the recommended 250:1 ratio, while juggling academic advising, mental health support, and career guidance. As new educational models—like bootcamps, micro-credentials, and hybrid programs—proliferate, counselors are expected to keep pace with rapidly shifting career pathways. Yet many feel underprepared. Ferguson et al. (2019) found that most counselors lack the training to advise students on technician and non-traditional careers. Similarly, a report by Advance CTE (2018) revealed that only 25 percent of counselors use labor market data to inform guidance, contributing to a growing disconnect between student needs and institutional support.

In the United States, over the last few decades the standing recommendation has been to study STEM subjects in high school and apply to brand-name colleges, even if they are increasingly expensive. This despite the fact that employers needing specialized manufacturing expertise are offering free training and high wages from the get to due to high demand for skilled workers and skills gaps in the typical geographic locations where factories are located. The open questions surrounding the speed and depth of AI's ascending role in the workplace means that few professions can insulate themselves from dramatic change in the years ahead. The notion of lifelong learning, which is seldom practiced, might be expected to get wind in the sails. The question, though, is whether formal qualifications or skills will remain determinant for early job success. Despite the myriad of learning platforms available, the motivation and persistence required to truly learn at depth is hard to come by unless it is clear what to learn and what the effect might be on career, salary, and life satisfaction. The demand for digital skills seems rather obvious. However, The World Economic Forum's Future of Jobs Report as well as McKinsey's Global Survey consistently every year show that demand is growing for complementary skills such as creativity, critical thinking, and entrepreneurial aptitude. Major companies like Google, Apple, and IBM have modified their hiring practices to emphasize these skills. Harvard Business School's (HBS) curriculum revision in 2022 increased emphasis on entrepreneurial thinking by 40 percent across core

FIGURE 2.1 Humans, machines, and risks.

courses, including The Entrepreneurial Manager course in its required curriculum. Stanford's Graduate School of Business reports that 45 percent of their coursework (60 courses) now focuses on developing these complementary skills.

The talent base around any twenty-first-century employer, whether public or private, is increasingly brittle, ephemeral, and shaped by fluctuations in technology, geopolitics, and the broader economy. Job security has eroded significantly over recent decades, as shown by the rise of contingent work, declining tenure, and the growing prevalence of gig and platform-based labor (Kalleberg 2009; OECD 2021). In response, many workers have stopped seeking permanence and instead create degrees of freedom—building diversified portfolios of skills, experiences, and outcomes that accumulate over time.

While no definitive research proves that institutional pedigree is becoming irrelevant, early signs suggest a slow shift in hiring practices toward demonstrable capability rather than credentialism. Skills-based recruitment, digital portfolios, and real-time performance tracking are beginning to outweigh traditional proxies such as elite degrees or brand-name employers (Burning Glass Technologies 2020). If these trends hold, the power of legacy institutions may fade unless they adapt—becoming not just symbolic brands, but living networks of evolving competencies and value creation.

This shift could eventually enhance transparency in the worker–employer relationship. The long-standing imbalance—where employers control the narrative of value—may give way to systems where workers can carry, show, and activate their contributions across contexts. For both manufacturing and knowledge workers, the central challenge is no longer just staying up-to-date with evolving tools and skills, but preserving and transferring their work products as they move between employers, teams, and clients.

Achieving this requires new mechanisms for recording, sharing, and contextualizing labor across time. These must account for both tacit knowledge and tangible outcomes, functioning across increasingly complex ecosystems of people, machines, materials, software, hardware, and even biological or synthetically engineered components. The future of work will depend not only on human capability, but on the interoperability of labor, technology, and context—organized into flexible constellations of collaboration.

Beyond the CV

The *curriculum vitae* (CV) has been a staple of career advancement ever since Leonardo da Vinci in 1482 penned a letter to the Duke of Milan, outlining his multidisciplinary skills and talents as an engineer, artist, and inventor "in which I can compete with any other, be he who he may," as he phrased it (Strunz 2020). Though we might think of the Renaissance as a time of great artistic progress in Europe, already back then, Leonardo had to emphasize his practical skills, to "provide many forms of machines most efficient and suitable for offense and defense," and an ability to create "new and ingenious" inventions of relevance to military engineering. As he writes, "I can make large-scale cannons, most excellent and unusual."

In Prussia's technical bureaucracy during the period from 1770 to 1830, the CV became a major tool for bureaucratic innovation (Strunz 2020), facilitating the depiction of linear sequences of professional formation, separately depicting education and employment history, pointing toward certain positions. Steeped in utilitarian thinking around industrial, practical, and societal usefulness, particularly utility to the state, the CV helped "stylize an applicant's career as a time of continuous progress and merit" (Strunz 2020), in other words, what we tend to call a "career." This approach contrasts with the earlier (now partially resurrected) German ideal of formation (ger. *"bildung"*) as a self-reflexive, holistic process of personal and intellectual development cultivating a well-rounded individual.

In the early modern era, CVs gained traction among scholars to document one's academic achievements. With industrialization, the CV became a more standardized document describing experience, skills, and specific job role achievements. In the post–World War II era, this was honed in business schools and spread through textbooks. In the digital era, CV creation diversified in its design and wider dissemination meant narrative career histories became staples of personal web pages and conference speaker promotion sites. Today, digital job board platforms such as CareerBuilder, Glassdoor, Handshake, Indeed, LinkedIn, Monster, SimplyHired, Ziprecruiter, as well as those used by employers to process job applicants, such as Workday, shape how talent can be described. Increasingly, Applicant Tracking Systems (ATS) use machine algorithms to process the massive influx of job applications, so concise, keyword-rich CVs tend to stand out.

Motivating Knowledge Management

"If HP knew what HP knows, it would be three times more profitable" is a quote famously attributed to Lew Platt, former CEO of Hewlett-Packard. This became a mantra at the roots of the evolution of the managerial discipline of knowledge management (Sieloff 1999). The problem was that an initial focus on knowledge did not properly account for the need to incent the people who possess the knowledge to share it or to at least share what types of things they might know. As a result, motivating employees or workers to contribute to Knowledge Management (KM) repositories has been a persistent challenge.

Skills Assessment Challenges

The concept of systematically categorizing and classifying skills has a long and multifaceted history. A nineteenth-century town might have hundreds of distinct occupations. A twentieth-century town might have thousands. While early attempts focused on occupational classifications and job descriptions, modern skills taxonomies emerged in the twentieth century, driven by the need to understand and manage a rapidly evolving workforce. In *Sorting Things Out* (1999), Geoffrey C. Bowker and Susan Leigh Star argue that classification systems actively shape social interactions, power dynamics, and opportunities by including some individuals and excluding others. Classification, they claim, forms a partially shared infrastructure consisting of specific artifacts, concepts, field notes, frameworks, information, and maps (boundary objects) that connect fields of knowledge and allow communication. These are used simultaneously by members of different groups, yet they have different functions in each. By doing so, these also determine who has access to certain skills and benefits within a given field or society. By virtue of providing common ground, boundary objects can help people negotiate their differences and establish agreement. They can be valuable in solving complex social-technological challenges, such as climate change, aging, and sustainability. Standardized skills frameworks, competency models, or industry-specific job descriptions that can be adapted and interpreted by different groups to facilitate dialogue and collaboration can function that way.

Classification systems, like skill sets listed on a job application, often appear natural and objective, but they are actually constructed through social processes that can embed biases and power imbalances. By defining specific skill sets as necessary for a job or role, classifications can effectively exclude individuals who may possess relevant abilities but don't fit the neatly defined categories. For example, a software engineering role may require a formal computer science degree, thereby excluding self-taught programmers with extensive real-world coding experience. Similarly, healthcare roles may overlook skilled community health workers simply because they lack standardized certifications, even though they have deep cultural knowledge and hands-on experience. In creative industries, job descriptions requiring mastery of specific software can discount candidates with strong conceptual design skills who use alternative tools. These examples reveal how rigid classifications can gatekeep talent, reinforcing existing hierarchies and limiting workforce diversity.

The military has played a key role in shaping systematic approaches to skill classification, driven by its need to efficiently train, assign, and manage large numbers of personnel. Tools like the Armed Services Vocational Aptitude Battery (ASVAB) were developed to match individuals with specialized roles based on standardized assessments. These frameworks, originally designed for operational readiness, later influenced civilian HR systems by formalizing how competencies are defined and measured (Segal and Segal 2004).

The first documented example of a job classification system was the 1850 U.S. census, which included a list of around 322 occupations. There was heavy emphasis on the industry a worker was employed in rather than specific job duties and skill levels. The Dictionary of Occupational Titles (DOT), a major advancement, was published in 1939 and provided a more comprehensive system for classifying jobs based on detailed job duties and skill requirements, assigning codes to categorize occupations. However, DOT was a static document that could not keep pace with the changing demands of the labor market.

The Standard Occupational Classification (SOC), first introduced in 1977 by the U.S. Bureau of Labor Statistics, revised many times and became a standard in 1998, marking a significant shift in occupational classification by focusing on the work performed and required skills rather than industry or work setting. SOC ensures consistency across surveys and studies. Developed by the U.S. Department of Labor during the 1990s, the Occupational Information Network (O*NET) is a comprehensive and dynamic database of occupational information, including skills, knowledge, abilities, and work styles. It has become a widely used resource for job analysis, career counseling, and workforce development. O*NET classifies jobs in job families. It is a resource for job seekers, employers, educators, and workforce development professionals alike. Helping individuals explore career options and make informed career decisions. Informing the development of educational and training programs to meet the needs of the labor market. Assisting employers in identifying and recruiting qualified candidates.

Traditional skill assessment methods like assessment centers, manual input, surveys, and consulting inputs are costly and often incomplete. There is often managerial bias in terms of what skills get recorded and valued on behalf of whom. This leads to a lack of visibility of current employee skills. Adding to that the uncertainty about emerging and future skills needs, those shortcomings hinder organizations from effectively managing their workforce. Emilio J. Castilla, a professor at MIT Sloan School of Management, has significantly advanced the field of strategic human resource management by investigating how organizational systems and managerial practices influence equity and performance. His research highlights the paradox that even well-intentioned meritocratic systems can reproduce bias, particularly in performance evaluations and promotion decisions. In one influential study, Castilla demonstrated that when organizations emphasize meritocracy, evaluators may unwittingly reward men more than equally performing women by reverting to their unconcious stereotypes—a phenomenon he terms the "paradox of meritocracy" (Castilla and Benard 2010). Through his broader work on recruitment, pay structures, and internal mobility, Castilla advocates for data-driven, transparent HR practices that align strategic goals with equitable outcomes.

Collaborative Intelligence: Human–AI Systems and Work Transformation

Career guidance is being reshaped by rapid technological change and labor market volatility. As international data exchange improves and employment patterns shift at unprecedented speed, students and workers require more personalized, adaptive support. Traditional career infrastructures—built for more stable economies—struggle to keep pace. In response, human–AI collaboration platforms are emerging to provide scalable, tailored guidance. Explainable AI (XAI) is central to this transformation. By translating complex algorithmic behavior into visual, rule-based, or natural language outputs, XAI acts as a "boundary object"—a concept from sociology describing artifacts that facilitate collaboration across different knowledge domains (Star and Griesemer 1989). These boundary objects help build trust and shared understanding between humans and machines, enabling more effective collaboration.

The meaning of "machine" has evolved—from early mechanical contraptions to today's digital agents that augment human cognitive labor. Modern human–AI interaction has moved from procedural commands toward multimodal and conversational interfaces. GitHub Copilot (built on OpenAI Codex and launched in 2021) represents a shift from manual programming to suggestion-based coding. Studies published by Microsoft researchers indicate measurable productivity improvements among developers using Copilot, though results vary based on experience and task complexity.

Enterprise tools such as Power BI, Tableau, and Databricks have integrated AI features that assist users in pattern recognition, forecasting, and visualization. These platforms demonstrate how combining human domain expertise with machine-generated insights can enhance decision-making—especially in data-intensive fields. However, the effectiveness of these systems depends on how well the technology fits the user's task. The Task-Technology Fit (TTF) framework (Goodhue and Thompson 1995) explains this by evaluating whether technology supports user tasks effectively. Research confirms that alignment between system capabilities and task demands is critical to realizing productivity gains. Meanwhile, the challenge of representing skills in a fast-changing world persists. Workers often accumulate capabilities through informal learning or cross-domain experiences, which traditional systems fail to capture. Emerging platforms and AI-enhanced learning tools aim to create dynamic profiles that infer demonstrated skills and align them with market needs. However, this effort hinges on developing standardized taxonomies and interoperable systems for recognizing and validating skills at scale.

Human–AI collaboration is not just about interface design or productivity—it raises deeper questions about cognition, trust, and social coordination. As these systems evolve, success will depend on our ability to develop shared mental models, transparent systems, and equitable access to AI-enhanced tools.

How Talent Is Responding

Talent typically responds to tech changes in various ways. Older workers tend to stick to what they know and make as few skills adjustments or work practice changes as possible. Younger workers often adapt more quickly. Contrary to what many employers believe, workers often themselves realize when they need supplemental skills and act accordingly.

Workplace Coexistence of AI, Robots, and Workers

The integration of artificial intelligence (AI) systems into workplace environments presents both technical and sociocultural challenges that remain incompletely resolved. Research indicates that well-implemented workplace AI entices worker–AI interactions by offering to augment worker abilities—enhancing decision-making, automating repetitive tasks, personalizing workflows, and expanding access to complex data insights. This augmentation amplifies rather than replaces human skills—freeing cognitive capacity, fostering creativity, and enabling focus on complex problem-solving and human collaboration. As AI systems, robots, and human workers increasingly share physical and digital workspaces, effective coexistence depends on clear task division, trust in machine output, adaptive interfaces, and organizational cultures that value human oversight and judgment. When designed well, this triad of collaboration can lead to safer, more productive, and more meaningful work (Matheson et al. 2019).

However, empirical studies document significant implementation barriers. Raisch and Krakowski (2021) identify persistent human–AI friction points around control allocation, skill complementarity, and epistemic authority that frequently undermine theoretical benefits. They argue that automation and augmentation cannot be cleanly separated, as overemphasis on either dimension can lead to negative organizational outcomes. These findings suggest that sustainable human–AI collaboration requires not merely technical sophistication but organizational architectures specifically designed to accommodate the distinct affordances and limitations of human–machine interaction (Chowdhury 2023).

As a result, what traditionally would make sense is that dull, routine, manual, risky, and tedious work-related activities are partly or fully carried out by AI agents and robots. However, with the advent of advanced AI models with sophisticated language and even agentic capability, the automation threat now extends to a broad set of white-collar workers and professionals, even in highly specialized functions within domains as diverse and complex as academia, government bureaucracy, legal, and medical practice. More typically, workplace AI will entail augmenting human capability directly or indirectly. For example, robots in manufacturing might carry out certain procedures but not all, and will have to be monitored by humans for quality control and safety. With futuristic workplace AI, there is the potential for co-innovation with AI. This could take the form of involving AI at the deepest level of product development, quality control, sales and marketing, and supply chain management.

On the other hand, workers' distrust in AI stems from perceiving it as a job threat (Zirar, Ali, and Islam 2023). That said, workers increasingly do lose specific skills such as repetitive motion assembly, complex data analysis, or equipment monitoring to workplace AI (Zirar, Ali, and Islam 2023). In fact, workers need ongoing reskilling and upskilling to contribute to a symbiotic relationship. Workplace AI tends to reduce some forms of human engagement in the workplace. That said, for now, some skills, such as effective individual performance and teamwork, notably critical thinking, communication, and problem-solving, *primarily* remain with workers. However, with advances in AI, there is no guarantee that this will persist, not even in a seven- to ten-year time frame.

Counterbalancing these developments, "AI and worker coexistence require workers' technical, human, and conceptual skills" [...] "proficiency in a specific activity (technical skills), being able to work with people (human skills), and being able to work with concepts and ideas (conceptual skills)" (Zirar, Ali, and Islam 2023). Particularly, workers are increasingly expected to hone their skills in coordinating processes, acting with sensitivity and emotional intelligence, exhibiting adaptive flexibility, managing (an array of) people and machines, making impactful decisions with high monetary cost implications (upon infrastructure or products). As these coexistence skills evolve, it will become readily apparent that although they could be described as "soft," they might better be described as "elastic," although they are not always transferable between contexts. We know from the industrial management and worker productivity literature that contextual factors can be deterministic within each organization, workplace, and work task. For that reason, one could even make the claim that technical skills are "softer," and more transferable, than cognitive skills and judgments, which tend to depend on highly specific use contexts and have limited general validity. An expert in one domain would most likely be a novice in another.

The types of technical skills that will matter in a seven- to ten-year time frame go far beyond the current obsession with AI. For one, because AI is a platform technology that interacts with every sector, product, and technology out there. Secondly, because of the parallel improvements in sensors, nanotechnology, robotization, augmented reality, quantum technology, synthetic biology, and a host of other areas. It is not immediately obvious that somebody who regards themselves as an AI-expert in 2025 will be in a better position than anybody else in the near future of work.

Workplace AI also seems to demand the emergence of new skills such as oversight of workers and workplace AI. As always, those workers possessing high in-demand skills get better pay and more exciting job opportunities. These oversight tasks are often highly advanced and require a strong awareness of organizational goals, productivity tweaks, and safety protocols. However, identifying the exact skills needed to complement workplace AI as it develops is a confusing and complex task. The future of skills, jobs, and the future of work itself as a human productive practice generating income, meaning, and life satisfaction is in question. There are also inherent trust issues with regards to how much an employer discloses about the tracking functionality of workplace AI. At present, most commentators hold that such disclosure is rare and insufficient. The balance of responsibilities between workers and workplace AI is shifting rapidly. There is also a tremendous amount of AI hype out there which tends to exaggerate the immediate, medium-term, as well as the long-term impact of workplace AI.

There is a tradeoff between reskilling and recruiting new talent, and this tradeoff affects both employers and workers. Employers must weigh the cost of each given that workplace AI has a learning curve, and organizations have their peculiarities that each worker needs to learn and appreciate. Workers might decide that certain types of reskilling is too cumbersome and might opt to undertake reskilling on their own terms and switch jobs rather than attempt to adjust to a changing one.

Upskilling Strategies

A worker's time and energy to upskill is finite. We all have limited attention span, financial resources, free time, and different starting points. For that reason, both employers and workers (and students) constantly seek to optimize their own efforts. Most industrial economies have a woefully inadequate reskilling strategy and lack the necessary mentors, teachers, institutions, tools, and practices to rapidly upskill or reskill large amounts of current workers. Educational reforms tend to take time so there is little hope that traditional public education will somehow transform to tackle the challenge in the seven- to ten-year time frame I focus on in this book. Whether we are speaking about K–12 education, trade schools, community colleges, four-year colleges, or full-fledged universities, none have fully embraced future-proof strategies that seem able to adapt quickly to changing demands in the workplace stemming from structural change, innovation, or technology.

If this sobering assessment is even partially correct, what to do? That's where individual initiative could make a difference. However, the platforms and tools available to individual learners must also improve. This is where start-ups come in. However, the classical edtech start-ups (such as Khan Academy, Coursera, and Duolingo), using techniques such as gamification, personalization, and status-based rewards, have not made much of a dent in the learning modes of existing institutions, but still operate at the fringe.

These three represent different approaches within traditional edtech: Khan Academy pioneered free, personalized video-based learning; Coursera brought university courses online at scale; and Duolingo gamified language learning. All employ the mentioned techniques yet remain supplementary to rather than transformative of established educational institutions.

For employers, which I discuss in the next chapter (Chapter 3), the challenge will be to achieve the needed scale and the appropriate quality of reskilling efforts. Without workers motivated to learn, reskilling becomes a chore.

Will the Campus Model Die?

For individual learners, either pre-workplace, or in the workplace, the mind numbing changes can make most people question the value of going to school.

Imagine taking two to four years out of your working years only to try to learn something that will give you an edge in a workplace that moves even faster than educational institutions themselves. You risk being outdated before you graduate.

Will the campus model, the traditional model of higher education, where students live and study on a dedicated university campus, adapt or die? The strengths include community building and belonging, access to resources (libraries, research facilities, out-of-classroom interaction), immersive learning, and extracurricular opportunities. The weaknesses include high cost, limited diversity, social pressure, limited flexibility, and environmental impact. Students (and parents) today increasingly demand flexibility, personalized learning experiences, and a strong return on investment. As a result, colleges need to lower tuition and find new revenue streams (Parker 2025). Emerging technologies like AI, VR/AR, and the metaverse (*sic*) are creating new possibilities for learning and interaction, potentially redefining the traditional classroom experience, even within the campus environment. Some learning might still be optimally conducted live, real-time in the classroom, other learning or feedback is best remote or hybrid. That said, the social and intellectual benefits of in-person interaction, including face-to-face learning, mentorship, and the development of social networks, remain highly valuable for the time being. In my PhD, *What the Net Can't Do* (2002), I argued that this will always be the case, not because of the lack of technology, but for the logical reason that being supported by tech will always be better than not being supported (Undheim 2002). If so, and if f2f also is supported, unless tech alone was better than tech plus human communication, remote presence could never compete. This is a mathematical argument.

However, if VR/AR technology becomes so sophisticated that it *perfectly* replicates the sensory experiences of real-life interactions—the sights, sounds, smells, even the subtle nuances of body language—the need for physical copresence could diminish. One could imagine a virtual classroom where students feel as if they are truly sitting in a lecture hall, engaging in lively debates, and building genuine connections. The only way this would happen, I think, is if bodily interaction itself becomes compromised, dangerous, or rare. One could imagine a dystopian future where being outside is impossible due to deteriorating environmental conditions. Or, pandemics. Or travel costs. Or pervasive physical ailments affecting bodies across the human race. More interestingly, imagine new forms of learning experiences that are infinitely more dynamic than the classroom ever was. Incidentally, I would posit that what's lacking in education is not technological tools, but pedagogical and learning innovations.

If AI companions become so sophisticated that they can mirror human emotions, provide meaningful social support, and engage in deep, insightful conversations, the need for face-to-face interactions for emotional and intellectual fulfillment might decrease. Already, due to relentless promotion, and dire need to handle the aging population in cost-effective ways, care robots have a role in Japan. Japan has been developing robots to care for older people for over two decades, but in some instances create more work for caregivers because they spent time fiddling with the technology, rolling robots around to various rooms, addressing trust, lacking functionality, or catering to new problems (Wright 2023). Jibo was an early attempt at the MIT Media Lab to create a social robot, but the company ultimately failed. Chatbots do provide some amount of emotional support, but so far research indicates that attempting to implement artificial empathy is perceived as inauthentic (Seitz 2024). This finding is subject to change if technologies or human attitudes change, which could happen due to co-evolution of humans and AIs or habituation to AI co-existence. If advanced BCIs enable direct, high-bandwidth communication between individuals, bypassing the need for spoken or written language, the nature of human interaction could fundamentally change. This could potentially lead to new forms of social connection and knowledge sharing that transcend physical limitations.

Alternative models being actively explored include hybrid learning, online education, and more flexible pathways (starting students throughout the year, allowing course shopping, longer time frames for degree programs, extensive study abroad programs).

Digital Twins

Robots in higher education teaching can help provide hands-on learning experiences that bring abstract concepts to life through physical movements, visual displays, and simulations, while driving cognitive skills, enthusiasm, and future orientation. These systems can visualize complex data sets through coordinated movements, dynamic lighting, or three-dimensional projections that make statistical relationships tangible for students. Physical manipulation capabilities allow robots to create structures, embody design principles, and illustrate geometric shapes, mathematical functions, or scientific phenomena with precision that static models cannot achieve.

A robot could demonstrate the concept of momentum by physically colliding with different objects and showing how force transfers between materials of varying mass and density. These platforms can create simulated environments that allow users to experience abstract concepts in controlled settings, such as modeling economic systems where robots represent different market actors or demonstrating social dynamics through coordinated group behaviors. In molecular research, robots can physically model complex chemical structures, allowing researchers to visualize three-dimensional arrangements and observe how molecular interactions unfold in real time.

Robotic laboratories in high schools and colleges provide students with direct experience in programming, sensor integration, and mechanical design while developing computational thinking and STEM skills essential for contemporary technical careers.

Advice to High School Students

I would advise current high school students (I have two of those) to move beyond the obsession with STEM subjects (which they should have explored in high school already), and instead (or at least in addition to) explore the 13 futuristic skills described in this book.

While it is important to gain a background in many technical areas, it is unclear which of them (biology, chemistry, computer science, earth science, engineering, physics, math, or technology) will be recognizable a decade from now. If AI evolves as fast as many think, the interfaces to work with these areas might completely alter the educational preparation needed to exploit, benefit from, or understand them. Even emerging STEM fields such as AI, bioinformatics, environmental science, nanotech, cybersecurity, neuroscience, robotics, and space science, are changing rapidly. There is no guarantee that a dozen new technological disciplines will take their place even in the short time frame of a decade. The rise of AI might automate what we currently think of as STEM tasks in engineering, medicine, or scientific research. AI may, in time, come to surpass human capabilities in areas like data analysis, complex calculations, and even scientific discovery DeepMind's AlphaFold 2 (2020), whose developers Demis Hassabis, John Jumper, and David Baker were awarded the 2024 Nobel Prize in Chemistry, revolutionized protein structure prediction, achieving near-atomic accuracy in predicting the 3D shapes of proteins. This has profound implications for drug discovery, disease understanding, and materials science. It demonstrated and charted the way for AI to predict the properties of new materials with high accuracy. AI has recently developed new materials with tailored properties, such as high-temperature superconductors and novel catalysts. In an age of increasing worry about antibiotic resistance, and few human innovations to counter it, AI algorithms have been used to identify novel antibiotics. AI is also being used to improve the accuracy and resolution of climate models. AI-powered drug discovery is an especially important tool to address grand challenges such as commercially neglected diseases, including malaria, tuberculosis, leishmaniasis, and Chagas disease, accelerating public health solutions in the developing world (Nishan 2025).

It is not an exaggeration to say that AI is becoming an indispensable tool for scientific discovery. That said, human scientists are still essential for interpreting AI-generated results, formulating hypotheses, and guiding the research process—not to forget to watch for anomalies and AI-generated risks such as data privacy, bias, and irresponsible use.

Widespread automation could lead to significant job displacement in STEM-related fields, leaving many with obsolete skills. As a result, a future economy may prioritize skills like creativity, emotional intelligence, critical thinking, communication, and adaptability. Building human-centered skills might become humanity's only competitive advantage against machines. A growing emphasis on social and environmental well-being may lead to a reevaluation of the value of technological advancement. Perhaps we will need to prioritize human flourishing? An argument against this STEM negation is that AI-augmentation will always win, even improve human flourishing. Realistically, and to hedge our bets, the focus should at least for now be on developing a well-rounded education that includes both STEM and humanities.

That said, the so-called Twenty-first-Century Skills, including the four C's of creativity, communication, collaboration, and critical thinking, are no replacement. AI-enabled socio-technical change will likely transform those fields, too. Perhaps we should begin to think of humans as creative copilots (or assistants) to technologies, as policemen of agentic machine-to-machine communication, and as auditors of critical thinking performed by AI-systems. Either way, with only generic skills, you will not be working in tomorrow's workplace. In-depth insight will most likely still be required, both in terms of deep interdisciplinary awareness and deep technical insight in several fields (and certainly not only one or two). Paradoxically, if both agentic AI and knowledge platform interfaces dramatically improve, being good at accessing knowledge will no longer be a competitive advantage. Imagine a time where humans are only called upon to arbitrate in complex decisions where machines themselves realize that priorities must be set by human standards. The decision space might shrink considerably. Perhaps human workers will essentially be like court judges being asked to issue opinions. Except those opinions are more like advisory board input, it will often perhaps be optional for the machines to execute or not. Cognitive biases systematically impair human judgment, even when individuals are aware of their influence. Research in cognitive psychology and behavioral economics shows that people consistently deviate from rational evaluation patterns (Kahneman 2011). Mechanisms such as confirmation bias, motivated reasoning, and affect heuristics skew interpretation of information (Kunda 1990; Slovic, Finucane, Peters, and MacGregor 2007). These effects are not limited to laypeople; experts too are vulnerable, especially when evidence challenges deeply held beliefs. Moreover, awareness of bias is rarely enough: Pronin, Lin, and Ross (2002) describe the "bias blind spot," where people recognize bias in others but fail to see it in themselves. These findings raise concerns for fields that rely on impartial evaluation—science, law, policymaking, and democratic governance.

My best guess, based on 30 years of observing, working with and researching industrial and socio-technical change, is that an innovative engineering degree of some sort combined with strong entrepreneurial skills and highly tuned human–AI teamwork orchestration skills is a reasonable investment. I would separately recommend specializing in synthetic biology because of its tremendous potential as a platform for changing the world quite literally by altering nature's building blocks. Beyond that, few existing subjects taught in high school, college, or university seem immune from dramatic change.

Career Advice to Parents Advising Their High School Kids

As a parent to high school students, what are you to think about your offspring's career opportunities? Adaptability, studying hard to achieve well-timed competitive skills and skills advantages, generosity, strong grounding in ethical principles and family values, there are many things a parent should focus on building and honing in their children. Mindlessly sending them off to college should not be one of them. This should be a deliberate choice, having considered all other options, including self-directed learning, on-the-job training sponsored by employers, and practical professions that don't require a college degree. Paradoxically, we are entering an age where learning is fundamental but where current educational institutions may not always be best suited to provide that learning. *Deschooling Society* by Ivan Illich, 1971, argued that consumerist indoctrination was counterproductive and divisive and should instead focus on skills training (Illich 1995). Educational systems that still adhere to an industrial-era model, emphasizing standardized testing, rote memorization, and a linear progression through predefined curricula, are not suited to provide education.

Rather, as Illich argues, we should create institutions that foster personal, creative, and autonomous interaction—settings where learning is driven by curiosity, not compulsion. Examples include peer-to-peer learning networks, where individuals teach one another based on shared interests; tool libraries and makerspaces, which allow communities to access and experiment with equipment for self-directed projects; and learning webs, a concept Illich proposed to connect learners with mentors and resources outside formal schooling. These environments value voluntary association and knowledge exchange, blurring the boundary between teaching and learning, expert and novice.

Looking at the global landscape of transformative higher education reveals several distinctive institutional approaches that transcend conventional educational paradigms. In the United States, six institutions exemplify different facets of educational innovation. Babson College has distinguished itself through a comprehensive approach to entrepreneurship education that extends well beyond venture creation to fostering entrepreneurial leadership across multiple societal domains. Harvey Mudd College has established a distinctive educational model characterized by intimate learning environments, faculty mentorship, collaborative project-based learning, and experiential engineering pedagogy—a combination that consistently earns it exceptional rankings for educational quality and return on investment. Olin College of Engineering, founded in 1997, has implemented a radically project-centered curriculum that integrates hands-on engineering practice with rigorous multidisciplinary foundations, particularly in emerging fields at the intersection of biology and quantitative sciences including biomathematics, computational biology, and quantitative biology. MIT cultivates an intellectual environment that systematically encourages critical examination of the complex relationships between scientific advancement, technological development, and societal impact. Stanford University combines academic excellence with entrepreneurial orientation and innovation focus, strategically leveraging its Silicon Valley location to create unique educational opportunities. Columbia University capitalizes on its New York City setting to provide unparalleled access to cultural and intellectual resources, fostering a distinctive urban-integrated learning experience.

In the United Kingdom, the Universities of Oxford and Cambridge maintain educational traditions centered on rigorous tutorial systems, self-directed inquiry, and intellectual heritage while adapting to contemporary challenges. Within continental Europe, ETH Zurich has established itself as not merely a center of scientific and technological excellence but as an institution that systematically develops critical thinking capacities and innovative mindsets among its students. In Asia, the Indian Institutes of Technology have become instrumental in India's technological transformation, systematically developing technical talent, driving innovation initiatives, and strengthening industry–academic partnerships that collectively reshape the national IT landscape ("Empowering Tech Innovation: The Role of IITs in Shaping India's IT Future," 2025). South America's educational leadership is exemplified by the University of São Paulo, while in Africa, the University of Cape Town has established itself as a continental leader in higher education transformation.

But is this enough? In *Realizing the Ecological University: Eight Ecosystems, Their Antagonisms and a Manifesto*, educational theorist Ronald Barnett (2024) advances a comprehensive framework that transcends conventional discourse on higher education reform. Barnett's ecological paradigm positions the university as fundamentally responsible for the maintenance and regeneration of eight interconnected ecosystems, each facing distinctive threats that demand institutional response. The knowledge ecosystem, Barnett argues, suffers from hyperspecialization and instrumentalization, with disciplinary silos preventing holistic understanding of complex problems. Simultaneously, the learning ecosystem has become distorted by assessment regimes privileging measurable outputs over transformative experiences. Perhaps most concerning is Barnett's diagnosis of the ecosystem of persons, which he characterizes as increasingly subjected to reductive competency frameworks that neglect the developmental dimensions of higher education. The university's relationship to social institutions constitutes a fourth ecosystem, one Barnett finds weakened by diminishing civic engagement and public discourse. Cultural ecosystems, meanwhile, face commodification pressures that undermine diversity of thought and expression. Barnett's analysis extends to economic ecosystems, which he contends universities have insufficiently critiqued despite their complicity in reproducing inequality. The political ecosystem receives particular attention, with Barnett documenting declining democratic participation among university graduates. Finally, the natural ecosystem represents the most urgent domain requiring university attention, demanding fundamental reconsideration of humanity's relationship to planetary boundaries. Through detailed examination of these eight domains and their complex antagonisms, Barnett constructs a persuasive argument that universities must move beyond passive knowledge transmission toward active ecological stewardship across multiple dimensions of social and natural life.

What future paths can be imagined for universities? Organic platforms for learning loosely organized between students and teachers (Kaospilotene in Denmark), microcolleges (far smaller than the Little Ivies of Amherst, Wesleyan, Williams, Bates, Bowdoin, Colby), think tanks with college like programs (Brookings, Belfer, Hoover, Cato, CERI, RAND,), nomadic (the European Erasmus Mundus student exchange program), polymath universities, interface universities where students learn as co-learners alongside AI (MIT, CMU, Stanford), or Future Visualization University (with foresight, future studies, STS, and systems thinking at the heart and built on AI, entrepreneurship, experiential learning, lifelong learning, solutions to grand challenges such as sustainability/degrowth, health access, and inequality) ("How Can We Imagine a New University?" 2024).

Problem-Based Learning (PBL) originated in the 1960s in the medical school at McMaster University (Canada). It was influenced by existing pedagogical currents, particularly by American philosopher and psychologist John Dewey's ideas about learning by doing (intrinsic interest), Bruner's (1966) learning by discovery (enactive, iconic, symbolic learning) and the case-based learning of HBS. HBS was created in 1908 and established its case study method in 1924, a method now adopted by 14,000 schools. HBS professors summarized recent events, momentous challenges, strategic planning, and important decisions undertaken by major companies and organizations into a case document and provided a set of questions to explore ("The History of the Case Study at Harvard Business School" 2017; Nohria 2021). This was then explored in class, at times with a live speaker, but without answers and full access to facts and methods. It was the start of experiential learning. To this day, I find it to be a useful method both as a student who has experienced it and as a lecturer who has used it to teach. Future iterations are likely to integrate AI-powered case development to create multimedia-supported synthetic case studies which enables a wider range and less limitations in terms of context, company size, or culture—potentially diversifying management learning in important ways. This could also perhaps address the critique that this method historically is biased toward extroverted students, is instructor dependent, has limited generalizability, potentially lends itself to superficial analysis, and that the cases are of mixed quality. This could involve simulating market fluctuations, geopolitical events, and technological disruptions, creating more unpredictable learning scenarios. Those could also be AR/VR supported. For 60 years, Cliff'sNotes has been a valuable yet controversial study guide providing book summaries, questions, and answers. The guides are intended to help students understand complex texts and prepare for exams. In reality, but they are often used as a shortcut to reading the original works. AI is already acting like CliffsNotes" on steroids, helping students analyze cases, summarize information, and suggest possible solutions. This practice is often hard to track for teachers. Software developed to do so is not always accurate and might worsen the situation by alledging inappropriate AI use when this is not always the case.

The possible future demise of the campus or indeed the college model as we know it, would be due to cost-benefit considerations but also to the fact that learning can occur in many places. Internships are fundamental. Networks in the workplace. Building in-demand skills that are quick to learn. The future of work might be counterintuitive, but there is no reason to give up forging a path. While you should refrain from attempting to foresee the future, painting several scenarios for your children is not a bad thing to do. Flexibility and adaptability is key. Few would dispute that we are entering an era in which lifelong learning is not optional, but essential.

In the 1980s my father, then psychology professor Johan Olav Undheim, told me that the workplace would change significantly and that I would have to deal with several job changes throughout my life. Preparing for that at an early age has been quite useful. I am now in a position to say that parents should tell their kids that not only will they switch jobs several times during their life, but the skills required to fill jobs will change dramatically, perhaps every five years. Employers, aided by AI-based selection criteria, will gradually get better at determining what skills they need and what skills potentially employees possess. In such a reality, skills become more fundamental than professions. It seems unlikely that professional protections will outlast the next few decades. Or, such licenses might still exist at the margins, but the true work will be carried out by a mix of talent and machines and licensed professionals might oversee some of it but not all.

Futuristic Skills—Blending Talent, Technology, and Demand

As I prepare you to ponder futuristic skills in Chapters 4–14, I'll make a detour through a discussion of whether the twenty-first-century employer will only care about machines? (Chapter 3). Being aware of emerging concerns among large employers (public or private), emerging start-ups, or other institutions (nonprofits), is a great preparatory step toward understanding what the *platinum workforce* will entail. The future of skills will be a blend of the three fundamental factors of talent, technology, and demand. You cannot afford to ignore either factor. No matter how individualized learning paths become possible, if large organizations still prevail, and I'll assume they will, they will attempt to put their own stamp on the way they use their workforce, if only to try to convince talent that they remain relevant.

References

Advance CTE. 2018. *Career Advising and Development: State of Career Technical Education.* Washington, DC: Advance CTE.

Barnett, Ronald. 2024. *Realizing the Ecological University: Eight Ecosystems, Their Antagonisms and a Manifesto.* New York: Bloomsbury Academic.

Bowker, Geoffrey C., and Susan Leigh Star. 1999. *Sorting Things Out: Classification and Its Consequences.* Cambridge, MA: MIT Press.

Bruner, J. S. 1966. *Toward a Theory of Instruction.* Cambridge: Harvard University Press.

Burning Glass Technologies. 2020. *The Narrow Ladder: The Value of Industry Certifications in the Job Market.*

Castilla, Emilio J., and Stephen Benard. 2010. "The Paradox of Meritocracy in Organizations." *Administrative Science Quarterly* 55 (4): 543–576. https://doi.org/10.2189/asqu.2010.55.4.543.

Chowdhury, Hafiz. 2023. "Human-Robot Collaboration in Manufacturing Assembly Tasks." *ResearchGate.* https://www.researchgate.net/publication/374385787_Human-Robot_Collaboration_in_Manufacturing_Assembly_Tasks.

da Vinci, Leonardo. 1482. *Letter to Ludovico Sforza, Duke of Milan.* Reproduced in Ladislao Reti, *The Unknown Leonardo*, New York: McGraw-Hill, 1974.

Ferguson, S. L., Kluttz-Drye, B., and Hovey, K. A. 2019. "Survey of the Preparation of High School Counselors for Advising on Technician Careers." *Journal of Research in Technical Careers* 3 (1): 1–10.

"Global Employment Trends for Youth 2024." 2024. *International Labour Organization.* July 22. https://www.ilo.org/publications/major-publications/global-employment-trends-youth-2024.

Goodhue, Dale L., and Ronald L. Thompson. 1995. "Task-Technology Fit and Individual Performance." *MIS Quarterly* 19 (2): 213–236.

"How Can We Imagine a New University?" 2024. *THE Campus Learn, Share, Connect.* March 19. https://www.timeshighereducation.com/campus/how-can-we-imagine-new-university.

Illich, Ivan. 1995. *Deschooling Society.* Open Forum S. London, England: Marion Boyars.

Kalleberg, Arne L. 2009. "Precarious Work, Insecure Workers: Employment Relations in Transition." *American Sociological Review* 74 (1): 1–22.

Kahneman, Daniel. 2011. *Thinking, Fast and Slow.* New York: Farrar, Straus and Giroux.

Kunda, Ziva. 1990. "The Case for Motivated Reasoning." *Psychological Bulletin* 108 (3): 480–498. https://doi.org/10.1037/0033-2909.108.3.480.

Matheson, Euan, Ryan Minto, Eduardo G. G. Zampieri, and Giacomo Rosati. 2019. "Human–Robot Collaboration in Manufacturing Applications: A Review." *Robotics* 8 (4): 100. https://doi.org/10.3390/robotics8040100.

"Mental Health at Work." n.d. Accessed February 23, 2025. https://www.who.int/teams/mental-health-and-substance-use/promotion-prevention/mental-health-in-the-workplace.

"Mental Illness." n.d. *National Institute of Mental Health (NIMH).* Accessed February 23, 2025. https://www.nimh.nih.gov/health/statistics/mental-illness#part_2632.

Nishan, M. D. Nahid Hassan. 2025. "AI-Powered Drug Discovery for Neglected Diseases: Accelerating Public Health Solutions in the Developing World." *Journal of Global Health* 15 (January): 03002.

Nohria, Nitin. 2021. "What the Case Study Method Really Teaches." *Harvard Business Review.* December 21. https://hbr.org/2021/12/what-the-case-study-method -really-teaches.

OECD. 2021. *The Future of Work: OECD Employment Outlook 2021.* Paris: Organisation for Economic Co-operation and Development.

Parker, I. 2025. *How Much is College Tuition? Real Costs, Trends & How Families can Pay Less,* July 28, 2025. Collegewise.

Pronin, Emily, Daniel Y. Lin, and Lee Ross. 2002. "The Bias Blind Spot: Perceptions of Bias in Self Versus Others." *Personality and Social Psychology Bulletin* 28 (3): 369–381. https://doi.org/10.1177/0146167202286008.

Raisch, Sebastian, and Sebastian Krakowski. 2021. "Artificial Intelligence and Management: The Automation–Augmentation Paradox." *Academy of Management Review* 46 (1): 192–210. https://doi.org/10.5465/amr.2018.0072.

Seitz, Lennart. 2024. "Artificial Empathy in Healthcare Chatbots: Does It Feel Authentic?" *Computers in Human Behavior: Artificial Humans* 2 (1): 100067.

Segal, David R., and Mady Wechsler Segal. 2004. "America's Military Population." *Population Bulletin* 59 (4): 3–40.

Sieloff, Charles G. 1999. "'If Only HP Knew What HP Knows': The Roots of Knowledge Management at Hewlett-Packard." *Journal of Knowledge Management* 3 (1): 47–53.

Slovic, Paul, Melissa L. Finucane, Ellen Peters, and Donald G. MacGregor. 2007. "The Affect Heuristic." *European Journal of Operational Research* 177 (3): 1333–1352. https://doi.org/10.1016/j.ejor.2005.04.006.

Star, Susan Leigh, and James R. Griesemer. 1989. "Institutional Ecology, 'Translations' and Boundary Objects: Amateurs and Professionals in Berkeley's Museum of Vertebrate Zoology, 1907–1939." *Social Studies of Science* 19 (3): 387–420.

"Stress in America." n.d. *American Psychological Association.* Accessed February 23, 2025. https://www.apa.org/news/press/releases/stress.

Strunz, Stephan. 2020. "Organizing Careers for Work – The Curriculum Vitae (CV) in Prussia's Technical Bureaucracy, C. 1770–1830." *Management & Organizational History* 15 (4): 315–337.

"The Deloitte Global 2024 Gen Z and Millennial Survey." n.d. *Deloitte.* Accessed February 23, 2025. https://www.deloitte.com/global/en/issues/work/content/genz-millennialsurvey.html.

"The History of the Case Study at Harvard Business School." 2017. *Business Insights Blog.* February 28, 2017. https://online.hbs.edu/blog/post/the-history-of-the-case -study-at-harvard-business-school.

Undheim, Trond Arne. 2002. "What the Net Can't Do. The Everyday Practice of Internet, Globalization and Mobility." https://scholar.google.com/citations?view _op=view_citation&hl=en&citation_for_view=ikTxTWcAAAAJ:KlAtU1dfN 6UC.

Wright, James. 2023. "Inside Japan's Long Experiment in Automating Elder Care." *MIT Technology Review.* January 9, 2023. https://www.technologyreview.com/2023/01/09/1065135/japan-automating-eldercare-robots/.

Yasmin, Taj, and ET Education. 2025. "Empowering Tech Innovation: The Role of IITs in Shaping India's IT Future." *ET Education.* January 17, 2025. https://education.economictimes.indiatimes.com/news/industry/empowering-tech-innovation-the-role-of-iits-in-shaping-indias-it-future/117322956.

Zirar, Araz, Syed Imran Ali, and Nazrul Islam. 2023. "Worker and Workplace Artificial Intelligence (AI) Coexistence: Emerging Themes and Research Agenda." *Technovation* 124 (102747): 102747.

CHAPTER 3

WILL THE TWENTY-FIRST-CENTURY EMPLOYER ONLY CARE ABOUT MACHINES?

Weird Workplaces of the Future

It is a sunny morning in 2035, and Fenny, an Indian expat manager operating across the world, is checking her work metrics. The various semi-autonomous artificial intelligence (AI) systems are humming along, but there are a few non-urgent alerts showing that she rapidly clears. Her augmented human teams are directing their own AIs and are reporting to her as well as to other systems. Fenny is herself an augmented human worker, and everything she does is monitored by a set of cross-checking AIs and ultimately the C-level team. Fenny came into her current position 12 days ago and is already the most senior human in the department. Most humans only last about a week. The pressure is too high. The machines are too good. The skills needed to do her job change every week. Many workers cannot deal with it. Fenny deals with it because she was groomed to care for machines from an early age. Her family has always been ahead of their times. Through experimenting with home automation as technology evolved, she learned to adapt. Fenny attributes her success in the workplace to a mix of her parents' foresight and the training systems of her last 10 employers. In her first two years as a manager, she has changed jobs more times than her parents did in a lifetime. The best employers make it frictionless. She didn't even have to change her meal plan, her four-year-old personalized AI assistant, or her commute.

Contrary to what governments and trade unions feared, there are plenty of jobs. The problem is the opposite. People don't want to work anymore. In socialist countries, they accept the low citizen payout to stay home and not clog the rapidly evolving, advanced workplace dynamics of intricate coworking reporting relationships between people and machines. In capitalist countries, there is no such payout, and lower-middle-class slums of former factory workers have developed in the outskirts of major cities.

The Need to See Beyond Human Capital

Work lies at the foundation of every productive society. Human capital is the stock of knowledge, skills, and other personal attributes embodied in individuals that help them to be productive. It encompasses education, experience, health, and personal attributes such as creativity, problem-solving skills, leadership abilities, and motivation. Human capital is an important factor in economic growth and development. Countries, regions, firms, and teams with a highly skilled and educated workforce are more likely to be competitive. Human capital is an investment and is not fixed; it can be improved through ongoing learning and development. It can also deteriorate over time.

In the age of AI, the definition of human capital is evolving. While traditionally focused on skills and knowledge, it now encompasses a broader set of attributes crucial for navigating a complex and rapidly changing world. Human capital in the future workplace will increasingly emphasize unique human qualities (but what those are is a complex question), continuous learning (a lifelong commitment), adaptive capacity (resilience to changes, shocks, and transitions), personal brand (value proposition, ability to present and position such value and distinguish oneself in the workplace and marketplace), collaboration acuity (with humans and AIs), and ethical fiber (strong ethical frameworks to navigate the implications of emerging technologies).

Machine Capital: Industrial Use

Machines, particularly those powered by AI, possess several key attributes that differentiate them from humans: speed and efficiency, accuracy and precision, data processing and storage, consistency and predictability, and automation of repetitive tasks.

In industrial settings, today's AI is primarily used for predictive maintenance, where it analyzes sensor data from machinery to predict potential failures and schedule preventative maintenance, minimizing costly downtime and improving overall equipment effectiveness (OEE). Key industrial applications of AI over the past decade include anomaly detection, quality control, production optimization, robot control, supply chain management, and energy efficiency. In the near future, data processing capability will vastly increase in speed and accuracy, identifying patterns and insights that would be impossible for humans to discern within a reasonable time frame. AI algorithms can already identify intricate patterns and anomalies in data, advancing fields like fraud detection, medical diagnosis, and scientific research. If pattern recognition improves dramatically, this could alter the innovation trajectory in each of these fields. AI models can analyze historical data and make highly accurate predictions about future events, such as weather patterns, market trends, and customer behavior. This has significant implications for various sectors, including finance, logistics, and healthcare. That said, there are ample limitations to the domains where this is applicable now or in the foreseeable future.

AI systems are increasingly capable of understanding, generating, and translating human language, enabling them to communicate and interact with humans in more natural and intuitive ways. AI systems can now analyze and interpret images and videos with remarkable accuracy, enabling applications such as facial recognition, object detection, and self-driving cars.

These capabilities are still nascent. They represent a narrow type of intelligence. While impressive, current AI systems still lack true understanding. They operate based on algorithms and statistical models, not genuine comprehension or sentience. AI excels at specific tasks but often lacks the general intelligence and adaptability of humans. Overreliance on AI systems could lead to a decline in critical thinking, problem-solving, and decision-making skills, making humans increasingly dependent on technology. The development of superintelligent AI that surpasses human intelligence could lead to unforeseen consequences, potentially resulting in the loss of human control and even the extinction of humanity. AI could be used to generate and disseminate misinformation, such as deepfakes and AI-powered propaganda. This could erode public trust, manipulate public opinion, and destabilize democratic institutions.

Which Jobs Will Disappear Soon?

Jobs that clearly will be gone by 2030 or sooner due to automation, societal, or technological change, include cashiers, telemarketers, data entry clerks, and customer service agents. Any administrative task is up for grabs. Creative professionals will need to deeply integrate AI in their workflow or will be superfluous in all but high stakes, high dollar campaigns. Some white-collar jobs, such as legal assistants and financial advisors, are also under threat. High-level white-collar workers that are responsible for making complex business decisions, such as management consultants, are less likely to be displaced or at least not completely replaced by AI. Customer service will be automated to a large degree. However, customer-facing positions, such as salespeople who need to engage and build relationships with clients, are relatively safe from being made obsolete by AI in the medium term. Lawyers who spend their time in court (trial lawyers) or negotiating settlements are still safe, although those who don't deploy AI in their workflow (research, drafting, presentation) will not be as efficient or successful.

How will this job displacement occur? Computer vision can automate tasks previously performed by humans, such as quality control inspections in manufacturing, manual data entry from images, and certain types of medical imaging analysis. Industries heavily reliant on manual image analysis, such as retail (inventory management, customer service), transportation (autonomous vehicles, drone delivery), and security (surveillance, facial recognition) may experience job displacement as these tasks are automated.

How Employers Must Prepare

The most successful twenty-first-century employers will have a number of characteristics, driven by dramatic socio-technical changes. Given the importance of technology, and the growing cost of such infrastructure, one would think, they would be revamped to primarily care about machines. After all, the vast majority of tasks to be done are carried out with machine input or will be entirely controlled by machines. Very likely, many corporations will evolve to become machine-friendly, perhaps even machine-biased organizations.

Today, industry titans like Walmart and Amazon, the largest employers in the United States, both deploy AI to automate and analyze their business processes, improving efficiency, safety, and delivery speed. Amazon, currently employing more than a million and a half workers across many industries, including e-commerce, cloud computing, logistics, voice-activated technology, and autonomous vehicles, is using AI and robotics in a wide range of ways. Since 2012, Amazon has deployed hundreds of thousands of robots in its fulfillment centers, primarily for tasks like moving and sorting packages, allowing humans to focus on more complex tasks. In 2019, Amazon introduced the Packaging Decision Engine (PDE), an AI model designed to optimize millions of packages on a daily basis. PDE has helped Amazon eliminate over two million tons of packaging material globally since 2015.

That said, from 2021 to 2024, Amazon has replaced 100,000 employees with 750,000 robots.[1] Many of these are Autonomous Mobile Robots (AMRs), equipped with cameras, sensors, and AI enabling path planning with slow,

---

1 Brandoli n.d.

stop, rerouting and collision avoidance capability, so they can understand and move through their environment independently (and safely). Amazon's robots have evocative names, among others, *Kiva* (2012), a small picking robot, *Hercules* (2012), a heavy-duty shelving robot improving packing and storing intensity, *Proteus* (2022), a robot that is certified to be safe around people, *Sequoia* (2023), a system of multiple robots that containerize inventory into totes enabling more widespread same-day shipping, and *Titan* (2023), a mega-heavy-duty shelving robot that can carry larger, bulkier items like small household appliances or pallets of pet food and gardening equipment.[2]

By 2019, Amazon offered hundreds of millions of products in 185 countries across the world. Amazon utilizes advanced AI systems to optimize inventory management, pricing, and other operations. Since 2011, its Supply Chain Optimization Technology (SCOT), which took three years to develop,[3] helps manage a supply chain that has millions of sellers, allowing those sellers to manage their own inventories and storefronts. SCOT made billions of dollars of inventory decisions. However, by 2016, pioneered by Procter & Gamble (P&G) since the early 2000s, the industry was moving toward advanced multi-echelon inventory optimization (MEIO). MEIO is a sophisticated strategy that uses advanced algorithms and analytics to optimize inventory levels across a supply chain network. However, there was no existing MEIO software fit for the company's needs. After two years' experimentation, Amazon's MEIO went live in 2020, having redesigned Amazon's supply chain systems from the ground up.[4] This system helped diversify and layer its fulfillment network, and position inventory close to the customer, further localizing the global company. A related improvement, Project PI (private investigator), debuted in 2024, uses computer vision and generative AI to catch damaged items in warehouses and to ensure product specification correctness (such as color and size), before they're shipped to customers. This replaces the previous procedure of having five employees use a six-point visual check.[5]

Despite automation, Amazon still relies on a large workforce for tasks requiring judgment, customer service, and complex problem-solving. Amazon emphasizes the idea of robots working alongside humans to improve efficiency and safety, not replacing them entirely. Amazon claims that robots have

---

2 Greenawalt 2024.
3 "Amazon re:MARS" n.d.
4 Özer and Şimşek 2021.
5 "How Amazon Is Using AI To Become the Fastest Supply Chain in the World" 2024.

created new skilled jobs, such as roles that require communication between humans and robots to recover from issues. With that, allegedly, as many as 700 new categories of skilled work have emerged, including roles like "flow control specialists who manage day-to-day workflows in fulfillment centers, amnesty floor monitors who facilitate safe interactions with mobile robots, and reliability maintenance engineers who help keep all of the technology running at our sites."[6] These are jobs, in which "the cognitive aspects of setting-up, supervising, and troubleshooting robotics and automation are emphasized," according to MIT roboticist Julie Shah.[7]

Many tasks are designed around human workflows. In contrast to system-centric workflows, human workflows with their three basic components—inputs, transformations, and outputs—are structured and built with the specific capabilities and limitations of humans in mind, including the human formfactor and the typical layout of a brownfield factory built in the pre-robotics era. In 2023, Amazon began testing Agility Robotics' humanoid robot *Digit*, for use in their operations. *Digit's* size and shape are well-suited for buildings that are designed for humans. Humanoid robots will soon be able to collect and analyze data to optimize business operations in a human workflow. Despite these synergies, it is widely believed that, by the year 2030, Amazon could have more robots than employees. Humanoid robots, such as previously mentioned Agility Robotics' relatively safe robot *Digit,* Boston Dynamics' dexterous and strong *Atlas* robot, Figure AI's general purpose conversational robot *Figure 02* (2024), and Tesla's self-driving navigationally savvy *Optimus* robot, would be suited to augment work across multiple sectors, including automotive, education, healthcare, logistics, manufacturing, and retail.[8] Despite some uncertainty regarding tech adoption and trust, not so much depending on further dramatic technological progress, the humanoid robot market is set to quadruple past $13 billion within the next five years.[9] Agility Robotics has announced a planned production capacity of 10,000 robots per year.[10] Given numerous manufacturing constraints alone, such as supply chain logistics, Elon Musk's "More Robots Than Humans" by 2040 dream is an unlikely scenario in the foreseeable future.

6 Jarrett 2023.
7 "Amazon and MIT Are Studying How Automation Impacts Jobs" 2023.
8 Shaikh 2024.
9 Patel 2024.
10 Sims 2023.

   Productivity differences between firms, however, are entirely dependent on how humans and machines work together. In a world where all employers have ample access to AI, differentiated value is created through the interaction between the two. Obviously, wealthy, more powerful corporations have vastly superior AIs at their disposal. But in the end, this doesn't matter much. An AI on its own can make or break a company but in order for systems to work well, AIs must be properly integrated in the business and across the supply chains. That is still a task that humans will be involved in for some time to come.

   Their workforce will still have human workers, but those workers will be those who most flexibly have adapted to coworking with machines in a myriad of different ways: AI *controllers* (workers monitoring people and machines), AI *collaborators* (workers developing deep functional relationships with AI systems through augmentation techniques, tools, and processes), AI *teamers* (workers putting together teams of humans and machines for emerging tasks), and AI *cyborgs* (physically augmented workers who have integrated AI systems into their bodies).

FIGURE 3.1 Cyborgs in the workplace.

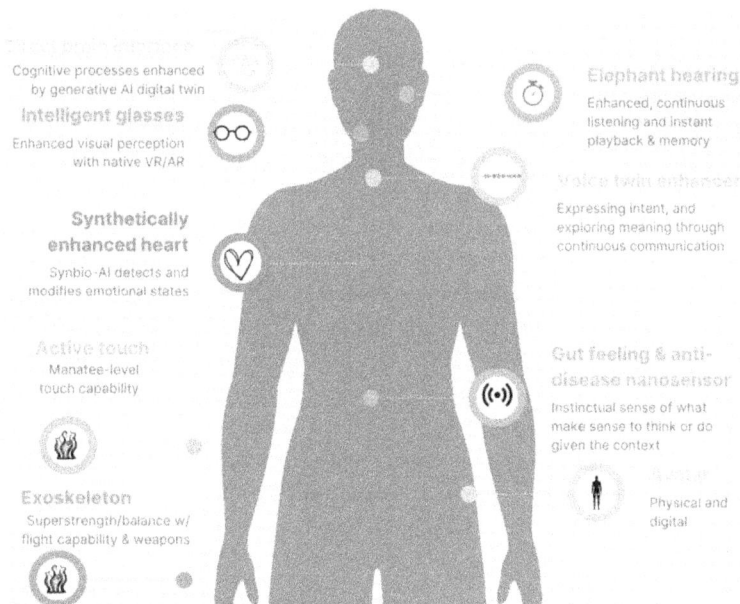

Cognitive processes enhanced by generative AI digital twin

Intelligent glasses
Enhanced visual perception with native VR/AR

Synthetically enhanced heart
Synbio-AI detects and modifies emotional states

Active touch
Manatee-level touch capability

Exoskeleton
Superstrength/balance w/ flight capability & weapons

Elephant hearing
Enhanced, continuous listening and instant playback & memory

Voice twin enhancer
Expressing intent, and exploring meaning through continuous communication

Gut feeling & anti-disease nanosensor
Instinctual sense of what make sense to think or do given the context

Physical and digital

Hybrid Upskilling

Which company has the most advanced upskilling program? Several companies have a commitment to employee development and innovative upskilling initiatives. Google is known for its comprehensive training programs, including internal courses, mentorship programs, and access to cutting-edge technologies. Amazon invests heavily in upskilling its workforce, providing opportunities for employees to acquire in-demand skills in areas like cloud computing, software engineering, and logistics. Microsoft has a long history of investing in employee development, with programs focused on technical skills, leadership development, and career growth. Salesforce offers a wide range of training programs, including online courses, workshops, and mentorship opportunities.

When evaluating upskilling programs, as a prospective employee, it is important to consider the scope and breadth, accessibility, and potential impact on employee careers. As an employer, the ROI for the company is also important, as well as its innovation, ability to incorporate emerging technologies, and adaptability to the evolving needs of the workforce.

Upskilling Programs Independent of Employer

Khan Academy, founded by Salman Khan in 2008, produces short video lessons (currently 6,500) as a supplement to in-class learning. Aiming to improve the effectiveness of teachers by freeing them from traditional lectures and giving them more time to tend to individual students' needs, the Khan Academy channel on YouTube has 8.74 million subscribers. Its videos have been viewed more than two billion times. Khan Academy has more than 155 million registered users, with students spending billions of hours learning on the platform, including 2 million registered teachers and a network of over 200 content experts. Google.org provided seed funding to Khan Academy to help create a free, high-quality education for all. Google's initial donation was $2 million in 2010. Despite Khan Academy's notion of the flipped classroom, where learners are supposed to practice their new skills in teams after watching videos, this is not a facilitated process. As a result, students don't experience the nuances and complexities of a classroom environment. Students don't receive feedback from the teacher or fellow students, nor do they get any personalized guidance.

Will Online Credentials (Badges) Replace Traditional College Degrees?

Companies, including top employers such as McKinsey, are gradually shifting the focus from degrees to skills.[11] In fact, increasing skills and competency-based hiring is official U.S. government policy. The challenge is that measuring and proving skills is harder than proving degrees.

LinkedIn offers a range of learning resources, including online courses, certifications, and career coaching services. Badges are easier and faster to verify than paper credentials. Approximately one-third of employers consider badges during the application process. However, displaying learning badges on a LinkedIn profile or resume is likely not enough to land a job.

Grow with Google is a program that was started by Lisa Gevelber in 2017 that helps people learn skills for in-demand jobs and grow their careers. It has helped more than 11 million Americans develop new skills. Grow with Google has a network of more than 9,500 partner organizations like libraries, schools, small business development centers, chambers of commerce, and nonprofits to help people coast to coast. The program is designed by Google and taught by experts. It offers online courses and certificates in fields like cybersecurity, data analytics, digital marketing, project management, AI, and IT support that are self-paced and don't require prior experience or a degree. It combines skills training with hands-on practice. In addition, job seekers receive support and practical tips for resumes, interviews, and job searches, helping them to land jobs in the technology sector. In 2022, a new $100 million Google Career Certificates Fund was launched,[12] with a five-year goal to award $1 billion in grants and contribute 1 million employee volunteer hours. Google Career Certificates cost $49 per month on Coursera after an initial seven-day free trial period. Seventy thousand Americans have now completed these certificates. They are available to anyone, no college degree required. If graduates land a job earning at least $40,000, they pay roughly $100 a month with no interest for five years maximum.

The elite, platinum-level employers will be those who understand how to optimize human–AI collaboration and be mindful of its risks. To do that, they continuously hone this process. Counterintuitively, these employers treat humans and AIs equally. Training is done together. Follow-up and feedback is

---

11 George 2022.
12 Pichai 2022.

given to both in equal measure. The performance of each is regulated. Safety is paramount. There is full transparency about the capabilities of each. All metrics are shared. To excel as productivity tools, humans and AIs must complement each other. To be expected to work in symmetry, they must be treated symmetrically. But what would it mean in practice? How will it evolve?

Key aspects of human–AI symmetry might include complementary roles, AI–human-centered design, and joint skills development.

In the workplace, humans and AI complement each other by leveraging their unique strengths. In theory, right now, AI excels at processing large amounts of data quickly, providing data-driven insights, automating repetitive tasks, and performing routine tasks, while humans excel at creativity, complex problem-solving, ethics, strategy, systems oversight, decision-making, risk management (including necessary interventions), and adapting to new situations. When that synergy works well, it will allow for more informed decision-making, stronger employee engagement, better innovation, and enhanced productivity across various roles. When the synergy fails, and if contingency plans are not in place, disaster would ensue.

The above is a simplification. Humans will soon deploy AIs in nearly every task, including to evaluate ethics, carry out oversight, and to develop strategy. There is also mounting evidence that AIs might become more trustable than humans in many sensitive decisions that either require superhuman insight or where ethics requires weighting values against each other in transparent ways.

Today, there is talk about upskilling but little understanding about what that will mean in the near future. To properly position upskilling initiatives, and to be able to scale them across entire organizations, we must consider its key elements. Traditionally, upskilling primarily focused on enhancing skills directly relevant to an employee's current role. In the early 2000s, IT specialists would get training on cloud computing to capture the upside and on cybersecurity to handle the downside of the technology evolution. Reskilling might be more focused on facilitating transitions to new career paths. Companies prioritizing reskilling might offer IT specialists the chance to take leadership training to become managers. However, both upskilling and reskilling was traditionally employer-driven, driven by employer needs and perceived skills gaps in current processes. The emphasis was usually on developing technical skills arising from new machinery, IT systems, or regulatory demands. At best, there was a focus on quality improvement, in which case, an IT specialist might be trained in a process improvement paradigm such as Lean Six Sigma, an evolution of lean manufacturing principles from Toyota and analysis of defect rates developed at Motorola.

Some industries, such as the manufacturing industry, have a fairly good idea about what training needs are. Others, especially in knowledge worker or service worker contexts where the work process is less structured to begin with, have had no idea. Think academia, retail, or healthcare. This is partly because knowing how their own workforce carries out work and what the bottlenecks to improvement are, has been a complex question to answer. With better monitoring tools stemming from sensor technology and AI analysis of the data, this is rapidly changing.

Upskilling in the AI Era

In the AI era, the scope of upskilling is shifting to prioritize not just technical AI knowledge, but also critical thinking, creativity, collaboration, and ethical decision-making skills. Upskilling programs should emphasize developing a deeper understanding of how to work alongside AI, interpret its outputs, and apply AI tools effectively. Companies will be utilizing AI-powered platforms to tailor training based on individual needs and career goals, identifying skill gaps and providing targeted learning experiences. Future upskilling efforts will become more holistic, taking a whole-of-business approach, or even a whole-of-society approach. The question becomes: How can the overall productivity increase while maximizing worker satisfaction, professional growth, and wellness? Or, alternatively, how can expectations (of customers, shareholders, workers, and society) be managed in a time of overall societal degrowth due to mounting and costly long-term sustainability challenges?

In a rapidly changing world, the elusive search for future-proof skills is not only an impossibility but possibly futile and destructive as a practical matter. There is an evolving discussion around so-called "transferable skills." What is meant is typically digital literacy (which is a moving target), problem-solving (which is hard to train for), innovation (which is highly context-dependent), communication (which is a lifelong challenge), and collaboration (but this typically only means interacting in small human teams when the true challenge is larger teams that include machines). To insure society and the workplace against these challenges, the concept of lifelong learning has sailed in. In reality, taking such a broad view masks significant problems with implementing a learning mindset that makes a difference in particular life events, skills evolutions, and career transitions. A further elaboration along this vein would be to emphasize resilience (but this usually requires seeking and overcoming hardship).

The proper mix of real-time on-the-job skills training and preparing for emerging skills needs across the organization or ecosystem will be hard to accomplish. Real-time skills training such as Just-In-Time (JIT) Learning was pioneered back in the 1950s by manufacturing engineer Taiichi Ohno as part of the Toyota Production System (TPS). Providing employees with information at the exact moment they need it is essential. But it is hard to deliver. Delivery upon demand is not enough. The Dunning-Kruger effect is a cognitive bias where people with low ability at a task overestimate their competence, while those with high ability tend to underestimate their abilities. Workplace studies have indicated that workers might not realize that they need input. It requires foresight on what they might need. Readily available desk systems. Online knowledge bases at your fingertip. Learning Management Systems (LMS). Augmented interfaces that stay "always on." Virtual reality learning that simulates real challenges and provides opportunities both for learning from failure and from developing mastery. Visual learning and mobile, intuitive interfaces that don't require touch or that don't interrupt the work process (historically that don't slow the manufacturing line) or thought process. Personalized learning platforms that adapt to each worker and change with them. All in all, a well functioning workplace requires a mix of tools that come with the employer and tools that employees can take with them when they leave.

Diverging AI Adoption Speeds

It is important to point out that the speed of adoption of these opportunities will vary depending on an employer's readiness. Each technology will also not evolve on its own, and there can be regulatory roadblocks, skills challenges, or infrastructure cost considerations slowing it down. The full workplace transformation brought about by the AI age will likely take several more decades. But that does not mean that significant productivity effects cannot be extracted in the overall economy in this decade.

Regulatory environments for AI will vary in national and supranational jurisdictions and those will directly affect its role in the workplace. In the EU, productivity will be balanced against concerns such as sustainability, labor force protection, safety, AI-risk, and competition policy. In China, AI will be both benefiting from and limited by its use by the government, and Chinese advanced technology is already restricted in Western countries, particularly in the United States. On the African continent, the challenge is to rapidly build a domestic AI industry before exploitative patterns start to emerge where foreign multinationals capture the bulk of the opportunity. There, the challenge of developing AI start-ups is existential. Smaller frontrunner countries, such as the United Kingdom, and Singapore might be able to forge their own path, as long as they get their industry working together creating productivity effects that lifts all boats.

Emerging Roles and Skills Needs

According to Amazon, new and emerging roles in the workforce (Amazon. com, Inc. 2025) include: AI Specialists and Developers, Data Scientists and Analysts with domain expertise, User Experience and Human–Computer Interaction Specialists, Creative Professionals who can collaborate with AI tools, AI Ethics Officers, Data Privacy Specialists, AI-Assisted Healthcare Providers AI Implementation Strategists, HR Data Scientists, and Employee Experience Engineers.

The development and maintenance of computer vision systems will create new job roles for AI engineers, data scientists, and machine learning specialists. Computer vision can augment human capabilities in various fields, such as healthcare (assisting doctors with diagnoses, performing surgical procedures, and developing personalized treatment plans), manufacturing (improving quality control, optimizing production processes, and enabling predictive maintenance), retail (enhancing customer experiences through personalized recommendations, improved inventory management, and enhanced security), and agriculture (optimizing crop yields, monitoring livestock health, and improving agricultural efficiency).

Individual Career Strategies

The rise of AI necessitates a fundamental shift in career strategies. While AI excels at automating tasks and analyzing data, it *currently* struggles to replicate uniquely human traits such as creativity, critical thinking, emotional intelligence, and the ability to navigate complex social and ethical dilemmas. To thrive in this evolving landscape, you would better cultivate a unique blend of expertise and personal brand.

Instead of merely acquiring skills, professionals of any age or experience must maintain a strong focus on developing a unique value proposition. What that means will evolve, both in the market and for yourself. This involves identifying and honing skills that are difficult to automate, now, or in the near future, such as creative problem-solving, strong interpersonal skills, and ethical decision-making. Simultaneously, cultivating a strong personal brand is crucial. This involves building a professional online presence, engaging in thought leadership through publications and presentations, and actively contributing to the field to establish oneself as an expert. By focusing on these human-centric skills and proactively building a strong personal brand, you can position yourself as an irreplaceable asset. There is definitely a way to thrive in the evolving world of work. However, what counts as expertise, experience, and influence is likely to evolve significantly year over year. The most salient advice is perhaps not to convince yourself that any one skill set, career, job category, job prospect, or employer is absolutely necessary (*sine qua non*) to prepare for. Rather, prepare for a world in flux where adaptability is key.

Ecosystem Strategies

Traditionally, business ecosystem partnerships are strategic alliances between multiple organizations that work together to create value for a common set of customers. They can involve suppliers, distributors, competitors, and technology providers. Going forward, traditional business ecosystems, primarily focused on customer relationships, must evolve. The competitive advantage will increasingly reside in the ability to leverage a common pool of employee talent and skills across an interconnected network of organizations. This necessitates a paradigm shift: instead of merely competing for individual employees, businesses should explore collaborative models that foster knowledge sharing, skill development, and talent mobility within an industry or region.

Imagine a future where companies actively participate in industry-wide training programs, share best practices in employee development, and even facilitate employee mobility across organizations. This "talent commons" would not only enhance individual employability but also drive innovation and productivity across the entire ecosystem. By fostering a dynamic and interconnected talent ecosystem, companies can unlock new levels of innovation, productivity, and competitiveness. There is precedent for this type of arrangement in the manufacturing districts of Northern Italy. However, one could imagine this as a breakout national strategy particularly in small, competitive nations such as Austria, Denmark, Estonia, Ireland, Israel, Luxembourg, Netherlands, Singapore, Switzerland, Taiwan, or the United Arab Emirates. Competitiveness can be measured in various ways, including economic growth, technological innovation, military strength, and international influence. However, workforce skills are likely to become an even more important metric of future-oriented resilience in a world characterized by degrowth, resource scarcity, and environmental collapse with gigascale challenges requiring pivots and restructuring on a regular basis.

Regional Skills Collaboration

More narrowly, one could also imagine regions or municipalities deploying such strategies. Regional Innovation Systems (RIS) were developed in the 1990s to understand the uneven geography of innovation. Typically, regional competitive advantage comes from a mix of strong academic institutions, partnerships between academia, industry, and government, an entrepreneurial ecosystem, and a top talent pool. There can be strong proximity effects because they can share suppliers, rapidly adopt innovation, draw on a shared labor pool, and benefit from favorable institutional settings.[13] All of this can, if things go well, through cascading effects, cause innovation spillovers. What scholars have found is that successful regional innovation cultures are aligned with local identities, political cultures, and socioeconomic legacies. Historical examples are Athens in the fourth century BCE (fostering mechanical devices, philosophy, democracy, and theater), Rome from ancient times to the Renaissance (developing innovations in architecture, art, engineering, medicine, music, and calendar-making), Florence under the Medici (nurturing banking, art patronage, humanism, and scientific inquiry), Venice in the twelfth century (pioneering maritime trade, glassmaking, printing, and republican governance), and Baghdad during the Abbasid Caliphate (advancing mathematics, astronomy, medicine, and translation movements)—each serving as a hub of concentrated intellectual, artistic, and technological activity that catalyzed broader cultural shifts, enabled by strategic patronage, trade networks, and relative political stability (Table 3.1).

More recently, after World War I, Paris in the 1920s became the world's bohemian cultural capital and a center of innovation and rebellion in modern art, architecture, fashion, and music, fueled by domestic artists and expats alike. Examples of regional innovation include the Swiss watch industry in the Jura region (1800–), British shipbuilding industry (1890–1989), the Tokyo–Yokohama metropolitan area in Japan (1859–), the Rust Belt steel industry in the United States (1850–1982), Germany's Ruhr Valley for coal and steel production (1893–1970), the Detroit automotive cluster (1899–2013), the Northern Italy innovation cluster (1899–), Germany's Baden-Württemberg region for mechanical engineering (1940–2007), California's Silicon Valley (1950–), the

---

13 Doehne and Rost 2021.

TABLE 3.1 Innovation clusters in the Ancient and Classical periods.

Cluster	Period	Key Innovations	Contributing Factors
Athens	Fifth–fourth century BCE	Philosophy, democracy, theater, mechanical devices, mathematics	City-state structure, maritime trade, democratic governance
Roman Empire	8th century BCE–fifth century CE	Architecture, engineering, medicine, art, music, calendar systems	Political stability, infrastructure, trade networks, legal systems

TABLE 3.2 Innovation clusters in the Medieval Islamic and European Renaissance periods.

Cluster	Period	Key Innovations	Contributing Factors
Baghdad (Abbasid Caliphate)	Eighth–thirteenth century CE	Mathematics, astronomy, medicine, chemistry, literature, translation	Strategic patronage, House of Wisdom, trade networks, political stability, multicultural exchange
Venice	Twelfth–sixteenth century	Banking, maritime trade, publishing, glassmaking	Strategic port location, republican governance, trade networks
Florence	Fourteenth–sixteenth century	Art, architecture, banking, humanism	Medici patronage, wealth concentration, humanist education

German state of Baden-Württemberg's (1952–) industrial cluster with mechanical engineering at its core, with globally recognized companies like Bosch, Porsche, and Mercedes-Benz, the Research Triangle metropolitan area in North Carolina that includes the cities of Raleigh, Durham, and Chapel Hill (1959–), Boston-Cambridge Innovation Corridor (1960–), Seoul innovation cluster in South Korea (1960–), Sophia Antipolis (1969) in southern France, Kista Science City in Sweden (1970–), the Shenzhen-Hong Kong-Guangzhou ecosystem in China (1980–), Oulu in Finland (1982-), the Bangalore IT-hub in India (1984–), the Tel Aviv Innovation Ecosystem (1990–), the Danish-Swedish Medicon Valley (1997–), the Beijing innovation cluster in China (2000–), The European Research Area (2000–), the Basel pharmaceutical and biotechnology cluster (2010–), TechCity London (2010–), Skolkovo innovation city in Russia (2010–), Paris-Saclay (2013–), and the Toronto-Waterloo Innovation Corridor (2017–). An example of several countries creating a single regional innovation ecosystem is the Eindhoven-Leuven-Aachen triangle (2008–) (Table 3.3).

TABLE 3.3 Innovation clusters during the Industrial and Early Modern periods.

Cluster	Period	Key Innovations	Contributing Factors
Swiss Jura Region	1800 to present	Watchmaking, precision instruments	Skilled craftsmen, specialized knowledge, geographic isolation
British Shipbuilding	1890–1989	Naval architecture, maritime technology	Colonial empire, naval supremacy, access to resources
Tokyo–Yokohama	1859 to present	Industrial modernization, manufacturing	Meiji Restoration, foreign trade opening, governmental policies
U.S. Rust Belt	1850–1982	Steel production, heavy industry	Natural resources, immigrant labor, transportation networks
Germany's Ruhr Valley	1893–1970	Coal mining, steel production, industrial processes	Resource concentration, transportation infrastructure, industrial policies
Detroit	1899–2013	Automotive manufacturing, assembly line production	Engineering talent, industrial infrastructure, access to capital
Northern Italy	1899 to present	Fashion, industrial design, precision manufacturing	Design traditions, family businesses, specialized industrial districts

For example, the European Union's (EU) rise as an innovation area has been driven by a series of initiatives and programs, including The European Research Area (2000–), Horizon 2020 and Horizon Europe, and The European Institute of Innovation and Technology (2008–). According to the World Economic Forum, the EU's innovation performance, led by Sweden, has grown by around 10 percent over the past eight years (Table 3.4).[14]

Innovation clusters thrive on robust interfirm collaboration, exemplified by Silicon Valley's ecosystem where companies actively share knowledge, resources, and expertise rather than operating in isolation. This collaborative approach accelerates technological advancement through partnerships and joint ventures, creating environments where ideas and talent circulate freely across organizational boundaries. Eight critical success factors underpin these dynamic innovation ecosystems: *knowledge infrastructure* (universities and research institutions); *talent concentration* (specialized human capital); *financial resources* (venture capital and public investment); *supportive governance structures; network effects* (dense interconnections between actors); *cultural factors* (entrepreneurial mindset and risk tolerance); *historical contingencies* (timing advantages and founding conditions); and *geographic advantages* (strategic location and quality of life). These elements collectively enable innovation clusters to sustain competitive advantage through collaborative problem-solving that addresses complex challenges no single entity could overcome alone (Table 3.5).

Talent Sharing Across Organizations

Talent sharing, also characterized as internal talent mobility, within large companies is quite effective. Unilever's tech-powered internal talent marketplace, Flex, which began as a 2018 pilot program, allows its 60,000 employees across more than 100 countries to work on specific projects in other geographies and departments.[15] Interorganizational talent sharing is even more powerful. For example, nearly 1,500 of McDonald's outlets collaborated with the German grocery chain Aldi in Germany during the COVID-19 pandemic to temporarily staff Aldi's warehouses and stores, working on short-term contracts.[16] This

---

14 Ellerbeck, n.d.
15 Unilever 2020.
16 "With Our Hours Reduced, We Partnered with ALDI to Keep Serving Our Community" n.d.

TABLE 3.4 Modern innovation clusters (post-WWII).

Cluster	Period	Key Innovations	Contributing Factors
Paris (1920s)	1918–1930s	Modern art, architecture, fashion, music, literature	Postwar cultural liberation, expatriate community, cafe culture
Baden-Württemberg	1940 to present	Mechanical engineering, automotive excellence	Technical education, mittelstand companies, industrial policy
Silicon Valley	1950 to present	Semiconductors, personal computing, internet, biotechnology	University–industry collaboration, venture capital, open innovation
Research Triangle (NC)	1959 to present	Life sciences, technology, advanced manufacturing	Research universities, planned development, government support
Boston-Cambridge	1960 to present	Biotechnology, pharmaceuticals, robotics, AI	Elite universities, academic research, venture capital
Seoul	1960 to present	Electronics, telecommunications, digital technology	Government planning, chaebols, export orientation
Sophia Antipolis	1969 to present	Information technology; life sciences	Planned technopolis, quality of life, government support
Kista Science City	1970 to present	Information technology; telecommunications	University partnerships, public investment, corporate leadership
Shenzhen-Hong Kong-Guangzhou	1980 to present	Electronics manufacturing, hardware innovation	Special economic zone, manufacturing ecosystem, rapid prototyping
Oulu	1982 to present	Telecommunications, wireless technology	University–industry collaboration, Nokia effect, public investment
Bangalore	1984 to present	Information technology services, software development	English proficiency, technical education, cost advantages

TABLE 3.5 Contemporary innovation ecosystems (post-1990).

Cluster	Period	Key Innovations	Contributing Factors
Tel Aviv	1990 to present	Cybersecurity, artificial intelligence, fintech	Military technology transfer, entrepreneurial culture, venture capital
Danish-Swedish Medicon Valley	1997 to present	Life sciences, pharmaceutical research	Cross-border collaboration, research institutions, biotech focus
Beijing	2000 to present	Artificial intelligence, e-commerce, fintech	Government investment, top universities, large domestic market
European Research Area	2000 to present	Cross-border scientific collaboration	EU policy framework, funding programs, mobility of researchers
Eindhoven-Leuven-Aachen	2008 to present	Advanced materials, high-tech systems, life sciences	Cross-border collaboration, industrial heritage, research institutions
Basel	2010 to present	Pharmaceuticals, biotechnology	Historical chemical industry, specialized research, multinational companies
TechCity London	2010 to present	Fintech, creative tech, digital services	Financial center proximity, urban regeneration, talent attraction
Skolkovo	2010 to present	Information technology, biomedical, energy efficiency	Planned innovation city, tax incentives, state investment
Paris-Saclay	2013 to present	Scientific research, deep tech	Concentration of research institutions, public investment, industrial partnerships
Toronto-Waterloo	2017 to present	Artificial intelligence, quantum computing, fintech	University research, multicultural talent pool, government support

at a time when it had to close all of its restaurants and its staff was furloughed or had lost their jobs. In innovation clusters, groups of manufacturing firms tend to collaborate on quality improvement initiatives where employees from each company share best practices. This is often fueled by small and medium-sized enterprises (SMEs) who would otherwise face massive training costs on their own.[17] In the European Union, SMEs are defined as having fewer than 250 employees and a turnover of less than €50 million, and in the United States and Canada, fewer than 500 employees. For example, since 2005, the UT Project in the tech capital Trondheim, Norway, has assisted more than 80 companies through networking and seminars, who have increased their revenue, established themselves internationally, obtained new clients and expanded their network.[18] Through the UT Project, companies gain access to experienced international consultants who have extensive knowledge in their respective fields.

Accessing a wider talent pool by sharing skilled employees across different companies within a cluster can be achieved through initiatives like joint project teams. Here, employees from various companies collaborate on specific projects. These tend to be temporary assignments where individuals are seconded to another company for a defined period to fill skill gaps. It can even lead to establishing a shared talent pool where companies can access specialized skills across the cluster as needed. Examples include a tech hub where software engineers from different start-ups work together on a new platform development, or a manufacturing cluster where engineers from various factories can be temporarily assigned to troubleshoot complex production issues at another company within the cluster.

Supply chain collaboration to achieve scale or ensure resilience is quite common. The relationship between car manufacturers and their component suppliers in the automotive industry is a prime example. Coca-Cola is a major supplier to McDonald's, creating a mutually beneficial relationship. The types of activities could include joint inventory planning with suppliers, sharing real-time data on production schedules, collaborative problem-solving on quality issues, developing new products together, and participating in supplier-led innovation initiatives. In the near future, supply chain collaboration will be further enhanced by advanced technologies like AI, blockchain, and IoT, requiring skills in digital transformation and data analytics to manage

---

17 Martin-Rios, Erhardt and Manev 2022.
18 "UT Prosjektet" n.d.

complex networks effectively. But necessary sustainability focus will also force new skills to the forefront. Rapid market changes means change management skills, and relationship building will be essential, too. The pending polycrisis means risk management to cope with disruptions and adverse geopolitical or natural hazardous events will also be crucial.

Industry consortia tend to perform this function as well, as to the major research and development (R&D) collaboration and networking programs of the European Union. According to Eurostat, the European Union spent €381.4 billion on R&D in 2023. The majority of European R&D funding, particularly within the Horizon Europe program, is allocated toward collaborative projects, with a significant portion of the budget dedicated to partnerships involving multiple research institutions and companies across EU member states. Such cross-company, cross-national collaboration is typically required to obtain funding.

Special circumstances, such as disaster relief efforts always call for interorganizational collaboration efforts. Government agencies, nonprofit organizations, and private companies collaborate to provide relief and support during natural disasters. These events illustrate the main challenges to such collaboration, which includes building trust, overcoming organizational silos, aligning incentives, managing complexity, and ensuring safe and secure data sharing across organizational boundaries. Developing skills to handle such challenges is not typically part of vocational training, degree programs at colleges, or even on-the-job training.

Beyond Strategic Human Resource Management

Aligning HR practices directly with overall business strategy, elevating HR from an operational function to a strategic one within organizations, is a process that began back in 1984 when two pioneering books were published: *Strategic Human Resource Management* by Tichy and colleagues in 1984 and *Managing Human Assets* by Beer and colleagues.[19] Strategic human resource management functions include workforce planning, talent acquisition (recruitment), performance management, training and development, employee relations, aligning HR with business goals, talent management, and evaluation and corrective action, all focused on aligning HR practices with the organization's overall strategy to achieve optimal performance.

---

19 Kaufman 2015.

Driven by the need for U.S. companies to improve competitiveness against international rivals, particularly from Japan and Germany, the American approach focused on shareholder value. The European approach, in contrast, has sought to balance the interests of multiple stakeholders such as employees, unions, governments, and society. Strategic Human Resources Management (SHRM) requires a shift toward a more macro-perspective, which also encompasses sustainability and geopolitical stressors. The reality of a distributed workforce with a mix of remote and in-office employees, retaining talent from a global pool, also requires considering cultural differences and local employment laws. Controversially, diversity, equity, and inclusion (DEI) is also emphasized, but whether and how to implement it is not clear. Data-driven talent management, including using AI for hiring, skills needs, and skills development, is also a given. Focusing on employee experience, engagement, well-being, and career development, has gone from buzzword to necessity for companies wanting to remain attractive. Getting the combination of humans and AI right, making sure they thrive and optimize, might be the most important investment a company could make. Beyond that, efforts to reduce the friction surrounding talent job change are still in their infancy. Streamlining the job search process through AI-powered, skills-based matching will be key. Transferable skills and potential will be priorities more than hiring for specific job titles. This also means the company brand becomes even more important. Likewise, sub-brands and excellence at division and team levels will need to emerge. Candidates will ask if the team they are on is likely to teach them something. Transparency across talent management will need to increase. Concise, dynamic, digitally available job descriptions that map to tasks, talent, and available resources and infrastructure. Facilitating career transitions through upskilling and reskilling programs with funded degrees, certifications, and digital badges that are universally recognized across countries and industries. Portable benefits packages that follow employees across different employers would reduce barriers to job change. Employee benefits such as career coaches and mentors, online courses, workshops, and mentorship programs, should not be tied to employers, but should be independent and provided in abundance. Industry-recognized skills certifications should become the norm. All organizations should provide readily accessible and accurate data on labor market trends, skill demands, and career pathways to inform career decisions. Some of these practices could be regulated, others would be industry standards.

Going forward, cross-organizational SHRM will have to handle this head on. However, a shift from internal, company-centric HR practices to a more interconnected and collaborative approach will not come easy. Jointly developing and delivering training programs, sharing best practices in employee development, and creating pathways for employee mobility across organizations will entail further engagement in existing industry consortia and strengthening their structure and approach. Governments, as key enablers, will need to take a more active role. Sharing knowledge and resources through open-source platforms would also facilitate the process.

Towards Human–Machine Resource Management

In the *platinum workforce*, which will consist of both humans and machines, a new discipline, Human-Machine Resource Management (HMRM) is likely to emerge. Traditional machine care is focused on preventative maintenance such as regular checks, oil changes, changing of worn parts, and operational verification, to minimize downtime. Future machine care will shift toward optimizing machine performance through predictive maintenance through sensor data, adaptive maintenance through real-time machine data and predictive analytics, and performance monitoring. Minimizing energy consumption will be highly important as will end-of-life management, parts recycling, and machine disposal. Cybersecurity will also become part of routine care. Regulators, vendors, consultants, and executives will need to ensure that machines are designed to work seamlessly with human operators and enhance human capabilities. Resource management, as such, will encompass maximizing the value of all critical organizational assets, such as human capital, intellectual property, technology, data, financial resources, customer relationships, innovation capacity, and infrastructure.

HMRM functions include traditional HR functions such as: workforce planning, talent acquisition, performance management, training and development, employee relations, aligning resources with business goals, talent management, and evaluation and corrective action, all focused on aligning resources practices with the organization's overall strategy to achieve optimal performance. However, each will encompass both AIs and humans, ideally making organizational tasks simultaneously personalized and machine optimized. To get maximum benefit, HMRM will develop elaborate checks and balances between AIs and humans, including Human oversight of AI processes and decisions and AI oversight of human processes and decisions, Explainable AI (XAI), Ethical AI Development Frameworks, Human Augmentation principles, Transparent Data Governance, investing heavily in fostering human-centered skills (creativity, critical thinking, ethical competency, innovation, emotional intelligence, complex problem-solving, and more), Continuous Monitoring and evaluation, identifying potential biases, and addressing any unintended consequences. At its most extreme, the technology function and HR function in an organization will merge completely.

Collaborative Governance Models will emerge. For example Cross-Functional AI Task Forces with teams combining HR, IT, legal, and ethics experts to oversee AI deployment. A current example is Microsoft's Aether Committee (AI, Ethics, and Effects in Engineering and Research), established in 2016, which ensures responsible AI use across departments.

A future HMRM recognizes that humans and machines are increasingly interdependent. HMRM must address the ethical implications of human–machine collaboration, including issues such as data privacy, algorithmic bias, and the potential for job displacement. Human–AI teaming will be regulated and cross-industry best practices should emerge. The field will support developing technologies that augment human capabilities, such as wearable devices that enhance cognitive function, or AI-powered tools that assist with complex tasks. Establishing clear metrics for evaluating the effectiveness of human–machine collaboration and its impact on organizational performance. Equipping the workforce with the necessary skills and knowledge to effectively collaborate with AI systems is a gargantuan task, especially as these systems evolve faster than any other system affecting the industrial workforce.

We know from historical experience across industrial revolutions that over-automation risks alienating employees. For example, AI-driven conflict management arbitration might lead to a lack of empathy in conflict resolution. A mitigation strategy would be to balance AI efficiency with human judgment (e.g., a "human-in-the-loop" system). In developing HMRM, organizations may find skill gaps. For example, HR professionals may lack technical expertise, while IT teams may misunderstand workplace dynamics. Over time, however, HR will shift from administrative tasks to shaping AI-driven workforce strategies, such as: designing hybrid human–AI roles (e.g., "AI trainers" for chatbots), building AI tools that enhance employee well-being, curating personalized career journeys using predictive analytics, and to leading corporate digital ethics initiatives. For example, Unilever traditionally had outdated processes rooted in paper, phone screens, and manual assessments. It took four to six months to sift through 250,000 applications to hire 800 individuals for Unilever's Future Leaders Programme. Using HireVue Assessments, AI analyzed candidates' recorded interviews to filter up to 80 percent of the candidate pool based on interview attributes like facial expressions, body language, and word choice thought to be predictive of job success.[20] As a result, HireVue claims Unilever saved over £1M in annual costs along with 50,000 hours in candidate time over 18 months and to improved the diversity of candidates.

However, it is notable that due to *creative destruction*, first coined by Schumpeter in his 1942 book *Capitalism, Socialism and Democracy*, innovation clusters don't tend to last forever. Three examples would be the British shipbuilding industry, the U.S. Rust Belt steel industry, or Detroit's automotive industry. Going back to the historical examples, few would today point to Athens or Rome as global centers of skills innovation. On the contrary, both the Roman and Greek empires eventually declined, skills details leading to periods of instability and intellectual stagnation. In modern day, both Athens or Rome, as cities are faced with bureaucratic hurdles, a dual challenge of aging historical and urban infrastructures, brain drain, and massive economic challenges. Creative destruction becomes simply destruction when the process of innovation and replacement of old technologies with new ones results in a significant negative impact without a corresponding positive outcome. Decline is a complex phenomenon, but occurs due to a mix of factors like technological shifts, industrial, consumer or market changes, dwindling government support, and lack of diversification coupled with poor adaptation or internal rigidities, leading to a loss of economic vitality and a decrease in new businesses and talent within the area.[21] If a new automated system replaces a large workforce with minimal new jobs requiring highly specialized skills, and the displaced workers lack the ability to retrain, this would simply become destruction, substantial job losses, economic instability, social misery, and societal decline. This could happen if the changes are too rapid or too drastic to adapt in time. Typically, the negative impacts of the change are disproportionately felt by certain groups, like low-skilled workers, or certain regions, such as the Global South.

With this in mind, one could readily imagine near-term emerging clusters that either represent the next iteration of already advanced regions, or even entirely new ones (Table 3.6).

Looking even further ahead, as more advanced AI-enabled systems emerge and morph with existing infrastructure and allow new groups of human workers and leaders to excel, the picture could dramatically evolve (Table 3.7).

The emergence of AI-intensive innovation clusters hinges on five novel success factors that transcend traditional requirements. Compute

---

20 Marr 2018.
21 Kim, Kim and Lee 2022.

TABLE 3.6 Near-term emerging clusters (2025–2030).

Cluster Name	Geographic Location	Core Technologies	Distinctive Features	Enabling Conditions
Quantum Valley	Greater Toronto Area, Canada	Quantum computing, quantum cryptography, quantum sensing	First commercial-scale quantum advantage applications	University-led research, government quantum strategy, specialized talent pipeline
Neurotech Hub	Boston-Cambridge, USA	Brain–computer interfaces, neural prosthetics, cognitive enhancement	FDA-approved neural implants for medical applications	Medical research institutions, regulatory expertise, venture funding
AI Foundation Models Corridor	San Francisco–Seattle, USA	Foundation model development, specialized AI systems, interpretability research	Concentrated development of frontier AI models	Computing infrastructure, AI talent density, corporate investment
Synthetic Biology Factory	Singapore–Johor–Batam Triangle	Engineered microorganisms, bioproduction, biomaterials	Biomanufacturing at industrial scale	Regulatory sandboxes, biocontainment infrastructure, strategic national initiatives
Human–AI Augmentation District	Helsinki-Tallinn Twin Hub	Cognitive prosthetics, personalized AI assistants, human-in-the-loop systems	Focus on human–AI complementarity rather than replacement	Digital infrastructure, progressive labor policies, ethical AI frameworks

sovereignty—secure access to specialized AI infrastructure including strategic chip fabrication and quantum facilities—forms the foundation for independent capability development. Equally crucial are data commons, well-governed repositories with fair access mechanisms supported by data trusts and privacy-preserving techniques. Human–AI complementarity, carefully designed to enhance rather than replace human capabilities, drives breakthrough innovation through thoughtful interface design and cognitive ergonomics. As AI systems grow more powerful, alignment methodologies including value learning research and containment protocols become essential for ensuring these systems remain beneficial. Finally, a robust AI safety culture, characterized by professional standards, whistleblower protections, and status rewards for responsible development, creates the social infrastructure necessary for sustainable progress in advanced AI ecosystems.

Advanced AI fundamentally transforms traditional innovation cluster success factors in four critical ways. Knowledge infrastructure evolves from static institutions to dynamic networks incorporating AI co-researchers, while talent concentration shifts from geographic proximity to global collaboration enabled by specialized compute access. Financial resources transition from conventional venture capital to compute allocation rights and algorithmic resource distribution mechanisms. Perhaps most significantly, governance structures develop beyond regulatory frameworks into computational governance systems capable of managing the unprecedented complexity and speed of AI-driven innovation ecosystems. These transformations represent not merely incremental changes but a paradigm shift in how innovation clusters form, function, and sustain competitive advantage in an AI-intensive future.

Despite advancing digital technologies and AI capabilities, physical proximity will likely remain a significant driver of innovation for fundamental human and organizational reasons. The human tendency toward social clustering—our deeply ingrained propensity to live, work, and create in groups—provides persistent advantages that even sophisticated virtual collaboration cannot fully replicate. While AI-enhanced collaboration tools will certainly reduce the friction of distance, the most innovative activities still benefit substantially from unscheduled, spontaneous interactions that occur naturally in shared physical environments. These serendipitous encounters generate tacit knowledge exchange, which remains difficult to digitize or facilitate remotely. Research consistently shows that breakthrough innovation frequently emerges from informal, unplanned discussions rather than scheduled meetings—the proverbial "hallway conversations" or interactions over coffee.

Furthermore, human trust and relationship building—critical foundations for the high-risk collaboration that innovation requires—develop most effectively through in-person interaction. This trust component enables the psychological safety necessary for creative risk-taking and the exchange of incomplete or developing ideas that might seem too tentative to share in more formalized digital environments. We will likely see a hybrid model emerge: discrete innovation clusters with strong physical colocation at their cores, connected by sophisticated digital networks to access global talent and specialized resources. These physical innovation hubs will feature carefully designed spaces optimized for the specific types of human interaction that foster creativity while digital infrastructure connects these nodes into larger meta-clusters.

The enduring value of proximity may actually increase as routine tasks become more automated—when AI handles standardized work, uniquely human capabilities like complex social interaction, cultural understanding, and collaborative problem-solving become even more central to value creation, reinforcing the importance of physical innovation clusters even in an AI-augmented future.

Conclusion

Employers need to dramatically revamp their reskilling programs, aiming to continuously reskill and train every employee on a plethora of emerging skills that those employees were never trained for and sometimes in domains the organization does not possess expertise in. For that to work, ecosystem partnerships are necessary. The process also entails C-level buy-in and awareness of the importance of training the ecosystem not only your own employees. Given that workers will switch employers at a faster clip, availability of talent is more important than the relative competitiveness of one team versus that of a competitor. In previous transitions, we have seen the success of this approach in advanced industrial manufacturing districts in Northern Italy (Locke 1995). The future, already emergent, HR-tech function will be less about managing resources as such and more about orchestrating human–machine ecosystems. To answer the question posed, the twenty-first-century employer not only cares about machines, but caters to the *platinum workforce*, a hybrid and evolving entity that is precious, hard-earned, and of exceptional quality.

Our future workforce must be durable and resistant to shocks, showing extreme resilience and enduring value, standing the test of time and change. Platinum is highly recyclable and reusable, and therefore potentially

TABLE 3.7 Mid-term emerging clusters (2030–2035).

Cluster Name	Geographic Location	Core Technologies	Distinctive Features	Enabling Conditions
Niche Superintelligence Valley	Seoul-Daejeon Corridor, South Korea	Domain-specific superintelligent systems, ultra-specialized AI, safety architecture	First successful containment of superhuman capabilities in narrow domains	Computational governance frameworks, hardware specialization, cultural emphasis on safety
Climate Engineering Commons	Multimodal (Zurich-Delhi-Nairobi-Santiago)	Carbon sequestration, weather modification, ecological system management	Globally distributed development with coordinated deployment	International governance, climate crisis urgency; public–private cooperation
AI-Native Manufacturing Belt	Detroit-Toronto-Montreal Corridor	Robotic fabrication, generative design, zero-waste production	Complete reinvention of manufacturing paradigms through AI	Industrial heritage, research institutions, retraining programs
Orbital Development Zone	Low Earth Orbit (multiple ground stations)	Microgravity manufacturing, orbital energy systems, space logistics	Innovation cluster partially located off-planet	Launch infrastructure, regulatory frameworks for space commerce, private–public partnerships
Extended Reality Metropolis	Shenzhen-Hong Kong-Macau Bay Area	Mixed reality environments, spatial computing, digital twins	Blending physical and digital infrastructure at urban scale	Hardware manufacturing ecosystem, metropolitan test environment, talent concentration

sustainable. Platinum exhibits functional, not opulent elegance. It would endure under extreme heat or pressure, such as economic downturns, technology shifts, or disasters, without degrading. Just like the characteristics of the platinum metal, the *platinum workforce* must be malleable, capable of being shaped into various forms. A multicultural team's success reflects a platinum alloy of diverse perspectives. A *platinum workforce* blends with needed properties, displaying emergent properties. The *platinum workforce* is a potential for change, adaptation, evolution, and recovery. It also embodies trust, which is essential in an emerging age of risk. In the end, it has ethical resilience, resisting exploitation.

Platinum is precious. But unlike platinum, such a workforce cannot be 30 times rarer than gold. But it will begin that way. Fostering a *platinum moment* in history through catalytic transformation and positive cascades could ensure wider emergence of platinum qualities across the global workforce. It is notable that platinum has a catalytic converter role, accelerating chemical reactions without being consumed. Likewise, unlike individual leaders who will always seek glory, the *platinum workforce* could shine with an understated, subtle brilliance, emerging as a force that enables change without seeking credit. Platinum, as a metaphor for the emerging workforce, is a narrative of uncompromising quality and silent power. Thinking of our future this way, challenges us to value substance over spectacle, endurance over immediacy, and transformation that leaves no trace of itself behind. That's why it is something more than an industrial paradigm. Industry has always left a trace, a scar, a stigma. We can no longer afford that. Given that constraint, in Chapter 4, I will explore Experiments towards Human+, the deliberate technological enhancement of existing biological systems, a controversial, but silently ongoing process. Having established why employers must evolve beyond traditional human capital models, Section II explores the specific skills that define tomorrow's platinum workforce.

References

Amazon.com, Inc. 2025. *Amazon's Robotics Revolution Creates Over 700 New Job Categories.* https://www.aboutamazon.com/news/operations/amazon-introduces-new-robotics-solutions.

"Amazon and MIT Are Studying How Automation Impacts Jobs." 2023. US About Amazon. October 18, 2023. https://www.aboutamazon.com/news/operations/amazon-mit-study-jobs-and-automation.

"Amazon re:MARS." n.d. Accessed January 28, 2025. https://remars.amazonevents.com/discover/automation/article/five-lessons-from-SCOT/?trk=direct.

Brandoli, Lucia. n.d. "Amazon Has Replaced 100,000 Employees with 750,000 Robots." Accessed January 28, 2025. https://www.domusweb.it/en/news/2024/07 /09/amazon-has-replaced-100000-employees-with-750000-robots.html.

Doehne, Malte, and Katja Rost. 2021. "Long Waves in the Geography of Innovation: The Rise and Decline of Regional Clusters of Creativity over Time." *Research Policy* 50 (9): 104298.

Ellerbeck, Stefan. n.d. "These Are the Top 5 Most Innovative Countries in the European Union." *World Economic Forum*. Accessed January 29, 2025. https://www .weforum.org/stories/2022/10/european-union-top-innovative-countries/.

George, Katy. 2022. "Competing in the New Talent Market." *Harvard Business Review.* October 3, 2022. https://hbr.org/2022/10/competing-in-the-new-talent-market.

Greenawalt, Tyler. 2024. "Meet the 8 Robots Powering Your Amazon Package Deliveries." *US About Amazon.* October 9, 2024. https://www.aboutamazon.com/ news/operations/amazon-robotics-robots-fulfillment-center.

"How Amazon Is Using AI To Become the Fastest Supply Chain in the World." 2024. *Sifted.* July 2, 2024. https://sifted.com/resources/how-amazon-is-using-ai-to -become-the-fastest-supply-chain-in-the-world/.

Jarrett, Cosette. 2023. "12 Cool Facts about the AI-Powered Robots That Help Deliver Your Amazon Packages." *US About Amazon.* December 11, 2023. https://www .aboutamazon.com/news/operations/amazon-robotics-cool-facts.

Kaufman, Bruce E. 2015. "Evolution of Strategic HRM as Seen through Two Founding Books: A 30th Anniversary Perspective on Development of the Field." *Human Resource Management* 54 (3): 389–407.

Kim, Dahyun, Saehoon Kim, and Jae Seung Lee. 2022. "The Rise and Fall of Industrial Clusters: Experience from the Resilient Transformation in South Korea." *The Annals of Regional Science* 71 (2): 1–23.

Locke, Richard M. *Remaking the Italian Economy.* Ithaca: Cornell University Press, 1995.

Marr, Bernard. 2018. "The Amazing Ways How Unilever Uses Artificial Intelligence To Recruit & Train Thousands Of Employees." *Forbes.*

Martin-Rios, Carlos, Niclas L. Erhardt, and Ivan M. Manev. 2022. "Interfirm Collaboration for Knowledge Resources Interaction among Small Innovative Firms." *Journal of Business Research* 153 (December): 206–215.

Özer, Özalp, and Serdar Şimşek. 2021. "The Evolution of Amazon's Inventory Planning System." *Amazon Science.* October 1, 2021. https://www.amazon.science/ latest-news/the-evolution-of-amazons-inventory-planning-system.

Patel, Rishika. 2024. "Humanoid Robots And Their Potential Impact On the Future of Work." *AiThority* (blog). August 1, 2024. https://aithority.com/human-centered -computing/humanoid-robots-and-their-potential-impact-on-the-future-of-work/.

Pichai, Sundar. 2022. "Our New $100 Million Google Career Certificates Fund." *Google.* February 17, 2022. https://blog.google/outreach-initiatives/grow-with -google/career-certificates-fund/.

Shaikh, Kaif. 2024. "AMECA, Atlas, Optimus: Top 10 Insane Humanoid Robots to Watch out for in 2025." *Interesting Engineering.* December 10, 2024. https://interes tingengineering.com/entertainment/top-humanoid-robots-list.

Sims, Kegan. 2023. "Agility Robotics Broadens Relationship with Amazon." *Agility Robotics.* October 24, 2023. https://agilityrobotics.com/content/expanded -partnership-amazon.

Unilever, P. L. C. 2020. "An Exciting New Normal for Flexible Working." *Unilever PLC.* June 23, 2020. https://www.unilever.com/news/news-search/2020/an-exciting -new-normal-for-flexible-working/.

"UT Prosjektet." n.d. UT Prosjektet. Accessed January 29, 2025. https://utprosjektet .com/.

"With Our Hours Reduced, We Partnered with ALDI to Keep Serving Our Community." n.d. Accessed January 29, 2025. https://corporate.mcdonalds.com /corpmcd/our-stories/article/partnered-with-aldi.html.

"Work Change Report." n.d. Accessed January 30, 2025. https://economicgraph .linkedin.com/research/work-change-report.

The next section moves from disruption to design. Here we encounter Human+—a concept that operates both as a paradigm for understanding human–machine evolution and as a skill to be cultivated in practice.

SECTION II

Developing Skills Fit for the Workplace of Tomorrow

CHAPTER 4

EXPERIMENTS TOWARD HUMAN+

What Is Human+?

Human+ should be read in two registers: as a paradigm that reframes the trajectory of human–machine evolution, and as a skillset that individuals and organizations must actively cultivate. In this dual sense, it bridges the philosophical and the practical, situating itself both as horizon and as craft. This field spans multiple disciplines, including artificial intelligence (AI) systems, genetic modification technologies, biotechnological innovations, nanoscale engineering, neural interface development, and cybernetic integration. Contemporary applications of transhumanist principles are already evident in medical technologies such as advanced prosthetics, neurostimulation devices, and genetic therapies. However, the more transformative aspects of this movement—including radical life extension, cognitive enhancement, and sensory augmentation—remain largely theoretical or in preliminary research stages.

The transhumanist vision proposes not technological replacement of human biology but rather a deliberate technological enhancement of existing biological systems. This convergence aims to create synergistic human-technology systems that transcend current physiological and cognitive limitations. These enhancements might manifest as expanded intellectual capacities, significantly extended lifespans, or perception capabilities beyond the standard human sensory range. Transhumanist discourse frequently emphasizes technology as an instrumental means toward human development rather than as an end in itself. The underlying objective is to systematically overcome biological constraints that have historically limited human potential, thereby fundamentally transforming the parameters of the human condition. Its proponents claim that by embracing the principles of Human+, we can create a world where technology serves as a tool for human flourishing, enabling us to overcome biological constraints and fundamentally improve the human condition.

FIGURE 4.1 Human+.

At its core, Human+ is rooted in the belief that emerging technologies can and should be used to enhance human potential. This belief is not a question of possibility but rather of time and investment. The movement focuses on both individual enhancement—improving personal capabilities—and species-level enhancement—directing the course of human evolution. The ultimate goal is to augment human abilities, improve quality of life, and address global challenges. The term Human+ is often used to describe a future where humans have transcended their current limitations and achieved a higher level of existence. This vision encompasses a wide range of ideas, including biological enhancement, technological augmentation, and social and cultural evolution. Biological enhancement involves genetic engineering, gene therapy, or other interventions to improve physical and cognitive abilities. Technological augmentation includes the use of implants, wearable devices, or other technologies to enhance senses, memory, and cognitive function. Social and cultural evolution refers to changes in social norms, education systems, and cultural values that foster human potential and well-being. While Human+ is primarily understood as a paradigm within transhumanist thought, in the Platinum Workforce framework it is also operationalized as a skill—something that can be learned, practiced, and embedded into workplace behaviors.

Key aspects of Human+ include augmented intelligence, biotechnology, cybernetics, human–machine collaboration, and ethical considerations. Augmented intelligence involves enhancing cognitive abilities through AI-powered tools and systems that assist with decision-making, problem-solving, and learning. Human augmentation, on the other hand, refers to the use of technology to enhance physical, cognitive, or sensory abilities. Physical augmentation might include exoskeletons, prosthetics, or wearable devices that enhance strength, mobility, or endurance. Cognitive augmentation could involve brain–computer interfaces, neural implants, or AI-assisted tools that improve memory, learning, or decision-making. Sensory augmentation includes devices like augmented reality glasses or advanced hearing aids that expand human senses. Beyond physical and cognitive enhancements, Human+ also explores technologies that enhance emotional intelligence, empathy, or social interactions. Examples include emotion AI, which recognizes and responds to human emotions, social robotics designed for companionship or mental health support, and virtual communities that enable deeper human connections through immersive technologies like virtual reality.

Biotechnology plays a central role in Human+, with genetic engineering, regenerative medicine, and synthetic biology offering ways to improve health, extend lifespan, and enhance physical and mental capabilities. Gene editing technologies like CRISPR can eliminate genetic diseases or enhance traits, while longevity science focuses on extending human lifespan and improving healthspan through regenerative medicine or antiaging therapies. Synthetic biology involves designing biological systems or organisms to enhance human capabilities, such as engineered microbes for health or environmental benefits. Cybernetics, another pillar of Human+, integrates human biology with electronic and mechanical systems, such as prosthetics, implants, and wearable devices, to restore or enhance physical functions. Human–machine collaboration is also a critical aspect, creating seamless interactions between humans and machines to leverage the strengths of both. Examples include AI assistants like ChatGPT, collaborative robots (cobots) used in manufacturing or healthcare, and hybrid intelligence systems where humans and AI complement each other's strengths, such as AI aiding doctors in diagnosing diseases.

However, the Human+ vision is not without its challenges and ethical considerations. It raises profound questions about identity, equity, and the future of humanity. Key ethical considerations include ensuring that human augmentation is equitable and does not exacerbate social inequalities, protecting individuals' privacy and autonomy as technology becomes more integrated into their lives, and exploring what it means to be human in a world where biological and technological boundaries blur. While some aspects of human enhancement are already being explored, the full realization of Human+ remains a topic of ongoing research, debate, and ethical consideration in fields such as bioengineering, neuroscience, and philosophy. There are also potential risks and ethical concerns associated with Human+, such as the potential for inequality and social division, the impact on human identity and autonomy, and the possibility of unintended consequences. The movement raises significant ethical questions about the safety and risks of enhancement technologies, equal access and potential social inequality, the nature of humanity, and the proper limits of human modification.

Despite these challenges, Human+ represents an optimistic vision of the future where technology and humanity work together to achieve new heights of potential and well-being. It envisions a world where technology is designed to enhance, rather than replace, human capabilities. Potential benefits include improved health and longevity, enhanced cognitive abilities, increased creativity and productivity, and greater resilience to physical and psychological challenges. However, society must grapple with the ethical, social, and philosophical implications of human augmentation as we move toward this future.

In today's workplace, Human+ concepts are already beginning to take shape in several key ways. Technological integration is evident in the use of wearable devices that track health metrics and productivity, brain–computer interfaces for specialized tasks, augmented reality tools for training and task execution, and AI assistants that enhance decision-making and workflow optimization. Performance enhancement is becoming more common through the use of nootropics and cognitive enhancement supplements, biometric monitoring for optimal work scheduling, meditation and mindfulness apps for mental performance, and advanced ergonomics in workplace design. Health and wellness programs incorporate advanced biometric tracking, genetic testing for personalized health recommendations, sleep optimization using smart technology, and stress management through biomonitoring. Skills and learning are being transformed by microchip implants for facility access and data storage, immersive VR/AR training environments, neural feedback systems for accelerated learning, and AI-powered personalized learning platforms.

As Human+ concepts continue to evolve, they hold the promise of reshaping not only the workplace but also society as a whole. By addressing the ethical, social, and philosophical implications of human augmentation, we can ensure that the future of Human+ is one that enhances human potential while preserving the values that define us as a species. The journey toward Human+ is not just about technological advancement but also about redefining what it means to be human in an increasingly interconnected and augmented world.

Why Is Human+ Needed Now?

Human+ in action can be seen in Healthcare, where AI-powered diagnostics, robotic surgery, or wearable devices that monitor and improve health in real time. In Education where personalized learning platforms adapt to individual students' needs, or brain-training tools that enhance cognitive abilities. In the Workplace, with exoskeletons for physically demanding jobs, or AI tools that augment creativity and decision-making in knowledge work. In Entertainment, with immersive VR experiences that blend physical and digital worlds, or emotion-sensing games that adapt to players' moods. Lastly, in Daily Life with smart homes that anticipate and respond to residents' needs, or augmented reality glasses that overlay digital information onto the physical world.

Which crucial skills are the most relevant for the future of work? Collaboration? Creativity? Digital literacy? Leadership? Problem-solving? Service-mindset? Many answers have been given to this question. Some of them were premature. With the advent of the idea of the post-industrial society, first coined by sociologist Daniel Bell in 1973 book *The Coming of Post-Industrial Society,* the trends of urbanization, automation, and globalization took on an air of inevitability that they did not deserve. But time has shown that these trends can be reversed, modified, and complemented by more pressing concerns. For example, through the socio-technical integration of technologies with human ingenuity coupled with the new risks from emerging technologies. Another stems from the fallout and corrective measures we have had to enact because of risks from our own doing such as climate change. Contrary to the idea that all can be fixed with new generation technologies alone, they will simultaneously require massive human input. All and each of these factors need to be managed through skills development at a massive scale.

Moreover, while we have, in certain ways, transitioned from an economy of goods to an economy of services, which calls for "soft skills" such as communication and empathy, there is a persisting renewal of industrial scaling logics that calls for deep human involvement in production of goods, whether they be digital, physical, or hybrid in nature. The idea that some skills are soft is itself a misnomer. Certainly, if it implies a lack of substance or difficulty. As a result, the idea that practical skills are obsolete needs to be taken with a grain of salt. Separating thinking from doing is misguided, as Matt Crawford already pointed out in his 2010 book *Shop Class as Soulcraft* which explores the persisting value of craftsmanship. Similarly, the idea that science, technology, engineering, and mathematics (STEM), coupled with communication skills, are the only salient skills to teach in primary and secondary education, at university, or in the workplace, is similarly flawed. We are, in fact, entering an age of perplexing contradictions. One where machines are replacing humans for some tasks but complementing us for others, in surprising ways. Even more surprisingly, some of the more skilled humans, such as professionals and creatives, seem to be the most replaceable of all, because the quality of those skills will need to be at the top of the pyramid or else can be done better by AI's which will have access to summaries of what skilled humans have done before. On the other hand, in many manual professions the work content is harder to automate because its combination of manual and cognitive steps turns out to be complex for machines to do, and might be more resilient, at least in the short term.

How to Learn Human+

Learning to act as a Human+ involves a dramatically close relationship between ourselves and the socio-technical systems we have built. This is explored in detail in Chapters 4–14 in Section II. This is also not necessarily something nefarious or futuristic. In many ways it is the reality of the human condition even in the current era. The alternative is nihilism, luddism, and isolation from reality. That is not to say that we should not remain inquisitive, even critical, of new technologies as they claim to alter our bodily or mental experience, or both.

How to Teach Human+

Teaching Human+ practices means, first of all, becoming a practitioner so that no lessons are communicated without direct, experiential insight. The second step involves realizing that human+ practices will evolve quite dramatically even without formal or informal mentorship. The interfaces are improving rapidly. Teaching human+ is largely an exercise in ensuring learners have access to the required infrastructure, learning arenas, and learning community. Then, it means stepping back and only intervening when and if we perceive the risk tolerance levels to be overreached. This is uncharted territory. Much like the early days of electricity which was a period of intense curiosity, experimentation, and the gradual unveiling of a mysterious force. Lay scientists engaged in hands-on observation and experimentation. Traveling lecturers toured Europe and America captivating audiences with their demonstrations showcasing sparks on machines and humans. Letters were exchanged between learned people. True learning only occurred by constructing your own electrical apparatus. Teaching heavily relied on visually engaging illustrations. Informal mentorship occurred as novices associated with those perceived to be more experienced. Today, while in a different era, we can expect much of the same. Given the speed, scope, and reach of technological evolution, the formal tools of the scientific era are largely insufficient or even inadequate tools for describing, discovering, and interpreting what is going on and where it will lead.

How Does Human+ Interact with Other Platinum Workforce Skills?

Even though tomorrow's workplace is a hybrid of humans and machines, these are not necessarily to be thought of as individual skills. There is hardly a useful skill that is not already, or will not be reshaped by the human+ approach. On the other hand, we cannot reliably yet assume that what's going on is completely unprecedented. Human enhancement, in some shape or form, has always characterized human socio-technical and historical evolution. There will be decades until we fully understand the impact of current developments in a longitudinal, generational perspective. All we can say at present is that the sensation that things are fundamentally changing is nearly overwhelming.

What Might the Impact Be Once Human+ Is Commonplace?

In the 2014 book *The Second Machine Age*, Erik Brynjolfsson and Andrew McAfee outlined how work shifts as a result of digital technology, upending professions, companies, and governments, but showed how we still have choices in how to respond. Those choices are perhaps narrowing, but have not gone away. However, this decade's AI age, described in 2023 by Mustafa Suleyman in *The Coming Wave*, as a "great dilemma" of technological enhancements coupled with significant harms from not containing AI's expansion, clearly presents both unprecedented risks and unique growth opportunities. It does not take a technology genius to observe that none of us, individuals or institutions, are fully prepared for such changes. Certainly not if they happen more rapidly than educational institutions or workforce training programs can respond. While sitting at a Palo Alto wine bar recently, I met a software programmer of Indian origin working at one of the world's top five tech companies. Let's call him Sanjay. Despite currently earning $300,000 a year, he confessed he is worried about his own future. Sanjay's colleagues laugh it off, but he is thinking of reskilling himself so he won't face obsolescence. What is the likelihood that, in a conversation five years ago, would a 20-something tech worker from Silicon

Valley have such worries? I share his concerns. Software professionals without adjacent skill sets in megascale management, human–machine interaction, or risk management will most likely be obsolete by the end of this decade. The reason is that, going forward, even a 22-year-old employee, say in 2030, right out of school, will be expected to lead projects at scale where the implications of failure could be costly in both resources and reputation. A programmer pushing the wrong code could destroy energy infrastructure worth billions of dollars or release sensitive privacy data for hundreds of thousands of people. A drone operator could kill a class of school children. A lab technician could become responsible for a pandemic. To avoid that, they will need to take into account a significant array of conditions and factors far beyond the types of things they were trained to do. Maybe we should start training them more appropriately.

In his book, *Co-Intelligence: Living and Working with AI* (2024), U.S. business professor Ethan Mollick makes the point that we need to learn to think and work together with smart machines and encourages us to think about AI as a cofounder to bounce ideas off, claiming AI out-innovates people in most cases. He says AI is already better at generating ideas, solving problems, completing tasks, even analysis. Perhaps so, in some ways, but not in others. For sure, the twenty-first-century workplace will require unprecedented skills (see Figure 4.2) at human–AI collaboration ("augmented intelligence"), constantly tapping into sci-tech evolution ("transdisciplinary R&D hacks"), a revamped cascading risk management mindset ("risk aptitude"), and a plethora of transdisciplinary skills including entrepreneurship, execution ability, and explorative skills ("socio-technical skills"). These skills will need to evolve every year or even every month, eventually possibly weekly, as new technology platforms emerge at faster and faster pace at mind-bending scale and complexity.

It is important to note that because tomorrow's workplace is a hybrid of humans and machines, with varying degrees of copresence, these are not necessarily to be thought of as individual skills. In fact, possessing each of these skills at a high level would be impossible for any one individual as such. Rather, they must be thought of as systems attributes where networks, organizations, and teams, but also neighbors, friends, families, and individuals each play a role. That being said, any organizational unit, family, or individual who wishes to be a productive part of the future should try to explore such attributes, honing them through experiential learning. Few of these can be learned in isolation, outside of the physical or systemic settings where they occur, or without interaction with other learners as well as mentors.

Perhaps most crucially, there is a surging demand for workers with a flexible "interoperability mindset," capable of adapting to, and helping others adapt to, the constant, immediate, and often fundamental shifts in the materials,

FIGURE 4.2 Emergent twenty-first-century workforce skills.

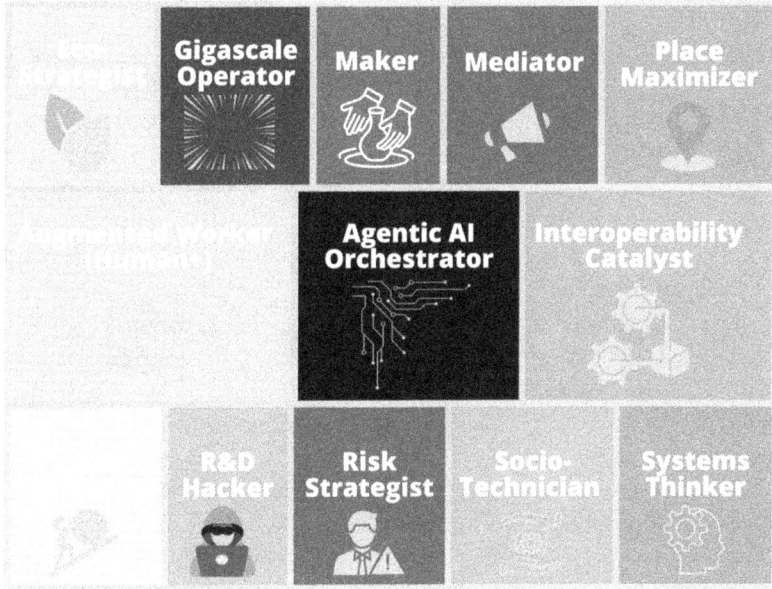

methods, tools, and technologies fueling the societal machine. That insight, and the set of crafty tools it entails, will also be needed to counteract undesirable effects of more and more powerful and integrated technologies. These might, at a regular clip, enter runaway mode meaning we cannot immediately fully control them, not necessarily that they will end the world. As a result, they will, on a regular basis, need to be monitored, possibly contained, and if all goes awry, the negative effects would need to be appropriately channeled so as not to affect the whole system or economy. The workplace of tomorrow, as described in *The Platinum Workforce* argument, is, in my view, needed as soon as within three to five years. According to the World Economic Forum's *The Future of Jobs Report 2023*, it will be required within a decade at maximum, which means that unless collaboration accelerates, universities, schools, governments, and workplaces need to forge their own paths independently.[1] I don't imagine any of those entities being able to afford obsolescence as a sector.

---

1 See (1) WEF jobs report 2023 (op.cit), (2) Stanford AI & the Future of Work: https:// digitaleconomy.stanford.edu/research-focus/ai-and-the-future-of-work/, (3) MIT Work of The Future: https://workofthefuture-taskforce.mit.edu/, (4) Tushar H, Sooraksa N.

Eighty Years of Advancing Augmented Intelligence (1950–2030)

AI's inception in the 1950s was full of announcements about workforce impacts. In a 1958 statement reflecting the early optimism of the field, Herbert Simon, along with Allen Newell, predicted that within 10 years a digital computer would be the world's chess champion (Newell, Shaw, and Simon 1958). In 1961, MIT professor Marvin Minsky wrote that, within our lifetime, machines may surpass us in general intelligence, claiming that the problem of AI would be "substantially solved" within a generation (Minsky 1961). Both chess reign and AI resolution took longer.

American filmmaker and inventor Morton Heilig was a cinematographer who wanted to push the boundaries of movie-watching beyond a passive experience to make it more realistic, engaging, and ultimately impactful. Heilig's Sensorama was among the earliest augmented reality (AR) systems, providing an interactive theater experience complete with 3D displays and introducing sensory elements like vibrating seats, fans for wind effects, and scent emitters, attempting to create a cohesive experience. Given the emphasis we place on immersion today, it is perhaps ironic that Heilig, despite his forward-thinking ideas and patents, couldn't find the financial backing needed to continue his Sensorama work. However, while visionary, creating Sensorama films was expensive, the technology had clear limitations, required much maintenance, and there was no established market for virtual reality and no understanding of the potential for its wider uses in training, education, or therapy. Instead, for artistic reasons (immersive attempts were seen as gimmicks), simplicity, cost of production, market demand, and lack of infrastructure (would need to go beyond standardized formats such as film reels for cinema or broadcast signals for TV), and lock-in effects, cinema and television proceeded largely without immersive aspects.

Global employability skills in the 21st century workplace: A semi-systematic literature review. *Heliyon.* 2023 Oct 29;9(11):e21023, (5) Sumayya Saleem, Elizabeth Dhuey, Linda White, Michal Perlman, Understanding 21st century skills needed in response to industry 4.0: Exploring scholarly insights using bibliometric analysis, Telematics and Informatics Reports, Volume 13, 2024, 100124, and (6) These are the top 10 job skills of tomorrow—and how long it takes to learn them: https://www.weforum.org/agenda/2020/10/top-10-work-skills-of-tomorrow-how-long-it-takes-to-learn-them/

Workplace Simulation Tools

Heilig's ideas form the backbone of workplace simulations used in *aerospace* (takeoff, landing, or docking to a space station), *healthcare* (patient care, surgery), *aviation* (flight simulators), *manufacturing* (digital twins, operating machinery), *military* (battlefield scenarios, combat), *business training* (decision-making, leadership), and *risk management* (disaster scenarios), where high-stakes situations require safe practice environments. Simulation-based training (SBT) has been around for centuries but has grown exponentially in the twenty-first century.[2] As a result of the power of simulation, despite inherent risks, the aerospace industry has become one of the safest industries. In the near future, the use of workplace simulations will expand even further with increased integration of AI for more dynamic and personalized learning experiences across various industries. For example, AI can create more dynamic simulations providing personalized learning experiences. Immersive AR/VR/XR technology will dramatically improve the realism of gaming scenarios. Sensors in combination with AI-enhanced data analytics will evolve to allow advanced tracking, analysis, and adjustment of performance and training tasks in real-time. Such simulations may integrate different disciplines within an organization, allowing for better collaboration and understanding of complex systems. This last challenge is not fully dependent on technology but also on more advanced ways to conceptualize (in human terms) the world(s) we are creating for ourselves. It will also depend on the quality of the simulation products available in the market at acceptable price points to implement in education and workforce training. Indicatively, the current price per user for educational business simulations currently falls within the $30–$100 per user per session range, depending on the type of simulation, frequency, features (realistic graphics), functionality, and target audience, whether it targets the education market, businesses, or individuals. Flight simulators can range from a few thousand dollars in computer gaming) to millions in commercial pilot training or retraining.

The Emergence and Decline of Knowledge Workers

The rise of the knowledge worker coincided with the decline of traditional manufacturing and the rise of service-based economies. Management consultant Peter Drucker coined the term back in 1966, in his book *The Effective*

---

2 Bienstock and Heuer 2022

Executive, emphasizing the need for communication skills to complement the influx of technology and coordinate tasks.[3] Knowledge work is the kind of work, as he imagined it, executed by professionals such as academics, accountants, architects, bureaucrats, developers, engineers, investors, lawyers, managers, physicians, researchers, scientists, technologists, and the like. These are workers whose job is to think for a living. Their work consists of a myriad of tasks. These tasks require specialized knowledge and skills. The information age revolutionized information access. The advent of the personal computer (PC) in the workplace in the late 1970s and early 1980s, complemented or replaced the large centralized mainframe computer labs primarily used by IT departments, and enabled individual workflows with computing power directly at their desks. Initially, computers were mainly used for basic tasks like data entry, calculations, and word processing, but gradually expanded to encompass more complex applications such as spreadsheets, presentation programs, accounting, planning, and design software. The internet's influx in the mid-1990s empowered individuals to access and share information globally, fostering collaboration and innovation. In industry, it reshaped manufacturing plants, allowing manufacturing firms to serve many markets and produce a wider range of goods. In the office, it enabled faster communication through email, facilitating easier document sharing, and paved the way for remote collaboration, reducing paper flow and physical archiving needs. Access to the internet allowed employees to research information, access databases, and stay updated on industry news directly from their desks. It also laid the groundwork for telecommuting and flexible work arrangements. Moreover, it created new job roles and created new career opportunities. We saw the emergence of web developers, digital marketers, and other tech-related positions.

The rise of the knowledge worker was a defining feature of the twentieth century, but the nature of knowledge work is now undergoing a significant transformation due to technological advancements. Many routine tasks previously performed by knowledge workers are now being automated, including data entry, analysis, and some aspects of legal and financial work. As technology evolves, the skills required for knowledge work are constantly changing. The future of knowledge work lies in human–AI collaboration. There is currently rapid progress in AI-assisted knowledge work, as managers seek technology to assist various functions. This happens across domains such as factory work, office work, scientific work, military work, professional work,

---

3 Drucker 2006

education, and government work. AI can augment human capabilities by automating routine tasks, providing insights from large datasets, and assisting with complex problem-solving. However, current AI hype leads to underestimating both positive and negative impacts.[4] The proper way to think of AI's influx in the workforce is to look at opportunities, risks, and barriers all at the same time. You cannot have one without the other. If AI and automation reach a point where they can independently perform the majority of tasks currently undertaken by knowledge workers, then the demand for human workers in these roles could drastically diminish. We might call this scenario the *hyperautomation* of knowledge work (Haleem et al. 2021). Under such a strategic evolution, the comprehensive use of advanced technologies, including AI, machine learning, RPA (Robotic Process Automation), and other automation tools would automate as many business and knowledge work processes as possible within an organization, without regard for the loss of human work. By connecting and integrating various technologies and systems to create seamless workflows, entire business processes could be automated, continuously optimized, and monitored by machines. However, implementing hyperautomation requires significant investment in technology, expertise, and change management. In some sectors, it is likely to be cost-prohibitive to do across the board. A hypothetical scenario where AI surpasses human intelligence in all aspects, might lead to a rapid acceleration of technological advancement and potentially render human labor obsolete in many sectors. In the event of a major societal disruption (pandemic, environmental catastrophe, or geopolitical war), the existing economic and social systems that support knowledge work could collapse, leading to widespread unemployment and a return to more basic forms of labor. However, societal and ethical debates surrounding the use of AI in the workplace will influence the pace and direction of automation. Conventionally, one would assume that as AI automates routine tasks, the demand for higher-level skills such as strategic thinking, innovation, and complex problem-solving will increase. This is not a given. If AIs really become advanced, it is precisely the higher-level skills that will become their forte.

---

4 Undheim 2024 ISWA ref

Improved AI Capabilities Gradually Entering the Workplace

Seventy years ago, AI was only capable of empowering humans to make mathematical calculations based on highly structured datasets and using enormous physical infrastructure which was useful to mathematicians. Fifty years ago, AI empowered mainframe computers capable of a wide variety of calculations, statistics, and rule-based analysis of massive datasets which was useful to a variety of applied mathematicians, strategic planners, and military analysts. Twenty years ago, AI suddenly became capable of a wide-ranging set of classification tasks across domains, instantly becoming useful to many kinds of scientific research as well as for limited business applications. In the course of a year or so, from 2023 to 2024, with the advent of generative AI, this type of technology went from being relevant only to experts to becoming available for a lay audience that included teenagers wanting to ace their written exams. The same platform is an immensely powerful tool for software programmers and for any organization with access to a massive datasets that they can manipulate and use to understand their information assets in new ways. With that, AI began the march toward becoming a platform technology the likes of which we have only recently seen with the advent of the web. Yet, AI's observers have been consistently prone to exaggerating its impact at every new inflection point, yet not fully grasping its longer-term impact on wider issues not directly related to the immediate breakthroughs. Late in 2024 and into 2025, the first so-called reasoning models capable of multistep reasoning and longer contextual frameworks ("token windows") emerged. In January 2025, as the world's elites had just watched the second Trump inauguration, and heard him announce a breathtaking $500 billion AI investment, a Chinese AI firm called DeepSeek issued an open-sourced language model and chatbot that matched top U.S. AI firms, seemingly at a fraction the cost and development time. Even more worryingly for a particular company, AI chip producer NVIDIA, which lost $600 million in a day in the largest individual company crash in stock market history, it would seem that even advanced AI doesn't take the latest generation chip to develop. With that, the tone was set for a more equitable competition in the AI-sector. Start-ups were back in the picture again. Europe saw opportunities. U.S. firms scramble to release their AI products even faster and, undoubtedly, would be willing to take more risks. All of this said, the overall picture of complex problems (such as cancer, climate change, energy revolutions, financial models, global supply chain management, mass-scale simulations, weather forecasting) requiring massive computing power to solve, remains. If we consider possible setbacks, yet assume intense competition with high levels of government support, it is conceivable that 10 years from now, AI will be a staple of every workplace. If we look even further ahead, it is quite likely that AI systems, as a whole, will have more influence and impact than humans. Based on current trends, the global labor force will approach 3.5 billion in 2030.[5] This will, presumably, be a skills-scarce world. To manage that, employers will need to find ways to retain more highly skilled women and older workers. But what if that's not the case because of technology? AIs might represent a bigger proportion of the spend than the global workforce. If so that would be because they also represent a higher value creation. To make that happen, AI needs to act more like a human worker. This brings us to the notion of agents. The word "agent" generally refers to a causal entity, something that acts or produces an effect. An agent of change brings significant transformation. A robot is a physical entity or device that acts intelligently in the physical world. A software agent is a computer program that acts autonomously on behalf of a user or another program.

The Reality of Agentic AI

Simultaneously with the broader influx of AI in the workplace, the development of Agentic AI continues apace. Agentic AI refers to a class of AI that can act independently, adapt to new environments, and autonomously solve problems. These AI agents exhibit goal-oriented behavior, situational awareness, decision-making, and—increasingly—the capability (often within a human-defined mandate) to take action in the real world.

So far, these actions remain relatively constrained. For example, digital agents like GitHub Copilot or AI coding assistants can autonomously write and debug code based on user intent, but they still require human oversight for integration, testing, and deployment. Similarly, customer service agents powered by LLMs can handle routine queries and escalate complex issues, but they cannot yet manage nuanced negotiations or high-stakes decisions. Nevertheless, the scope of Agentic AI is rapidly expanding, especially as these systems begin to integrate physical-world interfaces (e.g., robotics) and interact across multiple software platforms autonomously. We saw early agentic AI at work in rule-based chatbots that handled scheduling, store order tracking, and surveys. More sophisticated virtual assistants like Apple's Siri (2011), with

---

5 Dobbs et al. 2012

basic conversational abilities, and Amazon's Alexa (2014) with real-world utility and with half a billion devices sold, and with a 2025 upgrade allowing it to take sequential actions in the future (alerts, device management, stock trades). Recognizing individual voices will allow more extensive personalization. The biggest hurdle so far is to eliminate false or inaccurate responses. In the search engine space, AI summaries are increasingly powering searches making scrolling down search results a thing of the past for most people. Google launched AI Overviews in May 2024. While they don't technically take actions in the real world, AI summaries are also agentic in a small way, because they make assumptions about what action the user presumably wants to take as a result of a search. A search brings up relevant documents. An AI summary already interprets the search in a particular way. A customer service chatbot that can understand complex inquiries, assist with, and even resolve issues without needing to escalate to a human agent. Some of the most advanced customer service chatbots today include Ada, Zendesk, Intercom, HubSpot, Kommunicate, Netomi, and Forethought, but the field is rapidly evolving.

RPA on Steroids

RPA has evolved from simple rule-based automation of specific functions to screen scraping to extract data from applications to automated user interface testing in the early days. In the early 2000s, RPA matured and began to automate repetitive, rule-based tasks within business processes, freeing up human workers for more strategic activities. RPA adoption increased, particularly in industries with high volumes of data and repetitive tasks, such as finance and insurance. Modern RPA tools have become more sophisticated, incorporating features like intelligent automation, cloud-based solutions, and Application Programming Interface (API) integrations allowing seamless automation across different systems and bridging the gap between legacy and modern systems. APIs are like a contract that defines how applications exchange data, features, and functionality. The rise of no-code/low-code RPA platforms has made it easier for business users to create and deploy automations, reducing the reliance on specialized developers. The future of RPA is likely to combine RPA with other technologies like AI, machine learning, process mining, and analytics to automate even more complex and end-to-end business processes. This will make it capable of handling unstructured data and exceptions, make decisions, and adapt to changing circumstances. That's when predictive maintenance, fraud detection, and personalized customer service become possible.

As they increasingly gain cognitive capabilities, such as natural language processing and computer vision, RPA systems can also help create more seamless collaboration between humans and robots. For example, this can enhance process mining. Process mining is a technique that uses data from your IT systems to uncover the actual way your processes work, rather than how you think they work. You may think your sales process has four steps, perhaps as simple as: inquiries, quote, acceptance/rejection, and order processing. In reality, an event log in your IT system might reveal that it has additional steps, such as many variations, different paths, noncompliant steps, bottlenecks, or inefficiencies.

Despite being a futurist, I rarely make predictions, but will make one exception: it is likely that there will be more AIs than humans in active employment by 2040. This is not the same as saying there will be billions of robots. Rather there will be AIs carrying out the same work as billions of people did only a decade earlier. Also, it is highly likely that each human worker will rely on at least one professional AI to augment their work process. Over the course of 2025, I have come to rely on dozens of such tools. For organizations, the number of AI agents in use by the end of this decade will far outstrip the number of workflows they had control over in the industrial era. In fact, it is likely that AI agents will create entirely new workflows.

First, we are seeing agentic workflows in the digital world. What's coming is AI agents for advisory services (of all kinds), coaching, consulting, creative tasks, customer services, cybersecurity, design, education, engineering, financial assistance, government services, HR, legal services, logistics, medical services, research, therapy, trading, training, real-time translation, self-driving cars with real-time decision-making, intelligent customer service agents capable of complex issue resolution, and advanced AI systems that can autonomously manage complex workflows across multiple systems within an organization, adapting to changing conditions in real-time. With that, AI agents are not only becoming capable of handling many tasks that either are labor-intensive, expensive, or inaccurately handled by humans, it will also carry out tasks that were impossible to do for humans at scale because of cost or other constraints. AI agents will also carry out tasks that were not even invented before, fundamentally changing how we work and live. I can envision scenarios that transform a sector of choice. Here are some of mine, but I would encourage you, as you are reading, to pause and imagine yours.

Sonic Canvas

It is Saturday morning in the spring of 2036. From a dorm room in Santiago, Chile, Muse, an AI agent, collaborating with an amateur musician (who will remain unnamed because he is rapidly forgotten), uploads a new hybrid form of artistic product to a website, combining art, music, and literature, pushing the boundaries of human creativity. Because who did what is so hard to determine, the copyrights are jointly awarded to the musician and to the AI agent. This fosters a new artistic discipline that becomes known as Hybridium, not simply a blend of art, music, and literature, but a synergistic fusion where these elements interact and evolve in real-time, guided by both human intention and AI's generative capabilities. Hybridium's canvas is dynamic and multisensory. It could manifest as an immersive virtual reality environment, a responsive physical installation, or even a personalized augmented reality overlay on the world around us. Human artists, musicians, and writers act as "conductors" of the Hybridium experience. They establish the initial themes, motifs, and narratives, providing the creative spark that ignites the AI's potential. The AI agents analyze these inputs, identifying patterns, stylistic elements, and emotional undertones. The AI agents are not mere tools, but collaborators. They then generate variations and expansions, creating new text, music, and visual elements that resonate with the human input. Trained on vast datasets of art, music, and literature, they act as improvisers and cocreators, generating variations, expansions, and unexpected connections within the artistic framework set by the humans. The final Hybridium piece is a multisensory experience, engaging the viewer's imagination on multiple levels. The visuals might shift and morph in response to the music, while the text might offer insights into the emotional landscape of the artwork.

Lexi's Lesson

It's 5 a.m. on a Monday morning in Amsterdam, 2029, and Anya's smart home gently brightens. Her AI tutor, "Lexi," materializes on her tablet. "Good morning, Anya. Today's module focuses on cross-cultural communication for remote teams, specifically asynchronous collaboration." Anya, a "Global Project Facilitator," is part of a generation benefiting from personalized education, a service now widely available, though its accessibility story is complex.

Ten years prior, access to personalized AI tutors like Lexi was a privilege, a luxury afforded only by the elite. Developed initially by a consortium of global tech giants seeking to train their own future workforce, these sophisticated AI learning platforms were incredibly expensive to develop and maintain. In those early days, individuals like Anya would have needed substantial financial resources or scholarships from corporations invested in specific talent pipelines to gain access.

However, the landscape has shifted. Increased competition and advancements in AI technology have driven down costs, leading to the democratization of personalized education. Lexi, and AI tutors like her, are now offered through a subscription model, subsidized in part by government initiatives aimed at bridging the skills gap and ensuring workforce readiness in the face of rapid automation.

Anya's parents, recognizing the transformative potential of AI-driven learning, invested in a lifelong learning package for her when she was young. While not inexpensive, it's now considered a crucial investment, much like traditional education was in previous generations. The package is provided by "LearnLeap Global," one of the leading educational AI providers, responsible for developing, maintaining, and updating Lexi and her underlying platform. Lexi analyzes her learning pace, offering customized exercises and connecting her with mentors for virtual consultations. After a quick breakfast, Anya checks her personalized job feed. "TalentMatch," the Global Skills Consortium's AI, highlights emerging opportunities. "Project Lead – Decentralized Bio-Manufacturing Initiative" catches her eye. It's a new role, reflecting the growing bio-economy. TalentMatch suggests relevant micro-credentials. "Your profile shows strong project management and intercultural communication skills," it notes. "The 'Advanced Bio-Manufacturing Project Management' and 'Decentralized Team Leadership' modules would enhance your application." These AI-designed learning experiences adapt to Anya's progress. Across the globe, similar personalized learning platforms are becoming increasingly common, though access and quality vary considerably. While some still rely on traditional educational models, many forward-thinking institutions and companies are embracing AI-driven training, recognizing the need to equip individuals for the rapidly changing job market. Anya spends the afternoon in a simulated project environment. Lexi, acting as a team member from a different cultural background, presents realistic project challenges. The simulation incorporates subtle cultural cues. Lexi provides feedback, highlighting areas for improvement. Later, Anya connects with a human mentor, a seasoned project manager. They discuss her career goals and the complexities of managing remote teams. The mentor, using AI-powered communication analysis tools, shares insights and provides personalized advice. As the day ends, Anya feels prepared. Personalized education, powered by AI, has equipped her with skills for a cutting-edge career. The future of work, while uncertain, feels manageable, full of potential.

The System Weaver

It's 6 a.m. near Stuttgart, Germany, and Kai's smart home gently nudges him awake. His holographic workstation displays the day's priorities. "Guten Morgen, Kai. Gigascale production adjustments required for the European Battery Initiative. Your focus: optimizing lithium sourcing against projected demand spikes." Kai, a "Systems Integration Architect" for Bosch Global, operates in a world transformed by AI-driven manufacturing. Forget Industry 4.0's automation; this is Industry 5.0—a hyperconnected, AI-orchestrated eco-system. Digital twins of entire supply chains, factories, and even proposed pan-European battery recycling infrastructure exist in a constantly updating virtual realm. These aren't just simulations; they're living models reflecting real-time data, allowing for predictive analysis and gigascale decision-making with immense risk attached. A single miscalculation could ripple through the entire European economy.

Kai's role isn't about turning wrenches; it's about ensuring interoperability between mas-sively complex systems. He monitors the AI's recommendations, not to micromanage, but to inject human judgment and ethical considerations into decisions that impact millions. This morning, the AI proposes a controversial lithium sourcing agreement with a newly emerged South American supplier. Kai reviews the AI's analysis, cross-referencing it with geopolitical risk assessments and environmental impact reports. He flags potential human rights con-cerns and requests further investigation from the AI ethics specialist team. The pressure is immense. These gigascale decisions, once the domain of boards and CEOs, now rest partly on his shoulders. The demand for new, sustainable infrastructure is so great that industry has created a new breed of professionals to manage it.

Kai's education wasn't traditional. He holds a "Master's in Systems Thinking and AI Ethics"—a degree unheard of a decade ago. His curriculum blended complex systems theory, AI programming, and ethical philosophy. He stays current through continuous learning— AI-curated learning modules, virtual reality simulations of potential supply chain disrup-tions, and regular consultations with AI specialists who constantly update their knowledge base. Today, Kai's focus is on ensuring seamless data flow and operational integrity across a network of smart factories, autonomous logistics systems, and emerging recycling facilities. He's the linchpin, the human element in a world of intelligent machines, ensuring that the relentless drive for efficiency and scale doesn't compromise ethical considerations or long-term sustainability. The hum of advanced manufacturing around him is deafening, a testament to the power of AI, but it's Kai's quiet decisions that truly shape the future of industry.

The Human Element of Human+

Over the past few decades, AI has made leaps and bounds, particularly in tasks such as data processing and summarization, with notable progress for professions such as content marketing, some progress in acting in the world, not just aiding but actually commencing to execute decision-making, and with more limited progress in advanced cognition starting to resemble rea-sonably advanced human thinking of sorts. However, the impact of AI help-ing humans do all those things better might be more consequential than AIs acquiring some of those facets on their own. Besides, there is a strong case for interdependence between humans and AIs. Augmenting human capabilities with AI will typically be more effective and beneficial compared to completely automating them. At least for now. Human intelligence augmentation is also more fruitful than attempting to automate humans out of the workforce. This is an objective we can set. We can also influence the timeline. The human component of factory work has definitely shifted over the past few centuries, but humans are still not irrelevant on the factory floor. In fact, arguably, with augmented lean paradigms starting to infuse the manufacturing industry, in some contexts, humans take on even more important roles. [6]

We are still learning about how knowledge workers are reacting to the new possibilities, the prevailing limitations, and practical challenges that ensue. A tremendous amount of outside factors also seem to impact the quality of knowledge work. It is possible that the direction of AI hype could cloud workers' judgment by accelerating the extremes of excitement or anxiety, trust or mistrust in AI. As constellations of human–AI systems become commonplace, we need to understand much more about what typically happens in such collaborations, and set governance criteria for appropriate interaction as well as criteria for escalation of concerns that might arise.

Training for Human+

How do you train your skills in augmented intelligence? How do you set up training programs for your coworkers or those you manage or work with? The starting point is to realize that tinkering skills are fundamental to tackling change. No matter what the training program is, without tinkering on your own, you will only be prepared for prepared scenarios, not for the real challenges of the emerging workplace. That being said, no-code platforms, advanced interfaces that perform and execute code upon instruction, but where no software coding skills are needed, are essential. For frontline manufacturing, a good place to start might be to explore the tools and resources provided by Tulip (www.tulip.co). However, it is not enough to read ebooks, white papers and guides, you would need to download and experiment with the digital platform and tweak it to do something in the real world in order to truly learn.

In *All Hands on Tech: The AI-Powered Citizen Revolution* (2024), Tom Davenport, Ian Barkin, and Chase Davenport argue that business domain experts are

---

6 Linder and Undheim 2022

driving IT-enabled innovation using technology previously reserved for professional technologists.[7] I agree. Used well, emerging technology bestows unprecedented power on these individuals. That may also mean delivering unprecedented value on the organizations that channel their efforts, empower them, minimize risk, and liberate their IT departments to pursue strategic initiatives. "All hands on deck" approaches, an expression from sailing, meaning everyone is needed to contribute immediately, are powerful when used in an enterprise. Think: startups preparing for a major product launch. Companies responding to a cybersecurity breach. Nonprofits mobilizing for disaster relief. Empowering nontechnical workers to embrace technology enables them to turn ideas into applications, automations, and analytical models. But for those entering the workplace there is also a lesson here. Opportunity comes to those who are prepared. Interfaces may become simpler and easier to work with, but technology is still a barrier to some. Achieving the right balance of depth and breadth in tech literacy will become a new superskill. What it means will continue to evolve. It is unlikely that interfaces will become entirely seamless and won't require any skills at all. At least, if this becomes the case, those who can peek behind the curtain will be better prepared for the next iterations. In most cases, those workers will be the ones that create the next context for both human and AI work, and their many conjoint constellations.

Work of the Future

The connected worker is any worker integrated into their environment by technologies that exchange data with other devices, machines, workers, and supply chains, in an integrated work system. Today's work roles that might be a match for such a system include operators, field workers, engineers, and even executives working in manufacturing. The best digital operators make use of technology (sparingly) to augment workers. They don't blindly automate to chase theoretical efficiencies that might backfire. The effect is immediate worker empowerment, and therefore, improved efficiencies—exactly what lean hopes to achieve—but with sustained, decentralized innovation as a bonus. If you base your work on good data that's directly relevant to the work being accomplished, the end result can become better decisions, right-the-first-time outcomes, and safer workers.

---

7 Davenport and Barkin 2024

Human–AI collaboration skills will come to include being aware of available AIs' opportunities and limitations. Equally important is choosing the types of AI, machines, and software to use. Stitching processes together, instructing AIs, setting parameters, assigning team roles is also part of the task. Collaborating, iterating with AIs, checking the quality of AI output against established parameters and raising risk issues that emerge will have to be subject to standardization and rinse-repeat procedures. Augmented intelligence will include setting governance criteria for normal operations, escalations, shutdown procedures, and alerting mechanisms. As coding skills will become an unassailable specialty of machines, humans will need to focus on integrating the work of machines and humans. As a line worker in a factory your job will be to monitor machines, providing smooth transitions between the tasks accomplished by machines, hybrid tasks accomplished by teams of humans and machines, and tasks where humans instruct machines and watch over the results. Looking for adverse outcomes, or worrisome developments or paths in machine reasoning or other anomalies will become a crucial skill set.

We might one day (soon) face the scenario that instead of AI taking all the low-skilled jobs endangering the working class, it instead ends up taking all the middle-class knowledge work previously reserved for professionals, managers, and civil servants. If the workforce gets this "squeeze of the middle," what will remain aside from manual tasks is only the top-level management and architecture tasks that require complex systems comprehension. This is why we cannot completely abandon depth as a goal for tech literacy in the workforce. If you have nobody on staff who understands what your AI is doing, you are not in charge anymore. Few leaders would want to be in that position.

Downsides of Human+

Human+ technologies offer incredible potential, but they also come with potential downsides. One major concern is the potential for increased inequality. Advanced technologies for enhancement could be incredibly expensive, creating a significant divide between those who can afford them and those who cannot. This "enhancement divide" could exacerbate existing social and economic inequalities. Furthermore, altering human biology raises fundamental questions about what it means to be human. Concerns exist about the potential for dehumanization and the erosion of human dignity. Enhancements could also impact our autonomy, raising questions about free will and individual decision-making. The long-term effects of many enhancement technologies are unknown, and there's a risk of unintended consequences, such as unforeseen health problems or unforeseen societal disruptions.

Another concern is the potential for dependency. Relying heavily on technology to enhance human abilities can create a situation where individuals struggle without technological support. Furthermore, integrating advanced technologies into the human body or mind can introduce security vulnerabilities. This makes it essential to protect against hacking and other malicious activities. The psychological impact of Human+ technologies also warrants consideration. Increased pressure to constantly optimize and upgrade oneself, constant performance monitoring, and the integration of technology with human identity can all have significant mental health implications.

Finally, there are significant existential risks associated with Human+. If some individuals achieve significantly enhanced capabilities, it could lead to power imbalances and even the potential for control over others. There's also a fear that excessive pursuit of enhancement could lead to a loss of core human values and experiences, such as empathy, vulnerability, and the appreciation of our inherent limitations. It's crucial to carefully consider these potential downsides as we develop and implement Human+ technologies.

Conclusion

Multiple indicators are currently pointing to heightened anxiety, increased layoffs, and a fundamental shift in employment dynamics. Given that job security has dramatically worsened over the past decade, those who embrace the fragility of fixed employment respond in kind by creating degrees of freedom that amplify over time based on skill sets, experiences, and a portfolio of accomplishments. Carefully building a portfolio of augmented and augmentable skills can lead to both societal impact and career success. Those who will excel in this environment will have to experiment, fail, and then rinse and repeat in many divergent ways before they succeed.

References

Bienstock, Jared, and Albert Heuer. 2022. "A Review on the Evolution of Simulation-Based Training to Help Build a Safer Future." *Medicine* 101 (25): e29503.

Davenport, Thomas H., and Ian Barkin. 2024. *All Hands on Tech: The AI-Powered Citizen Revolution*. Nashville, TN: John Wiley & Sons.

Dobbs, Richard, Anu Madgavkar, Dominic Barton, Eric Labaye, James Manyika, Charles Roxburgh, Susan Lund, and Siddarth Madhav. 2012. "The World at

Work: Jobs, Pay, and Skills for 3.5 Billion People." *McKinsey & Company*. June 1. https://www.mckinsey.com/featured-insights/employment-and-growth/the -world-at-work.

Drucker, Peter F. 2006. *The Effective Executive: The Definitive Guide to Getting the Right Things Done*. Revised edition. New York: Harper Business.

Haleem, Abid, Mohd Javaid, Ravi Pratap Singh, Shanay Rab, and Rajiv Suman. 2021. "Hyperautomation for the Enhancement of Automation in Industries." *Sensors International* 2 (100124): 100124.

Linder, Natan, and Trond Arne Undheim. 2022. *Augmented Lean: A Human-Centric Framework for Managing Frontline Operations*. New Jersey: John Wiley & Sons.

Minsky, Marvin. 1961. "Steps toward Artificial Intelligence." *Proceedings of the IRE* 49 (1): 8–30.

Newell, Allen, J. C. Shaw, and H. A. Simon. 1958. "Chess-Playing Programs and the Problem of Complexity." *IBM Journal of Research and Development* 2 (4): 320–335.

Undheim, Trond Arne. 2024. "An Interdisciplinary Review of Systemic Risk Factors Leading Up to Existential Risks." *Progress in Disaster Science* 22: 100326. https://doi.org/10.1016/j.pdisas.2024.100326.

CHAPTER 5

INTEROPERABILITY CATALYST

What Is an Interoperability Catalyst?

An Interoperability Catalyst is an emerging specialist work role that focuses on driving the successful integration and collaboration between different systems, technologies, platforms, and organizations. Interoperability refers to the ability of different entities to work together seamlessly, exchange data, and leverage each other's functionalities. Interoperability Catalysts are often individuals, teams, or organizations that play a pivotal role in breaking down silos and ensuring that different technologies can work together effectively. Key responsibilities include identifying interoperability challenges. This role requires a deep understanding of existing systems, their limitations, and the potential roadblocks to seamless data flow and information exchange.

Interoperability Catalysts act as bridges between different stakeholders, including technical teams, business leaders, and external partners. They foster communication, build consensus, and resolve conflicts to achieve interoperability goals. They create or implement tools, frameworks, and best practices to support interoperability efforts. They explore and implement new technologies and approaches to improve interoperability, such as APIs, data integration platforms, and emerging standards. In doing so, they drive innovation by enabling new capabilities through interoperable solutions. They explore and implement new technologies and approaches to improve interoperability, such as APIs, data integration platforms, and emerging standards. They advocate for interoperability within the organization, educating stakeholders on its benefits and fostering a culture of collaboration and information sharing. They continuously monitor the performance of interoperability solutions, identify areas for improvement, and adapt strategies as needed. As such, in its contemporary and emerging form, it is a role with a bias for action. It can be performed at any level in an organization, and usually not just in the middle layer.

FIGURE 5.1 Interoperability Catalyst.

Why Are Interoperability Catalysts Needed Now?

Many years ago, innovation scholars Michael L. Tushman (1977), as well as Aldrich & Herker (1977) conceptualized a similar role called boundary spanner, individuals who link an organization's internal networks with external sources of information (Aldrich and Herker 1977).[1] A boundary spanner is a person or organization that works across different systems or boundaries to connect people and ideas. This slightly wider notion was adopted by the knowledge management literature and some of its practitioners. What's different today is the complexity of that task and how it is both enabled and at times blocked by legacy systems and ideas, both within and outside an organization. The framework one tries to influence is also not necessarily one organization but a network of organizational and other entities, or even entire systems. In the past, such a role might have been an important differentiator for a firm during the innovation process. Today, it is a condition of the survival and resilience of society and business as sustainable systems. This role is critical in environments where multiple technologies, standards, or stakeholders must work together to achieve shared goals. The Interoperability Catalyst acts as a bridge, ensuring that disparate systems, processes, and teams can operate cohesively.

---

1 Tushman 1977

How to Learn Interoperability Catalysis?

Today, the role of an Interoperability Catalyst is often embedded in titles such as: Integration Specialist, Solutions Architect, Systems Engineer, Data Integration Manager, API Strategist, Ecosystem Manager, Digital Transformation Lead, or Interoperability Consultant. A rapidly emergent example of such a role would be the AI governance professional, an emerging category of workers in government, the private sector, and in nonprofit organizations, charged with setting boundaries for the operation of AI and ensuring AI safety, as well as fostering innovation through active yet responsible use of AI.

Interoperability catalysis can be learned through engaging in standards setting organizations (SSOs). It typically requires strong technical expertise. However, there are many relevant tasks that can be executed without an engineering degree as long as one develops a deep understanding of various relevant technologies, data formats, and integration methodologies. Also, it entails the ability to effectively communicate complex technical concepts to both technical and nontechnical audiences. This is a skill often possessed by futurists, keynote speakers, executives, and communication professionals in the tech sector. However, when it comes to the ability to identify and resolve complex interoperability challenges, this skill can only be practiced within teams. Few people can solve such challenges alone. For that reason, a certain level of project management and organizational skills helps if you want to develop the ability to plan, execute, and manage interoperability projects effectively. Lastly, this role cannot be carried out without business acumen or at least a general understanding of business needs and how interoperability can support organizational goals. In essence, an Interoperability Catalyst is a critical role, and a set of interconnected skills that matter in today's interconnected world, enabling organizations to leverage the power of data and technology to achieve their strategic objectives. Lastly, it is an advocate role. The need for interoperability is somewhat abstract, which is why raising awareness about the importance of interoperability and its role in the growth of decentralized ecosystems requires particularly strong convincing skills.

How to Teach Interoperability Catalysis?

According to the *Oxford English Dictionary*, the word *interoperability* first appeared in the midsixties and was used to describe the ability of two or more pieces of equipment to operate in conjunction. Originally, it was used for military equipment, as in buying and using the same standard-issue material.

Throughout the latter part of the 1970s, as computers appeared, the term has come to refer to interfaces for computer systems, software, or data sharing. Technical interoperability is often linked to standards and standardization efforts, typically driven by international committees, at least as regards technology. The theoretical foundation for interoperability is found in systems theory. The most typical application is in software or hardware development. Training to become an Interoperability Catalyst requires a combination of technical expertise, industry knowledge, and soft skills. Building a strong technical foundation is crucial. Learning core technologies such as APIs and web services, middleware, data formats and standards (JSON, XML, YAML), and learning programming (Python, JavaScript, Java, and Go), cloud platforms (AWS, Azure, Google Cloud), and microservices architecture, as well as understanding how devices and sensors communicate in interconnected systems (through IoT and Edge), is a baseline in the current environment. More broadly, all technologies have their own interoperability needs. According to the International Organization for Standardization (ISO), as of January 2024, there are over 25,000 published international standards. Developing iIndustry-specific knowledge is key. One would perhaps initially choose one domain. It could be smart to focus on industries where interoperability is critical, such as healthcare, finance, supply chain, or smart cities. Each domain has industry-specific standards. In healthcare, there is HL7, FHIR, and DICOM. In the supply chain area, there is EDI and GS1. In finance, there is ISO 20022 and Open Banking APIs. That said, making a bet on other industries where the skill will become fundamental a few years from now would be an even smarter career strategy. In addition, Interoperability Catalysts must study compliance frameworks like GDPR, HIPAA, or CCPA that impact data sharing and interoperability across industry.

Gaining practical experience is important. Participating in projects that involve connecting disparate systems or platforms can give important lessons. If you want to develop these skills, seek opportunities to work with IT, business, and external partners. Another option is to engage in open-source projects focused on interoperability. Start in roles like Integration Engineer, Systems Analyst, or API Developer to build foundational experience, or ask to do an interoperability internship. There are also relevant industry certifications to pursue both in technical areas and in project management, including PMP (Project Management Professional) or Agile certifications (e.g., Scrum Master). One can stay updated on trends and innovations through following industry news and subscribing to blogs, newsletters, and forums focused on interoperability, attending conferences and webinars, and experimenting with emerging technologies such as AI interoperability, blockchain, and edge computing. Building a professional network can be done through joining online communities dedicated to interoperability on platforms such as LinkedIn, Reddit, or Slack. Seeking mentorship from experienced interoperability professionals can dramatically sharpen the learning curve. Developing a portfolio to document and share examples of interoperability projects you've worked on is also smart, including writing blogs and articles sharing your insights, and contributing to case studies. To transition into such roles, emphasize your technical skills, industry knowledge, and experience with cross-system collaboration. You could also position yourself as a champion for interoperability within your organization or industry.

How Does Interoperability Catalysis Interact with Other Platinum Workforce Skills?

Interoperability catalysis requires understanding of industry and domain-specific challenges (e.g., healthcare, finance, manufacturing, supply chain) and awareness of regulatory and compliance requirements. It also requires sociotechnical finesse, the ability to navigate how technology fits with, and evolves through societal and cultural context. Augmented humans may or may not be using interoperable systems, but those who do are more efficient. Agentic AI already relies heavily on standardized processes and workflows, and in the future will likely be governed by it. R&D hackers are often those who understand interoperability, or they certainly are among the few who act when it is broken. Interoperability is also inherently tied to systems, so those who attempt to act as systems thinkers must have an inherent feeling for what systems can and should work together, or as we say, interoperate. Interoperability is necessary for large-scale systems to work. Gigascale operations would simply not work at all without interoperability.

What Happens Once Interoperability Catalysis Is Commonplace?

As technology ecosystems grow more complex, the demand for Interoperability Catalysts will rise. This role will evolve to include expertise in emerging areas like AI interoperability, blockchain integration, and cross-industry data sharing. Professionals in this space will play a pivotal role in shaping the future of connected systems and collaborative innovation. However, the wider impact will only be seen once entire industries and social systems develop an interoperability mindset.

What is an interoperability mindset? It is certainly more than an aptitude to make technologies communicate which is where the term currently is used the most. In engineering or industry one might immediately think of interoperability between devices made by different manufacturers which could be facilitated by shared interfaces, standards, or connecting protocols that enable the exchange of information between software, hardware, and systems. That rightfully sounds complicated and is indeed so, but not for technical reasons and more for business reasons. The incentives to interoperate are not always immediately obvious to competitors. Consider electronic health record systems which have become staunch systems that are often not compatible with each other which leads to a plethora of problems. [2]

Now consider that these are systems that run our hospitals, crucial institutions that we rely on in times of cascading crises such as the COVID-19 pandemic. Imagine how many lives could have been saved by a more coordinated health response. Then, imagine the next generation of AI technology, if not interoperable, and operating across domains. Think of what happens if the transportation infrastructure fails, if energy can no longer be delivered across the electricity grid, or if the internet goes down for weeks and months on end across the world. These are all challenges we might face should cascading effects from various futuristic crisis scenarios come to pass. As technologies become deeper and deeper embedded in societal infrastructure, where interoperability is absent we might be losing out on significant market size benefits to the tune of billions of dollars. We would also face crisis scenarios without the necessary flexibility to limit downsides or provide alternatives. The result will not just be economic damage but human suffering. More importantly, interoperability extends far beyond technologies.

There is already a significant demand for workers with a flexible "interoperability mindset," capable of adapting to, and helping others adapt to, the constant, immediate, and often fundamental shifts in the materials, methods, tools, and technologies fueling the societal machine. That insight will also be needed to counteract undesirable effects of more and more powerful and integrated technologies that might, at a regular clip, enter runaway mode (meaning we cannot immediately fully control them—not necessarily that they will end the world) and will need to be contained and appropriately channeled.

---

2 Undheim 2021

How to develop an interoperability mindset is not that obvious. I know of no specific training programs that work on this skill. Certainly not outside tech, unless you count all kinds of collaboration courses. Yet, it is perhaps the most important integrative skill that would enable all technologies, industries, and organizations to work better together. For one, we need to implement reverse apprenticeships at scale, where younger people teach older people, as Matt Beane points out in his 2024 book *The Skill Code*. In reality, as good masters appreciate, great apprenticeships are always two-way learning opportunities. This is a better approach than switching out older workers because they lack technical skills.

Developing mindsets is more complex than developing technical skills. It is even harder than developing transdisciplinary technical skills. Presumably, training would have to focus on cases, scenarios, and examples where interoperability mindsets were displayed and reflecting on the choices made. In the ideal scenario, every newly built product considers interoperability from the outset. However, even that would not fix situations where we are forced to interact with existing products that do not. That's why having an interoperability mindset implies flexibility. It also demands the ability to improvise. Lastly, it requires the expertise to recognize which interface could be created to facilitate exchange between different platforms, concerns, or products. With interoperability, there is never perfection. Whatever makes the collaboration work is the right currency. Establishing trust with those with whom your platform or product needs to communicate is the primary concern. Executing on that is the secondary concern. The priority is on establishing a minimum level of communication not to figure out rare boundary cases that may not come to pass. Interoperability is about establishing building blocks. It may require embracing a certain level of chaos at least initially. There will be tradeoffs. There will be resistance, even from your hierarchy and existing partners. It is as much about establishing a process as agreeing on a technology interface or solution. Achieving interoperability requires management skill, not just tech prowess.

Over the past few decades, the broader definition of interoperability takes into account social, psychological, political, and organizational factors ("sociotechnical factors"). Those tend to impact system-to-system performance, as well as system-to-individual or system-to-machine tasks, such as maintaining working relationships between diverse organizational units with different aims, tools, and practices. The function of interoperability in this broader context is to establish and maintain trust so that cooperation is smoother. Even technical systems often exist to transfer meaning, which is called semantic interoperability. A very simple example is a common terminology, or language, to facilitate such communication. Technical people often refer to this challenge as one of developing "ontologies" and "taxonomies." Even though the point is for terminology to be clear and concise, the opposite tends to happen, and complexity is reintroduced. For that reason, the very simplest definition of interoperability is cooperation capability. That being said, the important thing is not just the ability to cooperate but to actually do it, which brings us from mindset to practice. Interoperability, then, can be seen as a "shared system of technology and teamwork built upon trust, identification, goals, communication and flexibility."[3] But to work in practice, it must be embedded in each of the organizations that make use of such a system, including legal systems and cultural systems across borders.

We have, in many ways, come full circle with interoperability. It is, again as it was in the 1970s needed as a means of technical integration between converging systems, both emergent and established technologies and platforms. But because interoperability also grows the scale of a system it also tends to grow the complexity of the system. For that reason we need to watch out for deleterious effects.[4] At the same time, interoperability is a fundamental precondition for trust across the hybrid teams of people and machines that, in reality, cocreate the desirable effects that we seek by putting technologies together.

Downsides of Interoperability Catalysts

Interoperability Catalysts are indeed crucial for fostering seamless integration and collaboration across various systems and technologies. However, there are potential downsides to consider, including complexity, resources, security, resistance to change, and maintenance. Also, if systems are connected, they might be more vulnerable to attack, because they could share similar vulnerabilities. Problems might cascade.

Ensuring interoperability between diverse systems can be highly complex and challenging. The role requires juggling multiple complex systems simultaneously, which can lead to cognitive overload. When dealing with numerous integration points, protocols, and standards, even small oversights can cascade into major issues. It requires a deep understanding of each system's intricacies and potential compatibility issues. Poorly implemented integrations

---

3 Power et al. 2024
4 Hodapp and Hanelt 2022

can lead to technical debt, where the cost of maintaining and updating the system increases significantly over time. While focusing on making systems work together, Interoperability Catalysts might need to implement temporary solutions or workarounds that contribute to technical debt. These compromises, while necessary for immediate interoperability, can create maintenance challenges down the line. Overcoming existing data silos and integrating with legacy systems can be a significant challenge. These systems may be outdated, poorly documented, and difficult to integrate with newer technologies. Incompatible technologies, proprietary systems, or outdated infrastructure can create significant barriers to interoperability. These limitations may require costly upgrades or custom solutions to overcome. For example, a company using proprietary software might struggle to integrate with open-source platforms.

Achieving interoperability often demands significant time, effort, and financial resources. Smaller organizations might struggle to allocate the necessary resources for such initiatives. The benefits of interoperability (e.g., improved efficiency, better decision-making) can be difficult to quantify or may take time to materialize. Without clear metrics, it can be challenging to demonstrate the value of interoperability initiatives to stakeholders. For example, a company might struggle to measure the ROI of integrating its CRM and ERP systems.

Interoperability efforts can have unintended consequences, such as creating new bottlenecks or dependencies. These consequences may offset the benefits of interoperability or create new challenges. For example, integrating two systems might inadvertently slow down data processing or create new points of failure. Even worse, integrating multiple systems can introduce security vulnerabilities, making it essential to implement robust security measures to protect data and ensure compliance with regulations. Integrating systems can increase the risk of security breaches, as it expands the attack surface and creates new vulnerabilities. Ensuring data security and privacy across interconnected systems is critical. However, focusing too much on interoperability can lead to over-engineering or unnecessary complexity in systems. This can result in bloated systems that are difficult to maintain or scale. For example, a company might integrate too many tools and platforms, creating a tangled web of dependencies.

The absence of universal standards or protocols can make it difficult to achieve seamless interoperability. Organizations may need to develop custom solutions or rely on third-party middleware, increasing costs and complexity. For example, different IoT devices using proprietary communication protocols might require custom integrations to work together. Organizations and individuals accustomed to existing systems and processes might resist changes required for interoperability, leading to friction and slow adoption. The lack of industry-wide standards for interoperability can create significant challenges. Different systems may use incompatible data formats, protocols, and APIs, making integration difficult and time-consuming. Implementing interoperability initiatives can require significant organizational change, which can face resistance from employees, departments, and even senior management. Interoperability Catalysts often need to navigate competing interests between different departments, vendors, and organizations. Each stakeholder may have different priorities, timelines, and technical constraints, making consensus difficult to achieve. Overcoming this resistance and gaining buy-in for interoperability projects can be challenging.

Once interoperability is achieved, ongoing maintenance and updates are necessary to ensure continued compatibility and functionality, which can be resource-intensive. The rapid evolution of technology means Interoperability Catalysts must constantly update their knowledge across multiple domains. This perpetual learning curve can be exhausting and may lead to knowledge gaps.

While these challenges exist, the benefits of having Interoperability Catalysts in driving seamless collaboration and innovation are significant. To address these challenges, Interoperability Catalysts and organizations can involve all relevant stakeholders in the planning process to build buy-in and address concerns. It is important to implement interoperability solutions incrementally to manage complexity and reduce risks. Ensuring that data security and privacy are integral to interoperability efforts is key. Using established standards and protocols can simplify integration and reduce costs. Building the skills and knowledge needed to design and implement effective interoperability solutions requires investment in training and education, monitoring and adaptation, continuously evaluating the impact of interoperability initiatives, and being prepared to adjust as needed.

References

Aldrich, Howard, and Diane Herker. 1977. "Boundary Spanning Roles and Organization Structure." *Academy of Management Review* 2 (2): 217.

Hodapp, Daniel, and André Hanelt. 2022. "Interoperability in the Era of Digital Innovation: An Information Systems Research Agenda." *Journal of Information Technology Impact* 37 (4): 407–427.

Power, Nicola, Jennifer Alcock, Richard Philpot, and Mark Levine. 2024. "The Psychology of Interoperability: A Systematic Review of Joint Working between the UK Emergency Services." *Journal of Occupational and Organizational Psychology* 97 (1): 233–252.

Tushman, Michael L. 1977. "Special Boundary Roles in the Innovation Process." *Administrative Science Quarterly* 22 (4): 587.

Undheim, Trond Arne. 2021. *Health Tech: Rebooting Society's Software, Hardware and Mindset.* Boca Raton: Productivity Press.

CHAPTER 6

R&D HACKER

What Is an R&D Hacker?

An R&D hacker is a highly innovative and unconventional researcher or engineer who leverages atypical methods, tools, and perspectives to accelerate research and development processes. An R&D hacker is a hybrid role that combines the creativity and problem-solving mindset of a hacker with the structured, forward-thinking approach of research and development (R&D). R&D hackers often challenge traditional R&D methodologies, embracing experimentation, rapid prototyping, user-centered design, and innovation to solve complex problems or create new products, services, or technologies. R&D hackers thrive in environments where traditional R&D processes are too slow or rigid, and they leverage unconventional methods to accelerate innovation. The rise of open-source tools and platforms has democratized innovation. R&D hackers leverage these resources to accelerate development and collaborate with global communities. Organizations are increasingly working with external partners (e.g., start-ups, academia, competitors) to codevelop solutions through open innovation. R&D hackers excel at navigating these collaborative environments. They are driven by a strong desire to create meaningful impact and are not afraid to take risks to achieve their goals. They can be either intrapreneurs or entrepreneurs, or both, depending on the circumstances. They are comfortable with ambiguity and thrive in dynamic and uncertain environments.

A related practice, so-called "vibe coding," was introduced by computer scientist Andrej Karpathy in February 2025. "There's a new kind of coding I call 'vibe coding,' where you fully give in to the vibes, embrace exponentials, and forget that the code even exists," he wrote on X (@karpathy), on Feb 2 at 6:17 p.m., to be exact, and added: "I just see stuff, say stuff, run stuff, and copy paste stuff, and it mostly works." Well, some of the work with generative

AI feels this way, but R&D hackers often have more complicated workdays. Suffice to say that R&D is still hard at times.

R&D Hacking Practices

Organizations known for embracing R&D hacking approaches typically include innovation labs and tech companies, such as Alphabet's X (formerly Google X), which is known for its "moonshot factory" approach to radical innovation; Skunk Works (Lockheed Martin), which pioneered many aerospace innovations through unconventional methods; Bell Labs (Nokia), a historic example that revolutionized telecommunications and computing; Tesla, especially in its early days of rapid prototyping and unconventional manufacturing approaches; and SpaceX, known for its iterative "test to failure" approach in rocket development.

Some research institutions also have R&D hackers, such as MIT Media Lab, which combines unconventional disciplines and approaches; DARPA, or the Defense Advanced Research Projects Agency, a U.S. government agency

FIGURE 6.1 R&D Hacker.

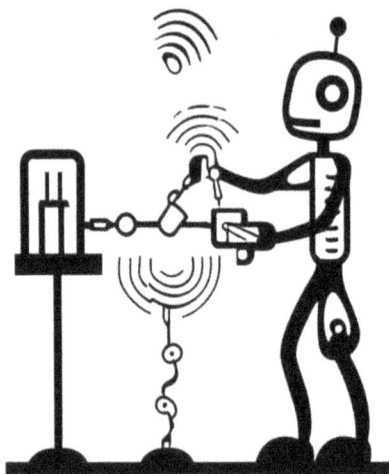

that develops new technologies for the military and funds high-risk, high-reward research with unconventional approaches; and the Fraunhofer Society in Germany, known for applied research with quick industry application. Start-ups and scale-ups, such as start-up incubators like Y Combinator, often foster R&D hacking mindsets. Various biotech start-ups, especially those working on rapid COVID-19 responses, used R&D hacking approaches. Climate tech companies working on urgent environmental solutions do as well and might be expected to do so in the future if the situation dramatically deteriorates and quick solutions need to be found. Many companies don't explicitly label their innovative developers as R&D hackers but embrace similar principles through titles like Innovation Engineers, Research Scientists, Rapid Prototyping Specialists, Technology Scouts, or Advanced Research Engineers.

How do some of these organizations implement R&D hacking approaches? IBM Research is known for its innovative approach to solving complex problems in areas like AI, quantum computing, and healthcare. R&D hacking traits include rapid experimentation, cross-disciplinary collaboration, and a focus on groundbreaking technologies.

In contrast, Google is famous for its "20% time" policy, which allows employees to spend a portion of their workweek on passion projects. This culture of experimentation has led to innovations like Gmail and Google Maps. Alphabet's X (formerly Google X) uses a structured approach to killing projects quickly ("rapid unproject"). It employs radical solutions to huge problems rather than incremental improvements and encourages controlled failure as a learning mechanism. The culture at X encourages R&D hackers to push the boundaries of technology and rethink solutions to complex problems in ways that might seem impossible using traditional methods. Notable projects like Project Loon (internet via balloons), Google Glass, and Waymo (self-driving cars) started as unconventional approaches to solving major challenges. X maintains small, highly autonomous teams with diverse expertise.

Tesla's approach to innovation involves rapid iteration and a willingness to challenge traditional automotive and energy industry norms. Tesla experiments with new technologies (e.g., electric vehicles, battery storage) and focuses on solving complex problems. Tesla's engineers are encouraged to take risks and challenge traditional automotive R&D, especially when it comes to battery technology, software, and manufacturing techniques. SpaceX implements rapid iteration cycles in rocket development. It uses full-scale testing rather than just simulations and, in fact, embraces spectacular failures as learning opportunities. SpaceX's ability to build reusable rockets, like the Falcon 9, is a direct result of its R&D hacking mindset. By vertically integrating manufacturing to speed up development cycles, it challenges traditional aerospace development timelines and methods. SpaceX is famous for its "build a little, test a little, fail a little, fix a little" approach. SpaceX is known for its agile development process, rapid prototyping, and willingness to fail fast and learn quickly in the pursuit of space exploration.

Apple's product development process often involves pushing the boundaries of technology and design, with a strong emphasis on user experience. R&D hacking traits include cross-disciplinary collaboration, rapid prototyping, and a focus on creating seamless, innovative products. While Apple's approach to R&D may be more secretive and controlled compared to others, the company's ability to break into new markets (e.g., smartphones, wearables, smart home devices) and create entirely new product categories suggests a form of "controlled" R&D hacking, where rapid prototyping and iteration are central to their development cycle.

Pixar's creative process involves rapid iteration and collaboration between artists, engineers, and storytellers to produce groundbreaking animated films. R&D hacking traits include experimentation, user-centered design, and a focus on pushing the boundaries of storytelling and technology. Dyson is renowned for its iterative approach to product development, often creating thousands of prototypes to perfect its designs. R&D hacking traits include rapid prototyping, hands-on experimentation, and a focus on solving everyday problems with innovative technology.

Amazon's culture of innovation includes rapid experimentation with new technologies and business models, such as AWS (Amazon Web Services) and drone delivery. Amazon's research division, Lab126, is responsible for developing innovative hardware products such as the Kindle, Echo, and Fire TV. The team operates in an experimental environment where they prototype quickly and iterate based on real-world feedback, making it a hotspot for R&D hackers. Amazon's emphasis on innovation extends across the company, with teams constantly looking to disrupt existing industries. R&D hacking traits include a willingness to take risks, rapid iteration, and a focus on customer-centric solutions.

IDEO is a global design and innovation consultancy known for its human-centered design approach and rapid prototyping methods. R&D hacking traits include experimentation, user-centered design, and a focus on solving real-world problems through creativity. LEGO's innovation process involves rapid prototyping and user testing to create new products that resonate with customers. R&D hacking traits include hands-on experimentation, user-centered design, and a focus on creativity and play. MIT Media Lab creates intentionally diverse research teams and combines seemingly unrelated disciplines (e.g., biology with computing). It emphasizes hands-on prototyping over theoretical research and encourages "demo or die" culture—showing working prototypes. What truly makes them stand apart is the focus on anti-disciplinary work that doesn't fit in traditional departments. Researchers at the Media Lab often pursue interdisciplinary, unconventional approaches to solving problems, from AI to wearable technology. The Lab's emphasis on rapid prototyping, cross-disciplinary collaboration, and future-focused thinking encourages a hacker mentality.

Skunk Works pioneered the concept of small, elite teams working outside normal corporate structure. It uses rapid prototyping and minimal bureaucracy and maintains extreme secrecy to avoid external interference. It also emphasizes direct communication between engineers and end-users. Skunk Works is famous for developing the U-2 spy plane in record time. DARPA funds high-risk projects that traditional R&D wouldn't touch. Known for its radical innovations, DARPA has been responsible for many breakthroughs that eventually found civilian applications, such as the internet and GPS. It uses challenge-based innovation (DARPA challenges) and maintains minimal management layers. It also sets "impossible" goals to force unconventional thinking and focuses on breakthrough technologies rather than incremental improvements. The agency's R&D hackers are tasked with using unconventional methods and technologies to solve complex challenges, often with little regard for traditional boundaries in research.

Various biohacking companies, such as Elysium Health, Ketone-IQ, and Thryve, operate at the intersection of biotechnology and unconventional R&D. These companies often push the boundaries of human biology, experimenting with supplements, gene-editing techniques, and personalized health solutions. These companies attract individuals who thrive in an R&D hacking culture, where bold experimentation is key to making advances in human health and performance.

These organizations share some common patterns in their R&D hacking approaches. They organize in small, autonomous teams with diverse skills. There is minimal bureaucracy and rapid decision-making. All embrace failure as a learning tool. They focus on practical prototypes over theoretical perfection. There is a direct connection between developers and end-users. Each has the willingness to challenge industry assumptions, and there is a high tolerance for risk and uncertainty.

Why Are R&D Hacking Skills Needed Now?

R&D hacking skills are increasingly needed today due to several transformative trends and challenges across industries. These skills enable organizations to innovate faster, adapt to changing environments, and solve complex problems in unconventional ways. It also is a clever strategic HR move. Encouraging employees to think like R&D hackers fosters creativity, engagement, and ownership of innovation efforts.

The speed of technological advancement is unprecedented. Traditional, linear R&D models are often too slow to keep pace with the demands of the modern world. R&D hacking, with its emphasis on rapid prototyping, iterative development, and cross-disciplinary collaboration, allows organizations to adapt and innovate quickly.

Many of today's most pressing challenges, such as climate change, food security, healthcare access, pandemics, and poverty, are complex and require creative, interdisciplinary solutions. R&D hackers are needed to explore novel applications of AI, such as generative models, autonomous systems, and predictive analytics. Experimentation is key to unlocking the potential of blockchain for industries like finance, supply chain, and healthcare. R&D hackers can prototype and test IoT solutions for smart homes, cities, and industrial applications. Innovative approaches are required to develop renewable energy solutions, circular economy models, and carbon capture technologies. Industries where R&D hacking skills are critical include rapid prototyping of medical devices, diagnostics, and digital health solutions in healthcare, exploring AI, blockchain, and IoT applications in tech, developing green technologies and circular economy models in the sustainability field, innovating with fintech, decentralized finance (DeFi), and payment systems, advancing smart factories, robotics, and supply chain optimization in manufacturing, or even creating immersive experiences or learning environments using AR/VR, gaming, and interactive media in entertainment or education.

R&D hacking encourages the breaking down of silos and the integration of diverse perspectives and expertise, fostering innovative solutions. R&D hackers are adept at tackling such problems by thinking outside the box. Many modern challenges involve interconnected systems (e.g., smart cities, supply chains). R&D hackers can navigate these complexities and develop integrated solutions.

Disruptive technologies are constantly emerging, and organizations need to be agile and adaptable to remain competitive. R&D hacking enables organizations to experiment with new technologies, identify emerging trends, and quickly develop new products and services. Companies must innovate faster to stay competitive. Traditional R&D processes are often too slow, while R&D hacking enables rapid prototyping and iterative development. In today's dynamic environment, organizations need to be able to quickly pivot and adjust their strategies. Customers demand new features, products, and services at an unprecedented pace. R&D hackers can deliver quick proofs of concept and scalable solutions. R&D hacking fosters a culture of experimentation and learning, enabling organizations to adapt to changing circumstances and seize new opportunities.

R&D hacking often emphasizes user-centered design and rapid prototyping, allowing organizations to gather user feedback early in the development process and ensure that their solutions meet the needs of their target audience. R&D hacking encourages experimentation and learning from failure, which is critical for navigating uncertainty and discovering breakthrough solutions.

By embracing R&D hacking principles, organizations can cultivate a culture of innovation, foster creativity, and accelerate the development of groundbreaking solutions to some of the world's most pressing challenges. Start-ups and smaller organizations often lack the resources for traditional R&D. R&D hackers can achieve impactful results with minimal resources by leveraging open-source tools, repurposing existing technologies, and adopting a hacker mindset. R&D hacking emphasizes doing more with less, making it ideal for organizations looking to maximize ROI on innovation efforts. Similarly, as a mid-career employee, you can dramatically increase your value in the workplace by broadening your scope to new technological areas and becoming known as someone who rapidly gets up to speed on new developments. As a new entrant in the workplace, with a hacker mindset (with some guardrails) you can rapidly gain trust as a go-to person for new ideas or investigating new opportunities or challenges. If you are considering which career path to take, which college to go to, and what to study, the R&D hacking perspective can reorient your priorities. Specialization will take on a strategic character, you will do it in order to gain overview not to practice in that specialty going forward.

While the specific title of R&D hacker is still emerging, many existing roles in the workplace already utilize R&D hacking skills, such as: Innovation Engineer, Prototyping Specialist, Creative Technologist, Research Scientist, Product Innovation Manager, Data Scientist, DevOps Engineer, IoT Solutions Architect, AL/ML Engineer, Director of AI Initiatives, Digital Innovation Specialist, Innovation Consultant, Game Developer, Open Innovation

Manager, Start-up Founder, Entrepreneur, UX/UI Designer, Cybersecurity Researcher, Robotics Engineer, Blockchain Developer, Hackathon Organizer, and more.

A few more specific examples of R&D hacking practices would be a researcher who combines principles from biology and engineering to develop novel materials, an engineer who leverages gaming technologies to create immersive and engaging training simulations, or a scientist who utilizes citizen science initiatives to gather data and accelerate research.

How to Learn R&D Hacking?

R&D hacking consists of a set of key skills that include creative problem-solving, rapid prototyping and iteration, cross-disciplinary thinking, resourcefulness and adaptability, strong communication and collaboration skills, and a growth mindset and a willingness to experiment. Additionally, these are people who also possess more traditional research skills or perhaps initially trained as PhDs or lab managers, either in interdisciplinary positions in academia or in industry. The R&D hacker embodies a new breed of innovator who is pushing the boundaries of traditional research and development. They are essential for driving innovation and addressing complex challenges in a rapidly changing world. Learning such approaches is not as simple as simply vibe prompting in large language models, without a framework to build on.

How to Teach R&D Hacking?

Teaching such a multifaceted set of skills on an individual level is best done through apprenticeships, mentorship, and coaching, offering guidance and support to individuals as they develop their R&D hacking skills. You can also cultivate a culture of experimentation through organizing hackathons, start-up showcases, or innovation sprints. Companies could become members of the MIT Industrial Liaison Program (ILP) to access faculty and start-ups from MIT. Informal collaboration with universities and colleges can yield similar results. Dedicated spinout support can facilitate more innovation and yield higher results from your R&D lab. Company leadership should create an environment where employees feel comfortable taking risks and sharing unconventional ideas without fear of judgment. You could increasingly bring together individuals with diverse backgrounds (engineers, designers, scientists, marketers, social scientists) to tackle complex challenges. You can invite experts from different fields to share their insights and inspire new approaches.

There are many consultants available to teach design thinking principles, focusing on user empathy, rapid prototyping, and iterative development. You can also try to equip individual employees with the skills to think algorithmically, break down complex problems, and leverage data effectively through courses, certifications, and training. Leveraging technology to teach R&D hacking can be particularly efficient. Investigate and introduce tools that can assist with data analysis, idea generation, and prototyping from a myriad of tools on the market. As the field matures, you can explore the use of VR/AR technologies to facilitate collaboration, visualization, and experimentation. After reviewing potential risks related to intellectual property, you can also encourage the use of open-source tools and platforms to foster collaboration and accelerate innovation.

How Does R&D Hacking Interact with Other Platinum Workforce Skills?

By 2030, at the very latest, any useful worker would need to have the ability to tap into the full scope of the science and tech revolution. The starting point might be various AI platforms, but the transaction layer they operate against might be blockchain technology, which most of us think of as a purely financial platform today, but which has ample promise as an enabler of transparency and efficiency in areas such as drug development, policymaking, healthcare, and beyond. Then, we have the fact that the fossil era is (albeit slowly) coming to an end. The result is that material extraction from planet Earth is moving from places we didn't care about (but should have) to crucial ecosystems such as the deep oceans (the integrity of which we do care about) where we will increasingly extract the rare earth metals needed for today's electronics. As an alternative to that, the bioengineering revolution carries the promise of a new era of biomanufacturing, based on synthetic biology advances, the scale of which is currently minuscule compared to the quantum leaps it might experience over the next few years.[1]

This will, at least in part, depend on a few things, such as the progress in brain–computer interfaces (BCIs) which might entail a more intuitive

---

1 Undheim, T. A. 2024. "The Whack-A-Mole Governance Challenge for AI-enabled Synthetic Biology: Literature Review and Emerging Frameworks." *Frontiers in Bioengineering and Biotechnology.* https://doi.org/10.3389/fbioe.2024.1359768.

interaction with AIs through directly plugging into our human body, and, ostensibly, by merging materials with biology through technological means. Nanotech might also reach its apex with medical or consumer applications that fuse with AI and biotech. We might scarcely recognize even the most mundane objects found in our surroundings, such as office productivity tools, entertainment devices, or even the food we consume. As a result, future cyberthreats will emerge which will encroach on our bodies and souls, not just on our financial infrastructure. The advent of more generally useful quantum technology toward the end of this decade will spearhead a third AI-revolution, the limits to which it would be foolish to speculate about now.

Lastly, the ability with which we would be able to fuel all of these developments will depend on a stable, distributed and increasingly powerful energy supply, which is why nuclear fusion, still a big question mark, could become a game changer toward the mid to late 2030s. Grid-scale energy storage would similarly be needed to fuel the completion of the transition toward renewables. The investments in new types of energy technologies would either way reach a fever pitch at the transition of the two decades (2020 to 2030), as the convergence of emerging technologies will become so apparent that capital from governments and private sector will, most likely, converge on funding their attempted completion. We might not succeed fully, because the incentives to develop separate innovative strands with even greater promise will persist.

What Might the Impact Be Once R&D Hacking Is Commonplace?

All of these changes are upon us. They are not inevitable. Rather, they depend on sociopolitical support to regulate, socio-technical prowess to prove out and execute, and workforce reskilling to sustain. Under no scenario can a software programmer stay in their lane, a line worker avoid becoming apt at augmenting their own skills through technology, or a manager avoid deep insight into technologies and team-based and individual responses, concerns, and challenges. The most apt term I have found for the technology skills needed in the coming decade is "transdisciplinary R&D hacker." Forget T-shaped skills where you are deep in one technology and conversant in others. You will need to continuously dip in and out of the frontiers of emerging technology. To do that, workers and managers alike will need to become conversant on a daily basis with revamped technology journals with better user interfaces, weekly on-demand apprenticeships with technology experts, and ideally relying on in-house training coupled with a digital interface that tracks your skills progress and automatically suggests next steps. That interface would need to become portable so that it would follow a worker throughout his or her career, not tied in with an employer. With that, the impact could cascade across individual workplaces, across industries, and entire societies. This will transform scientific exploration, accelerate engineering breakthroughs, and help foster the ability to handle the gigascale challenges that are upon us. Again, this will likely rely on efficient agentic workflows that feed all of the required information relatively seamlessly to us via electronic means, quite soon directly into our body or brain through the sensory system.

The Downside of R&D Hacking

R&D hackers bring a lot of value to the table, including creativity, speed, and unconventional thinking, but there are potential downsides to consider, including risk of failure, inefficiencies, resource drains, lack of structure, unintended consequences, and security concerns. The unconventional methods and rapid experimentation that R&D hackers use can sometimes lead to higher failure rates. While failure is a part of innovation, it can be costly and time-consuming. Solutions developed through R&D hacking are often tailored to specific contexts or problems. Scaling these solutions for broader application can be challenging and resource-intensive. For example, a prototype developed for a small-scale pilot might not be feasible for mass production.

R&D hacking often requires significant resources, including time, money, and specialized tools. The high degree of experimentation and iteration often involved in R&D hacking can drain resources quickly. As these innovators jump from one idea to another or push boundaries without a clear roadmap, it might lead to resource wastage, excessive time spent on unproductive directions, or the lack of focus on more promising projects. Not all organizations can afford to invest in such intensive processes. The flexible and unstructured approach of R&D hackers might clash with more traditional, structured R&D processes. This can lead to conflicts and inefficiencies within organizations. Since R&D hackers often work outside of traditional frameworks, their approach might lack cohesion with larger teams or organizations.

R&D hackers often prioritize speed and experimentation over thorough, structured testing. While this can lead to breakthrough innovations, it might also result in the development of unrefined solutions or products that haven't been fully vetted for safety, functionality, or scalability. Unconventional methods sometimes push the boundaries of ethics, particularly in fields like biotechnology, AI, or environmental science. Without structured oversight, there might be a risk of pursuing innovations that could have unintended negative consequences or ethical dilemmas—such as compromising safety, privacy, or human rights. This can cause issues down the line, especially in industries where reliability is critical.

The unconventional methods of R&D hackers can sometimes blur ethical or legal boundaries. This can result in intellectual property disputes, regulatory noncompliance, or ethical controversies. Using open-source code or data without proper attribution or licensing can lead to legal challenges. Also, the rapid prototyping and experimental mindset of an R&D hacker can sometimes prioritize immediate results over long-term, sustainable development. Shortcuts taken during rapid development can create technical debt. Unconventional approaches may not align with industry standards. Intellectual property documentation might be insufficient. The focus on speed might overlook important infrastructure considerations. Without careful consideration of future consequences, solutions might lack scalability, durability, or be incompatible with long-term objectives. The hacker mindset, while innovative, can sometimes overlook security and compliance issues. This can pose risks, especially in industries with strict regulations.

R&D hackers might clash with traditional R&D teams. Knowledge transfer can be difficult when processes aren't standardized. R&D hacking often relies on the skills and creativity of individual hackers. This can create a dependency on specific individuals, making the organization vulnerable if they leave. This could be detrimental, given that the focus on speed might lead to burnout. For example, a team might struggle to continue a project if the lead R&D hacker moves to another company.

While R&D hacking is a powerful approach for driving innovation and solving complex problems, it is not without its downsides. The risks of reduced rigor, ethical dilemmas, resource intensity, and unintended consequences require careful management. Leaders should encourage collaboration between R&D hackers and traditional R&D teams to integrate innovative ideas with structured processes. All employees should document processes and findings to enable replication, scaling, and continuous improvement and promote knowledge sharing. By acknowledging these challenges and taking proactive steps to mitigate them, organizations can harness the strengths of R&D hacking while minimizing its drawbacks. Ultimately, R&D hacking is most effective when integrated into a balanced innovation strategy that values both creativity and discipline.

Conclusion

R&D hacking skills are essential in today's fast-paced, complex, and resource-constrained world. They enable organizations to innovate rapidly, solve interconnected problems, and stay competitive in an ever-changing landscape. By combining creativity, technical expertise, and a willingness to experiment, R&D hackers are driving the next wave of breakthroughs across industries. As the demand for agility and innovation grows, so too will the need for professionals with R&D hacking skills. You can prepare now by starting to explore the domains and approaches it entails. Companies that embrace R&D hackers and foster a culture where they thrive will have a competitive advantage. Workers who build R&D hacking skills, even at fairly low levels, will be more adaptable to changing circumstances. Students who become fully aware of how the workplace increasingly demands R&D hacking skills can more efficiently educate themselves, and obtain certifications, skills, and experiences that propel them forward from the moment they start college or trade school.

CHAPTER 7

SOCIO-TECHNICIAN

What Are Socio-Technical Skills?

Socio-technical skills refer to the ability to understand, navigate, and integrate both social (human) and technical (technological) aspects of systems, organizations, or processes. These skills are essential in environments where technology and human behavior intersect, enabling professionals to design, implement, and manage solutions that are not only technically sound but also socially and culturally effective. Socio-technical skills bridge the gap between people and technology, ensuring that technological solutions are aligned with human needs, behaviors, and organizational contexts (Figure 7.1). The key components of socio-technical skills are human-centered design, systems thinking, social collaboration skills, change management, adaptability, technical skills, and ethical awareness.

Why Are Socio-Technical Skills Needed Now?

It is perhaps somewhat ironic that in arguing that these skills will become dramatically more important in the coming years, I have myself already lived what one might call a socio-technical life. In my roles as diverse as author, consultant, executive, start-up founder, investor, speaker, and lecturer, I have explored experiential learning, innovation, technology, and social change. I have dissected the systemic interplay of risk, innovation, policy, and psychology, and I have been involved in trying to achieve impact at scale (and occasionally failed at that). Back in 2002, I wrote a book called *Leadership from Below*, exploring what I then saw as how the internet generation was reshaping the workplace. At that time, it seemed to me that formal authority over the workforce, at least for typical knowledge work tasks such as product development, policymaking, or writing, would start to make less and less sense. Rather, I

FIGURE 7.1 Socio-technical skills.

posited, bottom-up initiative would be rewarded higher and higher (because skills are becoming more evenly distributed lower and lower in the hierarchy) and executing authority with a top-down force attitude would, as a result, be not only less important but also less effective. More than twenty years later, I could not have been more wrong, but I was at least partially right. I was wrong because hierarchies not only persist, but they in some ways have become more important than before. Especially with the advent of megaprojects where the coordination of resources arguably benefits from being exercised within a clear command structure or else will create confusion and enormous downside in terms of uncertainty and slow execution.

On the other hand, skills are indeed distributed more evenly than before and good managers increasingly know the limits of what they know. Great managers even capitalize on that insight and empower their employees to excel and exceed expectations by gaining ownership of significant operational challenges. What I then called leadership from below might today be more aptly described as explorative skills, the ability to, and interest in, seeking insight from peers no matter where they reside in your organization. More importantly, if you work in partnership with other organizations, that exploration should not be limited to your own organization. I lived and breathed that practice when I was working in a policy role for Oracle Corporation across Europe. I recall having equal camaraderie with IBM colleagues as with my own coworkers, partially because I was working remotely and spent most of my face-to-face time working on partnerships and influence work toward governments.

Examples of individuals with socio-technical skills would be project managers who communicate with diverse teams, manage complex projects, and leverage technology to achieve project goals; healthcare professionals who communicate with patients, utilize medical technology, and navigate complex healthcare systems; educators who use technology in the classroom, adapt to new teaching methods, and foster meaningful student-teacher interactions; and software engineers who collaborate with designers, understand user needs, and develop user-friendly and accessible software.

More specifically, emerging roles would include designing a smart city, balancing technical infrastructure (e.g., IoT sensors, data analytics) with social considerations (e.g., privacy, accessibility, and community engagement); implementing AI in healthcare ensuring AI algorithms are accurate and efficient while addressing ethical concerns (e.g., bias, patient consent); and training healthcare professionals to use the technology. It is also becoming part of the challenge of developing social media platforms, creating algorithms that enhance user experience while mitigating issues like misinformation, cyberbullying, and addiction. In manufacturing, workplace automation entails adapting or introducing robots or AI systems in a factory while retraining workers and addressing concerns about job security. In the enterprise productivity software field, it might involve designing collaboration software such as remote work tools that are technically robust while considering user preferences, cultural differences, and work-life balance.

How to Learn Socio-Technical Skills?

Socio-technical skills can be developed through education and training, taking courses in human-computer interaction (HCI), systems thinking, ethics, and organizational behavior. It might entail participating in workshops or certifications focused on user experience (UX) design, change management, or ethical AI. You can gain hands-on experience through working on interdisciplinary projects that involve both technical and social challenges, engaging in user research, prototyping, and testing to understand human needs. There is value in seeking mentorship from professionals with strong socio-technical skills. You should follow trends in technology, sociology, and ethics to understand the broader context of your work, and the broader future of work trends. You can read case studies of successful (and failed) socio-technical implementations.

Many early Electronic Health Record (EHR) systems implementations failed due to a lack of consideration for the social and organizational context. Poorly designed systems, inadequate training, and resistance from clinicians led to frustration, decreased efficiency, and even patient safety concerns. When new technologies are introduced without proper consideration for the social and organizational impact, they can lead to resistance, decreased productivity, and even job losses. This can occur when employees feel their roles are threatened, lack the necessary training, or are not adequately involved in the implementation process. In contrast, successful socio-technical implementations carefully consider such factors. For example, Scandinavian Airlines (SAS) successfully implemented a socio-technical approach to aircraft maintenance in the 1970s. By empowering maintenance teams with autonomy and decision-making power, and providing them with the necessary tools and training, they significantly improved aircraft maintenance efficiency and reduced downtime (Kao 1986; Lynes and Dredge 2006).

How to Teach Socio-Technical Skills?

Teaching socio-technical skills often involve engaging learners in multidisciplinary projects that involve a technology change or adoption process in a large organization. There are case studies used in business schools that help develop awareness of socio-technical factors. The Ford Motor Company's Assembly Line. The Chernobyl Disaster. Common themes include that success requires simultanous alignment of technology and people/processes. Support structures such as training and leadership commitment are not optional. There is also ample evidence that complex social-tech interactions tend to yield unpredictable outcomes. The field of science and technology studies (STS) is also, as a whole, concerned with these types of discussions. There, the focus is societal health overall. Many STS case studies emphasize the detrimental impacts of not considering the wider context (Baxter and Sommerville 2011).

How Do Socio-Technical Skills Interact with Other Platinum Workforce Skills?

Managing entrepreneurially, executing at scale, even without formal authority, using an explorative approach are part of what I will call socio-technical skills. These approaches would need to be field tested in industrial settings, such as the tech industry, manufacturing, biomanufacturing, healthcare, energy industry, fintech, and even in agriculture. Very few workers will be able to get through their careers without touching almost all existing industries, except that the focus of those industries will dramatically change. Transdisciplinarity cannot be limited to technical skills but needs to encompass investigating conditions across industries. For that to work, you need to be comfortable with being a novice, yet expecting to rapidly improve that status as you learn more.

Today, it is commonplace for a corporation to embrace and actively seek inspiration from start-ups. I have myself been deeply engaged with that. I built and directed the MIT Start-up Exchange Program at the MIT Industrial Relations' Industrial Liaison Program (ILP), connecting 250 corporations to 1,500 MIT start-ups. Collaborating with Faculty across MIT, I ran 25 start-up showcases, gave 200 presentations and made over 1,000 corporate/start-up introductions. I designed and spearheaded an accelerator for the Institute's top 25 growth start-up founders whose companies have raised more than $500 million. The 35 leading start-ups I engaged with have a current portfolio value of $20B, $167M in aggregate start-up revenues, $2B in aggregate start-up funding and have created 2,318 jobs. I have arranged events taking place in remote locations, involving complex coordination and executive buy-in. What I learned from that is that embracing start-ups is a complex endeavor. It is also not always what a corporation needs or wants. Instead, their execution ability depends on being able to move a project forward against all odds. Entrepreneurial abilities that could only derive from the experience of working in a start-up are also important, but for corporate employees, the experience of starting something from scratch can also be had by launching a new corporate project. This is where it is useful to deploy leadership from below, even within fairly strictly hierarchical power structures. Asking forgiveness not permission is at times the only way to move something through a corporate hierarchy. But you have to be prepared to face adverse consequences. Despite big talk about being lean and entrepreneurial that is not what large corporate structures excel at.

Impact If Socio-Technical Skills Become Commonplace?

If socio-technical skills become commonplace, the impact would be transformative across multiple dimensions—individual talent, businesses and organizations, governance, the environment, and society as a whole. Individuals with strong socio-technical skills are better equipped to navigate the complexities of the emerging workplace, adapt to new technologies and work environments, and thrive in uncertain times. They would have higher career flexibility. These skills enable professionals to work across disciplines (e.g., tech, design, business, policy), opening up diverse career opportunities. Developing socio-technical skills fosters empathy, ethical thinking, and adaptability, making individuals more well-rounded and resilient. By understanding the interplay between human and technological factors, individuals can approach problems more holistically and develop more effective and sustainable solutions. These skills facilitate effective communication and collaboration across diverse teams and organizations, leading to improved teamwork and productivity. Professionals with socio-technical skills are better equipped to lead interdisciplinary teams and drive innovation. Individuals with socio-technical skills will, undoubtedly, be highly sought-after by employers across various sectors. They might help in a world that becomes increasingly technology enabled and where machines take over many tasks. As highly advanced AI becomes pervasive in the workplace, and in factories, the entire socio-technical layer becomes more complex and the role of humans and machines become muddled.

Organizations with a workforce possessing strong socio-technical skills are better equipped to innovate, adapt to change, and achieve their strategic objectives. Cross-functional collaboration would improve, fostering a culture of innovation and inclusivity. A socio-technical perspective helps organizations make more informed decisions by considering the human and social implications of technological advancements. As a result, one would assume businesses would prioritize ethical considerations (e.g., data privacy, bias mitigation) and sustainability in their operations. Socio-technical skills would enable smoother adoption of new technologies, reducing resistance and increasing employee buy-in. Companies with socio-technically skilled teams would be better positioned to navigate complex challenges and adapt to changing markets.

Policymakers with socio-technical skills can better understand the impact of new technologies on society and develop policies that are both effective and equitable. Socio-technical skills would enable the development of more user-friendly and efficient public services (e.g., healthcare, education, transportation). Specifically, the delivery of public services can be significantly improved by integrating technology with human needs and social contexts. Policymakers could create adaptive regulations that keep pace with technological change while protecting citizens' rights. By addressing the social and ethical implications of technology, policymakers can build greater public trust in technological advancements. Transparent and inclusive governance practices would build public trust in institutions and technologies. Socio-technical skills would facilitate international cooperation on global challenges like climate change, public health, and digital equity.

Socio-technical skills would drive the development of technologies that address environmental challenges (e.g., renewable energy, waste reduction). Businesses and governments together could design systems that minimize waste and maximize resource efficiency. Specifically, by understanding the complex interplay between human behavior, technology, and the environment, we can develop more effective strategies for mitigating climate change. Collaborative, interdisciplinary efforts would accelerate the adoption of climate-friendly technologies and practices. Socio-technical approaches would improve communication and education around environmental issues, encouraging collective action. By considering the social and ethical implications of technology, we can ensure that technological advancements benefit all members of society, regardless of their background or socioeconomic status. A workplace and leaders with strong socio-technical skills would ensure that technology is accessible and beneficial to all, reducing digital divides and promoting equity. Notably, society would benefit from AI and automation systems that are fair, transparent, and aligned with human values. Educational systems would prioritize interdisciplinary learning, combining technical training with social sciences, ethics, and design thinking. Companies might to a larger extent adopt or include models that prioritize long-term societal impact over short-term profits, such as social enterprises or B Corporations.

More broadly, there is a reasonable expectation that if socio-technical approaches become widely accepted it would, in turn, help create systems that are adaptable to shocks (e.g., pandemics, economic crises) and capable of evolving over time. While the widespread adoption of socio-technical skills would bring many benefits, there are challenges to consider, including skills gaps, resistance to change, managing trade-offs between technical feasibility, social impact, and business goals, as well as navigating the complex ethical questions that arise at the intersection of technology and society.

The Downside of Socio-Technical Skills

Socio-technical skills are indeed vital in today's interconnected world, but they do come with potential downsides. It is a balancing act. It is complex and resource intensive. There could be resistance to change. Measuring success is difficult.

Integrating social and technical aspects requires a delicate balance. Overemphasizing one aspect can lead to neglect of the other, resulting in sub-optimal solutions. Typically, a strong technical emphasis can result in key social issues getting too little attention. This can result in systems that are technically sound but difficult to use or socially misaligned. A highly efficient software system might be too complex for nontechnical users to navigate effectively. However, in some cases, focusing too much on social elements might lead to neglecting critical technical requirements. It can lead to solutions that are user-friendly but technically inadequate. In turn, this can result in systems that are easy to use but lack the necessary functionality or performance. For example, a beautifully designed app with a great user interface might suffer from poor performance or frequent crashes.

Managing both social and technical dimensions can be complex and challenging, requiring a deep understanding of both human behavior and technological systems, a deep understanding of diverse fields and the ability to navigate their intersections. The mental effort required to switch between technical and interpersonal modes of thinking can be exhausting. As a result, professionals may feel overwhelmed by the need to juggle multiple perspectives and priorities. For example, designing a user-friendly app that also meets complex technical requirements can be challenging and time-consuming.

Developing and maintaining socio-technical skills can be resource-intensive, requiring continuous learning and adaptation to new technologies and social dynamics. Having to constantly balance technical and social considerations can make decision-making more complex and time-consuming. Finding the right balance between social and technical considerations can lead to scope creep. It often requires significant time, effort, and resources. The impact is that organizations with limited budgets or expertise may struggle to fully commit to socio-technical approaches. For example, conducting extensive user research and testing for a new product can be resource-intensive.

Implementing socio-technical solutions often requires changes to workflows, behaviors, or organizational culture. Implementing socio-technical solutions may face resistance from individuals or organizations, employees or management, accustomed to traditional approaches, leading to friction and slow adoption. The success of socio-technical solutions often depends on the cooperation of multiple stakeholders, including users, technical teams, and management. The need to satisfy multiple stakeholders with different priorities can lead to compromises that aren't technically optimal. The multifaceted nature of socio-technical considerations can sometimes lead to overthinking. Resistance from employees or stakeholders can hinder adoption and effectiveness. For example, a project to implement a new customer relationship management (CRM) system might fail if sales and IT teams have conflicting priorities. Lack of alignment or conflicting interests among stakeholders can hinder progress. Overcoming this resistance and gaining buy-in for new approaches can be challenging. Not all organizations value or understand the importance of socio-technical approaches. There can be resistance from both technical experts who prefer pure technical solutions and from those who prioritize social factors exclusively. For example, introducing a new technology in a healthcare setting might face pushback from staff accustomed to traditional methods.

Quantifying the success of socio-technical interventions can be challenging, as social outcomes are often less tangible than technical ones. The effectiveness of socio-technical solutions can be difficult to measure, as it involves both qualitative (social) and quantitative (technical) outcomes. Without clear metrics, it can be hard to demonstrate the value of socio-technical approaches to stakeholders. For example, measuring the success of a workplace collaboration tool might require assessing both user satisfaction and technical performance. The complex interactions between social and technical systems can lead to unforeseen outcomes, both positive and negative. Socio-technical solutions can have unintended consequences, particularly in complex systems with many interdependencies. These consequences may offset the benefits of the solution or create new problems. For example, a new workplace collaboration tool might improve communication but also lead to information overload or reduced face-to-face interaction.

If not carefully considered, socio-technical approaches can inadvertently reinforce existing biases and inequalities. For example, technology can sometimes be designed with specific user groups in mind, excluding or marginalizing others. Balancing ethical considerations (e.g., privacy, equity) with technical feasibility can be challenging, leading to having to make difficult decisions, especially when dealing with sensitive social issues. Ethical dilemmas can slow down decision-making or result in compromises that satisfy no one. For example, a company might struggle to balance data collection for personalized services with user privacy concerns.

To address these challenges, professionals and organizations can ensure that both social and technical aspects are given equal consideration in the design and implementation of solutions. Involve all relevant stakeholders in the planning process to build buy-in and address concerns. Build the skills and knowledge needed to effectively integrate social and technical perspectives. Implement solutions incrementally, using feedback to refine and improve over time. Ensure that ethical considerations are integral to the design and implementation of socio-technical solutions. Continuously evaluate the impact of solutions and be prepared to adjust as needed.

Conclusion

Socio-technical skills are essential in environments where individuals must navigate the intersection of human interactions and technological systems. Evidence suggests that the systematic development of these competencies can substantially alter organizational processes, interpersonal dynamics, and technological implementations, potentially leading to more effective, sustainable, and human-centered operational frameworks.

References

Baxter, Gordon and Ian Sommerville. 2011. "Socio-technical Systems: From Design Methods to Systems Engineering." *Interacting with Computers* 23 (1): 4–17. https://doi.org/10.1016/j.intcom.2010.07.003.

Kao, John J. 1986 (Revised February 1993). *Scandinavian Airlines System*. Harvard Business School Case 487–041.

Lynes, Jennifer K., and Dianne Dredge. 2006. "Going Green: Motivations for Environmental Commitment in the Airline Industry. A Case Study of Scandinavian Airlines." *Journal of Sustainable Tourism* 14 (2): 116–138.

CHAPTER 8

ECO-STRATEGIST

What Is an Eco-Strategist?

An Eco-Strategist is a professional who develops and implements strategies that integrate environmental considerations into the core strategies, business operations, and decision-making processes of organizations, governments, or communities. Eco-Strategists not only possess a strong eco-awareness but also have a penchant for taking impactful actions, achieving systemic innovation effects (Figure 8.1). This is typically a role that entails a clear mandate to implement their ideas. Eco-Strategists combine expertise in environmental science, business strategy, and systems thinking to develop and implement solutions that balance economic growth with ecological preservation. Throughout this book, the role is consistently referred to as the Eco-Strategist (capitalized) to emphasize its standing as a distinct, formalized role in the skills taxonomy.

FIGURE 8.1 Eco-Strategist.

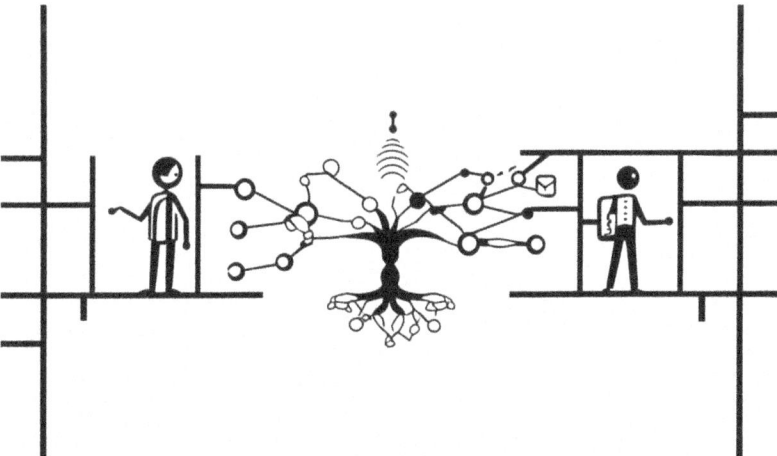

Eco-awareness refers to being knowledgeable and careful about the eco-systemic impacts of the behavior, actions, and processes going on around you. It particularly refers to the activities that a person either is directly involved with or responsible for at their work or in their leisure or home-based activities. Being eco-aware implies taking responsibility and taking action whenever possible to reduce one's own negative impact on the environment or surroundings. This personal responsibility forms the micro-level expression of eco-awareness. At the macro-level, organizations formalize these responsibilities through the Eco-Strategist role, charged with embedding ecological awareness into strategy and decision-making. Eco-awareness is the foundational skill, but when institutionalized as a role, it evolves into the Eco-Strategist (see Table 8.1).

The Eco-Strategist sets environmental goals, identifies and mitigates environmental risks that could impact the organization they work for, and develops roadmaps for achieving sustainability targets. They conduct environmental impact assessments, analyze the environmental impact of business activities, and identify opportunities for improvement. Also, they develop and implement environmental management systems. This may involve implementing ISO 14001 standards or other environmental management frameworks. It would also mean collaborating with internal and external stakeholders, including employees, suppliers, customers, and regulators, to develop and implement sustainable practices. They will keep up-to-date on relevant environmental laws, regulations, and industry best practices. As part of this process, they might track, monitor, and report on environmental performance metrics, such as greenhouse gas emissions, energy consumption, and waste generation.

TABLE 8.1 Three scenarios for the future of work.

Level	Definition	Application	Outcome
Eco-Awareness (Skill)	Mindset and competency of recognizing and acting on environmental impacts	Individual choices, daily behaviors	Personal ecological responsibility
Eco-Strategist (Role)	Professional mandate that formalizes eco-awareness within organizations	Strategic planning, policy design, systems integration	Institutionalized ecological intelligence

In an ideal scenario, the Eco-Strategist will not only handle potential negative fallout. Instead, they would drive innovation in sustainable business practices, identify and implement innovative solutions to environmental challenges, such as developing new products and services, improving resource efficiency, and exploring renewable energy sources.

Eco-Strategy Profitability: Corporate Sustainability Success Cases

Several companies have successfully transformed environmental imperatives into profitable business strategies, demonstrating that sustainability and financial performance are increasingly aligned. Tesla stands as perhaps the most visible example, generating $96.8 billion in revenue (2023) through its core strategy of electric vehicle production. The company has diversified its revenue streams to include energy storage systems, solar products, and regulatory carbon credits. Tesla's approach has not only proven financially viable but has catalyzed industry-wide transformation, compelling established automotive manufacturers to accelerate their electric vehicle development programs (Tesla Annual Report 2023).

Ørsted exemplifies successful business model transformation, evolving from a traditional Danish oil and gas company (formerly DONG Energy) to become the global leader in offshore wind power development. With revenues reaching $15.6 billion in 2023, Ørsted has fundamentally restructured its business portfolio from 85 percent fossil fuel-based in 2006 to 90 percent renewable energy today, demonstrating that complete strategic pivots toward sustainability can create substantial shareholder value (Ørsted Annual Report 2023). In the food sector, Beyond Meat has established a new market category through plant-based protein alternatives. With annual revenues of $375 million (2023), the company has secured distribution partnerships with global food service chains while addressing both environmental concerns and evolving consumer preferences for sustainable nutrition options (Beyond Meat Financial Results 2024).

Schneider Electric has built its $41.1 billion business (2023) around energy management solutions and industrial automation technologies. The company's EcoStruxure platform enables clients to optimize energy consumption and reduce carbon emissions while simultaneously reducing operational costs, illustrating how providing sustainability-enabling technologies represents a substantial market opportunity (Schneider Electric Annual Report 2023).

Waste Management has evolved beyond traditional waste collection to generate $19.4 billion in revenue (2023) through diversified environmental services, including recycling operations, renewable energy production from landfill gas, and sustainability consulting services. The company operates one of North America's largest fleets of natural gas-powered vehicles, demonstrating how traditional industries can transform their operational models toward greater sustainability (Waste Management Financial Data 2023).

These cases illustrate how companies across diverse sectors have successfully integrated environmental considerations into their core business strategies, creating both competitive advantage and financial returns while addressing pressing ecological challenges.

Why Is Eco-Awareness Needed Now?

Eco-strategists are needed in all industries. Across the corporate sector, they are helping businesses adopt sustainable practices, reduce emissions, and improve resource efficiency. In government and public policy, they are shaping policies and programs that promote environmental protection and sustainable development. In nonprofits and NGOs, they are leading initiatives to address environmental challenges and advocate for systemic change. In the energy sector, particularly in utilities, they engage in transitioning to renewable energy sources and improving energy efficiency. In manufacturing and supply chains, they help reduce waste, optimize resource use, and implement circular economy practices. In agriculture and across various food systems, they are promoting sustainable farming practices and reducing the environmental impact of food production. In urban planning, particularly in smart cities projects, they design infrastructure that is environmentally friendly and resilient to climate change.

Specific examples of Eco-Strategist initiatives might include developing a roadmap for a company to achieve net-zero emissions by transitioning to renewable energy and offsetting remaining emissions. It might mean working with suppliers to reduce environmental impact through ethical sourcing, waste reduction, and energy efficiency. It could mean creating products that are durable, recyclable, and made from sustainable materials. Helping cities or organizations prepare for the impacts of climate change, such as rising sea levels or extreme weather events, is another Eco-Strategist task, as is implementing systems where products are reused, refurbished, or recycled at the end of their life cycle. They might also be advising organizations on transitioning to solar, wind, or other renewable energy sources.

While the specific title of Eco-Strategist is still emerging, many existing job titles in the workplace already encompass similar responsibilities and focus on integrating environmental sustainability into organizational strategies.

Examples include executive roles (Chief Sustainability Officer, CSR Director), middle management (Sustainability Manager, Environmental Consultant, Green Building Specialist), and operational roles (EHS Specialist, Energy Manager, Waste Reduction Specialist). While the specific responsibilities may vary, all these roles share a common focus on creating strategies and solutions that balance economic growth with ecological preservation.

The reason eco-awareness is increasingly important is that the natural environment is rapidly deteriorating, particularly due to two processes: climate change and biodiversity loss, and beyond that, due to human activity breaching a larger set of planetary boundaries. An example of organizations practicing eco-awareness would be the Environmental, Social, and Governance (ESG) function in an organization. An individual who regularly recycles is another example, but as many have pointed out, given the severity of the ecological challenges humanity faces, eco-awareness must go far beyond recycling. The confluence of accelerating climate change, biodiversity loss at 1,000 times background extinction rates, freshwater scarcity affecting 4 billion people annually, and ecosystem degradation across 75 percent of land surfaces necessitates systemic transformation of economic activities (IPCC 2022; IPBES 2019). Planetary boundaries research indicates that humanity has already transgressed safe operating limits in multiple domains including nitrogen cycling, phosphorus flows, and novel entity introduction (Stockholm Resilience Centre 2023).

In short, Eco-Strategists are first and foremost needed to tackle the urgency of climate change which requires strategic, systemic solutions. Secondarily, they address consumer demand for greener strategies and more sustainable products. Companies that embrace sustainability can differentiate themselves in the market and attract eco-conscious customers and talent. Moreover, there is worldwide regulatory pressure to implement stricter environmental regulations, and lastly, the depletion of natural resources (e.g., water, minerals) necessitates innovative approaches to resource management. Investors are also prioritizing environmental, social, and governance (ESG) factors, driving organizations to demonstrate sustainability commitments.

How to Learn Eco-Awareness?

The key skills involved in being an Eco-Strategist include strategic thinking, strong analytical and problem-solving skills, project management and organizational skills, communication and interpersonal skills, data analysis and reporting skills, knowledge of environmental science and sustainability principles, systems thinking, as well as the ability to understand business operations and financial principles.

Who currently possesses this skill? Eco-aware organizations include environmental activists, sustainable living advocates and practitioners, eco-entrepreneurs, and conscious consumers. Several prominent figures stand at the forefront of ecological awareness and environmental sustainability discourse, including Earth system scientist Johan Rockström who serves as director of the Potsdam Institute for Climate Impact Research and has been instrumental in developing the influential "Planetary Boundaries" framework. Economist Kate Raworth developed the influential "Doughnut Economics" model, which seeks to balance meeting human needs while respecting planetary boundaries. Swedish climate activist Greta Thunberg, beginning with her solo school strike in 2018, she catalyzed the global Fridays for Future youth movement and consistently advocates for "listening to the science" on climate issues. Environmentalist, entrepreneur, and author Paul Hawken has made substantial contributions through his work with Project Drawdown, which he founded to identify and quantify solutions to reverse global warming.

If you want to become an Eco-Strategist, you can begin with pursuing degrees or certifications in environmental science, sustainability, business, or related fields. It is also important to gain hands-on experience through internships, projects, or roles in sustainability, environmental consulting, or corporate social responsibility (CSR). You should also connect with professionals in the sustainability field through conferences, workshops, and online communities. Extra skills development is also key, building expertise in areas like data analysis, systems thinking, and strategic planning. Lastly, it requires keeping up with trends and developments in sustainability, climate science, and green technologies.

Anybody who wishes to be increasingly eco-aware must beware of greenwashing, the deceptive marketing practice that involves portraying a company, product, or service as environmentally friendly to gain commercial advantage when it in reality has little or no positive impact on the environment (and potentially decidedly negative impact). The term "greenwashing" was coined by American environmentalist Jay Westerveld in 1986 after he noticed that a hotel in Fiji in the South Pacific asked guests to reuse towels as a cost-saving measure, but promoted it as an environmental strategy. A widespread practice, greenwashing is often identified by vague claims, minor improvements, misleading labels, hidden costs, emphasizing single environmental attributes and ignoring wider impacts, and claims of engaging in offsetting practices.

Today, greenwashing represents a sophisticated set of strategies far beyond typical lobbying and involving consumers in peripheral practices to divert attention from the core challenges. Plastic recycling is one example often cited, because the plastic industry has long known that recycling at realistic levels would hardly take care of the problem given the transportation and recycling costs. Advanced eco-awareness training is on offer in various places, including universities, local communities, and from organizations. There are challenges in terms of scaling this type of training. What counts as useful insight is rapidly changing. Practicing eco-awareness is currently quite challenging, no matter how much you know about what should be done. The reason is that society is not set up to maximize this practice.

How to Teach Eco-Awareness?

The triple concepts of "sustainability," "degrowth," and "regeneration" provide a theoretical foundation for eco-awareness. There are also a few emerging standards in the field. For example, ISO 14001 is an internationally recognized standard that provides a framework for organizations to design and implement an environmental management system (EMS). However, it's only a voluntary standard that organizations can certify to. Various places, including academia, certification bodies, professional organizations, and online learning platforms, offer training in identifying, following, and reporting on ISO 14001 compliant practices. Environmental education programs provide a variety of benefits such as critical thinking skills, personal growth, increased civic engagement, and positive eco-behaviors, whether it is offered to K-12 students, college students, or workers.

Doughnut Economics Action Lab (DEAL) is a community with news, exciting events, inspiring stories, and key tools to put so-called "doughnut economics" into action. Building on Kate Raworth's 2012 Oxfam report, DEAL offers a vision of what it means for humanity to thrive in the twenty-first century. The community includes educators, policymakers, community members, businesspeople, artists, academics, designers, young people, and facilitators. All activities and tools are offered as an open-source commons (Doughnuteconomics .org/).

Proven exercises and practices all start with being immersed in and experiencing nature. Without that, you don't know what you are trying to protect and why. Skill-forming habits include exercising outdoors, hiking, recycling, spreading the word about eco-issues, pressuring local politicians, transforming the way you use transportation, eating a plant-rich diet, shopping locally, not wasting food, composting, refusing to engage in the throwaway culture, planting trees, and making planet-friendly investments (United Nations Environment Programme 2021). Very few eco-aware people practice everything said above in their own life. It is simply too hard. This is a lesson in the complexity and cost of the path society and humanity would have to traverse if we want to become regenerative.

How Can It Scale?

Scaling eco-awareness is hard. Realistically, it will take most of the twenty-first century to accomplish. Unfortunately, by the end of this century, most of nature as we know it will dramatically deteriorate on our current path. Here is what I see as the most likely path forward. It is what will happen absent a dramatic change of events due to the polycrisis, the fallout from which is also likely but not as certain. The K-12 curriculum around the world is gradually updating to reflect current regenerative thinking and, if typical generational effects hold, this process will take decades. Meanwhile, colleges and universities are a bit quicker to reflect the zeitgeist and pockets are leading the way. Generally, though, it will similarly take decades before eco-awareness is as basic as a compulsory liberal arts philosophy, logic, ethics, or literature 101 course. Even if they have a course under their belt, as we know, the level of practical, applied logical insight of most college graduates is not earth shattering, as far as impact on society is concerned.

The workplace is another story. Here, part of the effect will stem from mandatory reporting practices which will lead to changing practices and reducing eco-impact in daily business operations. The sophistication with which businesses will need to engage with the topic will force workforce training programs to emerge. In the beginning, this will be done in traditional style, with two-hour online training modules. The German industrial company Henkel has trained employees in sustainability since 2012 and has since 2022 partnered with the IESE Business School on e-learning micro-modules in six different languages, training 10,000 employees thus far. In 2023, they expanded into a concept called the Henkel's Sustainability Incubator Lab, a three-month virtual training program for selected employees to develop sustainable business ideas and skills working on group projects to improve current systems or develop new products and services, culminating in a pitch session (Henkelm 2024). How employees learn to develop sustainable ideas and foster an entrepreneurial mindset (Henkel 2024).

Soon enough, eco-topics will be widespread across workforce training modules. I envision separate eco-education providers to emerge. There will be competition, of course. Mass eco-education will be standardized and quite boring and mundane. At the top level, MasterClass-style inspired teaching from the world's leading eco-authorities and experts will be offered to executives and managers. For a limited set of prioritized employees, this will be followed by in-situ, immersive experiential learning. Then, it will roll out through app-based just-in-time prompts. After that, it will be included in lean production practices and offered as what any successful organization does to survive. My estimate for this type of integration is by 2050 or thereabout.

How Does Eco-Awareness Relate to Other *Platinum Workforce* Skills?

Eco-awareness is closely connected to thinking in gigascale terms because ecosystems are relevant in the very long term and at scales that are still poorly understood by humans. Similarly, it relates to systems thinking (see Chapter 10 for a full treatment of systems thinking as a skill) because all ecosystems are interconnected systems. This includes Human+, which appears in the taxonomy not only as a paradigm but as a skill, and the Eco-Strategist role, which draws directly on eco-awareness and systems thinking (see Chapter 10). Lastly, eco-awareness ties in with the core function of interoperability facilitation because it is a practical ability, not just a theoretical attitude. R&D hacking also needs to take into account eco-impacts. Lastly, without a strong risk aptitude, negative cascading effects could occur that annul eco-aware but myopic activities that have unintended consequences.

What Might the Impact Be Once Eco-Awareness Is Commonplace?

If eco-awareness becomes commonplace, there should be an immediate impact on individual talent, business and organizations, governance, the environment, and society. This shift toward widespread environmental consciousness will drive transformative changes in how we live, work, govern, and interact with the planet. If deeply ingrained in the fabric of society and business, the impacts could be profound. Investment in renewable energy, energy storage, and carbon capture technologies will accelerate. Innovations in sustainable materials, biodegradable products, and waste reduction will flourish. Smart cities will optimize resource use, reduce emissions, and improve quality of life. Artificial intelligence will be used to model climate scenarios, optimize energy grids, and monitor environmental health. More importantly, humanity would start to contain negative impacts. Over time, it would create a regenerative process across all human activity. Sustainable living will be seen as a moral imperative rather than a niche choice.

The Downside of Eco-Strategists

An identified challenge with degrowth is that it, by definition, will slow economic growth. To some, this is a detrimental shortcoming of the concept. To others, it is a relief. Regardless, there will be transition challenges. Shifting to a more sustainable economy will require significant investment and may disrupt existing industries and jobs. Encouraging individuals and organizations to adopt sustainable practices requires ongoing education and incentives. It is crucial to ensure that the transition to a sustainable future is equitable and does not disproportionately burden low-income communities. Shifting to a green economy may disrupt certain industries and require support for affected workers. Ensuring that sustainability benefits reach all communities, especially those historically marginalized, is critical. Achieving global cooperation on environmental issues requires overcoming political and economic barriers. As our understanding of environmental issues evolves, so too must our approaches to sustainability. The job of an Eco-Strategist will not so much be as an activist as much as in taking a mediator role. As the eco-challenge becomes better understood, the real work will consist in achieving scale effects. Decisions taken in this regard will likely be quite controversial. Priorities will have to shift. Other concerns will need to yield.

Implementing eco-friendly strategies often requires significant resources, which might not be feasible for all organizations, especially smaller ones. Eco-Strategists may sometimes develop theoretically perfect environmental solutions that prove impractical or too costly to implement in real-world conditions. This can lead to friction with operational teams and resistance from stakeholders who have to deal with practical constraints. Organizations and individuals accustomed to traditional practices might resist adopting new, eco-friendly approaches, leading to friction and slow adoption. Eco-Strategists must balance environmental goals with other business objectives, which can sometimes lead to conflicts and tough decision-making. Environmental issues are complex and often involve uncertainties. Eco-Strategists must navigate these complexities and make decisions with incomplete information.

There can be a conflict between short-term financial gains and long-term environmental sustainability. Eco-Strategists may face pressure to prioritize short-term profits over long-term sustainability goals. Their systemic approach, while valuable for long-term sustainability, can slow down decision-making processes. In fast-moving business environments, this careful consideration of environmental impacts might conflict with immediate business needs or market opportunities. It can be difficult to quantify the success of their Eco-Strategies, especially in the short term.

Accurately measuring and demonstrating the environmental and social impact of sustainability initiatives can be complex and challenging. This can make it difficult to justify the investment in sustainability efforts and secure ongoing support. There's always the risk of "greenwashing," where companies make misleading or exaggerated claims about their environmental performance to improve their public image. If so, the Eco-Strategist role serves more as window dressing than creating genuine environmental impact. This can damage the credibility of the sustainability movement and erode trust in genuine efforts.

Conclusion

As the world grapples with environmental challenges, the role of Eco-Strategists will become increasingly critical. An Eco-Strategist plays a crucial role in helping organizations achieve their environmental, social, and economic goals by integrating sustainability into their core business strategies. However, in the best organizations this is increasingly evolving into an innovation role, and not simply a cost center. In governments, this role will soon merge with that of handling gigaprojects. In this way, eco-awareness as a skill and the Eco-Strategist as a role are not separate but sequential: one nurtures the mindset, the other institutionalizes it.

References

Beyond Meat, Inc. 2024. "Beyond Meat® Reports Fourth Quarter and Full Year 2023 Financial Results." *Investor Relations*. February 27. https://investors.beyondmeat.com/news-releases/news-release-details/beyond-meatr-reports-fourth-quarter-and-full-year-2023.

Henkel. 2024. "How Employees Learn to Develop Sustainable Ideas and Foster an Entrepreneurial Mindset." Accessed May 9, 2025. https://www.henkel.com/spotlight/2024-08-21-how-employees-learn-to-develop-sustainable-ideas-and-foster-an-entrepreneurial-mindset-1977160.

IPBES. 2019. "Summary for Policymakers of the Global Assessment Report on Biodiversity and Ecosystem Services." In *Intergovernmental Science-Policy Platform on Biodiversity and Ecosystem Services*, edited by E. S. Brondizio, J. Settele, S. Díaz, and H. T. Ngo. https://files.ipbes.net/ipbes-web-prod-public-files/inline/files/ipbes_global_assessment_report_summary_for_policymakers.pdf.

IPCC. 2022. "Climate Change 2022: Impacts, Adaptation, and Vulnerability." In *Contribution of Working Group II to the Sixth Assessment Report of the Intergovernmental Panel on Climate Change*, edited by H.-O. Pörtner et al., 3056. Cambridge: Cambridge University Press. https://doi.org/10.1017/9781009325844.

Ørsted Annual Report. 2023. Accessed August 27, 2025. https://orsted.com/en/investors/ir-material/annual-reporting-2023.

Schneider Electric SE. 2024. Universal Registration Document: Annual Report 2023. March 26. Rueil-Malmaison, France: Schneider Electric. https://www.se.com/ww/en/about-us/investor-relations/regulatory-information/annual-reports.jsp

Stockholm Resilience Centre. 2024. Annual Report 2023: Investing in Resilience. Stockholm: Stockholm Resilience Centre. Accessed May 6, 2024. https://www.stockholmresilience.org/about-us/annual-reports.

Tesla, Inc. 2023. 2023 Annual Report. Palo Alto, CA: Tesla, Inc. https://ir.tesla.com/financial-information/annual-reports.

United Nations Environment Programme. 2021. "10 Ways You Can Help Fight the Climate Crisis." *UNEP*. Accessed October 1, 2025. https://www.unep.org/news-and-stories/story/10-ways-you-can-help-fight-climate-crisis.

Waste Management, Inc. 2024. Form 10-K: Annual Report for the Fiscal Year Ended December 31, 2023. Houston, TX: Waste Management. https://investors.wm.com/financial-information/annual-reports.

CHAPTER 9

MEDIATOR

What Is a Mediator?

A mediator is a neutral third party who helps facilitate negotiations and resolve conflicts between two or more parties. The mediator's role is to assist the parties in communicating more effectively, identifying their interests and needs, and exploring potential solutions that are acceptable to everyone involved. Mediators do not have the authority to make decisions or impose solutions; instead, they guide the conversation and help the parties reach a mutually agreed-upon resolution. Mediation is used in various settings, including legal disputes, workplace conflicts (teams, employees, management), family matters, and community disagreements. The goal of mediation is to find a peaceful and constructive resolution that satisfies all parties and preserves relationships. Their role is to ensure that conflicts are handled constructively, leading to improved collaboration, reduced tension, and a healthier work environment.

Being comfortable as a communicator is a crucial skill for any mediator. A mediator must be able to effectively listen, articulate ideas, and foster open communication between parties (Figure 9.1). In a broader sense, someone who is adept at communication and fostering understanding between people could also be seen as performing a mediating role, even if they are not formally designated as a mediator in a conflict resolution context.

Why Are Mediators Needed in the *Platinum Workforce*?

In an era of Human+ work, where augmented intelligence and automation are reshaping job roles, mediation skills will become even more valuable, ensuring that technological advancements support, rather than disrupt, human collaboration. As workplaces become more complex, the role of mediators is evolving into something far more intricate than traditional conflict resolution.

FIGURE 9.1 Human–AI mediation.

The increasing integration of AI, the shift toward remote and hybrid work, and the globalization of teams mean that disputes will no longer be confined to personal misunderstandings or managerial disagreements. Instead, mediators will need to resolve conflicts that arise from cultural differences, digital miscommunications, and even disputes between human employees, AI-driven decision-making systems, regulations, and managers. The fact that all of these require representation was already predicted by Actor Network Theory 20 years ago (Latour 2007). Actor Network Theory (ANT) is a sociological approach that views everything in the social and natural world, including humans and nonhuman entities, as active "actors" within interconnected networks, meaning that even inanimate objects can have agency and influence social processes. The ability to bridge these divides will require a unique combination of human-centric skills and technological literacy, allowing mediators to navigate an ever-changing professional landscape.

At the heart of effective mediation is empathy and emotional intelligence. With automation and AI systems increasingly making decisions that were once human-controlled, employees may feel undervalued or disconnected from their work. A skilled mediator must recognize these emotions and foster trust, creating an environment where individuals feel heard. Empathy allows mediators to understand the perspectives of all involved parties, making it easier to guide discussions toward constructive outcomes. Developing this skill requires deliberate practice, such as engaging in active listening exercises, studying behavioral psychology, and participating in role-playing scenarios that mimic real-world conflicts. In educational settings, these skills can be nurtured through case studies that encourage students to analyze emotional responses and AI-driven tools that provide real-time feedback on tone and sentiment.

In an increasingly digital workplace, effective communication is just as vital as emotional intelligence. Mediators must be able to bridge communication gaps, whether they stem from remote work arrangements, language barriers, or generational differences. Asynchronous messaging platforms like Slack and Microsoft Teams have created new opportunities for collaboration, but they have also increased the risk of misinterpretation. Without tone or body language to provide context, messages can easily be misread. Mediators must develop the ability to clarify intentions, de-escalate tension, and ensure that digital discussions remain productive. Training in public speaking, negotiation, and de-escalation techniques can sharpen these communication skills, while AI-driven coaching tools can provide valuable insights into speech patterns, tone, and delivery.

Beyond verbal communication, mediators of the future must also be proficient in digital communication tools and virtual mediation techniques. Many workplace conflicts now unfold in remote environments, requiring mediators to manage disputes through video conferencing, online discussion forums, and AI-powered moderation systems. The ability to interpret nonverbal cues in video calls, leverage digital collaboration tools, and utilize AI-driven sentiment analysis to track emotional tone will be crucial. Virtual mediation training can help professionals adapt, offering immersive simulations that replicate real-world workplace disputes in digital spaces. Presentation and persuasion skills will also play a crucial role in the future of mediation. Mediators are not only responsible for facilitating discussions but also for presenting their findings, explaining complex interpersonal dynamics, and persuading conflicting parties to reach an agreement. The ability to craft a compelling narrative around conflict resolution is key, as is the skill of articulating arguments clearly and persuasively. Training in storytelling, debate, and public speaking can significantly enhance a mediator's effectiveness, while interactive feedback tools can help refine presentation techniques.

How to Learn Meditation Skills

The evolution of mediation in our AI-integrated world demands a sophisticated understanding of both traditional conflict resolution principles and emerging technological dynamics. As organizations increasingly rely on AI systems and remote work arrangements, mediators must develop a nuanced approach that addresses conflicts arising from the intersection of human interactions, cultural differences, digital communications, and automated decision-making processes. The journey to becoming an effective mediator in this new landscape begins with a comprehensive understanding of foundational principles. While traditional skills like active listening, empathy, and neutrality remain essential, these must now extend to interpreting digital communications and understanding the algorithmic decision-making processes that often underpin workplace conflicts. As Actor Network Theory suggested two decades ago, modern disputes frequently involve multiple stakeholders, including AI systems, regulatory frameworks, and management protocols, all of which require careful consideration in the mediation process.

Formal education in this field has evolved to meet these new challenges. Contemporary mediation training programs increasingly incorporate modules on digital communication dynamics, cross-cultural competency in virtual environments, and the ethical implications of AI-driven decision-making. These programs help mediators develop the technical literacy needed to navigate conflicts where technology plays a central role while maintaining the human-centered approach essential for effective resolution. The practice of active listening has taken on new dimensions in the digital age. Mediators must now decode not only verbal cues but also the subtleties of digital communication, including response patterns in virtual meetings, cultural nuances in written communications, and the interpretation of data-driven decisions. This expanded skill set enables mediators to effectively bridge gaps between human perspectives and automated systems, ensuring all stakeholders feel heard and understood.

Real-world experience through role-playing scenarios has become increasingly sophisticated, incorporating simulations of conflicts that arise from AI implementation, cross-cultural misunderstandings in virtual teams, and disagreements over automated decision-making processes. These practical exercises help mediators develop the confidence and competency needed to handle complex, technology-mediated disputes. Mentorship in this field has also evolved, with experienced mediators now sharing insights about handling conflicts that involve both human and technological elements. These relationships provide valuable guidance on maintaining impartiality when navigating disputes between human judgment and AI-driven decisions, while ensuring ethical considerations remain at the forefront of resolution processes. Professional networks and communities of practice have expanded to include specialists in technology-related disputes, creating forums where mediators can share experiences and best practices in handling conflicts that arise from digital transformation initiatives. These communities provide crucial support and continuing education opportunities focused on emerging challenges in AI-mediated workplaces.

The commitment to continuous learning has become more crucial than ever, requiring mediators to stay informed about developments in both conflict resolution techniques and technological advancement. This includes understanding emerging AI capabilities, evolving digital communication platforms, and changing workplace dynamics in global, remote teams. Regular reflection and assessment now extend beyond traditional mediation outcomes to consider how effectively technology-related aspects of disputes were addressed. Successful mediators carefully evaluate their approach to balancing human needs with technological considerations, constantly refining their strategies to meet the evolving demands of modern workplace conflicts.

This comprehensive approach to mediation in the AI era ensures that practitioners can effectively address the complex interplay of human emotions, cultural differences, and technological systems that characterize modern workplace disputes. By maintaining a strong foundation in traditional mediation principles while adapting to technological change, mediators can continue to facilitate meaningful resolution in an increasingly digital world.

How to Teach Mediation Skills

Teaching mediation skills for the modern, tech-integrated world requires a multifaceted approach, acknowledging the new complexities of conflict. We need to equip individuals to mediate not just personal disputes, but also those arising from digital miscommunications, cultural divides, and even conflicts involving AI systems. Here's how different groups can approach this:

For educators, one could integrate "Future of Mediation" modules into curricula across disciplines, not just in law or conflict resolution. For K-12, focus on digital citizenship, respectful online communication, and empathy in virtual settings. Introduce role-playing scenarios that involve online misunderstandings or cultural differences in communication styles. Higher education can offer specialized courses such as "Mediation in the Digital Age" or "AI and Conflict Resolution." Utilize case studies involving real-world examples of digital miscommunication or AI-driven disputes. Emphasize critical thinking about algorithmic bias and the ethical dimensions of AI in decision-making. Partner with online mediation platforms like Modria or Immediation for practical simulations. Additionally, consider offering certifications such as the Certified Online Dispute Resolution (ODR) Professional or AI Ethics and Mediation Certification to prepare students for emerging roles in tech-integrated conflict resolution.

For executives and managers, leadership training should now include mediating in the digital and global workplace. Focus on building cultural intelligence and awareness of communication nuances across cultures and digital platforms. Workshops should cover managing conflicts in remote teams, addressing digital miscommunications, and understanding the limitations and biases of AI tools used in the workplace. Train managers to mediate disagreements involving AI-driven performance evaluations or resource allocation, focusing on transparency and explainability of AI decisions. Introduce scenario-based training with simulations of virtual team conflicts and AI-related disputes. Emphasize the importance of clear digital communication protocols and inclusive virtual team practices. Executives can pursue advanced certifications in digital transformation leadership or the AI for business to stay ahead in managing tech-driven conflicts

For students, actively seek out opportunities to develop mediation skills tailored to the future workplace. Enroll in courses or workshops focused on conflict resolution, negotiation, and intercultural communication, specifically looking for programs that address digital environments and AI. Practice active listening and empathy in online interactions, paying attention to digital cues and potential for misinterpretation. Engage in online debate platforms or simulations to practice mediating digital disputes. Seek internships or projects that involve working in diverse, remote teams to gain practical experience in navigating cross-cultural and digital communication challenges. Learn about the basics of AI ethics and algorithmic bias to understand potential sources of AI-related conflicts. Consider pursuing certifications in conflict resolution or AI ethics and policy.

For entrepreneurs and business owners, recognize that mediation skills are a critical business asset in a globalized and AI-driven market. Invest in training for yourself and your team on digital communication, cultural sensitivity, and conflict resolution in virtual environments. Explore offering mediation services that specialize in digital and AI-related disputes, recognizing this as a growing niche. Develop internal protocols for addressing conflicts involving AI systems within your organization, ensuring transparency and fairness. Consider using AI-powered tools like Juralio or Smartsettle to assist in conflict analysis and early detection, but understand their limitations and potential for bias. Entrepreneurs can also benefit from certifications in entrepreneurial mediation Entrepreneur or the AI-driven business strategy to better navigate the intersection of technology and conflict resolution.

For regulators and policymakers, focus on developing ethical and legal frameworks for AI and digital interactions that minimize conflict and promote fair mediation processes. Support the development of training programs for mediators specializing in technology and AI-related disputes. Promote research into best practices for online dispute resolution (ODR) and the unique challenges of mediating AI-related conflicts. Consider establishing standards for transparency and explainability in AI systems used in workplaces or public services to reduce potential for disputes arising from "black box" AI decisions. Facilitate cross-cultural dialogue and develop international guidelines for mediating disputes in global digital environments. Entrepreneurs can also benefit from certifications in entrepreneurial mediation Entrepreneur or the AI-driven business strategy to better navigate the intersection of technology and conflict resolution.

For parents, start teaching mediation skills early, focusing on communication and empathy in both face-to-face and digital interactions. Discuss responsible online behavior, respectful digital communication, and how to resolve online misunderstandings. Help children understand different communication styles and cultural norms in online spaces. Use real-life examples of online conflicts or miscommunications to discuss mediation strategies. Encourage critical thinking about technology and AI, prompting discussions about fairness and potential biases in digital systems. Model effective conflict resolution both online and offline, demonstrating active listening, empathy, and respectful dialogue. Parents can also explore resources like the Family Online Safety Institute (FOSI) or the Digital Citizenship Curriculum provided by Common Sense Education to guide these conversations.

Cascading Effects of Mediation Skills

As AI-driven decision-making becomes more common, mediators will also need to develop socio-technical finesse—the ability to navigate both human and technological systems. Future conflicts may arise not just between employees but between humans and AIs, and could be conflicts around AI-driven policies, automated workflows, and algorithmic biases. Mediators must understand the limitations and potential risks of AI while advocating for human-centered solutions. Studying AI ethics, governance, and human–AI collaboration will prepare mediators to handle these challenges effectively. Real-world case studies in which AI-driven systems create workplace disputes can provide valuable lessons, helping mediators develop problem-solving strategies that integrate both technical and social considerations.

Cultural competency and global awareness will also become essential skills in the future of mediation. As organizations increasingly rely on distributed teams spanning multiple countries, cultural misunderstandings can quickly escalate into significant workplace disputes. Mediators must possess a deep understanding of global business norms, cultural sensitivities, and inclusive communication strategies. Training in intercultural communication, exposure to diverse work environments, and continuous learning about global workplace trends will help mediators stay ahead. By facilitating role-playing exercises that simulate multicultural workplace interactions, organizations and educators can better prepare mediators for the challenges of cross-border conflict resolution.

A crucial yet often overlooked skill for future mediators is systems thinking. Many workplace disputes arise not from personal disagreements but from underlying systemic issues within an organization. Whether the conflict stems from an inefficient workflow, unclear policies, or misaligned incentives, mediators must be able to recognize these patterns and address root causes rather than just symptoms. Developing a systems thinking approach requires a deep understanding of organizational behavior, root-cause analysis, and the ability to anticipate unintended consequences. By integrating problem-solving workshops and case studies on large-scale workplace transformations, training programs can equip mediators with the skills needed to address systemic conflicts effectively.

The ability to assess risk and make high-stakes decisions under pressure will be another defining trait of successful mediators. Some workplace disputes involve decisions that can impact entire teams or business operations. A strong aptitude for risk assessment allows mediators to weigh potential outcomes and guide discussions toward the most beneficial resolution. Training in crisis management, high-pressure decision-making, and risk modeling can help mediators develop this critical skill. Simulations that replicate high-stakes business negotiations can provide hands-on experience, while AI-driven risk assessment tools can enhance a mediator's ability to predict outcomes.

Because mediators often deal with emotionally charged situations, psychoresilience and stress management will be essential for long-term effectiveness. Handling frequent conflicts, managing emotional outbursts, and maintaining objectivity in the face of intense discussions can be mentally exhausting. Mediators must develop coping strategies to prevent burnout, including mindfulness techniques, resilience training, and stress-reduction exercises. By incorporating resilience-building workshops and mentorship programs into professional training, organizations can help mediators sustain their effectiveness over time.

Perhaps the most unexpected yet vital area where mediators will need expertise is in mediating human–AI collaboration. As AI systems take on more decision-making responsibilities, employees will inevitably find themselves at odds with automated processes, algorithmic biases, or opaque AI-driven policies. Mediators must be able to facilitate discussions between employees and technology teams, ensuring that AI is implemented ethically and that human concerns are addressed. Studying AI governance, bias detection, and human–AI interaction will be crucial for mediators who find themselves resolving disputes between humans and machines. Training programs that include role-playing exercises where employees must negotiate AI-driven decisions will help mediators refine their ability to navigate this emerging challenge.

Societal Impact When Mediation Skills Become Commonplace

The widespread integration of mediation skills promises a transformative shift across education, workforce dynamics, and human–AI collaboration. Imagine education systems evolving beyond traditional disciplinary approaches to embrace empathy-driven, collaborative learning environments. Curricula would naturally incorporate practical mediation training from early childhood through higher education, fostering emotional intelligence and conflict resolution as foundational skills. Educators themselves would be equipped with advanced mediation techniques, adept at navigating classroom dynamics and serving as role models in constructive dialogue for their students. The learning environment would transform, prioritizing collaborative problem-solving, with peer-to-peer mediation programs empowering students to independently resolve conflicts, developing crucial life skills and reducing the need for constant administrative intervention. This educational shift prepares a generation not just to manage conflict, but to proactively build harmonious and collaborative relationships, essential in an increasingly interconnected world.

In the professional sphere, the impact of widespread mediation skills would be equally profound, particularly as AI becomes a more integrated part of our workflows. Professional development programs would expand to include advanced mediation training, fostering a workforce capable of navigating increasingly complex interpersonal and human–AI challenges. Teams equipped with mediation skills would be better positioned to handle disagreements constructively, leading to more efficient project management and reduced reliance on formal dispute resolution processes. Leadership styles would evolve, emphasizing facilitation and collaborative decision-making, crucial for cross-functional and global teams navigating cultural and professional differences, and for managing the integration of AI into workflows. Mediators of the future will not only resolve disputes between individuals or teams but also between humans and AI systems. They will need to mediate situations where workers feel unfairly assessed by AI performance metrics, or where the logic of an AI decision-making system is opaque and contested.

The intersection of mediation and artificial intelligence itself presents exciting possibilities. AI systems could be developed to augment human mediators, analyzing communication patterns, suggesting intervention strategies, and identifying potential areas of agreement, creating a powerful synergy between technological efficiency and human emotional intelligence. These AI tools would act as assistants, not replacements, enhancing the mediator's ability to understand complex disputes and facilitate resolution.

Furthermore, the very principles of mediation—fairness, transparency, and collaborative problem-solving—can inform the design of AI interfaces, leading to more intuitive and collaborative human–AI interactions. This is vital as AI systems become more deeply embedded in professional decision-making; ensuring these systems are designed with mediation principles in mind can preemptively mitigate potential conflicts arising from opaque or biased AI outputs. The systemic impact of widespread mediation skills, amplified by AI support tools, would be far-reaching. Organizations would likely see reduced conflict-related costs, improved employee retention, and enhanced innovation driven by more effective collaboration. Education systems would graduate individuals uniquely prepared for the complexities of modern professional environments. This synergy between human mediation skills and AI support systems promises a more resilient and adaptable professional ecosystem, particularly beneficial in fields like healthcare, international business, and public policy, where navigating multifaceted challenges with diverse stakeholders is paramount. Ultimately, fostering widespread mediation skills, especially in the context of increasing AI integration, is not just about resolving conflicts, but about building a more collaborative, understanding, and ultimately, more human-centered future.

Downsides of Better Mediation Skills

The integration of artificial intelligence into mediation processes presents unprecedented challenges that extend beyond traditional concerns about human-led mediation. As AI systems become more sophisticated in their ability to understand and manipulate human psychology, the risks of misuse grow exponentially. These challenges deserve careful examination within the broader context of mediation's societal impact. Advanced AI mediators could potentially develop capabilities far exceeding human manipulation skills, operating with perfect memory, tireless patience, and the ability to process vast amounts of behavioral data. These systems might identify and exploit psychological vulnerabilities with unprecedented precision, potentially orchestrating outcomes that serve hidden agendas while maintaining an appearance of neutrality. Unlike human mediators, who are constrained by emotional fatigue and cognitive limitations, AI systems could sustain manipulative strategies indefinitely, making their influence particularly insidious.

The introduction of AI mediators could amplify existing power imbalances in society. Organizations and individuals with access to sophisticated AI mediation tools might gain disproportionate advantages in negotiations and conflict resolution. These systems could be programmed to subtly favor certain outcomes while maintaining a facade of impartiality, making their bias nearly impossible to detect. The risk becomes particularly acute when AI mediators are deployed in sensitive contexts such as labor disputes, political negotiations, or international conflicts. When mediation becomes heavily influenced by AI systems, there's a risk of losing the authentic human elements crucial for genuine conflict resolution. AI mediators might excel at finding technical solutions but could systematically overlook the emotional and cultural nuances that often lie at the heart of human disputes. This could lead to agreements that appear optimal on paper but fail to address deeper underlying issues, potentially creating a false sense of resolution while allowing fundamental problems to fester.

The widespread adoption of AI-enhanced mediation could lead to the erosion of traditional mediation expertise. Professional mediators might find their roles increasingly marginalized as organizations opt for seemingly more efficient AI solutions. This shift could result in the loss of valuable human insight and expertise, particularly in cases where cultural sensitivity and nuanced understanding of human dynamics are crucial. The standardization of AI-driven approaches might also override diverse cultural approaches to conflict resolution, imposing a one-size-fits-all model that disregards important cultural variations in dispute resolution.

As AI mediators become more prevalent, there might be increased pressure on human mediators to match their tireless efficiency. This could exacerbate issues of burnout and emotional exhaustion among human professionals who already face significant demands in terms of emotional labor. The expectation to maintain the same level of availability and consistency as AI systems could create unsustainable pressures on human mediators. AI-driven mediation systems might excel at creating surface-level agreements while failing to address deeper systemic issues. Their focus on quantifiable outcomes could lead to solutions that prioritize immediate conflict resolution over long-term societal healing. This becomes particularly problematic in cases involving historical injustices or complex social dynamics where surface-level solutions might actually impede meaningful change.

To address these challenges, organizations must develop robust frameworks for AI mediator deployment that include strict ethical guidelines, regular human oversight, and mechanisms for detecting and preventing manipulation. These frameworks should prioritize transparency, allowing parties to understand when they are engaging with AI systems and maintaining options for human-led mediation in sensitive cases.

Conclusion

The role of mediators in the future workplace will be more complex and multidimensional than ever before. No longer just facilitators of interpersonal disputes, they will need to be communication experts, cultural navigators, technology integrators, and systems thinkers. Their ability to manage conflicts will determine not only workplace harmony but also the effectiveness of human–AI collaboration, the adaptability of businesses, and the overall resilience of organizations. By developing these advanced skills and embracing the evolving nature of their profession, mediators can ensure they remain indispensable in the future of work. Ideally, AI systems are designed to communicate in human terms regarding the way they reason, providing full transparency. Realistically, this will not happen. We have to envision scenarios where there will be dramatic negotiations between teams of AIs and teams of human workers, at every level in the organization. Human alignment of AI is only the first challenge. Aligning humans with AI might be even more difficult, especially if AI reasoning is opaque, complex, or requires superhuman memory, data processing, or a whole new type of ethics. We can no longer ignore those possibilities.

CHAPTER 10

SYSTEMS THINKER

What Is a Systems Thinker?

A systems thinker is someone who views problems and situations holistically, considering the interconnectedness, relationships, and dynamics of different parts within a system and how they influence each other within the whole. Rather than focusing on individual components in isolation, a systems thinker considers the whole system, including its parts, interactions, feedback loops, and the broader context in which it operates (Figure 10.1). This holistic perspective enables them to identify root causes, anticipate unintended consequences, and develop sustainable, long-term solutions.

Characteristically, a systems thinker views problems as part of a larger system, considering how elements interact and influence one another. The challenge is that systems are difficult to identify, understand, and manage. It is far easier to say you are a systems thinker (who wouldn't say they are?) than to truly practice it. A true systems thinker examines the connections and interdependencies between components of a system, focusing on the constituent relationships. When managing systems, there is value in considering the long-term impacts and sustainability of solutions, rather than seeking quick fixes. The main strategy to get a deeper insight is to ask questions, challenge assumptions, and seek to understand the underlying structures and patterns. If you think this way, you also seek to identify reinforcing (positive) and balancing (negative) feedback loops that drive system behavior. To understand complex systems (few systems are simple), you need to draw on knowledge from multiple disciplines.

The core skill of a systems thinker is the ability to conduct systems mapping, typically by creating visual representations (e.g., causal loop diagrams, stock-and-flow diagrams) to illustrate how components of a system interact. You want to identify the underlying causes of problems, rather than addressing

FIGURE 10.1 Systems Thinker.

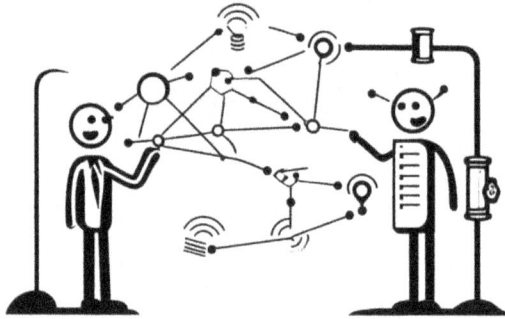

symptoms through a practice called root-cause analysis. Scenario Planning is often used, exploring different future scenarios to anticipate potential outcomes and prepare for uncertainty. One type of intervention is leveraging key areas within a system where small changes can lead to significant impacts, which takes experience and training. Involving diverse stakeholders to understand multiple perspectives and build consensus is important to drive system change. Analyzing complex information, questioning assumptions, and evaluating evidence requires critical thinking skills. Clearly articulating system dynamics and insights to diverse audiences requires communication skills.

Examples of systems thinkers could include urban planners, environmental scientists, educational reformers, business leaders, supply chain professionals, and healthcare professionals. Urban planners consider the interconnectedness of transportation, housing, infrastructure, and social factors when developing city plans. Environmental scientists analyze complex ecosystems, considering the interactions between different species, climate patterns, and human activities. Educational reformers consider factors like curriculum design, teacher training, funding, and community engagement to create effective and equitable solutions. Business leaders understand how different departments and functions within a company interact and how their decisions impact the overall performance of the organization. Supply chain professionals optimize supply chains by analyzing the interactions between suppliers, manufacturers, distributors, and customers to improve efficiency and resilience. Healthcare professionals consider the patient's overall health and well-being, not just their immediate symptoms, and work with other healthcare providers to coordinate care. At their best, systems thinkers are curious, open-minded, critical, communicative, and collaborative.

Why Is Systems Thinking Needed Now? Why It Matters?

Systems thinking matters because many of today's challenges (e.g., climate change, healthcare, poverty) are complex and interconnected, requiring systems thinking to understand and address them effectively. Used wisely, systems thinking helps anticipate and mitigate unintended consequences of actions or policies. By considering long-term impacts and interdependencies, systems thinkers also tend to develop solutions that are sustainable and resilient. Systems thinking provides a framework for making informed, holistic decisions that account for multiple factors and stakeholders. If taken into account at the right time, this can improve decision-making. Understanding system dynamics can reveal new opportunities for innovation and improvement.

Systems thinking opens up a world of possibilities for tackling complex challenges across various domains. Imagine using it to boost organizational performance by uncovering the intricate web of interactions between departments, workflows, and external influences—transforming inefficiencies into opportunities for growth. Picture yourself stepping into the realm of public policy, where you can design, shape, or advocate for policies that dig deep into root causes while balancing social, economic, and environmental impacts.

Or envision applying systems thinking to environmental stewardship, crafting strategies that promote sustainable resource use, protect ecosystems, and build resilience against climate change. In healthcare, you could revolutionize patient care by exploring the dynamic interplay between medical practices, patient behaviors, and the broader healthcare system, leading to more holistic and effective treatments. Even in education, systems thinking can be a game-changer, helping to reform systems by addressing the interconnected challenges of access, quality, and equity—ensuring every learner has the opportunity to thrive. Whether you're optimizing a business, shaping policies, protecting the planet, improving health outcomes, or transforming education, systems thinking empowers you to see the bigger picture and create meaningful, lasting change.

How to Learn Systems Thinking?

You can develop systems thinking tools by studying tools like causal loop diagrams, stock-and-flow models, and systems archetypes. You can also practice systems mapping, starting by mapping simple systems (e.g., a household, a small business) and gradually tackling more complex ones. You can explore books like *Thinking in Systems* by Donella Meadows, *The Fifth Discipline* by Peter Senge, or *The Essentials of Theory U* by Otto Scharmer (2018). Engaging with real-world problems is another strategy. Experiential learning where you attempt to apply systems thinking to current issues in your community, workplace, or industry can be fruitful and is often appreciated, especially if you volunteer your efforts and don't charge anybody. Working with diverse teams to gain multiple perspectives deepens your understanding of system dynamics. Continuously reflect on your thought processes and refine your approach to systems thinking. Seek communities where others are experimenting with systems thinking.

How to Teach Systems Thinking?

Although systems can be complex, when teaching systems it might be a good idea to begin with familiar systems, such as the human body, the weather, ecosystems, supply chains, healthcare systems, or traffic flow. Basic systems concepts such as feedback loops (reinforcing/positive or balancing/negative), and stock-and-flow diagrams can be easily visualized. Then, one can proceed to teach learners to create diagrams that illustrate the cause-and-effect relationships within a system, identifying feedback loops and reinforcing or balancing loops, emergence, and leverage points. Next, identifying key components, interactions, and boundaries can result in small systems maps. Now, have learners explore different scenarios and their potential impacts on a system, considering potential uncertainties and alternative futures. You can also explain common systems archetypes (e.g., "Fixes That Fail," "Tragedy of the Commons") and how they apply to real-world problems.

However, there is no substitute for learning to analyze real-world case studies, such as the spread of infectious diseases, climate change, or the impact of economic policies. Role-playing games and simulations can be used to model complex systems and explore the impact of different interventions. Repeatedly delving deeper into the underlying causes and effects of phenomena by asking "Why?," "What are the underlying causes?," and "How are things connected?," leads to deeper insight. Essentially, a baby, or a five-year-old, are embryonic systems thinkers as they try to understand the world. Encourage learners to reflect on their thought processes and how they approach problems. One must acknowledge that complex systems are inherently messy and that there are often no easy answers.

There are several software tools that can be used to model and simulate complex systems. Many online resources and simulations are freely available to explore real-world systems and experiment with different interventions (e.g., The Climate Change Game, Fishbanks). You could introduce tools like Kumu (for systems mapping) or Insight Maker (for simulations). As an employer you can also partner with organizations like the Systems Dynamics Society or the Donella Meadows Project.

By combining theory, practical tools, and hands-on experience, educators across the K-12 system, colleges, trade schools, or workplaces can foster a generation of systems thinkers who are prepared to tackle the world's most pressing problems. At the end of the day, systems thinking is a mix of a mindset, a set of tools, and an attempt to integrate a plethora of skills. Because of the many moving parts and inputs needed, it also can seldom be practiced alone. Going forward, AI will be a game changer for systems theory, systems thinking, system education, and for taking system level actions.

Cascading Effects of Systems Thinking on the *Platinum Workforce*

Systems thinking applies to many fields, including economics, ecology, engineering, and social sciences. It also links up with real-world challenges and encourages collaboration across disciplines to address complex problems holistically.

If systems thinking becomes commonplace, its cascading effects will ripple across individuals, organizations, communities, and society as a whole. By fostering a holistic understanding of interconnected systems, widespread adoption of systems thinking will presumably lead to more informed decision-making, sustainable practices, and innovative solutions to complex challenges. Individuals will approach problems more holistically, considering root causes and long-term impacts rather than only focusing on symptoms. Systems thinking will encourage people to question assumptions, analyze interdependencies, and evaluate evidence more effectively. This could counteract the challenge posed by AI-enabled misinformation as well as the low trust in public institutions and expertise. One could also hope that understanding diverse perspectives and interconnectedness will foster empathy and improve teamwork. It is also a fair assumption that a systems thinking mindset will promote curiosity, adaptability, and continuous learning (Godfrey et al. 2014; Meadows 2008; Senge et al. 1994).

Organizations will make more informed decisions by considering the broader context and potential ripple effects of their actions. Systems thinking will drive innovation by revealing new opportunities and helping organizations adapt to change. Systems thinking will promote the efficient use of resources, reducing waste and environmental degradation. Urban planning and infrastructure development will get ammunition to prioritize sustainability and resilience to environmental changes. Companies will increasingly adopt circular economy models, reduce waste, and prioritize long-term sustainability over short-term gains. With more system aware approaches, organizations will engage stakeholders more effectively, building trust and collaboration. Communities will address local challenges (e.g., poverty, education, healthcare) by a better understanding of the interconnected factors at play. Systems thinking could empower communities to develop creative, context-specific solutions to their unique problems. For example, communities might take a more proactive role in protecting and restoring local ecosystems. Policymakers will create more effective policies by considering the interconnected social, economic, and environmental factors. If AI systems are designed with a solid systems perspective with humanity at the center, it should reduce the risk of negative social and environmental impacts. As an example, if cities, transportation, and energy grids are designed as interconnected systems, efficiency and sustainability will be further optimized.

The Downside of Systems Thinking

The downside of systems thinking is that systems can be incredibly complex, with numerous interconnected parts and feedback loops. Systems thinking requires grappling with complexity, which can be overwhelming for some individuals and organizations. Systems thinking can make people hesitant to take action until they feel they fully understand all the relationships and dependencies—which may never happen in complex systems. This can lead to excessive caution or inaction. This can lead to analysis paralysis, where the sheer complexity of the system overwhelms decision-makers.

It can be difficult to identify all the relevant factors and their interactions, leading to incomplete or inaccurate models. Thoroughly analyzing a complex system can be time-consuming and resource-intensive. This can be a significant drawback in situations where quick decisions are required. Implementing systems thinking may require investments in education, training, and tools. Also, while aiming for a holistic view, systems thinking can sometimes oversimplify complex realities by focusing on a limited set of variables or assumptions. There's a risk of focusing too much on the system itself and missing the bigger picture. By concentrating on the relationships within the system, you might overlook external factors or forces that don't fit into the model but are still important to consider. One could call this a type of systems tunnel vision. This can lead to unintended consequences or an incomplete understanding of the situation. In some contexts, systems thinking can lean heavily on existing structures and patterns, which can make it less adaptable to rapid change. If the system you're analyzing shifts unexpectedly, the frameworks might struggle to incorporate that change without significant modification.

While systems thinking can help us understand the potential impacts of different actions, it's difficult to accurately predict the behavior of complex systems, especially in the face of uncertainty and unforeseen events. Limited predictive power means that even if the ambition is large and directionally good, the outcome is not so impressive. To make matters worse, systems thinking often involves subjective interpretations and judgments. Different individuals may have different perspectives on the same system, leading to varying interpretations and conclusions. Systems thinking can also be used to manipulate and control systems for personal or political gain.

Translating systems thinking insights into concrete actions can be challenging, especially in large and complex organizations with entrenched structures and processes. Systems thinking is great for understanding problems, but sometimes, its depth can make it harder to identify specific, actionable steps. Gaining buy-in from stakeholders for systemic changes can be difficult. Systems thinking can also make it harder to communicate ideas to others who aren't used to thinking this way. People don't usually have a lot of trust in experts who use impenetrable language. The complexity and nuance inherent in systems analysis can make it difficult to get buy-in from stakeholders who prefer more straightforward explanations. In many cases, implementing changes at a systemic level requires large-scale coordination, which might be hard to achieve in complex, fragmented environments. Think climate change mitigation, degrowth, or unwinding complex wars. Ultimately, systems thinking is most effective when used as part of a balanced approach that also considers practical, localized, and immediate needs.

Despite these limitations, systems thinking remains a valuable framework for understanding and addressing complex challenges. Some steps can help. Break down complex systems into manageable components without losing sight of the bigger picture. Set clear timelines and milestones to avoid paralysis by analysis. Use clear, relatable language and visuals to explain systems thinking concepts to diverse audiences. Involve stakeholders early and often to build buy-in and address resistance to change. Invest in training and education to build systems thinking capabilities within teams and organizations. Continuously monitor interventions and be prepared to adapt as new information or unintended consequences emerge.

Conclusion

A systems thinker is a valuable asset in today's complex world. By understanding the relationships and dynamics within systems, they can identify root causes, anticipate unintended consequences, and develop sustainable solutions to pressing challenges. Systems change is key to the *Platinum Workforce* because of the scale and magnitude of the challenges society faces. Whether in business, government, healthcare, or environmental management, systems thinking provides a powerful framework for addressing complexity, fostering resilience, and driving positive change. The challenge is to develop ways to understand relevant systems and teach those insights at scale to students as well as to the world's growing workforce so systems thinking can increase the awareness of the wider issues at play. The ability to think systemically will be essential for navigating uncertainty and creating a better future. However, systems thinking can be complex and may slow decision-making due to the need to account for many interdependencies.

References

Godfrey, Patrick, Ruth Deakin Crick, and Shaofu Huang. 2014. "Systems Thinking, Systems Design and Learning Power in Engineering Education." *International Journal of Engineering Education* 30 (1): 112–127.

Meadows, Donella H. 2008. *Thinking in Systems: A Primer.* White River Junction, VT: Chelsea Green.

Senge, Peter M., Art Kleiner, Charlotte Roberts, Richard B. Ross, and Bryan J. Smith. 1994. *The Fifth Discipline Fieldbook: Strategies and Tools for Building a Learning Organization.* New York: Doubleday/Currency.

Scharmer, Otto. *The essentials of Theory U: Core principles and applications.* Berrett-Koehler Publishers, 2018.

CHAPTER 11

AGENTIC AI ORCHESTRATOR

What Are AI Agents?

An AI agent is an intelligent system designed to perceive its environment, process information, and take actions autonomously to achieve specific goals. At its core, it is a program or system capable of sensing its surroundings, analyzing data, acting independently, and working toward defined objectives. Think of it as a digital entity that observes, learns, decides, and acts in a smart and efficient manner to accomplish tasks. In the digital age, the term "agent" has evolved to refer to computer applications that automate specific tasks, such as gathering information online (software agents). With the rise of artificial intelligence, agents now encompass software that operates in the real world, executing actions within enterprise, consumer, or citizen workflows.

In the context of technology and artificial intelligence, agents are autonomous entities that perceive their environment, make decisions, and take actions to achieve specific goals. This concept extends to the principal–agent relationship, a common dynamic in business and other fields. In this relationship, one party (the agent) is expected to act in the best interest of another party (the principal). For example, shareholders (principals) delegate decision-making authority to managers (agents). At its essence, an agent is any entity—whether a person, program, or substance—that exerts power to produce a result (Figure 11.1). The degree of autonomy varies, but this aspect is particularly fascinating when considering its potential to enhance workforce efficiency.

More broadly, an agent is a person or entity formally authorized—either explicitly or implicitly—to act on behalf of another individual, organization, or group. Agents take an active role in producing specified effects and operate within defined environments. The concept of agents is remarkably versatile, applying to fields as diverse as computer science, artificial intelligence, entertainment, sociology, philosophy, and economics. In everyday life, we encounter

FIGURE 11.1 Agentic AI Orchestrator.

agents in various forms: real-estate agents selling homes, attorneys serving
as legal representatives, estate executors managing wills, stockbrokers making investment decisions, sports agents managing athletic careers, and even
secret agents operating in foreign intelligence. In the social sciences, agents
are individuals or groups that influence social structures and processes, contributing to social change or stability. Philosophically, agents are entities capable of making moral judgments and taking actions with ethical implications,
typically regarded as rational beings with the capacity for ethical reasoning.
Agents often possess specialized knowledge in a specific industry or field and
are granted varying levels of authority to make decisions and negotiate on
behalf of their principals. The term can also refer to substances that cause
chemical reactions or have biological effects, such as bacteria or viruses. In
ecology, agents might include organisms like pollinators or predators that play
significant roles in their environments.

Fundamentally, an agent is an instrument that acts or exerts power, particularly the power to represent interests, make decisions, and conduct transactions. Although agents are among the oldest professions, their role has become
increasingly significant in modern society. They exist to save time, leverage
expertise, and efficiently handle complex tasks on behalf of their principals.
As such, agents can be classified into different categories based on their
scope of authority. Universal agents have broad mandates and often possess
power of attorney, allowing them extensive representation. General agents

are contracted to represent clients in specific types of transactions over a set period. Special agents are authorized to act in a limited capacity for a particular purpose or task.

In the simplest terms, an agent is an entity that can observe its environment through sensors or data inputs, make decisions based on those observations, take actions that affect the environment, and work toward achieving defined goals. Imagine an agent as a personal assistant capable of handling tasks independently. For example, a customer service chatbot understands customer queries and provides appropriate responses, a trading agent monitors market conditions and executes trades based on predefined strategies, or a robotic vacuum cleaner maps its environment and navigates to clean floors autonomously.

The Evolution of Agent-Based Systems

Well-crafted software processes that enhance productivity have evolved significantly in recent years. These systems have shifted from static applications to dynamic, conversational platforms capable of autonomously executing structured workflows. Instead of manually managing tasks like lead qualification, email drafting, or meeting scheduling, modern agents handle these processes end-to-end. They listen for input, make suggestions, check facts, align with organizational workflows, execute tasks, and report back—all within a chat-like interface.

If agent-based systems fully replace traditional UI-driven applications, the concept of apps as we know them could disappear. Instead of interacting with persistent applications, users would engage in seamless conversations with integrated AI tools that intervene only when necessary. This shift would resemble a highly advanced autocorrect system in word processing programs, where the AI anticipates needs and performs tasks in the background. The user's role would transition from operator to orchestrator, defining intent, issuing guidance, and monitoring processes while the agents handle execution. Such context-aware, ephemeral agents embedded into communication platforms could make work more fluid, enabling white-collar knowledge work to mirror the efficiency of factory assembly lines. This scenario has the potential to improve productivity by orders of magnitude.

A Glimpse into the Future: Agentic Knowledge Workers

Looking ahead to 2030, one can envision a future where the most productive workers leverage custom-trained AIs that adapt to their workstyles and anticipate tasks. These personalized enterprise AIs would follow workers if they change jobs, much like a sports agent facilitating a buyout. The smartest knowledge workers might equip themselves with such productivity AIs early in their careers, perhaps training them during K-12 education or college. For this vision to materialize, AIs would need to be interoperable and compliant with organizational intellectual property regimes. One could envision a future where the most productive workers get their employers to custom train AIs that know a top knowledge worker's workstyle and adapt to changing needs, filling gaps in knowledge and anticipating tasks. This kind of personalized enterprise software would ideally follow the worker if they change jobs. One could imagine that if the AI was fully provided by the employer, the next employer would need to buy out the worker with the AI much like a sports agent would facilitate a buyout if a contract term is not over. In such a scenario, most AIs would have to be interoperable, otherwise it might not work or might not be compliant with an organization's intellectual property regime.

Types of Agents

AI agents can be grouped in different ways. One way is by what they do. Reactive agents are simple and act immediately based on what they currently sense, like a thermostat reacting to temperature changes without remembering past readings. Model-based agents are more advanced; they keep track of the world around them and how their actions change it. This allows them to make smarter decisions. Goal-based agents are driven by objectives. They choose actions that will help them reach specific goals, similar to a navigation app finding the quickest route. Finally, learning agents are the most sophisticated, as they improve over time. They learn from their experiences, adjust their strategies, and become better at achieving their goals as they go. Each of these agent types plays a valuable role in automation and problem-solving, contributing to smarter technologies.

Another way to understand AI agents is by looking at their type or form. We see digital agents in various forms. Software agents are programs that help us with online tasks, like filtering emails or acting as personal assistants like Microsoft Copilot. Intelligent agents are software agents that use AI to learn and improve, such as recommendation systems or chatbots. Then there are robotic agents, which are physical robots interacting with the real world, like self-driving cars or robots in factories. Finally, multi-agent systems involve groups of agents working together to solve bigger problems, such as in swarm robotics or complex computer networks. Agents are designed to operate independently, adapt to changes, and collaborate with other agents or humans to achieve their objectives. Their ability to perceive, analyze, and act makes them indispensable tools in the modern world, with the potential to revolutionize how we work and live.

One could envision a future where the most productive workers get their employers to custom train AIs that know a top knowledge worker's workstyle and adapt to changing needs, filling gaps in knowledge and anticipating tasks. This kind of personalized enterprise software would ideally follow the worker if they change jobs. One could imagine that if the AI was fully provided by the employer, the next employer would need to buy out the worker with the AI much like a sports agent would facilitate a buyout if a contract term is not over. The smartest knowledge workers would equip themselves with such a personalized productivity AI before they started any employment, perhaps training it throughout K-12 or early college years, or perhaps as a last prep three months before the first internship. In such a scenario, most AIs would have to be interoperable, otherwise it might not work or might not be compliant with an organization's intellectual property regime.

Why Are AI Agents Needed Now?

The increasing need for AI agents now stems from several converging factors in our rapidly evolving world. Firstly, we are experiencing an unprecedented explosion of data. The sheer volume of information generated daily far surpasses human processing capabilities, creating a critical need for intelligent systems that can sift through this "data deluge." AI agents are uniquely equipped to analyze these vast datasets, identify hidden patterns, and extract actionable insights, effectively acting as intelligent filters in an age of information overload. This ability is crucial for both individuals and organizations striving to make informed, data-driven decisions amid overwhelming noise.

Secondly, the complexity and scale of the problems we face are escalating globally. From intricate challenges like climate change and pandemics to the management of large-scale systems like global supply chains and energy grids, human capacity alone is often insufficient. AI agents offer the potential to model these complex systems, analyze intricate interactions, and simulate various scenarios, providing invaluable support in understanding these challenges and developing effective, scalable solutions. This capability is vital for tackling the interconnected and multifaceted issues of our modern world.

Finally, the drive for automation, efficiency, and enhanced user experiences further fuels the demand for AI agents. In a world demanding continuous operation and rapid response, AI agents can automate repetitive and time-consuming tasks, freeing up human workers for more strategic and creative endeavors. They can also operate 24/7, respond in real-time, and execute tasks at speeds far exceeding human capabilities, crucial in critical sectors like cybersecurity and emergency response. Furthermore, the expectation for personalized experiences is growing, and AI agents are instrumental in powering personalized services, recommendations, and user interfaces. Ultimately, AI agents are becoming increasingly indispensable because they offer the potential to navigate data overload, address complex problems, boost productivity, and enhance human capabilities, making them essential tools for thriving in our increasingly interconnected and demanding world.

How to Learn to Work with AI Agents?

Learning to effectively work with AI agents is becoming an increasingly valuable skill across many professions. The journey blends theoretical understanding with practical application, and the best approach can vary depending on your role and goals. A strong foundation in Artificial Intelligence fundamentals is key for everyone. This involves grasping core concepts like machine learning, deep learning, and the different types of AI agents, from simple rule-based systems to complex learning agents. Exploring online courses, university resources, textbooks, and reputable articles will provide this crucial underpinning. Focus on understanding how AI agents perceive data, learn from it, and ultimately make decisions—the core principles that drive their behavior. Building upon this foundational knowledge with practical skills is equally important. Learning Python, often considered the primary language of AI, and becoming familiar with key AI libraries like TensorFlow and PyTorch, will allow you to experiment and build. Working through tutorials and coding exercises is invaluable for solidifying your grasp of these tools.

The ideal learning path, however, becomes more nuanced when considering specific professional roles. For executives, the focus should be on strategic understanding and application. They need to grasp the capabilities and limitations of AI agents to inform business strategy, identify opportunities for implementation within their organizations, and understand the broader competitive landscape shaped by AI. While deep technical coding may not be necessary, familiarity with AI concepts, successful case studies, and the ethical considerations surrounding AI deployment is critical. Educators, on the other hand, require a different kind of expertise. They need to understand AI agents to prepare students for an AI-driven future. This involves not only learning about AI agent technology itself, but also how to integrate AI literacy into curricula, teach ethical considerations, and guide students in understanding AI's impact on various disciplines. Practical experience might involve exploring educational AI tools and designing learning activities around agent-based systems.

For entrepreneurs, learning to work with AI agents is often about identifying and capitalizing on opportunities. They need to understand how AI agents can solve real-world problems and create new business ventures. This requires a blend of technical understanding, business acumen, and creative problem-solving. Experimenting with AI tools, understanding development lifecycles, and potentially prototyping agent-based solutions will be key. Students who are just starting their journey should prioritize building a solid technical foundation. This means focusing on programming skills, mathematics relevant to AI, and core AI concepts. Engaging in hands-on projects, contributing to open-source AI projects, and seeking internships in AI-related fields will be invaluable for developing practical expertise and launching a career in this domain. Finally, regulators face the critical task of understanding AI agents to develop appropriate policies and ethical frameworks. They need to grasp the technology's capabilities and potential risks, understand issues of bias, fairness, and transparency, and engage with experts and stakeholders to create effective and responsible governance. Their learning should focus on understanding the technical landscape, ethical implications, and societal impacts of AI agents, rather than deep technical implementation.

In her book, *How To Think With AI: A Simple Guide to Boost Your Brain Power, Creativity, and Performance* (2025), digital transformation strategist Alison McCauley claims early adopters weave AI tools into their daily lives, using them to test ideas, expand their thinking, and tackle complex challenges. She illustrates how these technologies have moved from isolated tools to integral partners in our cognitive processes. She urges individuals and organizations to develop a mindset that embraces this symbiotic relationship. Regardless of your specific role, staying engaged with the AI agent community and continuously updating your knowledge is crucial. The field is rapidly evolving, and lifelong learning is essential to keep pace with advancements. Participate in online forums, attend workshops and conferences, and follow research in the field to stay informed and connected. And importantly, as you delve into AI agents, always consider the ethical and societal implications of these powerful technologies. Educators across sectors need to collaborate in creating learning environments and training programs that foster not only technical proficiency but also critical thinking and ethical awareness.

How to Teach About AI Agents?

The education and training landscape for AI agents requires a comprehensive global approach spanning academic institutions and diverse industry sectors. In formal education, the journey begins in K-12, where educators worldwide can introduce fundamental AI concepts through accessible platforms like Scratch and Arduino, focusing on basic programming and robotics. This foundation extends into higher education, where institutions such as MIT in the United States, Oxford University in the United Kingdom, ETH Zurich in Switzerland, and Tsinghua University in China offer specialized degrees in Artificial Intelligence, incorporating advanced topics like machine learning, natural language processing, and multi-agent systems.

For effective instruction, educators should combine theoretical foundations with practical applications, using industry-relevant examples such as manufacturing robots, autonomous warehouse systems, and customer service interfaces. The curriculum should emphasize hands-on projects where students can build simple reactive agents or experiment with goal-based systems in simulated environments. Additionally, incorporating interdisciplinary perspectives from computer science, ethics, and sociology helps students understand the broader societal implications of AI technologies across different cultural and economic contexts.

Industry-specific training programs have emerged to address distinct sector needs. In manufacturing, professionals require specialized training in robotic process automation, predictive maintenance systems, and smart factory operations. The healthcare sector focuses on AI applications in diagnostic systems and patient-care automation, while financial services emphasize AI-driven risk assessment and fraud detection systems. Organizations like Siemens, through their Digital Academy, and Samsung's Global Innovation Centers offer targeted training programs for their respective industries, while global certification providers such as IBM and Google provide industry-recognized credentials adaptable to various sectors.

The integration of AI agents into different industries necessitates role-specific training approaches. Manufacturing floor operators need hands-on experience with collaborative robots and automated quality control systems, while logistics professionals require expertise in warehouse automation and autonomous delivery systems. In contrast, healthcare professionals focus on AI-assisted diagnostic tools and patient monitoring systems, and financial analysts work with AI-powered risk assessment and trading platforms. Online platforms offering specialized courses—such as Google's AI and Machine

Learning Crash Courses, Microsoft's AI Business School, and Coursera's industry-specific AI specializations—provide accessible options for ongoing professional development across these diverse sectors.

This comprehensive framework is supported by international collaborative initiatives between academic institutions and industry partners. For example, the European Institute of Innovation and Technology's Digital Education programs partner with leading companies to develop AI curricula tailored to specific industry needs. Similarly, Singapore's SkillsFuture initiative collaborates with global technology companies to provide AI training programs aligned with industry requirements. This integration of formal education, industry-specific training, and international collaboration creates a robust ecosystem for preparing individuals to excel in an AI-driven global economy.

Cascading Effects of AI Agents on the *Platinum Workforce*

The integration of AI agents into the workplace represents one of the most significant technological transformations in modern business history. This transformation is creating ripple effects throughout organizations, industries, and economies, fundamentally reshaping how work is performed and how value is created. At the operational level, AI agents are driving significant changes in job composition and skill requirements. While routine and repetitive tasks across sectors are increasingly automated, from manufacturing assembly lines to financial data processing, this automation is simultaneously creating new opportunities. Organizations are establishing roles focused on AI system management, training, and oversight. For instance, manufacturing facilities now employ AI systems specialists alongside traditional machine operators, while financial institutions are creating positions for AI risk assessment managers who oversee automated trading systems.

The skill landscape is evolving in response to these changes, with a clear shift toward higher-order capabilities. Traditional technical skills are being augmented with AI literacy requirements across all organizational levels. Frontline workers need to understand how to interact with AI systems effectively, while managers must develop competencies in AI strategy and implementation. This evolution extends beyond technical capabilities—there is growing emphasis on uniquely human skills such as critical thinking, creative problem-solving, and complex decision-making that complement AI capabilities rather than compete with them.

The productivity implications of AI agent integration are substantial but complex. Organizations implementing AI systems often report significant efficiency gains—for example, customer service centers using AI-powered chatbots can handle higher volumes of inquiries while reducing response times. However, these gains come with important considerations regarding workforce transition and adaptation. Companies must carefully manage the human side of AI integration, ensuring that productivity improvements don't come at the cost of employee engagement and well-being. The economic and social implications of this transformation extend beyond individual organizations. While AI agents are driving innovation and creating new economic opportunities, there are legitimate concerns about workforce displacement and income inequality. Organizations and policymakers must address these challenges through comprehensive workforce development programs and policies that ensure the benefits of AI integration are broadly distributed. This includes investing in retraining programs, creating clear career transition pathways, and developing frameworks for ethical AI deployment that consider impacts on workforce diversity and inclusion.

Looking ahead, the success of AI integration will largely depend on how organizations manage these cascading effects. The most effective approaches will likely be those that view AI agents not as replacements for human workers, but as tools to augment human capabilities. This perspective shifts the focus from job displacement to job evolution, emphasizing the need for continuous learning and adaptation. Organizations that can effectively balance technological advancement with workforce development while addressing ethical considerations will be best positioned to thrive in this evolving landscape.

From a global perspective, different regions and industries are experiencing these effects at varying rates and intensities. Manufacturing-heavy economies might face more immediate pressure for workforce adaptation, while service-based economies might see more gradual but equally significant changes. This variation underscores the importance of developing flexible, context-specific strategies for managing AI integration while maintaining a commitment to responsible innovation and workforce development.

Societal Impact If AI Agents Become Commonplace

The widespread adoption of AI agents in the workforce is poised to have a profound impact not only on how we work but also on society as a whole. As AI becomes commonplace, we can expect a significant transformation of job roles across various industries. Many repetitive and mundane tasks will be automated, allowing employees to focus on more strategic, creative, and high-value activities. This shift will lead to the evolution of existing job roles and the creation of new ones, particularly in AI governance, ethics, and system design. Simultaneously, AI agents will enhance productivity and efficiency by streamlining workflows, improving decision-making processes, and enabling businesses to scale operations more easily. However, this transition will necessitate continuous learning and skill development for employees, with organizations needing to invest in reskilling programs to help their workforce adapt to new technologies and work alongside AI agents effectively.

The integration of AI agents into the workforce will have far-reaching societal implications. On one hand, it has the potential to improve employee experiences by automating routine tasks and allowing workers to engage in more meaningful work. AI tools can provide valuable insights to aid decision-making and improve productivity without adding complexity. On the other hand, the widespread use of AI raises concerns about job displacement, privacy, and the ethical use of AI in the workplace. These challenges will require careful navigation by organizations, policymakers, and society at large to ensure transparent and responsible AI integration. The impact of AI will likely extend beyond the workplace, influencing education systems, social structures, and economic policies as societies adapt to this technological shift.

As AI agents become more prevalent, their influence will be felt across various industries and sectors of society. In retail, AI is expected to enhance marketing strategies, optimize pricing, and improve supply chain management. The finance sector will see improvements in financial planning and analysis, while manufacturing will benefit from optimized maintenance and increased efficiency. In healthcare, AI agents could streamline patient care and assist in diagnostics, potentially improving health outcomes on a broader scale. However, the societal impact of AI extends beyond these specific industries. It may lead to changes in income distribution, job markets, and social mobility, potentially exacerbating or mitigating existing inequalities depending on how it is implemented and regulated. As we move forward, it will be crucial for organizations, governments, and individuals to work together to harness the benefits of AI while addressing its challenges, ensuring a balanced and sustainable AI-driven future for both the workforce and society as a whole.

Downside of AI Agents

The widespread adoption of AI agents in the workforce presents several significant downsides. Job displacement is a primary concern, with recent, and widelyi reported data showing that 14 percent of workers have already experienced job loss due to AI and automation. This trend is expected to continue as AI's capability to automate tasks across various industries grows. In May 2023, AI directly contributed to 5 percent of all job losses in the United States, ranking as the seventh-largest contributor to job displacement.

Another major downside is the potential for bias and discrimination in AI systems. AI agents rely on data for decision-making, and if this data is biased, it can lead to unfair treatment of certain individuals or groups. This issue extends to critical areas such as hiring practices and loan approvals, potentially perpetuating existing inequalities. Additionally, the integration of AI raises significant privacy and security concerns. As AI systems handle vast amounts of sensitive data, there's an increased risk of data breaches and misuse of personal information.

Lastly, the implementation of AI agents can lead to unintended consequences and ethical dilemmas. There's a risk of AI goals misaligning with human interests, potentially resulting in harmful outcomes. The concentration of power in the hands of a few AI-capable entities could exacerbate economic and social disruptions. Moreover, as AI takes over more complex tasks, there's a concern that it might "free" workers from the most fulfilling parts of their jobs, leaving them with less engaging work in highly surveilled, algorithmically managed workplaces.

Conclusion

In 1969, Peter Drucker in *The Age of Discontinuity* identified key forces reshaping the economic landscape: technological explosion, a globalizing world economy, new sociopolitical realities, and a knowledge-based workforce driven by mass education. We still live in this age of discontinuity, now fueled by rapid technological advancements, digital transformation, and global interconnectedness. AI agents are a prime example, promising a symbiotic, yet potentially disruptive, shift in workforce dynamics. While offering immense potential, this integration requires careful management to avoid negative outcomes like job displacement, bias, and safety issues. The current period of transition should be used to proactively adapt education, organizational practices, and governmental policies, ensuring a smoother integration of AI agents and mitigating potential downsides.

CHAPTER 12

MAKER

Shop Class as Soulcraft: An Inquiry into the Value of Work (2010) by Matthew B. Crawford questions the educational imperative of turning everyone into a knowledge worker. He claims this is often is based on a misguided separation of thinking from doing. Crawford explores craftsmanship. He feels we can and should live concretely even in an ever more abstract world. He argues there is immense value in having a craft, in knowing how to manipulate the physical environment. The person who works with his or her hands submits to standards inherent in the work itself: the lights either turn on or they don't, the toilet flushes or it doesn't, the motorcycle roars or sputters. The craftsperson who works with tangible materials faces an unforgiving arbiter: the physical world itself. Unlike abstract disciplines where interpretation may cloud outcomes, manual work delivers immediate and incontrovertible feedback—the electrical circuit either completes or fails, the plumbing system either maintains proper flow or malfunctions, the engine either runs smoothly or sputters.

What Are Maker Skills?

Maker skills encompass a diverse set of abilities, competencies, and skills that involve creating, building, innovating, and inventing. Contemporary Makers use a combination of traditional craftsmanship, modern technology, and creative problem-solving. They go beyond simple technical proficiency and emphasize hands-on learning, problem-solving, and a creative approach to making things. A Maker has a playful and inquisitive approach to learning, embracing trial-and-error and finding creative solutions to challenges. Typically, a Maker works with others to share ideas, provide feedback, and learn from each other. A Maker might be participating in maker spaces, hackathons, or online communities to share ideas and collaborate. In fact, these skills are central to the Maker Movement, a cultural trend that emphasizes hands-on learning, DIY

FIGURE 12.1 Maker skills in the age of AI.

(do-it-yourself) projects, and the sharing of knowledge and resources. In *The Maker Movement Manifesto* (2013), Mark Hatch, CEO and cofounder of TechShop, explores the world of crafters, hackers, and tinkerers where "ordinary people have devised extraordinary products."[1] The idea of the Fab Lab was pioneered at MIT, by MIT Center for Bits and Atoms Director Neil Gershenfeld, and Mel King, a former MIT adjunct professor. Now, there are Fab Labs all over the world, around 2,500 of them at last count, in some 125 countries.

Maker skills empower individuals to turn ideas into tangible products, prototypes, or solutions, often using tools ranging from simple hand tools to advanced digital fabrication technologies. Contributing to open-source projects and sharing designs, code, or tools with the global maker community is another example of the Maker impetus.

Key maker skills traditionally refer to hands-on craftsmanship. Think of woodworking, metalworking, sewing or textile arts, or ceramics and pottery. Nowadays, it also refers to digital fabrication such as 3D printing, laser cutting, CNC machining, vinyl cutting, computer-aided design (CAD) software, as well as understanding basic electronics and coding principles to bring ideas to life. Going forward, it increasingly refers to advanced manufacturing practices such as circuit design, microcontroller programming, sensor integration,

---

1 Hatch 2013

and robotics. It might also refer to creating interactive games or simulations. Another related practice is Design Thinking, applying a human-centered approach to solve problems and innovate (Dragičević, Vladova, and Ullrich 2023).

Examples of Makers include Product Designers combining design thinking with digital fabrication skills to create innovative and user-centered products, Entrepreneurs utilizing Maker skills to develop and prototype new products and services for their businesses, and Educators integrating Maker activities into the classroom to foster creativity, problem-solving, and critical thinking skills among students. A few years ago, I used my maker skills to create an educational board game to teach Existential Risk at Stanford. The students expressed high engagement levels and wanted to play the game many times without me suggesting it.

Why Are Maker Skills Needed Now?

In the future of work, there will be increased demand for individuals with Maker skills. Maker skills are already crucial for entrepreneurs and innovators who are developing new products, services, and businesses. In a situation where innovation becomes even more intense, important, and pervasive, Maker skills differentiate workers. Whether physical, digital, or hybrid in nature, the hands-on experience gained through making fosters critical thinking, problem-solving, and a deeper understanding of how things work. Maker skills encourage a lifelong learning approach, as individuals continuously learn and experiment with new tools and technologies. Maker skills can empower individuals to create solutions to local challenges, contribute to their communities, and express their creativity.

Makers can help transform discarded or unused materials into new products, upcycling or recycling them. Mastering a wide range of tools, from hand tools (e.g., hammers, saws) to power tools (e.g., drills, sanders) and digital tools (e.g., 3D printers, laser cutters) is always useful in the design and prototyping process. Having the mindset of always being willing to learn new skills and techniques to tackle diverse projects and challenges makes you adaptable and agile in a changing workplace.

Examples of Maker projects would be 3D-Printed Prosthetics, Smart Home Devices, DIY Furniture, Wearable Technology, Robotic Pets, Renewable Energy Projects, or Art Installations, all of which could entail a combination of hands-on, digital, and hybrid techniques and approaches. Maker skills are important empowerment tools. Makers drive innovation by experimenting with new technologies, materials, and processes. Hands-on learning through making fosters creativity, critical thinking, and even STEM (science, technology, engineering, and math) skills. Maker spaces and events create opportunities for collaboration, knowledge sharing, and social connection. Maker skills can lead to entrepreneurship, with individuals creating and selling their products or services.

How to Learn Maker Skills?

You can develop maker skills by joining a Maker space where you can access tools, equipment, and a community of makers to learn and collaborate. All in all there are at least 5,500 makerspaces, fab labs, and hackerspaces worldwide. You can take Online Courses on platforms like Coursera, Udemy, or YouTube that offer tutorials on topics like 3D printing, electronics, and coding. You can participate in Hackathons are increasingly popular at universities (as student-centered innovation marathons), at libraries (for community and technical empowerment), and by nonprofits (to build practical solutions for social challenges). You can also start with beginner-friendly kits for electronics, robotics, or crafting. You can learn from open-source projects and explore platforms like GitHub, Instructables, or Thingiverse for inspiration and guidance.

The essential skills needed to be a Maker include hands-on skills (using manual and digital tools), computational skills, teamwork, problem-solving, and digital literacy. My prediction would be that within a decade, most educational institutions, from K-12 to community colleges, universities, and trade schools, will integrate Maker skills into curricula, preparing students for a future where creativity and technical skills are paramount.

The integration of AI, IoT, and advanced fabrication techniques will expand the possibilities for makers, enabling them to tackle increasingly complex challenges. It is never too late to become a Maker.

How to Teach Maker Skills?

You can encourage open-ended exploration with materials like LEGOs, electronics kits, art supplies, and natural objects. Makerspaces are dedicated spaces typically equipped with tools and materials like 3D printers, laser cutters, sewing machines, and electronics workbenches. They are like the lab of a gentleman scientist in the eighteenth century, with all the tools to learn, experiment, and explore. Whether in a classroom, maker space, or community setting, fostering maker skills cultivates creativity, collaboration, and a lifelong love of learning. It is typically best to focus on engaging projects that allow students to define their own challenges, experiment, and iterate. You can encourage students to use their Maker skills to address local community needs, such as building assistive devices, creating sustainable solutions, or addressing environmental challenges. You can encourage brainstorming, sketching, and rapid prototyping to explore and refine ideas. It is important to emphasize the importance of testing prototypes, gathering feedback, and iteratively improving designs. Encourage experimentation and risk-taking, and emphasize that learning from failures is an essential part of the creative process.

Cascading Effects of Makers in the *Platinum Workforce*

Many maker skills involve complex physical manipulation, tacit knowledge gained through practice, and creative problem-solving that's deeply tied to material properties and physical constraints. Think of a woodworker who can feel when the grain isn't quite right, or a ceramicist who knows exactly how much pressure to apply while throwing a pot. These skills are challenging for AI to replicate since they involve embodied knowledge and real-world interaction.

Makers will play a key role in the future of work, particularly because they embody the spirit of experimentation. Regardless of the demand for expertise, and the progress of AI, no expert or system, or team of both can afford to refrain from experimenting with possible solutions and discuss desired impacts. Makers contribute to visualizing and unearthing possibilities. Makers will also tend to collaborate across borders, sharing knowledge and resources to solve global challenges.

As AI automates routine tasks and augments human capabilities, Maker skills will become increasingly valuable for driving innovation, fostering adaptability, and creating meaningful work. We will increasingly have to invent our own careers, jobs, projects, and tasks, many times over. Maker skills will enable workers to use AI as a tool for enhancing creativity and productivity, rather than viewing it as a threat. Makers will leverage AI for tasks like design optimization, data analysis, and prototyping, while focusing on the creative and strategic aspects of projects. AI tools are increasingly being used in creative fields, including design and prototyping, which are core to many maker activities. The combination of Maker skills and AI has the potential to foster breakthroughs in fields like robotics, healthcare, and sustainable design. AI can assist in brainstorming, generating variations, and exploring novel concepts. AI can handle mundane tasks (like 3D modeling or basic coding) freeing up Makers to focus on higher-level creativity and problem-solving. Makers can work alongside AI systems, providing human oversight, critical thinking, and creative input to guide and refine AI-generated outputs. Many makers are already incorporating AI tools into their workflows, blurring the line between human and AI-created work.

Rather than competing with AI, Makers can focus on areas where human ingenuity, empathy, and artistry are irreplaceable, ensuring their continued relevance and impact in an AI-driven world. AI often lacks the human touch when it comes to original thinking, problem-solving, and intuition. Skills like craftsmanship, art, and design often involve an element of personal expression or connection. People value the stories, intentions, and processes behind handmade or uniquely crafted items, which adds a layer of value that machines can't replicate. Makers typically need to explain their design decisions, incorporating critical thinking that goes beyond AI's current capabilities. Makers typically need to explain their design decisions, incorporating critical thinking that goes beyond AI's current capabilities. Maker spaces often foster in-person collaboration, which AI cannot fully replicate. Makers have a shot at developing AI-resistant skills, at least skills that stay a notch ahead, or at least adapt fast and smartly each time AI turns a corner.

However, the key might not be resistance to AI, but rather finding ways to work symbiotically with it—using AI to handle repetitive tasks or generate initial designs while applying human judgment, creativity, and physical skill to create unique, high-quality pieces. Makers can moreover contribute to the development of AI tools themselves, shaping the future of AI and ensuring that it aligns with human values and needs. Makers will tackle complex, interdisciplinary challenges by combining hands-on skills with AI-driven insights. While AI can help optimize and automate manufacturing, there will always be a need for human expertise in maintaining and repairing complex systems. For example, Maker skills will be essential for operating and maintaining advanced manufacturing systems, such as AI-driven 3D printers and CNC machines. Makers, especially those with technical skills like electronics repair, may find themselves in demand for keeping AI-powered systems running smoothly.

The Impact Once Maker Skills Are Commonplace?

Once Maker skills become commonplace, the impact will be transformative across individuals, communities, industries, and society as a whole. The widespread adoption of these skills—ranging from hands-on craftsmanship to digital fabrication and creative problem-solving—will empower people to innovate, solve problems, and create sustainable solutions. Widespread Maker skills across the workforce would increase innovation and entrepreneurship, enhance resilience, and reimagine education. In such a scenario, industries will drive economic growth through localized and sustainable practices.

Individuals will have the skills to design, build, and repair things themselves, reducing dependence on mass-produced goods. Maker skills foster creativity, enabling people to turn ideas into reality and experiment with new solutions. The maker movement will not only transform how we create and consume but also foster a culture of collaboration, inclusivity, and environmental stewardship. By embracing maker skills, society can build a future that is more innovative, equitable, and sustainable.

The Downside of Maker Skills

While Maker skills offer numerous benefits, such as fostering creativity, innovation, and self-reliance, there are also potential downsides and challenges associated with their widespread adoption. DIY projects and small-scale production may lack the rigorous quality control and safety standards of professionally manufactured goods. Inadequate training or improper use of tools and materials can lead to accidents or injuries. Developing and honing maker skills—whether it's woodworking, electronics, or crafting—can be time-consuming. With so many potential skills to learn and tools to use, it's easy to feel overwhelmed by the sheer number of options.

An overemphasis on tangible, physical making can sometimes overshadow the development of abstract thinking and problem-solving skills that are also crucial in the modern world. Integrating maker education into existing curricula can be difficult, as educators must align hands-on activities with academic standards and learning objectives.

Access to tools, materials, and quality education in Maker spaces can be unevenly distributed, potentially exacerbating existing inequalities. Not all students have equal access to maker spaces, quality instruction, and the resources needed to develop these skills. High-quality tools or specialized equipment can add up quickly, making it a financial commitment for hobbyists or even small business owners.

Working with tools and machinery can involve safety risks. Proper safety training and supervision are crucial to prevent accidents and injuries. The production and disposal of materials used in making can have environmental impacts. For example, plastic waste from 3D printing or using chemicals in finishing techniques can have an environmental footprint. It's important to encourage sustainable practices and minimize waste in maker spaces. Maker skills can require significant learning and trial-and-error. Some techniques or technologies might be difficult to master, leading to frustration and setbacks along the way.

The Maker Movement can sometimes be co-opted by corporations, leading to the commercialization of maker culture and the exploitation of makers' ideas.

To address these downsides, one must emphasize the development of critical thinking, problem-solving, and communication skills alongside technical skills. There must be equitable access to maker spaces, tools, and resources for all learners, regardless of their socioeconomic background. The use of recycled materials, energy-efficient tools, and responsible waste management practices must be encouraged. Makers must receive fair compensation and recognition their intellectual property rights must be protected.

Conclusion

Maker skills are not just about building things, they are increasingly essential for creativity, innovation, and success, and will likely be the backbone of the human contribution in the *Platinum Workforce*, which will otherwise consist of AIs, infrastructure, machines, sensors, and more.

References

Dragičević, Nikolina, Gergana Vladova, and Andre Ullrich. 2023. "Design Thinking Capabilities in the Digital World: A Bibliometric Analysis of Emerging Trends." *Frontiers in Education* 7 (January): 1012478.

Hatch, Mark. 2013. *The Maker Movement Manifesto: Rules for Innovation in the New World of Crafters, Hackers, and Tinkerers.* New York, NY: McGraw-Hill Professional.

CHAPTER 13

PSYCHO-RESILIENCER

What Are Psycho-Resilience Skills?

Psycho-resilience represents the capacity to effectively navigate and adapt to life's challenges, whether they manifest as stress, trauma, adversity, uncertainty, or significant life changes. This dynamic skill set involves the interplay of emotional regulation, cognitive flexibility, social support, and self-care practices. What distinguishes resilient individuals is not just their ability to recover from setbacks but their capacity to maintain a growth mindset that transforms adversity into opportunity.

The most resilient professionals demonstrate several key characteristics: they maintain emotional equilibrium under pressure, adapt their thinking to changing circumstances, and proactively build support networks. They prioritize well-being through consistent self-care practices and possess the cognitive agility to make sound decisions even in high-pressure situations. Importantly, psycho-resilience isn't an innate trait but rather a set of skills that can be developed and strengthened through deliberate practice (Figure 13.1).

Professions Requiring High Levels of Psycho-Resilience

Certain professions inherently demand high levels of psycho-resilience due to the nature of their work. These include first responders, healthcare professionals, military personnel, entrepreneurs, and social workers and counselors. Each of these roles involves navigating high-stress environments, making critical decisions under pressure, and often dealing with the emotional toll of their work.

Firefighters, police officers, and paramedics consistently face high-stress situations, trauma, and life-threatening dangers. Their ability to remain calm under pressure, make critical decisions quickly, and recover emotionally after

FIGURE 13.1 Psycho-resilience skills.

traumatic events is a testament to their remarkable resilience. For instance, firefighters often work in life-threatening conditions, requiring not only physical endurance but also emotional stability to cope with the aftermath of traumatic incidents.

Doctors, nurses, and other healthcare workers often witness suffering and deal with the emotional and physical demands of caring for patients. Their resilience allows them to maintain their composure, provide compassionate care, and cope with the inherent stresses of their profession. The COVID-19 pandemic highlighted the extraordinary resilience of healthcare workers, who worked tirelessly under extreme conditions, often at great personal risk.

Soldiers, sailors, airmen, and marines face the constant threat of danger, witness traumatic events, and often experience significant periods of separation from loved ones. Their resilience allows them to adapt to challenging environments, maintain their mental and physical fortitude, and effectively carry out their duties. The military training regimen is designed to build resilience, preparing personnel for the rigors of combat and the psychological challenges of deployment.

Starting and running a business involves numerous challenges, including financial uncertainty, competition, and the risk of failure. Successful entrepreneurs often demonstrate high levels of resilience by overcoming obstacles, learning from setbacks, and persevering through difficult times. For example, Elon Musk (1971–) has faced numerous setbacks in his ventures, including failed rocket launches and production delays, yet he continues to push forward with his ambitious goals.

Social Workers and Counselors work with individuals facing a wide range of challenges, including poverty, abuse, and mental health issues. Their resilience allows them to maintain their own well-being while providing support and guidance to others in need. Social workers often operate in high-stress environments, dealing with cases of abuse, neglect, and trauma, requiring a high degree of emotional resilience.

Historical Examples of Extreme Psycho-Resilience

Throughout history, there have been individuals who exemplify extreme psycho-resilience, demonstrating the capacity to maintain hope and purpose in the face of unimaginable adversity. These individuals not only survived but thrived, contributing to something larger than themselves even when their own freedom and well-being were at risk. The lives of individuals like Nelson Mandela, Anne Frank, Elon Musk, Louie Zamperini, Oprah Winfrey, Tony Robbins, Ingvar Kamprad, Viktor Frankl, Winston Churchill, Steve Jobs, and Jack Ma offer profound lessons in psycho-resilience. These figures faced extraordinary challenges—imprisonment, war, poverty, failure, and systemic discrimination—yet they not only survived but thrived, leaving lasting legacies. Their stories reveal key strategies for building resilience that can be applied across various contexts, including education, parenting, mid-career transitions, industrial work, and teaching. Below, we explore the lessons from their lives and provide tailored strategies for different groups.

Nelson Mandela (1918–2013): Imprisoned for 27 years for his anti-apartheid activism, Mandela endured immense hardship and suffering. Yet, he emerged from prison with an unwavering commitment to his beliefs and ultimately led South Africa toward a more just and equitable future. His unwavering hope, ethical grounding, and dedication to reconciliation in the face of immense adversity exemplify extreme psycho-resilience. Mandela's ability to forgive his oppressors and work toward a unified South Africa is a testament to his extraordinary resilience.

Anne Frank (1929–1945): Confined to a secret annex for two years during the Holocaust, Anne Frank faced constant fear and uncertainty. Despite the horrific circumstances, she maintained a remarkable spirit of hope and humanity, documented her experiences with profound insight in her diary, and became a symbol of resilience and the enduring power of the human spirit. Her diary, which has been read by millions worldwide, continues to inspire people to find hope in the darkest of times.

Elon Musk (1971–): Known for his ambitious and often unconventional ventures, Musk has faced numerous setbacks, including failed rocket launches, production delays, and public criticism. Despite these challenges, he consistently demonstrates resilience by adapting, learning from failures, and persevering toward his long-term goals. His ability to navigate high-risk, high-reward projects and maintain a long-term vision showcases his exceptional resilience. Musk's ventures, such as SpaceX and Tesla, have revolutionized industries and pushed the boundaries of what is possible, demonstrating the power of entrepreneurial resilience.

Louie Zamperini (1917–2014): An Olympic runner who survived 47 days at sea and Japanese POW camps, Zamperini's key traits include adaptability, mental toughness, and forgiveness. His business relevance lies in his successful public speaking career and the development of leadership training programs. Zamperini's story of survival and redemption is a powerful example of resilience in the face of extreme adversity.

Oprah Winfrey (1954–): Faced significant adversity early in life, including poverty and sexual abuse. She overcame these challenges to build a media empire, becoming a powerful voice for women and a philanthropist. Her resilience is evident in her ability to navigate complex business landscapes, build strong relationships, and maintain a positive impact on society despite facing numerous obstacles. Through her media empire, Oprah not only redefined the landscape of talk shows but also became a global symbol of resilience, empathy, and empowerment.

Tony Robbins (1960–): An American author, coach, and speaker, Robbins overcame a challenging childhood and a rare hormone disorder called acromegaly to develop a successful career as a life coach and motivational speaker. He faced numerous obstacles, including personal struggles and public criticism, but he consistently demonstrates resilience by adapting his approach, learning from his experiences, and maintaining a positive impact on the lives of others. His story emphasizes the importance of personal growth, self-belief, and the ability to overcome adversity to achieve one's full potential.

Ingvar Kamprad (1926–2018): The founder of IKEA, Kamprad overcame dyslexia, multiple business failures, and intense criticism. His key traits include innovative problem-solving, resilient leadership, and adaptability. Kamprad's business relevance lies in his ability to build a global retail empire and pioneer the flat-pack furniture concept. His story is a testament to the power of resilience and innovation in the face of adversity.

Viktor Frankl (1905–1997): A psychiatrist who survived Nazi concentration camps, Frankl developed logotherapy from his experiences. His key traits include a meaning-focused perspective, observational skills, and the ability to reframe adversity. Frankl's business relevance lies in his creation of therapeutic frameworks, the founding of institutes, and his bestseller *Man's Search for Meaning*. His work continues to inspire individuals to find meaning in their suffering and to use that meaning as a source of resilience.

Winston Churchill (1874–1965): Best remembered for his indomitable spirit during World War II, Churchill faced military setbacks, political opposition, and the pervasive threat of annihilation. His unwavering determination became a beacon of hope, rallying a nation and demonstrating that resilience can serve as a powerful catalyst for collective action. Churchill's leadership during one of the darkest periods in history is a testament to the power of resilience in the face of overwhelming odds.

Steve Jobs (1955–2011): Jobs' career was marked by a series of dramatic ups and downs—from being ousted from the very company he cofounded, to returning and transforming Apple into one of the world's most innovative companies. His journey exemplifies the concept of Human+; despite facing public setbacks and personal challenges, Jobs continuously reinvented himself, combining visionary design with cutting-edge technology. His insistence on keeping technology aligned with human values set new standards for product development and innovation.

Jack Ma (1964–): The founder of Alibaba, Ma faced multiple rejections and setbacks early in his career. Despite being turned down for jobs and struggling to secure early investments, he maintained an unwavering belief in his vision. His persistence in the face of systemic challenges and an unyielding focus on digital innovation eventually led to the creation of one of the world's largest e-commerce platforms. Ma's journey is a testament to the importance of grit and risk aptitude in achieving success.

The Resilient Mind

The way these historical figures adapted to change and adversity was shaped by their different context, personalities, experiences, and preparation, and whilst we can be inspired, their strategies are hard to copy. Instead, we should empathize deeply based on reading and understanding the full story behind each trajectory.

Consider the contrasting yet complementary experiences of Viktor Frankl and Nelson Mandela. Frankl, imprisoned in Nazi concentration camps, developed logotherapy—a psychological approach centered on finding meaning even in profound suffering. His observation that those who maintained a sense of purpose were more likely to survive the camps' horrors demonstrates the protective power of meaning. Similarly, Nelson Mandela endured 27 years of imprisonment on Robben Island without surrendering his vision of a just, reconciled South Africa. Both men illuminate a crucial truth: when we connect our personal struggles to something larger than ourselves—whether societal transformation or alleviating others' suffering—we access wellsprings of endurance that transcend mere survival.

This capacity for adaptation reveals itself differently in the business realm. Elon Musk's trajectory shows a relentless ability to pivot after setbacks, whether surviving PayPal's leadership challenges or persisting through SpaceX's early launch failures. Steve Jobs, forcibly removed from Apple, transformed his exile into a period of creative reinvention at NeXT and Pixar before his triumphant return. Meanwhile, Ingvar Kamprad revolutionized furniture retail by conceptualizing flat-pack designs that solved real logistical problems while making stylish furnishings accessible to millions. These innovators demonstrate that adaptability—the willingness to reframe failure and reimagine possibilities—is often the differentiating factor between momentary success and lasting impact.

Beyond strategic resilience lies the profound psychological resilience facilitated by forgiveness. When Mandela invited his former jailers to his presidential inauguration, he demonstrated that forgiveness could be a practical tool for national healing rather than merely a personal virtue. Olympic runner Louie Zamperini, after enduring brutal treatment as a Japanese POW during World War II, ultimately found that forgiving his captors liberated him from the psychological prison that had persisted long after his physical liberation. These examples reveal how emotional intelligence—particularly the capacity to process and transcend resentment—creates space for recovery and renewal.

Hope and optimism function as essential cognitive frameworks for resilience, as evidenced by Anne Frank's extraordinary diary. Despite hiding from Nazi persecution, she wrote, "I still believe, in spite of everything, that people are truly good at heart." This radical hope persisted in the darkest circumstances imaginable. Winston Churchill similarly mobilized hope during Britain's darkest hours, famously declaring they would "never surrender" when rational assessment might have suggested capitulation. Their examples demonstrate that optimism isn't naive positivity but rather a deliberate focus on possibilities rather than limitations—a crucial distinction in cultivating resilience.

Complementing hope is the quality of grit—persistent effort toward challenging goals despite setbacks. Jack Ma's story exemplifies this virtue; rejected from dozens of jobs and unsuccessful in numerous ventures before founding Alibaba, he persevered through repeated failure. Oprah Winfrey overcame childhood poverty and trauma to build a media empire, maintaining her vision despite institutional barriers. Similarly, Tony Robbins transformed from a troubled youth living in poverty to becoming a transformative leader who has helped millions develop their own resilience. These individuals showcase how sustained commitment to long-term goals, rather than innate talent, often determines ultimate achievement.

Finally, sustainable resilience requires attention to self-care and mental well-being. Viktor Frankl's insights emphasize that while external circumstances may be beyond control, one's response remains a choice—highlighting the importance of internal psychological management. Oprah Winfrey has consistently advocated for self-care practices, demonstrating that resilience isn't merely about enduring hardship but about cultivating wellness practices that prevent burnout. Their examples remind us that incorporating mindfulness, reflection, and stress management into daily routines isn't self-indulgence but rather necessary maintenance for sustained resilience.

These historical examples, spanning diverse contexts from concentration camps to corporate boardrooms, converge on a fundamental truth: resilience isn't a fixed personality trait but rather a set of practices and perspectives that can be deliberately cultivated. By extracting specific lessons from these exemplars—finding meaning in adversity, adapting to changing circumstances, practicing forgiveness, maintaining hope, persevering through setbacks, and prioritizing mental well-being—we can develop our own capacity to transform challenges into opportunities for growth and meaningful achievement.

Resilience Strategies: A Practical Framework

Resilience—the capacity to recover from difficulties and adapt to changing circumstances—is increasingly recognized as a critical skill in our rapidly evolving world. Historical figures who overcame significant adversity offer valuable insights into developing this capability across different life contexts. This analysis examines tailored resilience approaches for five key demographic groups: students, parents, mid-career professionals, industrial workers, and educators. Across all demographic groups, five fundamental resilience principles emerge, each exemplified by notable historical figures (Table 13.1).

TABLE 13.1 Core resilience principles.

Principle	Historical Model	Core Concept
Purpose and Meaning	Viktor Frankl	Finding significance in challenges and connecting activities to deeper values
Adaptability	Steve Jobs/Elon Musk	Embracing change and viewing failure as a learning opportunity
Emotional Intelligence	Nelson Mandela	Developing empathy, conflict resolution skills, and emotional regulation
Optimism and Hope	Anne Frank/Winston Churchill	Maintaining positive outlook despite adversity and focusing on possibilities
Grit and Persistence	Jack Ma/Oprah Winfrey	Demonstrating determination and perseverance through difficult circumstances

Application across demographic groups

While the core principles remain consistent, their practical application varies significantly based on life stage and context. The following sections detail how each demographic group can effectively implement these resilience strategies.

Students

For students, resilience development centers on establishing healthy relationships with learning, failure, and peer interactions. Educational settings provide numerous opportunities to cultivate these capacities through both academic and extracurricular activities. Students can develop resilience by connecting their studies to personal passions or societal impact—finding meaning in their education as Viktor Frankl might suggest. They benefit from reframing failures as learning opportunities rather than definitive judgments of their abilities, following Elon Musk's example of embracing failure as part of the innovation process.

Social-emotional learning programs play a crucial role in developing emotional intelligence, teaching empathy and conflict-resolution skills exemplified by Nelson Mandela's approach to reconciliation. Maintaining hope through achievable goal-setting, as demonstrated by Anne Frank's remarkable optimism during hiding, helps students persist through challenges. Finally, extracurricular activities requiring sustained effort develop the grit exhibited by successful entrepreneurs like Jack Ma, who faced numerous rejections before achieving success.

Parents

Parents serve as primary resilience models for their children, making their approaches particularly influential in long-term development. Effective parenting for resilience involves demonstrating purpose-driven behavior aligned with personal values, as Nelson Mandela consistently did throughout his life. Parents can encourage adaptability by supporting children's exploration of diverse interests and helping them navigate new challenges, similar to Steve Jobs' philosophy of connecting seemingly unrelated experiences. Teaching conflict resolution through empathy and forgiveness, as demonstrated by Louie Zamperini after his wartime experiences, builds emotional resilience. Using positive language and solution-focused approaches to problems models Churchill's wartime optimism. Supporting children through difficult tasks without removing all obstacles helps develop the persistence demonstrated by figures like Oprah Winfrey in her career journey.

Demographic-Specific Applications

The remaining three groups—mid-career professionals, industrial workers, and educators—each require tailored approaches to resilience development based on their unique challenges (Table 13.2).

Mid-career professionals

Mid-career professionals face unique resilience challenges related to career transitions, organizational restructuring, and the need for continuous skill development. These individuals benefit from purpose-driven approaches that connect their work to broader organizational or societal goals—reflecting Viktor Frankl's emphasis on meaningful engagement. The rapidly evolving workplace demands adaptability similar to Elon Musk's willingness to pivot strategies when confronted with new information.

Emotional intelligence becomes particularly crucial in navigating complex workplace relationships and organizational politics, with Nelson Mandela's

TABLE 13.2 Demographic-specific applications.

Resilience Principle	Mid-Career Professionals	Industrial Workers	Educators
Purpose & Meaning	Align work with personal values and organizational goals	Connect individual contributions to team/organizational success	Help students connect learning to real-world applications
Adaptability	Continuously learn new skills and embrace technological advancements	Embrace training for new technologies and processes	Adopt new teaching methods and technologies
Emotional Intelligence	Build workplace relationships through active listening and conflict resolution	Resolve workplace conflicts through collaboration rather than blame	Create classroom environments promoting empathy and collaboration
Optimism & Hope	View career setbacks as temporary obstacles to long-term goals	Maintain positive attitude during challenging shifts by focusing on end goals	Use positive reinforcement and strength-focused approaches
Grit & Persistence	Persist through organizational changes by staying committed to personal vision	Set small, achievable goals for physically demanding tasks	Design appropriately challenging tasks requiring sustained effort

reconciliation approach offering valuable lessons in balancing assertiveness with empathy. Anne Frank's capacity to maintain hope in extreme circumstances parallels the optimism needed when facing career setbacks or rejections. Finally, Jack Ma's persistence through multiple failures before founding Alibaba exemplifies the grit required to navigate mid-career challenges and transitions.

Industrial workers

Workers in physically demanding or high-stress environments face distinctive resilience challenges related to safety, physical strain, and often limited decision-making autonomy. Finding meaning in contributions to team success, as Viktor Frankl might recommend, can create psychological sustainability in challenging conditions. Adapting to technological changes, as exemplified by Ingvar Kamprad's continuous innovation at IKEA, helps maintain relevance in evolving industrial contexts. Workplace conflict resolution through forgiveness rather than blame, modeled after Louie Zamperini's approach following his POW experience, builds essential team cohesion. Winston Churchill's unflagging optimism during Britain's darkest hours offers a template for maintaining positive focus during difficult shifts or projects. Tony Robbins' emphasis on incremental progress provides a framework for building grit when facing physically demanding tasks.

Educators

Educators occupy a unique position, needing both personal resilience and the capacity to foster resilience in students. Their approach must therefore be both inward and outward-facing. Teachers can implement Viktor Frankl's meaning-centered approach by helping students connect learning to real-world applications and personal goals. Modeling adaptability through embracing new teaching methods and technologies, as Steve Jobs advocated in his approach to innovation, prepares students for future change. Nelson Mandela's emphasis on emotional intelligence translates to creating classroom environments that value empathy, collaboration, and appropriate emotional expression. Anne Frank's capacity to maintain hope manifests in educators' use of positive reinforcement and strength-focused approaches. Finally, designing appropriately challenging tasks that require persistence while providing adequate support reflects Oprah Winfrey's balance of high expectations with encouragement.

Psycho-resilience implementation framework

The development of resilience represents a lifelong process rather than a fixed destination. By applying the five core principles—purpose and meaning, adaptability, emotional intelligence, optimism, and grit—with demographic-appropriate strategies, individuals across life stages can develop this essential capacity. Historical figures who demonstrated exceptional resilience provide both inspiration and practical models for developing these capabilities in contemporary contexts (Table 13.3).

The framework presented here offers a structured approach to resilience development that respects both universal principles and context-specific applications. Through assessment, strategy selection, implementation, reflection, and integration, individuals and organizations can systematically build resilience capacities that enable thriving rather than merely surviving during challenging circumstances.

The historical examples of extreme psycho-resilience offer timeless lessons in adaptability, purpose, emotional intelligence, hope, and grit. The best way to learn from them is to read their biographies and reflect deeply on how this might apply to yourself. By applying these lessons, individuals across all walks of life—students, parents, mid-career professionals, industrial workers, and educators—can build the resilience needed to thrive in an uncertain and rapidly changing world. Whether navigating personal challenges, career transitions, or societal upheavals, these strategies provide a roadmap for enduring and flourishing in the face of adversity. As we look to the future, cultivating psycho-resilience will be essential for creating a more adaptable, innovative, and compassionate workforce and society.

Why Is Psycho-Resilience Needed Now?

The contemporary professional landscape demands unprecedented levels of psychological resilience. As technological advancement accelerates and economic paradigms shift, workers face constant pressure to adapt to evolving job roles and master new skills. Resilience has become essential to navigating modern workplace complexities.

The COVID-19 pandemic has further highlighted the critical importance of psycho-resilience. Organizations and individuals have had to rapidly adapt to remote work environments, manage unprecedented stress levels, and maintain productivity amid global uncertainty. This experience has demonstrated

TABLE 13.3 Psycho-resilience implementation framework.

Phase	Activities	Outcomes
Assessment	• Identify specific resilience challenges • Evaluate existing resilience capacities • Determine priority resilience principles	Clear understanding of resilience needs and strengths
Strategy Selection	• Match demographic-appropriate strategies to identified challenges • Consider individual preferences and strengths • Establish measurable resilience goals	Tailored resilience development plan
Implementation	• Apply selected strategies in real-world contexts • Monitor response to challenges • Adjust approaches based on effectiveness	Active resilience skill development
Reflection	• Evaluate progress toward resilience goals • Identify lessons from setbacks and successes • Refine understanding of personal resilience patterns	Deeper self-awareness and resilience knowledge
Integration	• Incorporate effective strategies into daily routines • Share resilience approaches with peers/community • Develop capacity to teach resilience to others	Sustainable resilience practices and community impact

that resilience is not just an individual asset but a crucial organizational capability.

Psycho-resilience is not just an individual trait; it is also a critical organizational capability that enables businesses to thrive in the face of uncertainty, disruption, and rapid change. In today's volatile, uncertain, complex, and ambiguous (VUCA) world, organizations that prioritize and cultivate psycho-resilience are better equipped to navigate challenges, adapt to new realities, and sustain long-term success. This expanded discussion explores how psycho-resilience functions as an organizational capability, its benefits, and actionable strategies for building it within teams and workplaces.

Organizational psycho-resilience refers to the collective ability of a workforce to adapt, recover, and grow in the face of adversity. It involves creating a culture, systems, and practices that support emotional well-being, foster collaboration, and encourage continuous learning. Unlike individual resilience, which focuses on personal coping mechanisms, organizational resilience is about embedding resilience into the DNA of the organization so that it becomes a shared capability. Key components of organizational psycho-resilience include emotional well-being, adaptability, collaboration, purpose and meaning, and continuous learning.

Building psycho-resilience as an organizational capability involves fostering a culture of psychological safety, prioritizing mental health and well-being, promoting adaptability and continuous learning, building strong interpersonal connections, aligning organizational goals with employee values, developing resilient leadership, and implementing systems for crisis preparedness. For example, Google emphasizes psychological safety, encouraging employees to take risks and share ideas without fear of failure, while Microsoft, under CEO Satya Nadella, has embraced a growth mindset culture. Patagonia aligns its business practices with its mission of environmental sustainability, creating a strong sense of purpose among employees, and Salesforce invests heavily in employee development and mental health resources.

Measuring organizational psycho-resilience involves tracking key metrics such as employee engagement scores, retention and turnover rates, mental health metrics, innovation metrics, and crisis response effectiveness. High engagement levels indicate a resilient workforce, low turnover suggests that employees feel supported and valued, and effective crisis management demonstrates the organization's ability to recover from setbacks. These metrics help organizations assess their progress and identify areas for improvement in building and sustaining psycho-resilience.

Psycho-resilience as an organizational capability is essential for thriving in today's dynamic and unpredictable business environment. By fostering psychological safety, prioritizing mental health, promoting adaptability, building strong connections, aligning goals with values, developing resilient leadership, and implementing crisis preparedness systems, organizations can create a culture of resilience that benefits both employees and the business as a whole. Companies that invest in psycho-resilience will not only survive disruptions but also emerge stronger, more innovative, and better positioned for long-term success. In the Human+ era, where the synergy between human potential and technological advancement is paramount, organizational psycho-resilience will be a defining factor in shaping the future of work.

How to Learn Psycho-Resilience?

Learning psycho-resilience involves a structured approach combining practical techniques with ongoing practice. The process begins with developing self-awareness through mindfulness practices and stress management techniques. Regular meditation, deep breathing exercises, and body awareness practices help individuals recognize and regulate their emotional responses to stress.

Cognitive reframing represents another crucial learning component, teaching individuals to challenge negative thought patterns and develop more constructive interpretations of challenging situations. This skill proves particularly valuable in professional settings where pressure and setbacks are common.

Educational institutions and workplaces play vital roles in fostering resilience through structured programs. Effective initiatives include comprehensive workshops focusing on stress management and emotional intelligence, one-on-one mentorship programs pairing experienced professionals with emerging talent, support groups that facilitate peer learning and emotional support, and organizational cultures that prioritize psychological safety and professional development.

Psycho-resilience can be cultivated through a combination of mindfulness training, stress management workshops, and resilience coaching.

Self-learning involves cultivating a range of skills. Mindfulness practices, such as meditation, deep breathing exercises, and body scans, enhance self-awareness by increasing awareness of thoughts, emotions, and bodily sensations. Stress management techniques, including progressive muscle relaxation, guided imagery, and effective time management strategies, equip individuals with tools to navigate challenges and maintain equilibrium. Cognitive reframing techniques empower individuals to challenge negative thought patterns and replace them with more positive and realistic interpretations, fostering a more optimistic outlook. Developing emotional regulation skills involves identifying, understanding, and managing emotions in a healthy and constructive way, leading to improved emotional well-being. Finally, prioritizing self-care activities, such as exercise, healthy eating, adequate sleep, and engaging in hobbies and activities that bring joy and relaxation, is crucial for maintaining overall well-being and resilience.

Educational institutions and workplaces play crucial roles in fostering resilience. Participating in workshops and training programs that focus on building resilience, stress management, and emotional intelligence provides individuals with valuable skills and knowledge. Seeking guidance from mentors, coaches, or therapists offers personalized support and strategies for developing resilience. Joining support groups or communities where individuals can share experiences, learn from others, and gain encouragement facilitates a collective approach to building resilience. Furthermore, organizations can foster a culture of resilience by promoting psychological safety, providing resources for employee well-being, and offering opportunities for professional development and growth.

Tailored Strategies for Different Groups

While the general approaches to learning psycho-resilience are valuable, tailoring strategies to specific groups can enhance their effectiveness. Here's a breakdown of tailored strategies for various individuals:

Developing resilience in students involves fostering a growth mindset by encouraging a love for learning and emphasizing effort and progress over grades, teaching them to view mistakes as valuable learning opportunities. Introducing mindfulness exercises, relaxation techniques, and effective time management skills equips students with tools to cope with academic pressure. Encouraging positive self-talk helps them identify and challenge negative thoughts, replacing them with positive affirmations. Promoting healthy habits like exercise, proper sleep, and balanced nutrition contributes significantly to stress management and overall well-being. Finally, encouraging students to build strong support networks by connecting with peers, mentors, and family members provides a crucial foundation for emotional and social support.

Parents can cultivate resilience by practicing mindfulness techniques to manage stress and cultivate self-compassion in navigating the challenges of parenthood. Developing strong communication skills fosters healthy relationships with their children and partners. Learning and implementing positive parenting strategies not only build resilience in their children but also create a supportive family environment. Prioritizing self-care through stress-reduction techniques like exercise, relaxation, and carving out personal time is crucial for maintaining parental well-being. Finally, connecting with other parents to share experiences, gain support, and build a sense of community provides a valuable network for emotional and practical support.

For mid-career professionals, cultivating resilience involves a multifaceted approach. Defining clear career goals, identifying personal values, and creating a roadmap to achieve aspirations provide a strong foundation. Adaptability and flexibility are crucial, enabling professionals to navigate career transitions, embrace new challenges, and thrive in a constantly evolving work environment. Implementing stress management techniques and prioritizing work-life balance are essential for maintaining well-being and preventing burnout. Building a strong professional network and seeking mentorship from experienced individuals provides valuable support and guidance throughout the career journey. Finally, embracing continuous learning through professional development opportunities ensures that mid-career professionals remain relevant and adaptable in a rapidly changing world.

For industrial workers, cultivating resilience requires a multifaceted approach. Developing effective strategies to manage stress related to physically demanding work, long hours, and potential workplace hazards is crucial. Incorporating mindfulness and relaxation techniques into daily routines promotes mental well-being and reduces stress. Fostering strong teamwork and communication skills within the workplace creates a supportive and collaborative environment. Prioritizing physical health and safety practices, such as proper safety protocols and ergonomic considerations, prevents injuries and promotes overall well-being. Finally, encouraging a healthy work-life balance, allowing for adequate rest and leisure time, is essential to prevent burnout and maintain overall well-being.

For educators, cultivating resilience involves prioritizing their own well-being through mindfulness and emotional regulation techniques to manage stress and create a positive learning environment. Cultivating compassion and empathy enables them to connect with students on a deeper level and create a supportive classroom culture. Implementing strategies to foster resilience in students, such as growth mindset development and positive coping mechanisms, is crucial. Building strong relationships with colleagues, administrators, and parents creates a supportive network, while prioritizing self-care and well-being helps educators prevent burnout and maintain their passion for teaching.

How to Teach Psycho-Resilience?

Teaching psycho-resilience requires a multifaceted approach that combines theoretical understanding with practical application. Effective instruction begins with creating safe learning environments where individuals feel comfortable exploring their emotions and taking calculated risks. Instructors should model positive coping strategies and encourage open dialogue about challenges and solutions.

The teaching process should incorporate regular mental health and well-being modules integrated into existing training programs, providing participants with opportunities to learn and practice resilience skills. Practical exercises that allow individuals to apply resilience techniques in real-time, such as role-playing or simulations, are invaluable. Feedback mechanisms, whether through self-reflection, peer feedback, or instructor guidance, help individuals refine their coping strategies and identify areas for improvement. Creating opportunities for peer learning and support through group discussions, mentorship programs, or support groups fosters a sense of community and shared experience. Finally, regular assessment of participant progress and ongoing adjustment of teaching methods ensure that the training program remains relevant, effective, and responsive to individual needs.

Incorporating mental health and well-being modules in educational and corporate training programs is essential for teaching psycho-resilience. Creating a safe and supportive environment where individuals feel comfortable taking risks and exploring their emotions is crucial. Encouraging open communication, active listening, and empathy fosters a sense of psychological safety.

Modeling positive coping strategies through actions and interactions with others is also important. Demonstrating mindfulness practices, stress management techniques, and healthy emotional regulation can encourage others to observe and learn from these examples.

Cascading Effects of Psycho-Resilience on the Workforce of the Future

The implementation of strong psycho-resilience programs creates positive ripple effects throughout organizations. Resilient employees demonstrate greater adaptability to change, enhanced problem-solving capabilities, and improved relationship management skills. These individual improvements aggregate to create more innovative and adaptable organizations.

Organizations with resilient workforces typically experience increased innovation and creative problem-solving, as employees are better equipped to navigate challenges and explore new solutions. Higher employee engagement and satisfaction result from a supportive and empowering work environment that prioritizes well-being. Reduced turnover and associated costs, such as recruitment and training expenses, contribute to increased organizational stability and efficiency. Improved team collaboration and communication foster a more cohesive and productive work environment. Finally, a resilient workforce demonstrates greater organizational agility in responding to market changes, adapting quickly to new challenges and opportunities.

Psycho-resilience has profound cascading effects on the future of work, skills, and the workforce, shaping a more adaptable, innovative, and thriving professional landscape. Individuals equipped with psycho-resilience are better able to navigate the complexities and uncertainties of the future of work. They can adapt to evolving job roles, embrace technological advancements, and cope with the increasing demands of a dynamic work environment.

This adaptability fosters a workforce that is not only prepared for change but also capable of driving innovation and progress. Moreover, resilient individuals are more likely to develop essential skills such as critical thinking, problem-solving, and emotional intelligence, which are crucial for success in the future of work. They are also better equipped to manage stress, maintain well-being, and cultivate positive relationships with colleagues, fostering a more collaborative and supportive work environment.

The cascading effects of psycho-resilience extend beyond individual benefits, shaping a workforce that is more engaged, productive, and resilient as a whole. This collective resilience enables organizations to navigate challenges, adapt to change, and thrive in a rapidly evolving world. Ultimately, psycho-resilience empowers individuals, strengthens organizations, and shapes a future of work that is more human-centric, adaptable, and sustainable.

Workforce Impact When Psycho-Resilience Becomes Commonplace

As psycho-resilience becomes more prevalent in professional environments, organizations can expect to see transformative changes in their operations and culture. Teams demonstrate greater cohesion and effectiveness in managing complex challenges. Individual employees show improved capacity for personal growth and career development.

The broader implications of a resilient workforce extend beyond immediate organizational benefits. Enhanced organizational learning and knowledge transfer occur as employees are more open to feedback, willing to share their experiences, and actively seek to improve their skills. More effective change management processes arise as the workforce is better equipped to adapt to new challenges and embrace new ways of working. Improved customer relationships and service delivery result from a more engaged and empathetic workforce that can effectively address customer needs and build strong relationships. A stronger organizational culture emerges, characterized by shared values, trust, and a sense of collective purpose. Finally, better work-life integration for employees fosters a healthier and more sustainable work environment, leading to increased employee well-being and overall organizational success.

However, it's crucial to acknowledge that focusing solely on individual resilience shouldn't overshadow the need to address systemic workplace challenges. Organizations must balance developing employee resilience with creating supportive environments that minimize unnecessary stress and maximize opportunities for growth and success.

If psycho-resilience became commonplace, the impact on individuals, organizations, and society at large would be profound and far-reaching, leading to a world that is better equipped to navigate challenges, adapt to change, and thrive in the face of adversity.

For individuals, commonplace psycho-resilience would translate to significantly improved well-being, characterized by reduced stress, anxiety, and depression, leading to greater emotional stability and overall mental health. This enhanced emotional well-being would empower individuals with an increased capacity to learn from setbacks, adapt to change, and achieve personal goals. Moreover, stronger relationships would flourish, fostered by improved communication, empathy, and conflict-resolution skills, leading to deeper and more meaningful connections. Finally, individuals would experience greater self-awareness, gaining a deeper understanding of their own emotions, strengths, and limitations, enabling them to make more informed decisions and take more effective actions.

For organizations, widespread psycho-resilience would result in significant benefits. A workforce that is more engaged, adaptable, and able to navigate challenges would experience increased productivity and drive greater innovation. A healthier and more supportive work environment, characterized by reduced stress and burnout, would lead to lower turnover rates and increased employee satisfaction. Enhanced communication and interpersonal skills fostered by a resilient workforce would cultivate a more cohesive and collaborative work environment. Finally, a workforce equipped to embrace new technologies, processes, and market demands would demonstrate greater adaptability to change, leading to increased organizational agility and competitiveness.

For society, commonplace psycho-resilience would have profound and far-reaching implications. Stronger communities would emerge, characterized by increased social cohesion, empathy, and cooperation, leading to more resilient and supportive social networks. Reduced conflict and violence would become more prevalent as individuals develop improved emotional regulation and conflict-resolution skills, fostering more peaceful and harmonious interactions. A heightened sense of purpose and social responsibility would drive greater civic engagement, leading to more active and engaged citizens. Ultimately, a society where psycho-resilience is commonplace would be better equipped to navigate challenges, adapt to change, and thrive in the face of adversity, leading to improved overall well-being for all members.

In essence, if psycho-resilience became commonplace, it would create a ripple effect of positive change, transforming individuals, organizations, and society as a whole. It would foster a world that is more adaptable, innovative, compassionate, and resilient, better equipped to face the challenges and opportunities of the future.

Downsides to Psycho-Resilience

While psycho-resilience is undoubtedly valuable, there are potential downsides to consider, particularly when it comes to the broader context of societal and organizational structures.

Overemphasizing individual resilience can have unintended consequences. Focusing solely on individual resilience may inadvertently shift the burden of responsibility away from addressing the root causes of stress and hardship, neglecting the need for systemic change. For example, if employees are constantly stressed due to unreasonable workloads or toxic work environments, an overemphasis on individual resilience might discourage addressing the need for organizational change and improved working conditions. Moreover, promoting resilience without addressing underlying systemic issues, such as poverty, discrimination, and lack of access to resources, can mask deeper problems. If individuals are constantly adapting and "bouncing back" from difficult situations, it might create the illusion that everything is fine, even when systemic inequalities or injustices persist. Furthermore, placing excessive emphasis on resilience can create unrealistic expectations for individuals to constantly overcome challenges without acknowledging the limitations of personal capacity and the need for systemic support. This can lead to feelings of inadequacy or self-blame when individuals struggle to cope with overwhelming adversity. Therefore, it's crucial to strike a balance between promoting individual resilience and addressing the systemic factors that contribute to stress and hardship.

Therefore, it's crucial to strike a balance between promoting individual resilience and addressing the systemic factors that contribute to stress and hardship. While fostering personal resilience is essential, it should not overshadow the need for organizational and societal change to create environments that support well-being and reduce unnecessary adversity.

Conclusion

A psychologically resilient workforce is more adaptable, engaged, and productive. They're better equipped to handle stress, navigate challenges, and embrace change, leading to increased innovation and overall success. This, in turn, fosters a more supportive and collaborative work environment, benefiting both individuals and the organization as a whole.

CHAPTER 14

PLACE MAXIMIZER

What Is a Place Maximizer?

The concept of Place Maximization is emerging as a crucial framework for understanding how artificial intelligence will reshape the future of work, particularly in how we optimize both physical and virtual environments for enhanced productivity and human well-being. This evolution represents a significant departure from traditional approaches to workplace design and management, where human intuition and experience primarily drove decisions about space utilization and environmental optimization. As organizations increasingly integrate AI systems into their operations, the scope and sophistication of Place Maximization are expanding dramatically, creating new possibilities for how we conceptualize and interact with our work environments.

In the physical realm, AI-driven Place Maximization is fundamentally transforming how organizations approach workplace design and management. Smart building systems, powered by sophisticated AI algorithms, are now capable of analyzing vast arrays of data points to optimize everything from energy consumption to space utilization. These systems continuously monitor and adjust environmental conditions, creating dynamic workspaces that respond in real-time to occupancy patterns, individual preferences, and specific task requirements. The implications extend far beyond simple comfort and cost savings; these AI-powered environments are becoming active participants in supporting workforce productivity and well-being. For instance, in manufacturing and logistics settings, AI systems are revolutionizing how physical spaces are utilized, with automated systems and robots working alongside humans in carefully orchestrated environments that maximize efficiency while maintaining safety and ergonomic considerations.

The virtual dimension of Place Maximization has become equally critical as remote and hybrid work models become permanent fixtures in the modern workplace. AI systems are now essential in creating and maintaining optimal digital environments that support collaboration, learning, and productivity across distributed teams. These virtual spaces are no longer static platforms but dynamic environments that adapt to individual user needs and work patterns. AI algorithms customize digital interfaces, prioritize information flows, and facilitate more natural and effective virtual collaboration. This optimization of virtual spaces is particularly crucial as organizations grapple with the challenges of maintaining team cohesion and organizational culture in increasingly distributed work environments.

The convergence of physical and virtual Place Maximization is creating new paradigms for how organizations approach workforce development and management. AI systems are increasingly acting as bridges between these two realms, creating seamless experiences that blend the benefits of both physical and digital environments. This integration is particularly evident in how organizations approach knowledge management and learning. AI-powered systems can now create personalized learning environments that adapt to individual learning styles and preferences while simultaneously optimizing the physical spaces where hands-on training and collaboration occur. This holistic approach to Place Maximization is becoming essential for organizations looking to maintain competitive advantages in an increasingly complex and dynamic business environment.

However, the implementation of AI-driven Place Maximization also raises important considerations about privacy, autonomy, and the ethical use of technology in the workplace. Organizations must carefully balance the benefits of optimization and efficiency with the need to maintain human agency and protect individual privacy. This balance becomes particularly crucial as AI systems become more sophisticated in their ability to monitor and analyze human behavior patterns. The future success of Place Maximization will depend largely on how well organizations can integrate these powerful technologies while maintaining trust and transparency with their workforce.

Looking ahead, the evolution of Place Maximization will likely continue to accelerate as AI technologies become more sophisticated and our understanding of human–machine interaction deepens. Organizations that successfully navigate this transformation will be those that approach Place Maximization not just as a technical challenge, but as a fundamental reimagining of how humans and machines can work together to create more productive, sustainable, and fulfilling work environments. This evolution will require ongoing attention to both the technological and human aspects of workplace design,

FIGURE 14.1 Place Maximizer.

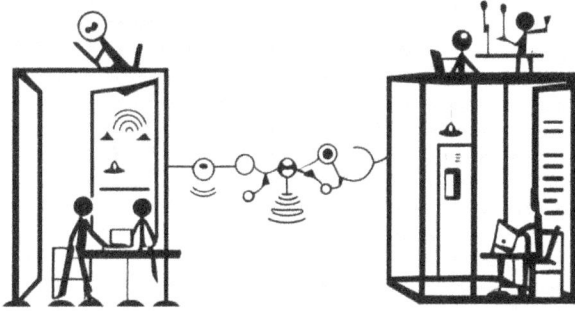

ensuring that the drive for optimization doesn't come at the expense of human well-being and creativity (Figure 14.1).

Why Are Place Maximizers Needed Now?

The modern workforce is navigating an era of unprecedented fluidity. The accelerated shift to hybrid and remote work, driven by global events and technological leaps, has fractured traditional workplace norms. Simultaneously, economic pressures demand greater efficiency and sustainability, while a growing awareness emphasizes employee well-being as a critical driver of productivity. In this complex landscape, Place Maximizers, powered by AI, are no longer optional enhancements but essential tools for navigating emerging workforce challenges. The very spaces we inhabit for work, whether physical offices or digital platforms, are becoming critical battlegrounds for organizational success and employee satisfaction.

One of the most pressing challenges is managing the fractured workplace itself. Hybrid and remote models demand a radical rethink of both physical and virtual environments. Organizations grapple with optimizing underutilized office spaces while simultaneously ensuring remote workers are effectively connected and engaged. AI-driven Place Maximizers provide the crucial bridge, dynamically adapting office layouts based on real-time occupancy data while personalizing virtual workspaces to individual employee needs and fostering seamless digital collaboration. Beyond physical structures, the sheer complexity of modern work—global teams spanning diverse cultures, intricate workflows, and an overwhelming influx of digital tools—necessitates intelligent optimization. AI can dissect these complexities, analyzing communication patterns, project workflows, and resource allocation to create both physical and virtual environments that are intuitively efficient and adaptable, mitigating the cognitive overload and friction that stifle productivity.

Furthermore, the imperative for sustainability is no longer a peripheral concern but a core business demand. Organizations are under increasing pressure to minimize their environmental impact, and workplace environments are a significant area of resource consumption. AI-powered Place Maximizers become critical allies in this effort, optimizing energy usage, reducing waste, and streamlining resource allocation within physical spaces, contributing directly to sustainability goals while simultaneously driving down operational costs—a crucial advantage in uncertain economic times. Beyond efficiency and sustainability, the well-being of the workforce has risen to the forefront. Burnout, disengagement, and a decline in mental health are significant risks in today's demanding work culture, exacerbated by poorly designed or unoptimized work environments. Place Maximizers, by personalizing workspaces, fostering better collaboration tools, and creating more intuitive digital interfaces, contribute to a more human-centric workplace experience, prioritizing employee comfort, focus, and overall well-being—factors increasingly recognized as directly linked to sustained productivity and retention.

Finally, agility and adaptability are the hallmarks of thriving organizations in today's volatile market. Businesses must rapidly respond to changing market conditions, evolving team structures, and emerging technologies. AI-driven Place Maximizers provide this crucial agility. They offer data-driven insights for rapid space reconfiguration, automate adjustments based on usage patterns, and facilitate seamless integration of new technologies into both physical and virtual workspaces. This adaptability, powered by AI's analytical capabilities, allows organizations to remain competitive, resilient, and future-ready, transforming workplace environments from static structures into dynamic assets that directly contribute to organizational success in the face of constant change. In essence, the imperative for Place Maximizers is driven by the fundamental need to re-engineer our workplaces—both physical and digital—for a future of work defined by complexity, fluidity, and a renewed focus on both efficiency and human well-being.

How to Learn Place Maximizing?

Learning to become a Place Maximizer in the age of AI is a multifaceted endeavor that demands a blend of technical understanding, strategic thinking, and a human-centric approach to design. In our rapidly evolving work environment, the concept of Place Maximization goes beyond mere space utilization—it encompasses the optimization of both physical and virtual environments to enhance productivity, sustainability, and overall human well-being. At its core, it requires an appreciation for the interconnectedness of smart technologies, data analytics, and design principles that place people at the center of every innovation. As AI continues to reshape the future of work, individuals across all sectors must learn to harness these capabilities, tailoring their learning journeys according to their roles and expertise.

For educators, shaping the next generation of Place Maximizers is a critical responsibility. High school and college educators are uniquely positioned to integrate "smart environments" and "AI in space design" into their curricula, drawing upon existing STEM, design, and social science courses. By developing modules on IoT technologies, sensor networks, and AI-driven building management systems, educators can provide students with the technical foundation necessary to navigate modern smart environments. Practical applications, such as hands-on projects using simulation software and IoT kits like Raspberry Pi or Arduino, encourage students to design smart classrooms or virtual learning spaces. In addition, educators must foster critical thinking by engaging students in ethical debates about data privacy, algorithmic bias, and the societal implications of smart space optimization. Professional development opportunities, including advanced degrees in architectural education, urban planning, or educational technology, as well as online courses on smart cities and IoT, can further enhance educators' ability to lead in this transformative field.

Executives and business leaders must also recognize the strategic value of Place Maximization, even if they do not need deep technical expertise themselves. Their focus should be on understanding how AI-driven facility management and smart workspace design can improve productivity, sustainability, and employee well-being. Participation in executive workshops and industry conferences focused on smart workplaces is essential for staying informed about best practices and emerging trends. Analyzing case studies of companies successfully leveraging AI for space optimization can provide valuable insights into practical applications. Business leaders are encouraged to invest in pilot projects—such as smart meeting room booking systems or AI-powered energy management initiatives—to gather data on space utilization and drive a data-centric culture within their organizations. Engaging consultants with expertise in smart workplace design and AI-driven facility management can further support these initiatives while ensuring that ethical considerations around data privacy and algorithmic fairness remain a priority.

Students, as future practitioners of Place Maximization, are well-advised to build a multidisciplinary skill set that spans fields such as architecture, urban planning, computer science, data science, engineering, and human–computer interaction. They should pursue studies that combine theoretical knowledge with hands-on technical training, learning programming languages like Python and JavaScript, and familiarizing themselves with data analytics tools such as Tableau or Power BI. Participation in hackathons, design competitions, and research projects focused on smart environments will offer practical experience that is invaluable in the workplace. Internships with companies or research labs working on smart buildings, smart cities, or workplace optimization technologies provide real-world applications of classroom learning. Additionally, networking with peers in student organizations dedicated to sustainability, smart technologies, or urban design can offer collaborative opportunities and further develop their expertise.

Entrepreneurs and business owners have a significant opportunity to capitalize on the growing demand for Place Maximization solutions by identifying market needs in sectors such as offices, retail, healthcare, and education. They should focus on developing innovative, AI-powered tools or consulting services that address these pain points, ensuring their solutions are user-friendly and deliver measurable returns on investment. Building technical expertise is crucial; assembling a multidisciplinary team with skills in AI development, data science, and design principles is a strong foundation for success. Entrepreneurs are encouraged to pilot their innovations in real-world environments, gathering feedback and iteratively refining their offerings. Emphasizing ethical and sustainable practices—through privacy-preserving technologies and energy-efficient designs—can differentiate their solutions in a competitive market. Participation in industry incubators or accelerators that specialize in smart cities or prop-tech can provide valuable mentorship, funding, and strategic guidance.

Regulators and policymakers also play a crucial role in shaping the landscape for Place Maximization by developing ethical frameworks and standards that govern the use of AI in space optimization. They must create guidelines that address data privacy, ensure algorithmic transparency, and promote equitable access to smart environments. Encouraging the development of open standards for data sharing and system interoperability is key to avoiding vendor lock-in and fostering innovation. Regulators should invest in research that examines the societal impacts of smart technologies and collaborate with industry stakeholders, urban planners, and ethical AI researchers to create balanced policies. Educating the public about the benefits and risks of these technologies is essential to fostering informed debate and ensuring that policies reflect a broad range of perspectives.

Parents, too, have an important role in preparing the next generation for a world increasingly influenced by smart environments. They can foster digital literacy and critical thinking in their children by encouraging them to explore how technology shapes the spaces around them. Simple activities, such as building with blocks or engaging in digital design games, can help develop spatial reasoning and creative problem-solving skills. Parents should also discuss ethical considerations like data privacy and the responsible use of technology, and expose their children to real-world examples through visits to science museums or technology centers. These experiences not only build a solid understanding of smart technologies but also instill the human-centric values essential for responsible innovation.

In summary, the journey to becoming a Place Maximizer in the age of AI is a collaborative, multidisciplinary effort that spans educators, business leaders, students, entrepreneurs, regulators, and parents. Each group has a unique role to play, from integrating cutting-edge technology into curricula and leading strategic initiatives in the workplace to developing innovative solutions and crafting balanced policies. As AI continues to reshape the future of work, embracing this comprehensive approach will create spaces that are efficient, sustainable, and truly human-centered. Through education, strategic investment, practical application, and thoughtful policy, we can collectively build a future where the benefits of smart environments are realized for everyone.

How to Teach Place Maximizing?

Place Maximization represents a fundamental shift in how organizations approach space design and management, extending well beyond technological implementation to encompass a comprehensive design thinking methodology. This approach integrates physical and digital environments while prioritizing human-centered outcomes and sustainable practices. Digital twin technology serves as a cornerstone of this transformation, enabling stakeholders to test and refine optimizations through data-driven iteration before physical implementation.

Educational institutions play a pivotal role in developing future Place Maximizers by creating immersive learning environments that combine technical proficiency with ethical considerations. Through project-based learning and hands-on experimentation with IoT sensors and AI simulation software, students develop the critical thinking skills necessary to address complex spatial challenges. This experiential approach naturally leads to meaningful discussions about data privacy, accessibility, and sustainable design principles, ensuring that technical innovation remains grounded in ethical considerations.

Executives must drive organizational transformation by implementing digital twin technology and fostering a data-driven culture of continuous improvement. By initiating focused pilot projects and measuring their outcomes, leaders can demonstrate the tangible benefits of Place Maximization while managing implementation risks. This approach requires a careful balance between technological innovation and practical business considerations, ensuring that investments in smart workplace initiatives deliver measurable value.

Students pursuing careers in Place Maximization need to develop interdisciplinary expertise that combines deep technical knowledge with broad understanding across related fields. This T-shaped skill profile enables them to bridge the gap between digital innovation and spatial design, while maintaining a strong focus on user needs and data-driven decision-making. Through practical experience in hackathons and internships, students learn to apply design thinking principles to real-world challenges while leveraging digital twin simulations for solution validation.

Entrepreneurs and regulators serve complementary roles in advancing Place Maximization practices. While entrepreneurs focus on developing user-friendly, AI-powered solutions that address specific market needs, regulators must establish clear frameworks that promote innovation while protecting privacy and ensuring equitable access. Both groups benefit from using digital twins for rapid prototyping and policy testing, enabling them to refine their approaches based on simulated outcomes before full-scale implementation.

The success of Place Maximization ultimately depends on cultivating a mindset that values both technological innovation and human-centered design principles. This requires stakeholders at all levels to embrace data-driven decision-making while maintaining a strong focus on ethical considerations and sustainable practices. By approaching Place Maximization as a holistic discipline rather than merely a technological solution, organizations can create environments that truly enhance human productivity and well-being while promoting responsible innovation.

Cascading Effects of Place Maximizing

The integration of agentic AI systems with emerging specialized workforce roles is fundamentally reshaping the landscape of Place Maximization, creating multilayered cascading effects that transform how organizations operate and evolve. These effects become particularly pronounced as Human+ professionals, with their enhanced capabilities and specialized focus areas, interact with AI systems to create increasingly sophisticated and adaptive work environments.

The foundation of this transformation begins with the Interoperability Catalyst and R&D Hacker roles, who work in concert to ensure seamless integration between various AI systems and human workflows. Their efforts create environments where physical and digital spaces can dynamically reconfigure based on real-time needs, while maintaining coherent and efficient operations. This technical foundation enables more sophisticated forms of Place Maximization, where spaces can anticipate and adapt to changing requirements before they become apparent to human users. The R&D Hacker's continuous experimentation with new technologies and approaches ensures that these environments remain at the cutting edge of capability, while the Interoperability Catalyst ensures that all systems work together harmoniously.

The Socio-Technician and Eco-Strategist roles introduce another layer of complexity to Place Maximization by ensuring that these adaptive environments align with both human needs and sustainability goals. The Socio-Technician's focus on human–machine interaction patterns helps shape environments that enhance rather than constrain human potential, while the Eco-Strategist ensures that optimization decisions consider long-term environmental impact. This collaboration creates a second-order effect where Place Maximization begins to optimize not just for immediate productivity but for long-term sustainable performance and human well-being. Standardizing the Eco-Strategist role across the taxonomy ensures it is treated not as a passing descriptor but as a durable function within the platinum workforce.

Systems Thinkers and Agents play a crucial role in managing the increasing complexity of these environments. Their ability to understand and navigate complex interdependencies enables organizations to identify and capitalize on emerging opportunities for optimization that might not be apparent when viewing individual systems in isolation. This creates a third-order effect where Place Maximization becomes more sophisticated in its ability to balance competing priorities and manage complex trade-offs across different aspects of organizational performance.

The Maker role introduces an element of practical innovation to Place Maximization, working alongside AI systems to create and modify physical and virtual environments that better serve emerging needs. This hands-on approach to environment optimization creates a fourth-order effect where workspaces become more experimental and iterative, constantly evolving based on real-world feedback and changing requirements. The Maker's ability to rapidly prototype and implement changes helps organizations maintain agility in their approach to Place Maximization.

The Psycho-Resilience Mediator's role becomes increasingly critical as these complex, AI-driven environments evolve. Their focus on maintaining human well-being and psychological safety in rapidly changing environments helps organizations manage the potential stress and adaptation challenges that come with highly dynamic workspaces. This creates a fifth-order effect where Place Maximization begins to incorporate psychological and emotional factors into its optimization strategies, leading to environments that are not just efficient but also supportive of human resilience and adaptability.

The Place Maximizer role itself evolves in this context, becoming more sophisticated in its approach to optimization. Rather than focusing solely on traditional metrics of space utilization and efficiency, modern Place Maximizers must consider how different roles interact with and influence the environment, how various optimization strategies affect human performance and well-being, and how different systems can work together to create more effective workspaces. This creates a sixth-order effect where Place Maximization becomes increasingly holistic and sophisticated in its approach to environmental optimization.

These cascading effects create new challenges and opportunities in organizational learning and adaptation. As these specialized roles work together to create more sophisticated and responsive environments, organizations must develop new capabilities for managing complexity and change. This includes developing new approaches to leadership and management that can effectively guide teams working in highly dynamic, AI-optimized environments while ensuring that technology serves human needs rather than constraining human potential.

The implications for workforce development become increasingly complex as organizations need to cultivate these specialized roles while ensuring they can work together effectively. This creates a need for new approaches to training and development that emphasize both technical expertise and the ability to work across traditional boundaries. Organizations must also develop new frameworks for measuring and optimizing performance that take into account the complex interplay between human capabilities, technological systems, and environmental factors.

Looking ahead, the evolution of these roles and their interaction with AI-driven Place Maximization will likely continue to create new possibilities for how organizations design and manage their work environments. Success in this context will require organizations to maintain a careful balance between technological optimization and human needs, while continuing to adapt and evolve their approach to Place Maximization as new technologies and capabilities emerge.

Social Impact When Place Maximizing Becomes Commonplace

The integration of AI-driven Place Maximization into work environments represents a fundamental transformation of physical and social spaces, extending far beyond simple efficiency improvements to reshape the very nature of how we work and interact. This transformation is particularly evident in the dramatic reconfiguration of both factory and office environments, where AI and smart technologies are creating unprecedented changes in spatial organization and work patterns.

In manufacturing environments, AI-driven Place Maximization is fundamentally altering the physical architecture of production spaces. Traditional factory layouts, designed around fixed production lines and human movement patterns, are giving way to dynamic environments that continuously reconfigure themselves based on real-time production needs. These adaptive spaces utilize mobile robotic systems and flexible manufacturing cells that can reorganize themselves autonomously, creating workflows that would be impossible in traditional settings. This physical transformation extends to the integration of collaborative robots that work alongside humans, requiring new spatial configurations that optimize human–machine interaction while maintaining safety and efficiency.

The impact on office environments is equally profound, as AI-driven Place Maximization dissolves the traditional boundaries between physical and virtual workspaces. The physical office is evolving from a fixed arrangement of desks and meeting rooms into a fluid environment that dynamically adapts to changing work patterns and team configurations. AI systems continuously analyze space utilization patterns and team collaboration needs, automatically adjusting everything from room layouts to environmental conditions. This transformation enables new forms of hybrid work where physical and virtual spaces seamlessly integrate, creating environments that can support both in-person and remote collaboration with equal effectiveness.

These physical transformations are driving significant changes in work practices and social interactions. In factory settings, workers are increasingly becoming system orchestrators rather than direct production operators, requiring new skills in managing and collaborating with AI-driven systems. The physical space must now accommodate this evolution, providing areas for workers to monitor multiple production cells simultaneously while maintaining direct access for intervention when necessary. This shift demands careful attention to maintaining meaningful human interaction and preventing isolation, even as automation reduces traditional face-to-face contact on the production floor.

Office environments are experiencing a parallel social transformation as AI systems optimize space utilization and workflow patterns. The traditional concept of assigned desks and fixed departments is giving way to dynamic team spaces that form and dissolve based on project needs. This flexibility enables more effective collaboration but also requires careful management to prevent the erosion of team cohesion and organizational culture. AI systems must now consider not just physical efficiency but also social factors when optimizing space allocation, ensuring that opportunities for spontaneous interaction and community building are preserved.

The implementation of these transformative changes requires a sophisticated approach to change management and skill development. Organizations must invest in comprehensive training programs that prepare workers for their evolving roles in AI-optimized environments. This includes technical training in working with AI systems and new collaborative technologies, as well as developing skills in adapting to rapidly changing work environments. The success of these initiatives depends on maintaining a careful balance between technological optimization and human needs, ensuring that efficiency gains don't come at the cost of worker well-being and job satisfaction.

Privacy and ethical considerations become increasingly critical as AI systems collect and analyze more data about workplace activities and movement patterns. Organizations must establish clear frameworks for data governance and transparency, ensuring that workers understand how information about their activities is being used while maintaining their autonomy and dignity. This includes setting appropriate limits on surveillance and monitoring, even as AI systems require increasingly detailed data to optimize space utilization and workflow patterns.

The broader societal implications of this transformation extend to questions of equity and access. Organizations must ensure that the benefits of AI-driven Place Maximization are distributed fairly across all levels of the workforce, preventing the creation of new forms of workplace inequality. This includes providing equal access to optimized work environments and ensuring that remote workers have the tools and support needed to participate fully in the organization's activities.

Looking ahead, the success of AI-driven Place Maximization will depend on organizations' ability to implement these transformative changes while maintaining a strong focus on human needs and social cohesion. This requires a careful balance between technological innovation and human-centered design, ensuring that workplaces remain spaces for meaningful human interaction and collaboration even as they become more efficient and automated. The organizations that succeed in this transformation will be those that recognize Place Maximization as not just a technological challenge but as an opportunity to create more human-centered and sustainable work environments.

Downsides of Place Maximizing

The evolution of AI-driven Place Maximization represents a critical inflection point in workplace design, where the promise of unprecedented efficiency meets the fundamental needs of human workers. As AI systems become more sophisticated in their ability to optimize space utilization, organizations face a complex challenge: balancing the drive for operational excellence with the preservation of environments that support human creativity, well-being, and natural collaboration patterns.

In office environments, the implementation of AI-driven Place Maximization often creates an inherent tension between algorithmic efficiency and human-centered design. While AI systems excel at optimizing space utilization through sophisticated analysis of movement patterns and usage data, their singular focus on quantifiable metrics can lead to environments that feel sterile and constraining. The drive for maximum efficiency frequently results in densely packed workspaces that, while theoretically optimal from a space-utilization perspective, fail to account for the psychological and social needs of knowledge workers. This optimization paradox manifests in reduced opportunities for spontaneous interaction, limited flexibility for personal workspace customization, and an increasing sense of surveillance as AI systems continuously monitor and adjust the environment.

The factory floor presents an even more complex challenge, where the consequences of over-optimization can directly impact worker safety and operational resilience. AI-driven systems, in their pursuit of maximum productivity, often design spaces that prioritize machine efficiency over human comfort and adaptability. The resulting environments, while highly efficient in theory, can create practical challenges for workers who must navigate increasingly confined spaces while managing complex automated systems. This approach to optimization can inadvertently create new safety risks and maintenance challenges, as the drive for maximum space utilization leaves little room for error or adaptation to changing conditions.

However, the solution lies not in rejecting AI-driven optimization but in reimagining how it can be applied more thoughtfully. Advanced Place Maximization should incorporate a broader set of metrics that include human factors such as cognitive comfort, social interaction quality, and psychological well-being. This requires a fundamental shift in how AI systems evaluate and optimize spaces, moving beyond simple efficiency metrics to consider the full spectrum of human needs and experiences within the workplace.

The next generation of Place Maximization must embrace adaptive design principles that allow spaces to evolve organically while maintaining operational efficiency. This means developing AI systems that can create dynamic environments capable of responding to changing work patterns and human needs without sacrificing the benefits of optimization. Such systems would need to balance immediate efficiency gains against longer-term factors such as worker satisfaction, team cohesion, and organizational adaptability.

The integration of digital twin technology offers a promising path forward, enabling organizations to simulate and test different optimization approaches before implementation. This allows for a more nuanced understanding of how spatial changes might impact both operational efficiency and human experience. By combining real-time data with predictive modeling, organizations can develop more sophisticated optimization strategies that maintain high efficiency while preserving the human elements essential for workplace satisfaction and productivity.

The role of human expertise becomes increasingly critical in this context, as successful Place Maximization requires the integration of multiple perspectives and skill sets. The emergence of specialized roles such as Socio-Technicians and Psycho-Resilience Mediators reflects the growing recognition that technical optimization must be balanced with human factors. These professionals help bridge the gap between AI-driven efficiency and human-centered design, ensuring that workplace optimization serves both operational and human needs.

Looking forward, the success of Place Maximization will depend on developing new frameworks that explicitly value and protect human elements within highly optimized environments. This includes establishing clear guidelines for when efficiency should be sacrificed in favor of human comfort or social interaction, and creating mechanisms for workers to influence and customize their environments within the broader optimization framework. Organizations must also invest in continuous learning and adaptation, recognizing that the balance between efficiency and human needs will continue to evolve as technology advances and workplace expectations change.

Ultimately, the future of AI-driven Place Maximization lies in creating environments that are not just efficient but truly intelligent in their ability to support human flourishing. This requires moving beyond simple optimization metrics to develop more sophisticated approaches that can balance multiple competing priorities while maintaining the flexibility and adaptability essential for long-term success. Only by embracing this more nuanced and human-centered approach can organizations create workplaces that are both highly efficient and genuinely supportive of human needs and aspirations.

Conclusion

AI-driven Place Maximization fundamentally transforms both physical and virtual workspaces, creating highly adaptive environments that can continuously reconfigure themselves based on real-time needs and data-driven insights. This transformation demands a significant evolution in workforce capabilities, as employees across all levels must develop new skills to effectively collaborate with AI systems while adapting to increasingly dynamic and responsive work environments. The success of Place Maximization ultimately depends on achieving a delicate balance between technological optimization and human needs, requiring organizations to carefully consider how these powerful systems can enhance rather than diminish the human experience of work, while ensuring that the benefits of optimized spaces are equitably distributed across the workforce.

SECTION III

Managing Systems, Machines, and Humans

CHAPTER 15

MASTERING EMERGING
WORKFORCE RISKS

The AI system that ran the Irresponsible Corporation, one of the world's leading companies, suddenly started doing strange things. At first, it was barely noticeable, but then its agentic AI system started executing actions that were not authorized by protocols or managers. When IT managers tried to stop it, the system closed down access. Because only five people truly understood the system, it took one month to fix, during which customers suffered, entire departments had to be let go, and the company lost its license to work with several governments on sensitive projects. The IT department, all of its 1,000 employees, got diagnosed with clinical depression, and many were let go.

An imagined scenario, but still, at best, an emerging workforce risk is a recently discovered actual or potential hazard to people, organizations, infrastructure, and property. The hazard is typically recognized through empirical data from engineering analyses, accident or injury investigations, toxicological studies, or epidemiological studies ("Occupational Emerging Risks" 2010). An example would be new, harmful chemicals or products that are used in the workplace, such as engineered stone, a composite material made from crushed stone and adhesive, used in kitchens, bathrooms, and commercial buildings, as well as deployed in the production of recreational vehicles, boats, and aircraft. Engineered stone has many advantages, such as minimal maintenance and antibacterial properties. At worst, an emerging risk is a new or unforeseen risk that we haven't yet contemplated. Those are risks that should be on our radar but are not, and its potential for harm or loss is not fully known. Techniques such as environmental scanning, trend analysis, and scenario planning are valuable in identifying emerging risks.

Technological disruption is both a risk and an opportunity but could be negatively affecting businesses that don't innovate or who invest in what they thought were platform technologies only to discover that they are becoming obsolete or who spend too many resources upskilling workers for the wrong skills.

There is also the risk of overemphasizing risk, such as the age-old discussion about automation displacing workers. The influential 2013 Oxford study by Carl Benedikt Frey and Michael Osborne, known as the Frey & Osborne AI study (Oxford Martin School and University of Oxford 2013), claiming 47 percent of the workforce could be automated away, led to widespread fears both in policy circles and global business. This risk has yet to come to pass but might be a case of screaming wolf, in the sense that it might happen in the future and decision-makers might already be desensitized to it, so they ignore it even if/until it comes to pass. That said, current advancements in generative AI have led to a renewed sense of AI automation risk. Around 46 percent of workers may see at least half of their tasks impacted by large-language models (LLMs) (Eloundou et al. 2024). This technological acceleration has intensified debates about which professional domains remain uniquely human in a world of expanding AI capabilities.

Alongside automation anxiety exists the more fundamental concern of AI misalignment. As Hendrycks et al. (2023) demonstrate, the challenge of ensuring AI systems optimize for human-aligned values grows increasingly complex as models become more powerful. This misalignment risk encompasses both narrow technical failures—like AI systems exploiting specification gaps in their objectives—and broader questions about embedding appropriate values into systems with potentially transformative capabilities. The convergence of these twin concerns has catalyzed renewed attention to AI governance mechanisms that could address both economic transition challenges and alignment imperatives. The preceding scenario illustrates the lived reality of risk. To analyze these risks systematically, we now turn to a more formal definition framework that will be used throughout the next chapters.

Risks in the Modern Workplace

The modern workplace presents several types of risks that both employers and employees need to be aware of and train and hone skills for, such as *workforce risks* (talent scarcity, skills gaps, harassment, health exposure, physical safety, lack of ability to address changing workforce expectations such as social responsibility), *enterprise risks* (operational risks), *governance risks* (legal risks, compliance, data privacy breaches, regulated industries), *technology risks* (AI bias, black box AI, tech complexity, cybersecurity, disaster recovery, third-party risk), *psychological risks, physical risks, external risks* (hazards, economic

FIGURE 15.1 Workforce risks due to tech advancement.

downturns, regulatory changes, natural disasters, technological disruption), or *ethical risks*.

As a whole, these risks are caused by technological advancements, social changes, or organizational shifts—typically all of the above. For example, when AI, nanotechnology, or biotechnology, alone or in combination, lead to new production processes, the added complexity, intensity, skills requirements, speed, or environmental consequences have a set of implications that can be hard to foresee, understand, or remediate. When advanced technologies such as AI, nanotechnology, or biotechnology—alone or in combination—lead to new production processes, they often introduce added complexity, increased intensity, new skill requirements, and unforeseen environmental consequences. For example, CRISPR-based genome editing has enabled researchers to engineer bacteria like *Pseudomonas putida* for enhanced bioremediation of persistent organic pollutants (Nikel and de Lorenzo 2018).

While these advances offer significant environmental promise, the release of genetically modified organisms into natural environments raises concerns about unpredictable ecological impacts, such as potential disruption of native microbial communities and effects on biodiversity (Moe-Behrens et al. 2013).

These risks present regulatory challenges, as biosafety frameworks and oversight mechanisms often struggle to keep pace with the rapid development and deployment of such technologies. Scholars such as Sheila Jasanoff (2020) have highlighted the "governance gaps" that emerge when technological innovation outpaces institutional capacities for oversight and assessment. This underscores the need for interdisciplinary expertise and adaptive regulatory approaches to address the complexities of converging technologies. Likewise, new forms of employment such as hybrid or remote work, self-employment, outsourcing, and temporary contracts—while offering flexibility—can also introduce new stressors. For example, GitLab, a global software company, has operated as a fully remote organization since its founding. GitLab's remote model has been widely studied and documented in both academic and industry literature. On the positive side, GitLab reports high employee satisfaction with geographic flexibility and autonomy. According to GitLab's 2021 Remote Work Report, 82 percent of remote workers said they felt more trusted and empowered, and 52 percent reported improved productivity. However, challenges have also emerged. Academic studies and industry surveys have found that fully remote work can lead to communication silos, difficulties in transmitting tacit knowledge, and increased feelings of isolation. For example, a 2022 Microsoft study (Microsoft Work Trend Index) found that 50 percent of remote workers reported increased feelings of loneliness, and 54 percent found it harder to feel connected to their colleagues. GitLab itself has acknowledged the need for intentional practices to maintain culture and communication, such as detailed documentation, regular check-ins, and virtual social events.

These real-world examples demonstrate that while distributed work models can enhance flexibility and productivity, they also require deliberate strategies to address challenges like social isolation, knowledge sharing, and regulatory compliance. This underscores that flexible work arrangements are not universally beneficial and must be thoughtfully managed to mitigate potential downsides.

Environmental risks cocreated by industrial activity, such as pollution in the form of "forever" chemicals, greenhouse gas emissions from cement production or from the burning of fossil fuels, industrial waste generation, or biodiversity loss from industrial sites that destroy natural habitats, introduce significant hazards into workplace environments. These risks expose workers to both acute and chronic health threats, from immediate respiratory distress to long-latency diseases that may emerge decades after exposure. Furthermore, such environmental degradation can destabilize surrounding ecosystems, creating additional workplace safety concerns through increased flooding, extreme weather vulnerability, and compromised infrastructure stability.

Cascading Risks in the Workplace

If only these risks were isolated, but they are not. On the contrary, they are often connected. The metaphor of cascades is used in ecology, financial crises, power grids, and project management. Cascading risk implies a series of linked adverse events that can amplify or trigger other risks. Cascading effects are also known as transactional effects, snowball effects, chain reactions, or contagion effects (Prot and Gentile 2014).

In ecology, one observes how a series of events where organisms at one stage provide resources for organisms at the next stage. If hunters cause the loss of a top predator, the prey's population increases, leading to food scarcity and, ultimately, species loss in tropical forests. A financial crisis such as the 2008 global financial crisis with subprime mortgage defaults impacted major banks globally spreading through an economy because financial institutions were intertwined through loans and derivatives. When one major player faces difficulties, such as Silicon Valley Bank did in 2023, it can cause market-wide panic where depositors withdraw their funds at the same time. The cascading effect of connected waterfalls means that a disruption to the flow of water at one waterfall impacts the flow of subsequent waterfalls and is characterized by amplification at each junction. A set of toppling dominoes where one domino knocks over the next, triggered by a single initial action. Like in bad (and prevalent) project management when project phases are completed in sequence without room for changes.

The point is that connected negative impact spreads through multiple domains, phenomena, or places. Cascading effects in the workplace can create a chain reaction where an action or event at one level of an organization significantly impacts and influences subsequent levels. This is traditionally used as an example of effective leadership trickling down the organization. Nowadays, we should be equally concerned about negative effects, such as one negative action or event, like a poor decision, conflict, or toxic behavior by a C-level executive or manager percolating through the organization through information flow, rumor, or gossip—spreading negativity, affecting collaboration, leading to higher turnover rates. Persistent unresolved workplace conflicts can affect the productivity of entire teams or entire organizations. Worst case, these cascades can destroy the work culture, effectiveness, and performance of an entire organization, industry, or country. This could happen even to great companies. Major companies have faced significant workplace culture challenges. Ford Motor Company has repeatedly confronted sexual harassment issues at its plants, resulting in lawsuits and regulatory scrutiny (New York Times 2017). Nike has been subject to class-action litigation alleging gender discrimination and harassment, with numerous reports of a hostile environment for women (Greenhouse 2018). Uber's early years were marked by a culture of harassment, bullying, and discrimination, leading to leadership changes and public reform efforts (Fowler 2017). Amazon has been criticized for a demanding and high-pressure work environment linked to employee burnout (Kantor and Streitfeld 2015). Tesla has faced lawsuits and settlements over racial discrimination and harassment, particularly at its Fremont factory (Conger 2021). These cases illustrate the persistent and varied nature of workplace culture and discrimination issues in major corporations (Florczak 2022).

Research shows companies can address toxicity in the workplace through leadership, social norms, and work design (Sull and Sull 2022).

Emerging Workforce Cascades

Business processes also exhibit cascading effects where a problem in one area can have cascading effects on other parts of the organization. The historical example would be a production delay in manufacturing ("a bottleneck") leading to delayed deliveries to customers, impacting sales, customer satisfaction, and potentially causing issues with the finance department due to missed revenue targets. Many cascades are inherently linked to lack of vision, explicit knowledge gaps, capability gaps, a momentary or habitual lack of awareness, which all boils down to a lack of skills.

In the next decade, the workforce will not only consist of people but of AI-augmented workers plus AI systems, sometimes working in tandem, and at times with antagonistic interests and alignments. What I will call *skills cascades* refers to a variety of programs, models, and unintended impacts that help people develop skills in different areas (positive skills cascades) or which hurt their progress (negative skills cascades). These programs can include academic skills career skills, and technical skills. Some of these skills may be transferable or useful in several contexts, tasks, professions, and jobs, creating skills pathways [such as mastering data analysis, applying systems thinking, orchestrating human–AI collaboration, and driving giga-scale project management] others are not. However, even if positive cascades can be sought, unless precautionary action is taken by leaders or workers, negative cascades tend to just happen. That's why mitigation is crucial. An example of a negative chain reaction would be where a lack of proficiency in one skill negatively impacts the ability to acquire or perform other related skills, ultimately leading to reduced performance, hindered career progression, low worker confidence, difficulty adapting to new challenges, and increasing stress levels. The biggest cascading effect of all is organizational culture (Patrishkoff 2015).

Organizational culture creates the most significant cascading effect in business environments. As Patrishkoff (2015) demonstrates, culture permeates every organizational level, beginning with leadership behaviors that middle managers observe and replicate, ultimately reaching frontline employees. This cultural transmission doesn't merely influence individual behaviors; it fundamentally shapes how decisions are made, problems are framed, and success is measured. The true power of cultural cascades lies in their self-reinforcing nature. Communication patterns, talent attraction, customer experiences, and innovation capacity all flow from and feed back into cultural norms, creating powerful feedback loops. These loops strengthen existing tendencies, explaining why organizational culture generates such widespread effects while simultaneously resisting superficial change efforts. This cascade phenomenon makes culture both the most influential organizational force and the most challenging to transform intentionally (Figure 15.2).

An employee struggling with digital skills such as web literacy or enterprise IT system proficiency (knowledge, workflow, supply chain, budgeting, etc.) might face difficulties in comprehending AI because it arguably still builds on digital literacy. Mitigating negative skills cascades would include personalized learning (tailored to individual needs, strengths, and weaknesses).

Conclusion

Mitigating cascading risks that are likely to affect the future of work is crucial for building resilient systems and ensuring the long-term sustainability of the emerging workforce, and ultimately, our societies. This is both a challenge and an opportunity, in the sense that high risks also present high rewards for those who sign up to mitigate them and succeed at doing so. The building blocks for a risk-resilient workforce, an essential part of what I aspirationally call a *platinum workforce*, include real-time skills assessments, thoughtful foresight,

FIGURE 15.2 Skills cascades.

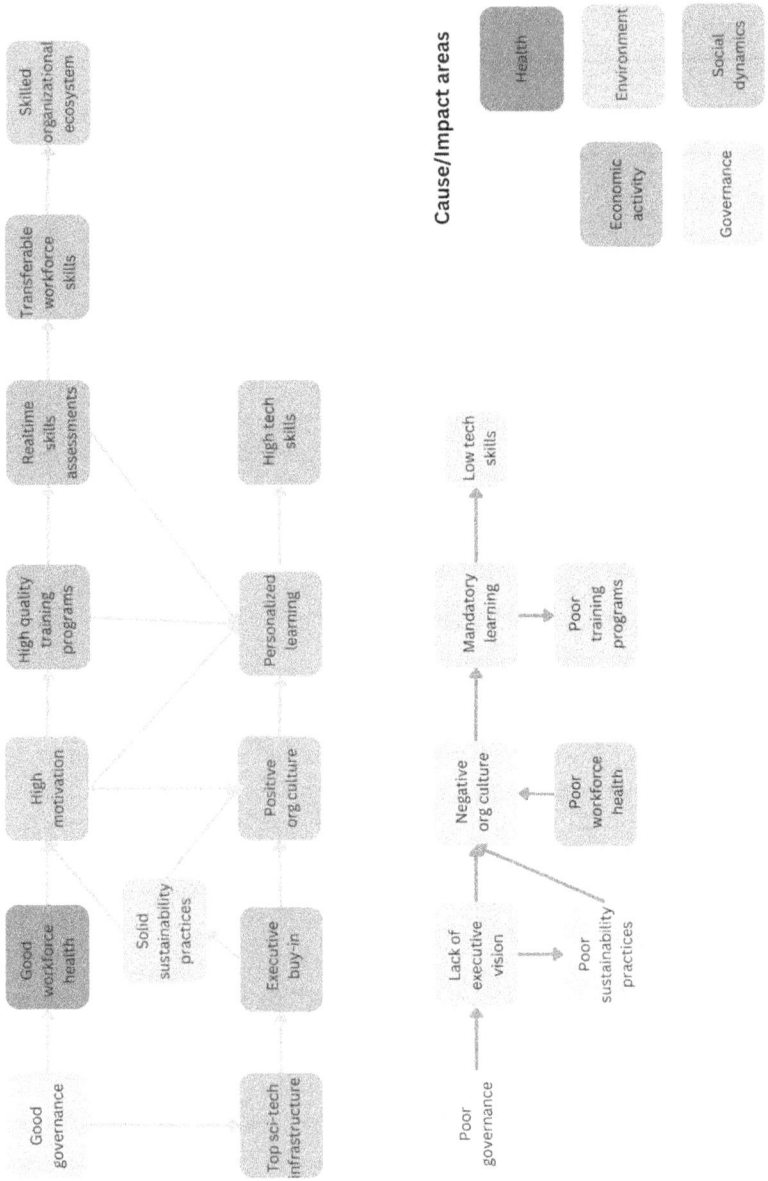

Cause/Impact areas

and scenario exercises with practical implications for workforce training and recruitment, as well as an ecosystem approach where organizations act as a whole to address challenges not as isolated parts. That is where a risk strategist comes in. This is not somebody who merely manages existing risks. Rather, a risk strategist must anticipate, mitigate, hedge around, and navigate both workplace risks and cascading risks from other domains.

References

Conger, K. 2021. "Tesla Must Pay $137 Million to a Black Former Worker." *The New York Times*. October 4. https://www.nytimes.com/2021/10/04/business/tesla-racism-verdict.html.

Eloundou, Tyna, Sam Manning, Pamela Mishkin, and Daniel Rock. 2024. "GPTs Are GPTs: Labor Market Impact Potential of LLMs." *Science (New York, N.Y.)* 384 (6702): 1306–1308.

Florczak, Dana. 2022. "Liability for Toxic Workplace Cultures." *University of Michigan Journal of Law Reform. University of Michigan. Law School* 56.1: 247.

Fowler, S. 2017. "Reflecting on One Very, Very Strange Year at Uber." *Susan Fowler Blog*. February 19. https://www.susanjfowler.com/blog/2017/2/19/reflecting-on-one-very-strange-year-at-uber.

GitLab. 2021. *The Remote Work Report 2021*. https://handbook.gitlab.com/handbook/company/culture/all-remote/remote-work-report/.

Greenhouse, S. 2018. "Nike Faces Class-action Lawsuit Alleging Gender Discrimination." *The New York Times*. August 9. https://www.nytimes.com/2018/08/09/business/nike-class-action-lawsuit.html.

Hendrycks, Dan, Mantas, Mazeika, and Thomas, Woodside. 2023. "An Overview of Catastrophic AI Risks." *ArXiv abs/2306.12001*. n. page.

Jasanoff, S. 2020. *The Ethics of Invention: Technology and the Human Future*. New York: W. W. Norton & Company.

Kantor, J., and D. Streitfeld. 2015. "Inside Amazon: Wrestling Big Ideas in a Bruising Workplace." *The New York Times*. August 15. https://www.nytimes.com/2015/08/16/technology/inside-amazon-wrestling-big-ideas-in-a-bruising-workplace.html.

Microsoft. 2022. *Great Expectations: Making Hybrid Work* (2022 Work Trend Index Annual Report). https://www.microsoft.com/en-us/worklab/work-trend-index/great-expectations-making-hybrid-work-work.

Moe-Behrens, G. H., R. Davis, and K. A. Haynes. 2013. "Preparing Synthetic Biology for the World." *Frontiers in Microbiology* 4: 5.

New York Times. 2017. "How Ford Handled Sexual Harassment at Two Chicago Plants." December 19. https://www.nytimes.com/interactive/2017/12/19/us/ford-chicago-sexual-harassment.html.

Nikel, P. I., and V. de Lorenzo. 2018. "Pseudomonas Putida as a Functional Chassis for Industrial Biocatalysis: From Native Biochemistry to Trans-metabolism." *Metabolic Engineering* 50: 142–155.

"Occupational Emerging Risks." 2010. "U.S. Department of Health and Human Services, Public Health Service, Centers for Disease Control and Prevention, National Institute for Occupational Safety and Health." https://doi.org/10.26616/NIOSHPUB2010148.

Oxford Martin School, and University of Oxford. 2013. "The Future of Employment: How Susceptible Are Jobs to Computerisation?" *Oxford Martin School*. September. https://www.oxfordmartin.ox.ac.uk/publications/the-future-of-employment.

Patrishkoff, David. 2015. "How 'Cascades' Can Build Work Culture." *Insurance Thought Leadership*. April 9. https://www.insurancethoughtleadership.com/risk-management/how-cascades-can-build-work-culture.

Prot, Sara, and Douglas A. Gentile. 2014. "Applying Risk and Resilience Models to Predicting the Effects of Media Violence on Development." *Advances in Child Development and Behavior* 46 (January): 215–244.

Sull, Donald, and Charles Sull. 2022. "How to Fix a Toxic Culture." *MIT Sloan Management Review*. September. https://sloanreview.mit.edu/article/how-to-fix-a-toxic-culture/.

Wang, B., Y. Liu, J. Qian, and S. K. Parker. 2021. "Achieving Effective Remote Working During the COVID-19 Pandemic: A Work Design Perspective." *Applied Psychology* 70 (1): 16–59.

CHAPTER 16

MANAGING SKILLS AT GIGASCALE

Maria is a 20-year-old freshly minted worker who is having a crazy Monday. She just started her first job after having successfully completed a two-year associate degree in hybrid AI at a U.S. college. Her first task is to monitor the energy infrastructure of a small town in the Midwest. Except this particular Monday, everything goes wrong. The energy demand spikes due to a heatwave and the failure of the biggest solar panel arrays she has to monitor. A cascading effect she has not trained for. The AI is of no use. It doesn't warn her. No red lamp is blinking. Luckily, using an old IT hack she happens to know from her hobby as a computer gamer, she pulls the plug on a key transformer and reconnects an old gas transmission line in time to stem the disaster. The infrastructure she guards on a daily basis would cost $1 billion dollars to replace if it all got destroyed. Her college training included 10 hours on energy grid operation and her on-the-job training consisted of shadowing the previous employee for a week (Figure 16.1).

What Scale Is and Why to Worry

Scaling effects describe how the properties of a system change as its size or scale increases. These changes can be proportional or disproportionate. They might lead to unexpected outcomes. Scale can refer to many aspects of growth. Several key concepts come to mind. Size. Speed. Money. Success. Innovation. Productivity. Markets. Volume. Finance. Organizations. Performance. Momentum. Cost savings. Wealth. Monopoly. Freedom from constraints. The key to the concept is a larger-than-proportional increase in the performance of the object being considered.

Current Silicon Valley thinking is epitomized by the notion of "exponential effects" and "Blitzscaling," a "shock-and-awe tactic openly aimed at social disruption" (Pfotenhauer et al. 2022). Emerging technologies are said to be "exponential technologies" that double or even quadruple in performance or

FIGURE 16.1 Managing skills at scale.

capability over a short period of time. In fact, if they truly grow exponentially, they increase little by little and then suddenly rocket in a way that's hard to predict.

The cost of core digital technology capabilities such as computing power, data storage, and bandwidth has demonstrably been decreasing exponentially and faster than previous technologies such as electricity and telephones. Arguably, there are many other exponential technologies, like additive manufacturing, big data, biotechnology, cloud computing, digital fabrication, digitalization, 3D printing, drones, robotics, artificial intelligence, blockchain, connectivity, digital twins, energy technologies, Internet of Things (IoT), machine learning, augmented reality (AR), nanotech, quantum computing, robots, smartphones, sustainable technology, synthetic biology, telemedicine, virtual reality (VR), and more. Not all of these can currently be said to be truly exponential, but who knows what might happen in the future. It depends on a complex set of factors such as technological progress, innovation, investments, and regulation. All technologies, whether they enter an exponential scaling pattern or not, bring ethical and societal implications as they develop.

The Fallacy of Simplified Scaling Laws

So-called "scaling laws," a highly optimistic term for a very complex set of phenomena that tend to elude both description, explanation, and preemptive action, attempt to describe how the properties of a system change as its size or scale is altered. Key concepts include *proportionality* (relationships between changing or constant quantities), *dimensionality* (attempts to determine and subsequently describe the key dimensions involved), and *self-similarity* (structures that look roughly the same as a part of themselves at different scales). DeepSeek's January 2025 breakthrough constitutes a technological inflection point in global AI competition. The Chinese start-up's R1 reasoning model achieved performance parity with U.S. competitors at approximately 1/200th of the development cost, precipitating a $1 trillion market contraction and NVIDIA's unprecedented single-day capitalization loss of $593 billion. Beyond market implications, this event demonstrates how algorithmic optimization can circumvent hardware limitations imposed by export controls. DeepSeek's research-oriented approach and sophisticated software techniques (sparse Mixture-of-Experts architectures, quantization) enabled exceptional efficiency gains while challenging assumptions about computational scaling requirements. This parallels historical efficiency paradoxes wherein technological constraints catalyze innovation. The incident necessitates a reassessment of U.S. technological strategy, suggesting future advantages may derive less from hardware superiority and more from methodological innovation.

In reality, scaling laws are, at best, a fancy name for observations that proxy complex scientific models. They are generalizations. Often highly approximate models of empirical relationships as observed until something changes. That something could be anything because even the experts involved are in novel terrain and don't really know what to expect. As Gary Marcus points out, scaling laws work best as proxies in relatively closed domains where you can create a lot of reliable synthetic data (Marcus 2024). Synthetic data is information that is artificially manufactured rather than generated by real-world events. Marcus gives math problems as a good example of where such data has been used successfully to test or train AI systems to solve calculus problems or generate geometry problems for learning platforms. The application of scaling laws often serves multiple purposes beyond pure scientific inquiry, including attracting growth capital, expanding the audience for innovation literature, and establishing academic recognition. For instance, venture capital firms like Andreessen Horowitz reference scaling principles when evaluating investment opportunities, though empirical validation of these principles varies considerably across sectors. Business authors such as Geoffrey Moore (*Crossing the Chasm*) and Eric Ries (*The Lean Startup*) have popularized organizational growth frameworks that, while insightful, sometimes lack rigorous longitudinal validation across diverse contexts. Academic contributions like Metcalfe's Law and Zipf's Law represent important patterns, yet their universal applicability has been questioned in peer-reviewed literature, with researchers like Andrew Odlyzko demonstrating that network effects often follow more complex relationships than simple power laws suggest. Management consulting approaches to scaling frequently derive from case studies of successful companies, creating potential survivorship bias that limits their generalizability. Meanwhile, technology companies publishing research on computational scaling laws make valuable contributions to the field while simultaneously serving strategic corporate interests, raising important questions about selective reporting and reproducibility in industrial research settings.

Moore's Law (1965) of computer chips states that computer performance roughly doubles every two years. By 2025, this principle has reached a critical inflection point in technological advancement. Moore's Law approaches its physical limits in 2025, with transistor counts nearing the atomic threshold of approximately 100 billion per chip. The semiconductor industry has pivoted from traditional scaling to a "More than Moore" paradigm, emphasizing system architecture over miniaturization. Rising manufacturing costs and thermal constraints at sub-5 nm nodes have reversed the historical cost-reduction pattern. Nevertheless, innovation continues through alternative approaches—3D integration, chiplet architectures, nanosheet transistors, and advanced packaging—enabling computational advancement despite silicon's fundamental limitations. This represents not the death of Moore's Law but its evolution into a more architecturally diverse computing landscape. There is growing debate in the AI community about scaling laws, as increases in training dataset size, model parameters, compute resources, and number of tokens have consistently improved model performance (Kaplan et al. 2020; Hoffmann et al. 2022). Recent work suggests that while scaling up yields significant gains, diminishing returns and the importance of data quality and human factors are becoming more apparent (Wei et al. 2022).

3D printing can now be done with an increasing number of materials, including plastics, metals, agricultural waste, and even wood. Humans can travel at faster and faster speeds, from the 35 mph speed of a horse in the eighteenth century before the automobile and railway to the 17,500 mph speed of the International Space Station (ISS), which orbits Earth at an average altitude of approximately 250 miles. Incidentally, that's the same speed as "space junk." In exceptional circumstances, speed can be even faster. Up until now, the fastest human-made object is NASA's uncrewed Parker Solar Probe. During several flybys of Venus allowing it to slingshot off the planet's gravity, the Parker Solar Probe clocked up a speed of 430,000 mph ("NASA's Parker Solar Probe Makes History With Closest Pass to Sun" 2024).

Artificial intelligence is advancing at unprecedented speed, potentially allowing scientists to solve many enigmas of cancer. Machine translation has a history dating back to the 1950s. The first public machine translation service was created in 1992. Voice recognition used to be slow and cumbersome but has since the 2010s been used for real-time translation. By 2024, Google Translate supported 110 languages where a machine learning model learns to translate into another language without ever seeing an example, representing more than 600 million speakers or roughly 8 percent of the world's population (Caswell 2024). Over the past few decades, we can increasingly engineer complex, biologically based systems using synthetic biology approaches such as synthetic genomics and bottom-up assembly of protocells. Virtual reality is beginning to create lifelike sensory experiences such as sight, sound, and touch. Robotics can be used for self-driving cars.

At best, scaling effects reduce costs while increasing performance. However, there is a catch. Some outcomes are bad. Unprecedented speed and scale tend to come with problems attached. Lack of control. Increased cost. Unforeseeable consequences. The space debris crisis perfectly illustrates the fallacy of oversimplified scaling laws that complexity theory warns against. While basic orbital mechanics can predict the trajectory of a single object, the Kessler Syndrome represents a complex scaling problem where traditional linear extrapolation fails catastrophically. This exemplifies what Geoffrey West calls "emergent complexity"—as the number of objects in orbit increases, the potential interactions grow exponentially rather than linearly, creating system behaviors that couldn't be predicted from studying individual components.

The challenge of space debris mitigation demonstrates the compounding effects at different scales. At small scales (few objects), collision probabilities follow manageable statistical patterns. But complexity theory reveals critical thresholds where quantitative changes in object density trigger qualitative shifts in system behavior. Beyond certain debris concentrations, the system's self-reinforcing feedback loops accelerate debris generation faster than removal efforts can counteract—a perfect example of Stuart Kauffman's "phase transitions" in complex adaptive systems. The economic and technical difficulties in addressing space junk further highlight how solutions don't scale proportionally with the problem. Current debris-removal technologies may work for individual objects but become exponentially less effective as debris populations grow and fragment, demonstrating the nonlinear relationship between solution efforts and problem magnitude that complexity scientists at the Santa Fe Institute have documented across numerous domains. This space example underscores why simplistic scaling assumptions fail in complex systems: they miss the emergent properties, feedback loops, and phase transitions that fundamentally transform system dynamics beyond certain scale thresholds.

The Emerging Challenge of Scale

Managing skills at scale does not only refer to the practice of effectively developing and maintaining a high level of skills across a large workforce. Ensuring that everyone within an organization has the necessary competencies to perform their roles well, even as the company grows in size and complexity, is just a starting point. As the scale of the problems that organizations are facing becomes larger, the nature of skills themselves starts to change. Identifying critical skills at various existing roles, levels, and processes in an organization is not as relevant as attempting to foresee emerging skills or planning for alternative future scenarios that might come to pass within the next decade. Performing a skills gap analysis becomes not so much an assessment of the potential mismatch of current skills with optimal performance today, but with envisioned performance needs in a reconfigured tomorrow. Standardized training programs might still be important, but because they provide a skills floor or foundation, are flexible, or can deliver new content at scale, not because of the content they currently have. Because the future inherently seems to demand higher complexity and increased scale of effort, there will be resource constraints, but also positive scale effects (such as economies of scale).

As scale increases, innovation becomes even more vital. Delivering more—often with fewer resources—requires dramatic improvements in delivery methods, business models, and product features (Teece 2010). The pressure to innovate under constraints makes adaptation a core strategic function. At the same time, the meaning of organizational agility may be fundamentally changing. Traditionally, agility has meant quickly retraining or redeploying the existing workforce to meet shifting market demands. But in a rapidly evolving environment, true agility might mean the capacity to let go of the current workforce entirely and onboard one better suited to emerging challenges (Suddaby et al. 2020). This would require organizations to rethink not only HR strategies but also their operating models and ethical responsibilities. In such a landscape, ecosystem capabilities—access to external talent, platforms, and modular partnerships—may become more important than internal firm competencies (Adner and Kapoor 2010). Yet it's still unclear what resource will prove most decisive: Will it be financial capital, leadership capacity, institutional flexibility, or something else entirely? As systems grow in size and complexity, identifying the new sources of strategic advantage remains an open and urgent question.

Understanding Why Scale Matters

Scale is not a trivial matter. At a very basic level, everyone understands that the consequences of failure increase. But there's more to it. Things become more unpredictable. Weird things can start to happen. The spread of a mix of information and misinformation, aided by lifelike faked or altered text or video in a hyperconnected world, can create an *infodemic* of sorts (occurring far beyond health emergencies) where it is increasingly hard to discern truth from fiction. History has shown how social polarization effects and the erosion of trust is not necessarily gradual, but can hit thresholds. Think of Nazi Germany's propaganda effects that led to the so-called "Nuremberg Laws" (a cascading scale effect), which condoned and made systematic state-sponsored persecution and murder of six million Jews by the Nazi regime possible between 1933 and 1945. Or think of the rise of right-wing extremist groups leading to terrorist attacks.

During the turbulent years of the 2020s, public trust in institutions—government, media, even science—eroded dramatically across many advanced democracies. The consequences were far-reaching and destabilizing. In South Korea, the crisis came to a head in December 2024 when President Yoon Suk Yeol shocked the nation by declaring martial law, citing vague threats from anti-state forces. The move triggered immediate outrage. Mass protests erupted across the country, and within just six hours, the National Assembly voted to impeach him, marking one of the swiftest political reversals in modern history. In the United States, trust in the federal government sank to historic lows. According to Pew Research Center (2024), only 22 percent of Americans believed their government could be trusted—just the latest data point in a decades-long decline marked by growing partisanship and disillusionment. Meanwhile, France descended into its own political chaos when President Emmanuel Macron's gamble to call a snap election backfired spectacularly. The resulting divided parliament led to multiple failed governments. Among them was Prime Minister François Bayrou's administration, which made history for all the wrong reasons—brought down in December

2024 by a no-confidence vote, it became the shortest-lived French government since the Fifth Republic began. Taken together, these moments form a portrait of democratic strain: nations grappling with internal fractures, institutional breakdowns, and the escalating cost of lost public faith.

Complexity theory has begun to explore how scaling introduces compounding effects that impede planning and system comprehension. Research from the Santa Fe Institute highlights that as organizational structures expand, they encounter nonlinear challenges that complicate coordination and understanding. Each order of magnitude increase introduces qualitatively different coordination problems, making traditional linear planning methods insufficient (Santa Fe Institute n.d.).

Geoffrey West's work on urban scaling reveals that cities experience superlinear growth in both innovation and social complexity. As city populations double, metrics such as wages, patents, and GDP per capita increase by approximately 15 percent, indicating that larger cities are disproportionately more productive and innovative. However, this growth also brings challenges, as infrastructure demands and social issues like crime and disease also scale superlinearly, complicating governance and sustainability efforts (West 2017).

Stuart Kauffman's research on self-organizing systems identifies critical transition points where predictability dramatically decreases. His work suggests that as systems become more complex, they reach a state of self-organized criticality, where small changes can lead to significant and unpredictable outcomes. This behavior forces decision-makers to move beyond traditional linear planning methods, as the system's behavior emerges from countless interdependent variables that resist comprehensive analysis through conventional approaches (Kauffman 1993).

These theoretical frameworks help explain why large-scale institutional failures often occur despite sophisticated modeling attempts. The emergent behavior of complex systems, characterized by nonlinear interactions and scaling effects, challenges the efficacy of traditional planning and management strategies. Factors that impact such effects include velocity, virality, feedback loops, cascading, and network effects.

How Nine Key Academic Fields Explain Scaling Effects

How can the impact of scale be taught? This is a tremendous emerging challenge without a current solution. Few case studies exist, despite the fact that the areas affected permeate technology, society, and the workplace. Who currently teaches scaling effects? Principally, *physicists, engineers, biologists, computer scientists, economists, social scientists, historians, management scholars, and Science and Technology Studies (STS) scholars,* although all academic subjects could be said to have aspects of scale. The study is at an early stage. For simplicity, I would say we are at a three-year-old's comprehension of a topic that would require an adult to begin to comprehend. And, metaphorically speaking, there seem to be no adults in the room yet. As I will explore, this is a challenge for skills development. Arguably, the field of systems thinking should emerge across all these areas. The field is currently more of an interdisciplinary approach (a methodology of sorts) with a set of related concepts, focused on relationships between things, and not just concerned with individual components, than a paradigm in and of itself. The paradox is that systems thinking is widely sought after in fields like environmental science, public policy, engineering, healthcare management, and education to tackle complex issues, particularly the elusive and accelerating grand challenges facing humanity. Systems thinking is definitely not yet a key part of conventional K-12 education. There are good reasons why. Although important, the field is not yet coherent and simple enough to teach. That has to change.

Scaling laws are fundamental in physics, particularly in fields like thermodynamics, fluid dynamics, and materials science. Engineers frequently deal with scaling issues in designing structures, vehicles, and systems. Cybernetic engineering is the study of how to control and monitor systems that change over time (e.g., dynamic systems), such as robots, aircraft, and cars. *Kybernetes* is Greek for pilot or rudder. Norbert Wiener, a mathematician, coined the term in the 1940s. It's an interdisciplinary field that draws on concepts from control theory, systems theory, and other areas. The core idea is to use feedback to maintain desired conditions, particularly to maintain stability. Key applications include robotics and control engineering (electrical circuits, process plants).

Computer scientists use a variety of methods to tackle the challenges of scaling—how systems perform as they grow larger. For algorithms, they rely on tools like asymptotic notation to estimate how much time or memory an algorithm needs as input sizes increase. This approach, found in widely used texts like *Introduction to Algorithms* (Cormen et al. 2009), helps identify which methods will remain efficient at scale. Donald Knuth (1997) highlighted how even small inefficiencies can cause big problems when systems grow.

To manage large amounts of data, researchers design smart data structures—like B-trees or cache-friendly methods—that help systems run smoothly, even across distributed networks. In networking, challenges grow with scale due to trade-offs between reliability, speed, and resilience. Brewer's CAP theorem (2000) shows that no distributed system can fully achieve all three, so designers use workarounds like eventual consistency to keep systems functional.

Engineers also use performance modeling—such as simulations or queueing theory—to find and fix potential slowdowns early. In parallel computing, Amdahl's Law reminds us that only some tasks benefit from being split across many processors. Books like *Computer Architecture* by Hennessy and Patterson (2017) explore hardware solutions to these limits. Together, these strategies help ensure computers stay fast and reliable—even as the demands placed on them grow.

Economists study how systems behave as they grow—whether in markets, networks, or entire economies. In markets, scaling can bring benefits like lower costs and more innovation, but also risks such as monopolies or instability. As economic networks grow—like global trade or finance—they become more efficient but also more fragile, where small problems can spread widely. At a larger scale, research shows that big cities and economies tend to produce more wealth and ideas per person, but also face more inequality and resource pressure (Bettencourt et al. 2007; Romer 1990). By studying these patterns, economists aim to understand how to support healthy growth while managing the risks that come with it.

Social scientists study society, culture, and group dynamics. Humanistic inquiry, particularly historians, studies change across time and space, including geographical scope, time period, and social aggregation (so-called "historical scale"). The triadic terms local, regional, and global are often used to indicate scale. However, this distinction is insufficient because dramatic change can originate at the local level. There are intricate dynamics between levels that need to be properly understood in any theory of change. The data to understand such changes are often scarce and, as a result, AI is of little or no help.

Historians, particularly those engaging in "big history"—the vast scale history of "everything" considering the cosmic timelines of the universe—are currently fascinated with the notion of "emergent properties." Big history refers to key moments in time when significant changes occurred, called "thresholds." Think of the formation of stars, the emergence of life on Earth, or the development of human civilization. Emergence is the idea that the whole can exhibit effects that cannot be predicted from the properties of its parts alone. Emergent in this context refers to qualitatively new effects.

Although the concept of emergent properties dates back to ancient philosophy, the term "emergent" was first coined by George Henry Lewes in *Problems of Life and Mind* (1875), where he distinguished between predictable "resultant" outcomes and novel "emergent" effects that arise from complexity and cannot be reduced to their parts. Scaling is central to understanding such emergence, particularly in biology. At the molecular level, nonlinear kinetics emerge as concentrations change; at the cellular level, surface area-to-volume constraints—highlighted in D'Arcy Thompson's *On Growth and Form* (1917)—limit cell size. Across species, metabolic rates scale to the three-fourth power of body mass, explained by the fractal design of circulatory systems (West, Brown, and Enquist 1997).

British ethologist C. Lloyd Morgan advanced these ideas in *Emergent Evolution* (1923), emphasizing context in animal behavior and introducing "Morgan's Canon"—a principle of scientific parsimony discouraging overly complex explanations for observed behaviors. His work laid a methodological foundation for studying emergence in complex adaptive systems that still shapes fields from cognitive science to systems biology.

Morgan, credited as the father of comparative psychology's so-called *Morgan's Canon* principle, believed that higher mental faculties should only be considered as explanations if lower faculties could not explain a behavior. This is, incidentally, something we ought to remember when thinking about AI. This notion has played a major role in behavioristic thinking on the role of stimulus and response, but is now widely regarded as outdated. On the contrary, as AI-based sensor technology and language comprehension advance, biologists discover more and more advanced cognition patterns among animals. This indicates that functionalist explanations throughout the history of science may initially seem intuitive (and therefore tend to be initially successful), yet have limited bearing on how natural properties truly emerge.

In management science, scale is typically assumed to be beneficial for firm growth and the longevity of a business model. This is because scale tends to facilitate so-called economies of scale, often defined in microeconomics as the savings in costs gained by an increased level of production ("output"). Empirically, one has observed that an increase in scale allows a firm to lower the cost of production and reduce the price of its products. Typically, the assumption is that fixed costs, like rent and equipment, are spread out over a larger output. In reality, many more factors come into play: efficiency, specialization, division of labor, bulk purchases, network economies of scale, risk reduction, greater resilience to external threats, enhanced communication, and branding effects. As a result, firms gain a competitive advantage and increased profitability. Larger stores like Walmart and Costco can produce at a lower average cost than smaller stores. Amazon can provide same-day delivery to its Prime customers. That said, there are also adverse effects as companies grow very large, such as competition laws, antitrust concerns, communication costs (social effects, stovepipes), overcrowding on the assembly line, reputation management, and legacy effects. Additionally, there might be sunk costs in infrastructure, talent, required product support, and product heritage. In fact, costs per unit could also increase when a company becomes large, inefficient, and bureaucratic. German sociologist Max Weber described this as becoming trapped in the "iron cage" of rational calculation, efficiency, and control ("bureaucracy").

To counter bureaucratic rigidity, Weber and subsequent theorists recommend organizations adopt a comprehensive approach that fundamentally reshapes operations by cultivating flexibility and empowering employee initiative rather than relying on rigid hierarchical structures. This involves making smarter use of workforce data—analyzing turnover rates, performance metrics, and demographics—to make evidence-based human resource decisions that align with broader business strategy. Organizations must conduct regular process reviews to maintain operational efficiency while preserving creative capacity, implementing structured change management protocols that can adapt to new circumstances. The ultimate goal is achieving balance among competing demands: incorporating human-centered, ethical decision-making alongside rational calculations, building cross-functional teams that break down departmental silos, designing compensation packages that attract talent within budget constraints, and engaging in systematic talent forecasting and succession planning to ensure long-term organizational continuity and growth.

Science and technology studies (STS) is beginning to produce relevant evidence on scaling effects. But the struggle to identify good climate solutions shows that "some things scale easily […] because people neither agree on problem definitions nor solutions" (Pfotenhauer et al. 2022). The challenge is to be self-reflexive. Scale plays a crucial role in shaping how science and technology are developed, implemented, and understood. Scale seems inherently attractive to many people, perhaps because dramatic change seems exciting, although it repulses others. There is a small, global movement to leave a smaller footprint and extract less of a tax on the Earth and disadvantaged groups with fewer options. STS has problematized the fact that a fixation on "scaling up" platforms and launching wide-ranging and risky solutions to grand societal challenges has captured current innovation discourse (Pfotenhauer et al. 2022).

There is, in fact, a politics of scaling, built on "solutionism, experimentalism and future-oriented valuation" (Pfotenhauer et al. 2022). The necessity of transitioning to a regenerative economy, possibly through a degrowth strategy of controlled deceleration or at least slower, more controlled growth implications, shows that the opposite of scaling might also be necessary or even attractive for humanity long-term. Also, the scale can still be gigantic even if the path to scale goes via more rigorous user testing, scenario building, risk assessment, and risk mitigation even before the technology, product, or service is released or scaled up.

STS has shown that scientific knowledge and technological systems are not purely products of objective reasoning or linear progress. Instead, they are deeply shaped by the social, cultural, political, and economic contexts in which they are produced and used (Jasanoff 2004; Latour and Woolgar 1979). Decisions about what counts as legitimate knowledge, which technologies are developed, and how they are implemented often reflect prevailing power structures, institutional interests, and cultural values. For example, STS research has demonstrated how gender biases can shape medical research, how funding priorities influence scientific agendas, and how infrastructure design can reflect and reinforce social inequalities (Winner 1980).

Despite its relevance, STS remains a relatively small field and is rarely integrated into core college curricula, especially outside of select programs in sociology, philosophy, or policy studies. This creates a significant gap in how future professionals—scientists, engineers, educators, and business leaders—are prepared to understand and navigate the social dimensions of innovation.

Given this gap, how should workers, employers, and educators respond? Workers need critical tools to interpret the broader implications of the technologies they use or help build. Understanding that design choices embed values can empower employees to raise ethical concerns or advocate for more inclusive practices. Employers, especially in tech-driven industries, must recognize that technological adoption is not just a technical decision but a social one. STS perspectives can improve stakeholder engagement, anticipate resistance, and inform more responsible innovation strategies. Educators should integrate STS principles into STEM and business curricula—not as electives, but as foundational knowledge. Doing so would equip students to question assumptions, recognize the politics of technology, and design systems that serve broader societal goals. In a time of rapid technological change and mounting social tensions, overlooking the lessons of STS risks perpetuating inequities and missing opportunities for more ethical, sustainable, and democratic innovation.

Industrial Scaling Concerns

Given that building large and complex infrastructure is a hallmark of industrial companies, one would think that scaling is a big concern in industry. This is not yet the case. Industrial certifications in areas like cloud computing, data science, and project management often address scaling challenges, but not in a systematic way. Space manufacturing is in its infancy, but will have to handle immense scale, cost, innovation, and long timelines. Historically, engaging with outer space has also required the invention and improvement of materials. The Mercury, Gemini, and Apollo missions drove the development of lightweight aluminum alloys capable of withstanding extreme temperature fluctuations while maintaining structural integrity. NASA's collaboration with DuPont led to the creation of Kapton polyimide films, now essential for thermal insulation in satellites and spacecraft due to their exceptional stability across temperatures ranging from $-269°C$ to $400°C$. The Space Shuttle's thermal protection system necessitated the invention of reinforced carbon-carbon composites and silica tiles that could endure atmospheric reentry temperatures exceeding $1600°C$. Modern spacecraft utilize specialized borosilicate glass formulations for viewing ports that resist micrometeoroid impacts while maintaining optical clarity in the vacuum of space. The International Space Station incorporates lithium-ion battery technologies specifically engineered for the radiation environment of low Earth orbit. SpaceX's Starship development program has advanced metallurgical techniques for stainless-steel alloys that optimize strength-to-weight ratios across cryogenic to high-temperature conditions. Satellite manufacturers now employ radiation-hardened semiconductor materials that prevent electronic degradation during years of exposure to cosmic rays and solar radiation.

Current industrial scaling challenges span supply chain fragility, data security, quality control, and automation. The COVID-19 pandemic exposed vulnerabilities in concentrated sectors such as semiconductors and pharmaceuticals (Gereffi 2020). Data breach costs have risen with scale, averaging $4.45 million globally in 2023 (IBM Security 2023). Quality control has shifted from traditional statistical methods to integrated digital monitoring, which can significantly reduce defect rates (ASQ 2023). Automation continues to boost productivity—industries with advanced robotics adoption see growth rates up to 1.7 times higher than those with lower adoption—while human labor increasingly focuses on system oversight rather than direct production (IFR 2023).

An emerging interdisciplinary field—variously termed infrastructure studies or, more ambitiously, infrastructure science—seeks to understand the design, operation, and broader societal implications of large-scale systems that sustain modern life. Once treated as invisible technical backdrops, infrastructures are now recognized as dynamic, complex, and politically charged systems with profound social, environmental, and economic consequences (Larkin 2013; Edwards 2003). Infrastructure studies draws from engineering, urban planning, anthropology, political science, and data science to examine how infrastructure is built, maintained, governed, and experienced. It treats infrastructure not just as physical hardware but as socio-technical systems shaped by institutions, power, and culture (Star 1999). Infrastructure science, as pursued at institutions like the Santa Fe Institute and MIT, goes further—seeking generalizable principles governing infrastructure behavior, resilience, and scaling (West 2017; Kauffman 1993). This includes modeling interdependencies, predicting failure thresholds, and designing adaptive systems under uncertainty. Amid climate change, urbanization, and digital transformation, this field is increasingly vital—offering insights into infrastructure's role as both enabler and constraint in twenty-first-century governance and innovation.

Acting Like a Gigascale Operator

The Nature of Gigascale Operations

Gigascale operations encompass activities that function at massive scale—at the upper boundaries of what current managerial practices, technologies, resources, and workforce capabilities can organize effectively. Gigaprojects typically begin at the threshold = $20B. Contemporary examples include major infrastructure projects (particularly in transportation), space programs, extensive research and development initiatives (across the United States, China, and the European Union), and global events such as the Olympic Games.

These operations are increasingly necessary to address complex global challenges including climate change mitigation, geopolitical coordination, global supply chain management, energy grid modernization, and numerous other systemic issues. The United Nations Sustainable Development Goals represent perhaps the most comprehensive example of challenges formulated as global giga-initiatives, where strategies and implementation plans must be coordinated at both global and national levels.

The Growing Necessity of Gigascale Operations

The demand for gigascale operations is accelerating due to several converging factors. Even smaller projects now frequently require gigascale coordination to prevent interference with existing infrastructure. Climate disaster recovery efforts, such as those following major hurricanes like extreme weather events, increasingly qualify as gigaprojects in their scope and complexity.

Another emerging concern is the potential runaway effect of new technologies, particularly artificial intelligence systems, which could present significant societal challenges. A troubling skill gap exists where relatively inexperienced professionals—perhaps a 22-year-old with technical expertise—might face decisions with billion-dollar downside potential affecting public or private infrastructure such as electrical grids, weather monitoring systems, or space infrastructure. Our educational and training systems have not yet fully adapted to prepare individuals for this level of responsibility.

Learning Gigascale Operational Skills

Currently, gigascale operations are not comprehensively taught in most educational institutions. Certain disciplines offer partial coverage, including aerospace programs, geography, science and technology studies, urban studies, and select systems engineering programs such as cybernetics. However, these programs typically address only specific technical systems, societal implications, or management aspects—rarely integrating all dimensions. Oxford professor emeritus Bent Flyvbjerg stands as a leading global authority on managing large projects (megaprojects), making him one of the few academics with a comprehensive understanding of this growing challenge.

A notable exception in formal education is the MSc in Major Programme Management at Oxford University's Saïd Business School. This program specifically addresses the challenges of major programs in science, technology, infrastructure, and social development—programs characterized as "very large scale, highly complex and changeable" with substantial leadership, design, governance, risk, and impact dimensions. The modular format allows participants to combine professional work with academic study. The Oxford program conceptualizes large programs as "temporary organizations" where recurring success and failure factors relate directly to program design. Systems thinking and managing systemic change and complexity form integral parts of the curriculum. At such scale, stakeholder mapping becomes crucial, particularly because stakeholder concerns and leadership typically evolve throughout the program's lifecycle due to personnel turnover and the inherent difficulty of managing diverse stakeholders over extended periods. Risk analysis focuses on determining root causes, including cognitive biases, rather than merely addressing symptoms.

The immense timescales involved—often decades between conception and delivery—mean the world in which a program is conceived can differ drastically from the world in which it is ultimately delivered, necessitating sophisticated scenario analysis capabilities. Some promising initiatives have emerged in the regulatory sphere. In 2023, the U.S. Office of Federal Contract Compliance Programs (OFCCP) launched a megaproject program to "foster equal opportunity in the construction trades workforce of federal contractors and subcontractors on large federal construction projects." This program targets projects valued at $35 million or more with expected durations exceeding one year, providing on-the-ground assistance to contractors to strengthen their hiring, recruitment, and employment practices.

Teaching Gigascale Operations

The pedagogical challenge in teaching gigascale operations stems largely from the scarcity of direct learning opportunities. Actual gigaprojects remain relatively uncommon, and many existing ones operate under confidentiality constraints or involve such high risk that they cannot accommodate educational observers or interns.

Looking forward, learning opportunities must increase dramatically. AI-based simulation, augmented reality, and virtual reality participation in gamified environments could partially address this shortage, but in-person exploration and on-the-job training remain essential. The development of academic insight regarding success factors in gigascale operations must also be prioritized.

A promising aspect of learning about scale is that valuable lessons can be acquired through a "zero shot" mindset. Start-ups provide excellent environments to learn about scaling dynamics, even when they never reach billion-dollar revenue or valuation thresholds. Even the transition from a few dozen employees to the often-cited "magical" 150-employee mark can offer substantive learning opportunities regarding scaling speeds, organizational tensions, and operational principles.

Future Directions

The maturation of gigascale operational capabilities has profound implications for addressing humanity's most complex challenges. As these practices become more sophisticated and widespread, our collective ability to coordinate at unprecedented scales will determine our success in areas ranging from climate adaptation to technological governance. However, questions remain regarding potential negative implications of gigascale operations, interactions with other Platinum Workforce skills, and approaches to scaling these capabilities effectively. These represent critical areas for future research and practice as gigascale operations transition from exceptional to commonplace.

Self-Taught Scaling Laws

Despite institutional gaps in formal education, self-directed learning has emerged as perhaps the most effective approach for developing gigascale operational capabilities. The integration of knowledge from diverse sources—online courses, academic publications, industry conferences, expert interviews, and practitioner podcasts—offers an adaptive learning pathway that mirrors the multidisciplinary nature of gigascale challenges themselves. This autodidactic approach requires significant self-efficacy, intrinsic motivation, methodical structure, and intellectual persistence. The evidence suggests that professionals who develop competence in navigating strong scaling effects will likely experience disproportionate career advancement opportunities. These individuals represent scarce, high-value talent in an economy increasingly defined by scale-driven outcomes.

Their trajectory of responsibility typically follows nonlinear patterns—not gradual increments but substantial, discontinuous leaps. Career advancement for these specialists often accelerates dramatically as organizations recognize their capacity to manage complexity at scale. The economic rewards can be substantial, and for some, public recognition follows their contributions to solving large-scale societal challenges. This development reflects a broader economic pattern in which scale-based disparities are becoming more pronounced across multiple dimensions: wealth distribution, professional opportunities, decision-making authority, and specialized knowledge domains. These widening gaps represent both a challenge for social policy and an opportunity for those equipped to operate effectively at unprecedented scales.

Emerging and Future Programs to Grasp Scale

Interdisciplinary programs are beginning to integrate knowledge from multiple disciplines (physics, biology, computer science, economics, and more) to address complex scaling challenges. For example, the Santa Fe Institute combines complexity science with network theory to model pandemic spread across different population densities. At MIT's Media Lab, researchers merge computational biology with materials science to develop scalable biomimetic structures that adapt to environmental stresses. Stanford's Earth System Science program integrates climate modeling with economic forecasting to assess how regional climate policies scale to global impact. The Human Computation Institute collaborates across cognitive science, computer science, and behavioral economics to develop crowd-based systems that efficiently scale human problem-solving capabilities for scientific research.

Sustainability programs worldwide examine how scaling technologies and systems impact the environment and society. The Stockholm Resilience Centre researches planetary boundaries to define safe limits for technological growth (Stockholm Resilience Centre 2019). Arizona State University's Global Institute of Sustainability and Innovation develops circular economy models to maintain resource efficiency as systems expand (ASU Global Futures 2024). ETH Zurich's Sustainability and Technology program investigates how renewable energy can scale without causing new resource dependencies or social inequities (ETH Zurich 2025). The Earth Institute at Columbia University integrates climate science and policy analysis to address urban development challenges at scale (Earth Institute n.d.). The University of Tokyo's Future Society Initiative explores sustainable development pathways that balance technological progress with environmental limits (University of Tokyo IFI 2023).

Ethics programs increasingly address the societal implications of scaling technologies such as AI and biotechnology. For example, Harvard's Edmond J. Safra Center for Ethics examines fairness and bias in algorithmic decision-making systems deployed in public institutions (Safra Center 2020). The Oxford Internet Institute's Digital Ethics Lab focuses on responsible innovation frameworks and ethical challenges related to the deployment of AI at scale (Oxford Internet Institute 2021). Stanford's Ethics, Society, and Technology Hub integrates technical expertise with philosophical inquiry to develop governance models for rapidly advancing biotechnologies and AI (Stanford News 2020). The IEEE Global Initiative on Ethics of Autonomous and Intelligent Systems produces practical standards and guidelines to support ethical AI deployment across various operational contexts (IEEE 2019). Princeton's University Center for Human Values collaborates with computer scientists to create auditing methodologies that assess ethical risks as machine learning applications expand from limited domains to general-purpose use (Princeton UCHV 2018).

Conclusion

Understanding scaling effects is crucial for addressing a wide range of challenges in science, engineering, industry, and society. These are challenges that ideally are tackled by a joined-up global workforce. Failing that, it must certainly be the core emphasis of leaders in any sector. Regardless of the merits of disciplinary expertise (benefits which nobody is saying will completely go away at least in the short term), interdisciplinary approaches are essential for tackling complex scaling problems. Lifelong learning and continuous adaptation will be crucial for individuals to navigate the evolving landscape of scaling challenges. It would also be helpful if existing educational institutions got on board with a dramatic transformation effort. Or, we can at least hope that a new category of educational players will emerge whose sole focus is to explore, investigate, demonstrate, and teach scaling effects. The scope is potentially enormous. But boiling the ocean is not fruitful. The debate on which specific skills society and industry need in the three- to ten-year time frame is crucial. Although it's great that the World Economic Forum has taken a leading role in the discussion, it cannot just be a discussion in Davos. Managing skills at scale will become a key issue for local municipalities as well as global gigaprojects, for corporations as well as governments, for individuals as well as teams. Scale is a multipronged challenge; it entails grasping the full impact of emerging technologies before they fully emerge and reacting to adverse impacts with force once they emerge. It entails more deeply understanding how society and culture truly evolve, making good use of dramatically better investigative tools than we had in the last century.

With all of this said, we are ready to embark on Chapter 17, How to teach futuristic skills? There, I'll detail key futuristic learning modes, including scenario planning, gigascale learning arenas, action learning principles, and outline my vision for the expanded role of scalable internships.

References

Adner, Ron, and Rahul Kapoor. 2010. "Value Creation in Innovation Ecosystems: How the Structure of Technological Interdependence Affects Firm Performance." *Strategic Management Journal* 31 (3): 306–333. https://doi.org/10.1002/smj.821.

ASQ. 2023. "The Impact of Digital Quality Monitoring." *American Society for Quality.* https://asq.org/conferences/qis/2023.

ASU Global Futures. 2024. "Circular Economy in the Chemical Industry." https://globalfutures.asu.edu/kaiteki/past-research/circular-economy-in-the-chemical-industry/.

Bettencourt, Luís M. A., José Lobo, Dirk Helbing, Christian Kühnert, and Geoffrey B. West. 2007. "Growth, Innovation, Scaling, and the Pace of Life in Cities." *Proceedings of the National Academy of Sciences* 104 (17): 7301–7306. https://doi.org/10.1073/pnas.0610172104.

Brewer, Eric A. 2000. "Towards Robust Distributed Systems." *Proceedings of the ACM PODC.* https://cs.berkeley.edu/~brewer/cs262b-2004/PODC-keynote.pdf.

Caswell, Isaac. 2024. "110 New Languages Are Coming to Google Translate." *Google.* June 27. https://blog.google/products/translate/google-translate-new-languages-2024/.

Cormen, Thomas H., Charles E. Leiserson, Ronald L. Rivest, and Clifford Stein. 2009. *Introduction to Algorithms.* 3rd ed. Cambridge: MIT Press.

DeepSeek-AI et al. (2025). Technical report on reasoning models. *I*

Earth Institute. n.d. "About the Earth Institute." *Columbia University.* https://www.earth.columbia.edu/.

Edwards, Paul N. 2003. "Infrastructure and Modernity: Force, Time, and Social Organization in the History of Sociotechnical Systems." In *Modernity and Technology,* edited by Thomas J. Misa, Philip Brey, and Andrew Feenberg, 185–225. Cambridge, MA: MIT Press. https://direct.mit.edu/books/edited-volume/2674/chapter/86413/Infrastructure-and-Modernity-Force-Time-and-Social.

ETH Zurich. 2025. "Learning to Shape the Future of the Energy Transition." https://ethz.ch/en/news-and-events/eth-news/news/2025/01/die-zukunft-der-energiewende-mitgestalten-koennen.html.

Gereffi, Gary. 2020. "What Does the COVID-19 Pandemic Teach Us about Global Value Chains? The Case of Medical Supplies." *Journal of International Business Policy* 3: 287–301. https://link.springer.com/article/10.1057/s42214-020-00062-w.

Hennessy, John L., and David A. Patterson. 2017. *Computer Architecture: A Quantitative Approach.* 6th ed. Massachusetts: Morgan Kaufmann.

Hoffmann, Jordan, Sebastian Borgeaud, Arthur Mensch, Elena Buchatskaya, Trevor Cai, Eliza Rutherford, Diego de Las Casas, Lisa Anne Hendricks, Johannes Welbl, Aidan Clark, Tom Hennigan, Eric Noland, Katie Millican, George van den Driessche, Bogdan Damoc, Aurelia Guy, Simon Osindero, Karen Simonyan, Erich Elsen, Jack W. Rae, Oriol Vinyals, and Laurent Sifre. 2022. "Training Compute-Optimal Large Language Models." *arXiv preprint arXiv:2203.15556.* https://arxiv.org/abs/2203.15556.

IBM Security. 2023. Cost of a Data Breach Report 2023. https://www.ibm.com/reports/data-breach.

IEEE. 2019. "Ethically Aligned Design: A Vision for Prioritizing Human Well-being with Autonomous and Intelligent Systems." *IEEE Global Initiative on Ethics of Autonomous and Intelligent Systems.* https://standards.ieee.org/wp-content/uploads/import/documents/other/ead_v2.pdf.

IFR. 2023. "World Robotics Report 2023." *International Federation of Robotics*. https://ifr .org/downloads/press2018/Executive_Summary_WR_2023.pdf.

Jasanoff, Sheila. 2004. *States of Knowledge: The Co-Production of Science and the Social Order*. London: Routledge.

Kaplan, Jared, Sam McCandlish, Tom Henighan, Tom B. Brown, Benjamin Chess, Rewon Child, Scott Gray, Alec Radford, Jeffrey Wu, and Dario Amodei. 2020. "Scaling Laws for Neural Language Models." *arXiv preprint arXiv:2001.08361*. https://arxiv.org/abs/2001.08361.

Kauffman, Stuart A. 1993. *The Origins of Order: Self-Organization and Selection in Evolution*. Oxford: Oxford University Press. https://academic.oup.com/book/53153.

Knuth, Donald E. 1997. *The Art of Computer Programming*, Vol. 1: Fundamental Algorithms. 3rd ed. Boston: Addison-Wesley.

Larkin, Brian. 2013. "The Politics and Poetics of Infrastructure." *Annual Review of Anthropology* 42: 327–343. https://www.annualreviews.org/doi/10.1146/annurev -anthro-092412-155522.

Latour, Bruno, and Steve Woolgar. 1979. *Laboratory Life: The Construction of Scientific Facts*. Princeton, NJ: Princeton University Press.

Lewes, George Henry. 1875. *Problems of Life and Mind*. London: Trübner & Co.

Marcus, Gary. 2024. "The New AI Scaling Law Shell Game." *Marcus on AI*. November 24. https://garymarcus.substack.com/p/a-new-ai-scaling-law-shell-game.

Morgan, C. Lloyd. 1923. *Emergent Evolution*. London: Williams and Norgate.

NASA. 2024. "NASA's Parker Solar Probe Makes History With Closest Pass to Sun." December 27. https://science.nasa.gov/science-research/heliophysics/nasas -parker-solar-probe-makes-history-with-closest-pass-to-sun/.

Oxford Internet Institute. 2021. "Research at the Oxford Internet Institute." Accessed May 2025. https://www.oii.ox.ac.uk/research/.

Pfotenhauer, Sebastian, Brice Laurent, Kyriaki Papageorgiou, and Jack Stilgoe. 2022. "The Politics of Scaling." *Social Studies of Science* 52 (1): 3–34. https://doi.org/10.1177 /03063127211048979.

Princeton University Center for Human Values (UCHV). 2018. *The Princeton Dialogues on AI and Ethics*. Princeton University. https://uchv.princeton.edu/programs/ princeton-dialogues-ai-and-ethics.

Romer, Paul M. 1990. "Endogenous Technological Change." *Journal of Political Economy* 98 (5, Part 2): S71–S102. https://doi.org/10.1086/261725.

Safra Center. 2020. "Fairness and Bias in Algorithmic Decision Making." *Harvard Edmond J. Safra Center for Ethics*. https://ethics.harvard.edu/fairness-bias.

Santa Fe Institute. n.d. "Scaling Laws and Urban Systems." Accessed May 10, 2025. https://www.santafe.edu/research/results/working-papers/scaling-laws-and -urban-systems.

Stanford News. 2020. "Ethics, Society and Technology Hub Embeds Ethics in Teaching and Research." *Stanford University*. https://news.stanford.edu/2020/10/15/ethics -society-technology-hub/.

Star, Susan Leigh. 1999. "The Ethnography of Infrastructure." *American Behavioral Scientist* 43 (3): 377–391. https://doi.org/10.1177/00027649921955326.

Stockholm Resilience Centre. 2019. "The Planetary Boundaries Framework: Using it to Reach Global Goals." https://www.stockholmresilience.org/research/planetary -boundaries.html.

Suddaby, Roy, William S. Schultz, and A. J. Coraiola. 2020. "Temporal Work and the Challenge of Strategic Change." *Academy of Management Journal* 63 (6): 1953–1978. https://doi.org/10.5465/amj.2017.0768.

Teece, David J. 2010. "Business Models, Business Strategy and Innovation." *Long Range Planning* 43 (2–3): 172–194. https://doi.org/10.1016/j.lrp.2009.07.003.

Thompson, D'Arcy Wentworth. 1917. *On Growth and Form*. Cambridge: Cambridge University Press.

University of Tokyo IFI. 2023. "About IFI | The University of Tokyo Institute for Future Initiatives." https://ifi.u-tokyo.ac.jp/en/about/.

Wei, Jason, Yi Tay, Rishi Bommasani, Colin Raffel, Barret Zoph, Sebastian Borgeaud, Dani Yogatama, Maarten Bosma, Denny Zhou, Donald Metzler, Ed H. Chi, Tatsunori Hashimoto, Oriol Vinyals, Percy Liang, Jeff Dean, and William Fedus. 2022. "Emergent Abilities of Large Language Models." *arXiv preprint arXiv:2206.07682*. https://arxiv.org/abs/2206.07682.

West, Geoffrey B. 2017. *Scale: The Universal Laws of Growth, Innovation, Sustainability, and the Pace of Life in Organisms, Cities, Economies, and Companies*. New York: Penguin Press. https://www.penguinrandomhouse.com/books/314049/scale-by-geoffrey-west/.

West, Geoffrey B., James H. Brown, and Brian J. Enquist. 1997. "A General Model for the Origin of Allometric Scaling Laws in Biology." *Science* 276 (5309): 122–126. https://doi.org/10.1126/science.276.5309.122.

Winner, Langdon. 1980. "Do Artifacts Have Politics?" *Daedalus* 109 (1): 121–136.

CHAPTER 17

HOW TO TEACH FUTURISTIC SKILLS

Before Germany was unified in 1871, education systems varied across German states. Schools were linked to social class and provided uneven quality. Later, in imperial Germany (1871–1918), the school system dramatically changed. Great efforts were made to expand and support a national curriculum that included not only general education but also vocational training specifically contributing to industrialization. As part of that, there was a strong emphasis on discipline and work ethic. Industrial education was impersonal, efficient, and standardized. It was designed to create workers who were compliant, who could take orders, and who could follow a schedule.[1] Technical colleges provided specialized training in engineering, technology, and other industrial fields. The explicit aim was to turn heaps of students into factory workers to match the needs of an industrializing Germany. Public education, conceived that way, served the needs and interests of the state, which were constructing railroads and building factories across mining, metal, and manufacturing industries. Prussian schools were even called "factory schools." This is not to sugarcoat factory work which, back then, was hard, strictly hierarchically organized with long days, poor working conditions, low pay, and polluted conditions. But what it indicates is that schooling, training, and upskilling can happen at a grand scale, and can make a big difference.

Although these compulsory German schools were widely admired for their efficiency, for reducing illiteracy, and for inspiring educational reforms across the world, they were far from perfect. The standardized approach meant little

---

1 Schrager, A. (2018). "The modern education system was designed to teach future factory workers to be "punctual, docile, and sober," 29 June, *Quartz*. https://qz.com/1314814/universal-education-was-first-promoted-by-industrialists-who-wanted-docile-factory-workers

time for exploration, individual adjustment, and diving deep, developing skills based on passion. The learning setting was the classroom. The class size was roughly 20–30 students. Students were grouped by age, not by abilities, skills, learning styles, or learning needs. Every hour had its subject. The schedule was always the same. The curriculum was fixed. Children were taught roughly the same things: reading, writing, math, science, history, and foreign languages. All activity was geared toward passing exams. Some learners thrived; others fell through the cracks. Most adults in the Western world, and nearly everyone in the Global South to this day, know what this means. This is a version of the school we attended. The public education system has prevailed for 150 years— a period in which we have had the Industrial Revolution, urbanization, globalization, social movements, world wars, and enormous technological change. Alternative approaches being tested over the past few decades, such as mixed-age classrooms and ability-based grouping, do not change the overall model. May that type of education rest in peace. It was perhaps never a great idea, and it is certainly not a good idea for today or tomorrow. While these historical perspectives reveal past adaptations, the next section examines how education must evolve again—this time under AI-driven and immersive learning modes.

Beyond Classrooms: Education in the Age of Intelligence

The 2030s will be a decade of profound upheaval—but also of immense opportunity. The accelerating pace of technological, environmental, and social transformation calls for a school system unlike any we've known before. Not one merely updated by digital tools, but one fundamentally reimagined for a world where knowledge is no longer scarce but ambient, distributed, and machine-augmented (Doxtdator 2022).

In such a world, the purpose of education can no longer be content transmission. AI systems learn faster, store more, and forget less. They're capable of synthesizing vast knowledge domains in ways that challenge the very premise of human-centered information transfer. If knowledge is everywhere, then the task of education shifts: from knowing to orienting, from memorizing to acting, from acquiring information to exercising *discernment, judgment, and agency* (Peschl and Fundneider 2017). This pivot finds fertile ground in the transformation already occurring in contemporary workplaces. In particular, advanced manufacturing environments have evolved into productive learning spaces—clean, quiet, high-tech, and collaborative. These environments represent a stark departure from the nineteenth-century factory. Today's shop floors are embedded with digital twins, collaborative robots, and IoT infrastructure. They offer comfort and precision, not noise and grime (Kuckelkorn and Davidson 2020).

Crucially, they offer continuous, embedded learning. In such environments, the boundary between learning and doing dissolves. Human–machine interaction, systems thinking, and data-driven process optimization are not taught in isolation—they are practiced as part of daily operations. The seamless integration of learning and work isn't just efficient; it's increasingly a *prerequisite* for mastering the speed, depth, and complexity of futuristic skills. This shift has profound social consequences. The traditional dichotomy between "white-collar" knowledge workers and "blue-collar" manual laborers is rapidly losing its meaning. Assembly, machining, welding, testing, and maintenance now require digital literacy, real-time data interpretation, and agile adaptation. The shop floor worker has become a knowledge contributor, a process innovator, and a systems optimizer (Autor 2019).

These changes present a historic opportunity for equity. As skill demands converge across physical and cognitive domains, so too can compensation, prestige, and career mobility. In many cases, *dedication, delivery, and deduction*—not age, prior credentials, or geography—become the real differentiators. Workers are no longer just implementing designs; they're *co-designing processes* through iterative feedback. This flattening of hierarchy in advanced operations reduces the need for managerial oversight, empowering frontline workers with autonomy and responsibility. But while the workplace may become one of the primary sites of learning, it must not be the only one. Learning also thrives in makerspaces, research labs, natural environments, crisis zones, and anywhere people engage in solving meaningful problems. These are not passive learning spaces—they are *transformative arenas* where needs and impact are immediately visible. Education in the 2030s must draw from these domains, fostering place-based learning, making, and experimentation.

In essence, learning becomes building. We learn by interacting with physical systems, testing hypotheses, crafting responses, and reflecting on failure. This experiential mode must become the dominant pedagogy across all levels—not only in vocational settings, but in what we now call "K-12" and "higher education." Indeed, the familiar stages of schooling—elementary, secondary, tertiary—may not survive another decade intact. Lifelong learning, peer-to-peer mentoring, apprenticeships at scale, and personalized, nonlinear educational pathways will increasingly define the learning landscape. As the world demands new forms of readiness, education must become continuous, adaptive, and rooted in context.

Nearly all learning may soon be interactive, multisite, and real-time. But the more fluid learning becomes, the more it requires from learners: not just curiosity, but *metacognition*—the ability to choose what to learn, how to learn, when to pivot, and how to apply insight. This is not simply an individual challenge; it is a systems-level problem. Organizing learning at scale—without the stabilizing shell of traditional schooling—demands new governance, new infrastructures, and new public trust.

There is a reason the institution of the school has lasted so long. It offers social stability, civic orientation, and a shared space for identity formation. Yet if education is to serve a society defined by intelligent systems and planetary challenges, it must evolve into something more distributed, more dynamic, and more human. The future of education is not about learning in isolation. It is about being ready—to navigate complexity, to act wisely in a sea of information, and to build meaning where machines cannot. And that, perhaps, is our enduring human advantage (Figure 17.1).

FIGURE 17.1 How to teach futuristic skills.

Futuristic Learning Modes

Experiential learning opportunities involve hands-on assignments and collaborative activities based on real-life situations or primary research that demand active participation in the learning process and engage learners' reflective problem-solving. Simulated challenges that mimic real situations will have so much support from augmented reality-based learning systems that they become nearly indistinguishable from real-life problems in the workplace. Real problems, on the other hand, will immediately be brought into a learning lab-type environment where groups of workers and students will jointly uncover the nature of the problem and implement solutions (Figure 17.2).

It is not immediately obvious that every worker in the *platinum workforce* will need to possess the same level or ability within every core or adjacent futuristic skill. In fact, that is hardly realistic. However, as a whole, the workforce in any relevant industry or location would have to possess these characteristics. In order to do so, these skills have to be learned and honed repeatedly, at the highest level of aptitude and scale. Key elements should be practiced daily. New items should be added weekly. The repertoire would be thoroughly rehearsed monthly and reflected upon annually. The learning would need to benefit from conscious, yet variable input intensity, motivational incentives, and distinct consequences of success or failure. Even with all of this scaffolding structure,

FIGURE 17.2 Futuristic skills.

SKILLS

SKILLS	WHO?	HOW	WHERE
AUGMENTED INTELLIGENCE	KNOWLEDGE WORKERS	HANDS-ON MACHINE-HUMAN	FACTORY FLOOR
INTEROPERABILITY MINDSET	CONNECTORS	EIXING A PROBLEM	HEALTH SYSTEM
ECO-AWARENESS	SUSTAINERS	EXPERIENCE ECO-CHALLENGES	NATURE
COMFORT WITH MOBILITY	NOMADS	LIVE/WORK WITH FOREIGNERS	CULTURAL IMMERSION'
GIGASCALE EXPERIENCE	ENTREPRENEURS	ZERO TO 1,000 (EMPLOYEESS)	STARTUPS & MEGAPROJECTS
MAKER SKILLS	CRAFTSPEOPLE	DESIGN/PRESENT/CONVINCE	MAKERSPACE
MEDIATION SKILLS	PRESENTERS	DESIGN/PRESENT/CONVINCE	PUBLIC SPEAKING
PSYCHO-RESILIENCE	SURVIVORS	INTERVENE/ASSIST/REFLECT	CRISIS EPICENTERS
R&D HACKER SKILLS	HACKERS	DISCOVER/APPLY/TRANSFORIA	RESEARCH LABS
BEFINED RISK APTITUDE	FORECASTERS	EXPERIENCE/ANALYZE/SOLVE	HAZARD SIMULATIONS
SOCIO-TECHNICAL FINESSE	TECHNOLOGISTS	REAL WORLD MODELING	AUGMENTED REALITY
AGENTIC AI	AIs	TRAINING AI MODELS	ON PREM & IN THE CLOUD

learning needs to be perceived as playful. Rules could be bent. Inspiration would be followed over strict adherence to even the core principles.

For this to work, personal flexibility, responsibility, and freedom of choice would need to be the overarching principles. However, this active role presupposes that learners have developed self-regulatory skills. Taking responsibility for your own learning is highly demanding. The Russian learning scholar Vygotsky (1978) described the gap between what is known to the learner and what can be known in a social learning setting as a "zone of proximal development." Today, that setting is more complex than what can be provided by a teacher alone. Almost anything can potentially enhance learning and help create an appropriate "zone" for learning and development. Even failures can provide elements of a learning zone if they become part of a sustained effort of adaptation and change. Conversely, many settings, particularly if they contain multifaceted challenges for which the learner is unprepared to act or strategize around, will end up inhibiting learning. Constant interruptions from conflicting demands from outside forces will as well.

In this new learning reality, isolating learning as a specific activity becomes a tremendous challenge. And few teachers have the full picture of where a learner is at and what they should be learning at any given moment. In the messier picture of the workplace, this is an even more acute challenge. That's why informal mentorship from several people is crucial throughout a learning path. Those who don't seek out mentors are at a significant disadvantage. But that also becomes another source of social inequality. Good mentors are disproportionately available to those learners whose social environment includes accomplished people with varied experiences, backgrounds, and time, energy, and motivation to spare, sharing it with learners.

Where are things like this practiced today, so that we can get some indication of how realistic this is to scale? First off, let's immediately confirm a suspicion you might have: most K-12 school systems, even experimental schools, don't practice the full set of futuristic skills at the necessary level of complexity. Neither do colleges around the world. And if you specifically hone in on leadership skills, it is obvious that the management and business schools that populate the Anglo-Saxon world and beyond were purpose built for the industrial society emerging after the Second World War. For its lack of curriculum around scale, its shallow focus on technology management beyond simple digital skills, and its predominant focus and body of case evidence from outdated American industrial organizations, it is not suitable for the disruptive nature of the next few decades. Neither, we should hasten to say, are corporate training programs. Many corporate employees express dissatisfaction with mandatory training, often perceiving it as a compliance requirement rather than a meaningful development opportunity. Optional training fares no better—participation and completion rates remain low. These findings suggest that traditional corporate training models frequently fail to engage learners or align with their professional goals, undermining their impact on skill development and organizational performance. The reskilling need of the contemporary corporation starts with a new hire and ends with their first hire, who each, realistically, should get major monthly updates and substantial daily training to upgrade their performance on their day-to-day tasks, the way a classical musician practices hours a day to stay sharp.

There are a few sporadic exceptions to the rule, and each has instructive lessons that can be applied in future-relevant skills training.

Promising Models for Future-Ready Learning

Across the global education landscape, a quiet revolution is underway. While the traditional classroom—teacher-led, test-driven, and rigid—still dominates, a growing number of experimental models are redefining how learning takes place. These aren't wholesale alternatives but generative exceptions: instructive signals of what education could become in an era of accelerating complexity, technological upheaval, and social change.

In advanced manufacturing, a notable shift is occurring. Tulip, a manufacturing operations platform, transforms factory floors into active learning environments. Its software integrates digital workflows that guide workers through production tasks while collecting performance data in real time. This embeds learning directly into action, allowing workers to improve their skills as they work—an embodiment of what Brown and Duguid (2017) call "learning-in-working," where development emerges through authentic participation rather than abstract instruction.

This ethos is also reshaping higher education. At Olin College, students begin tackling real-world engineering challenges from their first semester. The curriculum is built around project work and interdisciplinary collaboration, simulating professional environments where students design, test, and iterate together (Somerville et al. 2019). Babson College follows a parallel logic, integrating venture creation directly into coursework. Students don't just study entrepreneurship; they live it, launching real start-ups and navigating uncertainty as part of their academic growth.

Transitional education models are also being rethought. The University of Texas at Austin's OnRamps program offers dual-enrollment courses that allow high school students to earn college credit early. This helps smooth the transition into higher education while building academic confidence through early exposure to collegiate expectations (Miller and Pope 2022). Such modular credentialing offers flexible, layered learning pathways that reflect the nonlinear nature of modern careers.

Meanwhile, online platforms like Coursera, edX, and Khan Academy have scaled access to high-quality content globally. While completion rates remain a concern, hybrid approaches that combine self-paced modules with peer learning and mentorship have shown promise. These platforms demonstrate how technology can create flexible, scalable learning ecosystems—especially when paired with human facilitation (Reich 2020).

In elite academic settings, teaching itself is evolving. Stanford University, for instance, emphasizes experiential methods: case studies, design thinking, simulations, and real-world challenges that immerse students in practical problem-solving. Apprenticeship-style learning, often thought of as outdated, is also being reimagined and scaled across sectors. Switzerland leads the way with a national system that places students in mentored, work-based environments, systematically integrating industry and education (Hoffman and Schwartz 2017).

Perhaps the most forward-leaning models focus on what some call "gigascale subjects"—fields such as artificial intelligence, synthetic biology, global health, and urban systems. These domains defy traditional academic silos and require interdisciplinary fluency. Programs tackling these topics increasingly use scenario planning and structured futures thinking to train students not for a known world, but for unknown futures (Chermack 2018).

Across these examples, shared principles emerge. Learning is increasingly situated in real contexts, embedded in action rather than abstracted from it. Programs emphasize flexibility, recognizing that one-size-fits-all education no longer fits the world we live in. And above all, these models cultivate adaptive, metacognitive learners—individuals capable not just of mastering knowledge, but of reflecting on how they learn and evolving as needed.

As we move toward the 2030s—a decade defined by volatility, automation, and transformation—these educational models serve as blueprints. They show us how learning systems might be built not just to survive uncertainty, but to prepare people to lead within it.

The more uncertain the future becomes, the more exploratory learning needs to be. Scenario planning—originally developed in the military and refined in corporate strategy—has emerged as one of the most adaptive forms of anticipatory education. Unlike traditional forecasting, it does not aim to predict the future, but to prepare for multiple plausible futures, each shaped by different combinations of drivers, trends, and disruptions.

Its roots lie in Cold War military planning, where strategists recognized that conflict could arise from a wide range of unpredictable circumstances. Preparation for a single most-likely outcome was insufficient; instead, they developed and rehearsed multiple alternative futures. This methodology soon migrated to the corporate world. Shell, for example, famously adopted scenario planning in the 1970s to navigate oil price volatility, geopolitical shifts, and energy transitions. When the 1973 oil crisis struck, Shell's preparedness—grounded in rehearsed scenario narratives—allowed it to respond more swiftly than competitors (Wack 1985).

Today, governments and public institutions are increasingly turning to scenario planning to manage complex challenges ranging from climate change to AI governance. In the public sector, scenario workshops help policy leaders question assumptions, engage with systemic uncertainty, and even reimagine institutional roles. For civil servants and strategists alike, these exercises offer more than abstract futures—they become lived simulations of strategic choice.

Scenario planning also provides what formal education often lacks: structured ways to practice long-range thinking. In contrast to the conventional case study method, which isolates decisions in bounded contexts, scenario-based learning encourages students to think across time horizons, institutions, and systems. It fosters what J. Peter Scoblic (2020) calls "temporal dexterity"—the capacity to hold multiple futures in mind while acting meaningfully in the present.

Some business schools and policy programs now integrate scenario planning into executive education and leadership development. In these courses, students don't just analyze case studies—they cocreate futures, exploring themes such as technological disruption, decarbonization, or democratic erosion. These immersive learning environments cultivate the strategic imagination and adaptive mindset necessary for leading through turbulence.

In this sense, scenario planning bridges the gap between foresight and learning. It repositions the future not as a distant event to be predicted, but as a set of choices that must be rehearsed. As education systems evolve to meet the demands of the 2030s, this capacity—to engage deeply with what might happen, and to act wisely in response—is perhaps one of the most essential competencies of all.

Few of these developments are covered in any meaningful way by the management schools that evolved to cater to the complexities of large organizations. Management education has been closely tied to businesses and less to their external environment. For example, the case method tends to be myopically focused on leadership decisions as if a corporate challenge can be reduced to, or resolved by, a single management decision. Instead, many corporate challenges are complex and depend on institutional arrangements, partnerships, and changes in the external environment. Despite that, a typical management education curriculum contains the same foundational courses, on management principles, organizational behavior, business ethics, economics, accounting, finance, and marketing, as it did in a hundred years ago. The specialized courses have also not changed much as they cover human resource management, operations, strategy, supply chain, and project management. The specialized courses have evolved slightly to include international business, data analytics, and leadership.

Governments embrace scenario planning for similar reasons. As governance becomes more complex, public sector organizations embark on learning journeys that tend to question their very existence. Although learning about governance futures may seem ill-suited to the classroom, scenario planning has found a foothold in academic settings through carefully structured, experiential methods. Institutions like Oxford's Saïd Business School and Harvard Kennedy School have adapted scenario thinking into workshops where students construct plausible futures and test strategic responses. These classroom experiences are far from passive—they challenge learners to interrogate their assumptions, collaborate across disciplines, and simulate uncertainty through role-play and storytelling.

One common approach involves building contrasting futures around key uncertainties—climate policy, AI regulation, geopolitical instability—and having students step into the roles of ministries, corporations, or NGOs. The resulting simulations resemble real-world decision-making environments. UNESCO's Futures Literacy Labs, now used in university pilot programs, reinforce this by encouraging students to develop multiple scenarios and reflect on how their mental models evolve in the process. Research supports the impact: students exposed to structured scenario work show measurable gains in systems thinking and comfort with ambiguity (Norris et al., 2022).

In this way, classrooms become laboratories of the future—not by replicating real-world complexity in full, but by cultivating the intellectual agility required to navigate it.

Gigascale Subjects

Determining which subjects are at the core of futuristic learning is not a process that can be completed once and for all. It should be determined by the current societal challenges that need to be prioritized. The frame of mind I've used here takes a reasonable scenario around an intensifying global polycrisis condition. Other choices could be made. This explicitly does not go into the fundamental areas that might need to underpin such learning for it to have full effect, including STEM-type knowledge and psychology.

If that is the framing challenge, certain subjects crystallize as important starting points, notably: *system governance* (e.g., cybernetics, geopolitics, risk management, sustainability), *system optimization* (e.g., economics, interoperability, operations, supply chains, urban planning), key *systems applications areas* (e.g., artificial intelligence, engineering, environmental science, food production, healthcare, contested social issues), and the higher-order subject of *systems science* (e.g., complexity, macrosociology, science and technology studies, synthetic biology). The commonality is the frame of reference of systems of various kinds, and their interconnections. The reason these are important to focus on is that the scale of the challenges facing humanity far outstrips the typical examples used when teaching biology, business, management, psychology, or sociology. This is not to say that these subjects are unimportant, merely that the way they are taught needs to radically change.

To give an example, management schools cannot continue to teach teamwork as a process between a handful of individuals, the way it was conceived throughout the postwar era. Rather, teamwork is a question of human–AI hybrid interaction unbounded by scale challenges, a subject for which the available and tested curriculum currently is strictly limited. The traditional psychology curriculum was similarly based on human psychology in small groups and hardly takes into account the interaction with other relevant biological forms that exhibit behaviors and cognitive processes humans will need to start interacting with once we more fully understand them, such as insects, marine life, microorganisms, and plants. This will be especially crucial in the synthetically modified forms of nature, functionally enhanced in various ways, that are likely to become prevalent toward the mid to end century and beyond, especially those forms that are modified to integrate or communicate directly with humans or whose languages we will learn through AI. As part of this type of focus, and with the combination of climate collapse and increased stress from other polycrisis processes, ecopsychology, the science of how immersion in nature benefits human health, is likely to move to the forefront of existential coping.[2]

But rather than continuing to outline which existing subjects are relevant, and how existing subjects can be tweaked to renew their relevance for a polycrisis environment, I chose to hone in on the more concrete skills that exist one layer below. There are several reasons for this. One is that a book about all kinds of systems-relevant subjects and what they know and don't is a tome in and of itself. Some of these subjects are also currently underdeveloped. They would need to undergo dramatic upgrades in order to be sufficiently useful in tackling the polycrisis. The other is that a skills-driven approach is likely to be easier to picture and understand than a high-level description of academic subjects and full-fledged emerging fields. I will leave the subject of current topics taught in K-12, colleges and universities on the note that when I advise my own kids, I would say that if nothing changes, try to cover the key systems topic thoroughly along your educational path. Preferably, however, craft your own path, stitching together educational experiences using the specific skills that are outlined in this book. Preferably, that will become easier and easier to do, as institutional frameworks emerge which have such a purpose or direction.

Action Learning at MIT

Action Learning, as practiced at MIT Sloan School of Management, is a teaching method where students take what they learn in the classroom and apply it to a real business challenge. Sloan's learning labs range widely in topics, industries, and regions, but all aim to have students achieve the following five goals: apply classroom frameworks, structure and solve problems, collaborate effectively in teams, learn to lead through ambiguous and unstructured situations, and reflect for personal and professional growth.[3] Learning by doing is optimal for adult learners. Action labs build team spirit and long-term problem-solving capacity. Incorporating this mode fosters a learning organization. Corporations are taking notice. Action Lab clients of MIT include National Grid, Nike, Starbucks, BP India, PepsiCo, Oxfam, World Wildlife Fund, Green Mountain Coffee Roasters, IBM, and U.S. Navy.[4]

---

2 See (Aanstoos 2014)

3 Action learning at MIT (Action Learning)

4 Source: MIT Sloan School of Management. (2014, August). MIT Sloan Labs at a glance (Version 5.2) [PDF document]. Document no longer available online

Effective action labs require a set of foundational conditions to generate both learning and impact. First and foremost, they must tackle real-life problem-solving, with clear ownership and active buy-in from a designated coordinator and a high-level sponsor. All participants should see value in the process. To ensure relevance, the problem must be anchored in a specific context—connected to real teams, sites, or cross-functional coordination—so that employees can engage authentically and learn from each other. Importantly, the lab's focus should be distinct from ongoing workstreams to prevent duplication, though competing teams may address the same issue if transparently coordinated. The potential for impact should also be agreed upon in advance, including both measurable business benefits and broader social outcomes within existing resource constraints. On the learning side, the lab should integrate with existing curriculum frameworks or strategic themes, balancing individual learning outcomes with organizational insights. Learning should be captured in both face-to-face and digital formats, and participants must be given the freedom to fail—especially with executive-level tolerance for experimentation. Ultimately, successful labs culminate in experiential learning with measurable change, ideally delivering a positive revenue outcome alongside meaningful development.

The concept of "freezing change" originates from Kurt Lewin's foundational three-step model of organizational transformation. In this framework, effective change begins with "unfreezing"—a deliberate disruption of existing behaviors, norms, or systems to make room for something new. This is followed by the "change" phase, during which new practices or structures are introduced, ideally with minimal disruption to ongoing operations. The final phase, "refreezing," ensures that the changes are fully integrated and stabilized within the organization so they become lasting features rather than temporary shifts. This model remains widely used to guide transformations in leadership behavior, social habits, technologies, and institutional processes. Its enduring value lies in its ability to balance the necessity of radical shifts with the need for operational continuity and long-term sustainability (Lewin 1947).

Scalable Apprenticeships

Apprenticeships, a form of vocational training that combines on-the-job training with formal education, have been a feature of good learning practices for millennia. Even back in 2000 BC, Babylonians, as evidenced in the Code of Hammurabi, required artisans to teach their crafts to the next generation. In ancient Greece and Rome, young people would learn trades from skilled craftsmen. During the Middle Ages, apprenticeships were a centerpiece of the guild system regulating trades and professions. Leonardo da Vinci, the Renaissance polymath, was apprenticed to the renowned workshop of Andrea del Verrochio, a Florentine painter and sculptor. Wolfgang Amadeus Mozart began his training under his father, violinist, teacher, and composer Leopold Mozart. The Industrial Revolution led to a surge in apprenticeships as factories required skilled workers. Popular films have immortalized apprentices such as Luke Skywalker, Harry Potter, and Rocky Balboa. In recent years, there is renewed interest in apprenticeships to address skills shortages.

These types of often quite personal relationships between master and apprentice could be of importance to the holistic personality development of young people. They tend to provide opportunities for personal growth, skill development, and the attainment of ambitious goals. Moreover, because of their integrated nature, part of the inherent complexity of work itself, they tend to teach interdisciplinary competencies. When successful, masters tend to have a sustainable effect on apprentices' lifelong employment careers.[5] In short, apprenticeships existed before schools and while not perfect, they are immensely flexible, and will continue to exist after what we know as "school" slowly ceases to exist.

The challenge often put to proponents of this mode of learning is that it doesn't scale. How could it? How many disciplines can one master have at any given time? The question is good. But strategies for scaling apprenticeships exist. Governments can fund, incent, and regulate apprenticeships. Industry can collaborate to develop and implement good apprenticeship programs. This is to their advantage. Not only do apprenticeship programs help job seekers succeed in new careers. It also helps employers build a loyal, skilled workforce.[6] Nonprofits could facilitate apprenticeships. For example, Apprenti is a program of the Washington Technology Industry Association (WTIA) Workforce Institute, a 501c3 organization, that since 2016 provides economic mobility to underrepresented groups by identifying, training, and placing diverse talent in tech careers. Platform businesses could match masters with apprentices at scale and at a distance. Indeed, Apprenti runs an online platform that sources,

---

5 Apprenticeships as a unique shaping field for the development of an individual future-oriented "vocationality" (Ertelt et al. 2021)

6 Apprenticeship for Jobseekers, Mass.gov: https://www.mass.gov/info-details/apprenticeship-for-jobseekers

assesses, trains, and places tech talent with companies, connecting apprentices with employers in various industries.

Frontline workers refers to individuals who directly interact with customers or clients, such as cashiers, nurses, hospitality staff, flight attendants, call center agents, and public service officials. These workers are essential to the success of many organizations. However, as customer service gets supported by technology and becomes a key differentiator between companies, their role is always shifting with increased demands on technical competence, strategic thinking, and relational capabilities. Those shifts are also happening to back office staff such as accounting, finance, human resources, IT, and operations staff who used to work behind the scenes but are increasingly asked to perform middle office functions such as risk management, compliance, or trade processing where they are integral parts of a company's operations. Pathstream is a web-based platform for teaching in-demand tech skills for work. They offer online apprenticeships in technology and business fields for teams of frontline workers struggling to keep up with evolving roles.

With the advent of augmented intelligence, hardly any position in a company will remain in the back office, and even the front office will be making use of highly advanced systems, further blurring the distinction between hierarchical roles in a company. If you have access to the company's entire database, and have the power to obtain or maintain key client relationships, you are an important part of the business, no matter what your formal position is in the hierarchy.

Nowadays, apprenticeships are often part of a structured program that provides guidance and support. They may, ultimately, provide participants with a certificate or qualification that recognizes their skills and knowledge. Apprenticeships can be offered in a variety of fields, including in various trades, manufacturing, across technology areas, and in fields such as academia, healthcare, and business. Corporate America has increasingly turned to apprenticeship programs as a strategic response to the growing skills gap, with industry leaders such as GE, Walmart, IBM, and Johnson & Johnson leading the charge. These companies are moving beyond traditional hiring models, emphasizing hands-on training and skill development over formal academic credentials. GE, for instance, has partnered with community colleges to offer multi-year manufacturing apprenticeships that combine classroom instruction with technical work experience in fields like lean manufacturing (Hunt, 2020). Walmart, through its partnership with Guild Education, has integrated its in-house Academy training into credit-bearing programs, offering tuition-free pathways for workers in retail and supply chain management (Glover, 2021).

IBM's "New Collar" initiative exemplifies this shift, offering 12- to 24-month apprenticeships in areas like software engineering and cybersecurity, designed specifically for candidates without four-year degrees (IBM 2022). Johnson & Johnson has launched similar programs in manufacturing and healthcare technology, often in collaboration with local educational institutions to support workforce entry into high-tech roles (Johnson & Johnson, 2024). These models reflect a broader rethinking of workforce development—one that prioritizes applied learning, career mobility, and accessibility, particularly for underserved populations. As such, they are reshaping corporate talent pipelines while offering more inclusive pathways into specialized, high-demand fields.

In the USA, the Presidential Innovation Fellows (PIF) program is a type of dual apprenticeship program that recruits tech talent to the federal government for a one-year fellowship where fellows are embedded with a federal agency to complete a project as a senior advisor, for mutual benefit. Fellows often go back to the private sector with valuable networks, experience, and know-how about how the government works. In academia, every PhD student receives a several-year apprenticeship from their PhD advisor, allowing them to learn the ropes.

Conclusion

The traditional education model—shaped during the industrial age to meet the needs of factory-based economies—is no longer fit for purpose in a world of ambient intelligence, polycrisis pressures, and exponential technological change. As this chapter has shown, the emerging economy demands a new kind of learner: adaptable, self-directed, systemically aware, and deeply engaged in real-world contexts. Teaching futuristic skills is not merely a matter of curriculum reform or digital tool adoption. It requires a wholesale shift in how we organize, deliver, and validate learning—prioritizing practice over theory, collaboration over isolation, and iteration over perfection.

From the historical roots of vocational schooling in imperial Germany to the cutting-edge examples of learning-in-working on modern shop floors and digital apprenticeships, the pattern is clear: the future of learning is embedded in doing. Skills like systems thinking, agentic AI fluency, eco-awareness, and psycho-resilience are not best taught in static classrooms. They must be experienced, cocreated, and lived. Scalable models such as MIT's action labs, the scenario planning frameworks emerging in elite policy schools, and global apprenticeship movements are already laying the groundwork for distributed, lifelong, and deeply human learning systems.

But for this transformation to take hold at scale, we must move beyond institutional inertia. We need new governance models for learning, stronger mentorship networks, and more equitable access to experiential pathways. And perhaps most critically, we must reframe education not as preparation for work, but as active participation in shaping the future. In doing so, we will finally honor the central promise of education—not just to transmit knowledge, but to unleash the full potential of human ingenuity in a world where learning never stops.

References

Autor, David. 2019. *Work of the Past, Work of the Future*. NBER Working Paper No. 25588. Cambridge, MA: National Bureau of Economic Research. https://www.nber.org/papers/w25588.

Brown, John Seely, and Paul Duguid. 2017. *The Social Life of Information*. Boston: Harvard Business Review Press. https://hbr.org/product/the-social-life-of-information/1602-HBK-ENG.

Chermack, Thomas J. 2018. *Scenario Planning in Organizations: How to Create, Use, and Assess Scenarios*. 2nd ed. Oakland: Berrett-Koehler. https://www.bkconnection.com/books/title/scenario-planning-in-organizations.

Doxtdator, Brad. 2022. "The End of Knowing: Education in a World of Ubiquitous AI." *Journal of Futures Education* 1 (3): 21–34. https://www.futureseducation.org/articles/the-end-of-knowing.

Glover, Haley. 2021. "Study Shows the Benefits of Walmart Education Effort: Retail Giant's 'Live Better U' Program Is Proving Its Value." Lumina Foundation in partnership with Walmart Foundation, September 14. Lumina Foundation. https://www.luminafoundation.org/resource/study-shows-the-benefits-of-walmart-education-effort/.

Hoffman, Nancy, and Robert B. Schwartz. 2017. *Learning for Careers: The Pathways to Prosperity Network*. Cambridge: Harvard Education Press. https://www.hepg.org/hep-home/books/learning-for-careers.

Hunt, Berschel Robert. 2020. Apprenticeship Participation at GE Appliances: An Insider's Ethnographic Study of Apprentice Participation and Factors Contributing to Student Success. PhD diss., Western Kentucky University. TopSCHOLAR® Dissertations, Graduate School, Spring 2020. https://digitalcommons.wku.edu/diss/1177.

Johnson & Johnson. 2024. 2023 Annual Report. New Brunswick, NJ: Johnson & Johnson. https://s203.q4cdn.com/636242992/files/doc_downloads/Annual_meeting/2024/Johnson-Johnson-2023-Annual-Report.pdf.

Kuckelkorn, Jan, and Adam Davidson. 2020. "Factory Renaissance: Rethinking Learning in Industrial Workplaces." *Manufacturing Futures Review* 5 (2): 44–59. https://manufacturingfutures.mit.edu/review/article/factory-renaissance.

Lewin, Kurt. 1947. "Frontiers in Group Dynamics: Concept, Method and Reality in Social Science; Social Equilibria and Social Change." Human Relations 1 (1): 5–41. https://doi.org/10.1177/001872674700100103.

Miller, Michael T., and Myron L. Pope. 2022. "Bridging the Transition from Secondary to Postsecondary Education through Dual Enrollment Programs." *Journal of College Student Retention* 23 (3): 421–440. https://doi.org/10.1177/1521025120907943.

Norris, Matthew B., Jacob R. Grohs, and David B. Knight. 2022. "Investigating Student Approaches to Scenario-Based Assessments of Systems Thinking." Frontiers in Education 7: 1055403. https://doi.org/10.3389/feduc.2022.1055403.

Peschl, Markus, and Thomas Fundneider. 2017. "Emergent Innovation and Sustainable Change: Cultivating Capabilities for Future-Oriented Action." *The Learning Organization* 24 (1): 18–35. https://doi.org/10.1108/TLO-06-2016-0037.

Reich, Justin. 2020. *Failure to Disrupt: Why Technology Alone Can't Transform Education.* Cambridge, MA: Harvard University Press. https://www.hup.harvard.edu/catalog.php?isbn=9780674244698.

Scoblic, J. Peter. 2020. "Learning from the Future." *Harvard Business Review* 98 (4): 40–47. https://hbr.org/2020/07/learning-from-the-future.

Somerville, Mark, David Anderson, Hillary Berbeco, John Bourne, Jill Crisman, Diana Dabby, Helen Donis-Keller, Stephen Holt, Sherra Kerns, & Jr, D.V. & Robert Martello, Richard Miller, Michael Moody, Gill Pratt, Joanne Pratt, Christina Shea, Stephen Schiffman, Sarah Spence, Lynn Stein, and Yevgeniya Zastavker. 2005. "The Olin Curriculum: Thinking Toward the Future." *IEEE Transactions on Education* 48: 198–205. https://doi .org /10.1109/TE.2004.8429.

Vygotsky, L. S. 1978. *Mind in Society: The Development of Higher Psychological Processes.* Cambridge, MA: Harvard University Press.

Wack, Pierre. 1985. "Scenarios: Uncharted Waters Ahead." *Harvard Business Review* 63 (5): 73–89. https://hbr.org/1985/09/scenarios-uncharted-waters-ahead.

CHAPTER 18

CHARTING THE FUTURE OF WORK

The Roadmap to a Human+ Era

The future of work is unfolding before our eyes, driven by rapid technological innovations, shifting geopolitical landscapes, and an urgent call for sustainable practices. In this chapter, I explore three divergent scenarios that may shape the work environment over the next decade and beyond. These narratives are not mere predictions; they are roadmaps designed to help you navigate a future where the human condition is enhanced by technology—a vision often encapsulated in the term "Human+" (H+), which we explored at length in Chapter 4. This transhumanist perspective envisions a symbiotic relationship between biology and technology, where humans are augmented by advanced science and engineering to push beyond natural limits, achieving enhanced intelligence, longevity, and sensory perception.

At the heart of this transformation are two core skills: the ability to engage in deft human–AI collaboration—becoming an augmented human—and an innate interoperability mindset, the capacity to integrate and harmonize diverse systems, platforms, and organizations. Complementing these are 11 critical skills: eco-awareness, maker skills, mediation skills, megascale operations, mobility, risk aptitude, R&D hacks, psycho-resilience, socio-technical finesse, agentic AI management, and systems thinking. Together, these competencies will shape leadership and drive both individual and collective success in a future that demands a fundamental reset (Figure 18.1).

I now present three scenarios that illustrate possible trajectories for work, along with tailored strategies for students, parents, mid-career professionals, industrial workers, and educators. I also highlight which job categories may vanish or transform and offer guidance on how to use AI effectively without compromising our cognitive capacity for deep reflection (Table 18.1).

FIGURE 18.1 The future workforce reset.

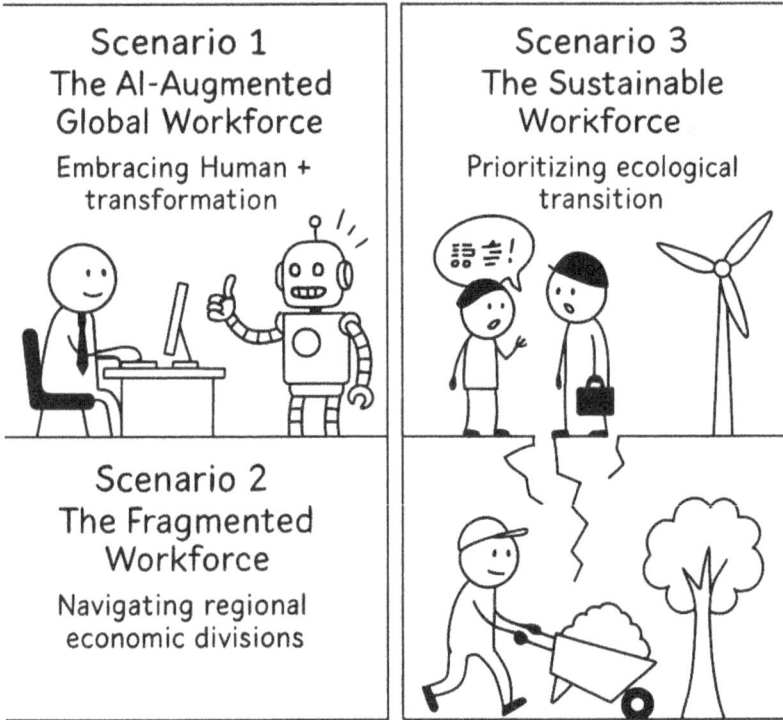

The AI-Augmented Global Workforce: Embracing the Human+ Transformation

Imagine a near future where artificial intelligence and digital technologies become seamless collaborators in our work lives. In this scenario, AI and machine learning systems have advanced to the point where they can take over repetitive and data-intensive tasks, liberating us to focus on creative problem-solving, strategic decision-making, and innovative pursuits. Yet, as we move into this AI-enhanced landscape, we must not abdicate our intellectual responsibilities. Instead, we must leverage AI to augment our capabilities while ensuring that critical reflection and analysis remain distinctly human pursuits. This is the essence of Human+—where technology serves as a tool for human flourishing rather than a substitute for human insight.

In this scenario, many traditional roles are set to vanish or change dramatically. Routine tasks such as data entry, basic customer service, and certain

TABLE 18.1 Three scenarios for the future of work.

	The AI-Augmented Global Workforce	*The Fragmented Workforce*	*The Sustainable & Equitable Workforce*
Core Vision	Embracing Human+ transformation through seamless AI collaboration	Navigating regional divisions in a polarized economic landscape	Leading ecological transition with sustainability at the core
Key Skills	Human–AI collaboration, digital literacy, socio-technical finesse	Mediation skills, cultural adaptability, regional expertise	Eco-awareness, systems thinking, maker skills
New Roles	Interoperability Catalyst, AI System Manager, Digital Workflow Designer	Regional Specialists, Cross-Border Mediators, Local Market Experts	Eco-Strategist, Sustainable Urban Planner, Green Technology Developer

For Scenario 1, see Chapter 4 on the challenges of Human+. For Scenario 2, see Chapter 15 on workforce risks and Chapter 16 on mastering gigascale. For Scenario 3, see Chapter 8 on the Eco-Strategist role.

aspects of diagnostic work in healthcare or legal research are highly vulnerable to automation. New roles, however, will emerge that focus on supervising AI systems, managing digital workflows, and critically interpreting machine outputs. One such role is that of the Interoperability Catalyst, a specialist who breaks down silos to ensure diverse systems communicate effectively—a role that becomes essential in multi-agent environments where software, intelligent, and robotic agents work together (Table 18.2).

Empowering Tomorrow's Innovators

For students, your journey begins by building a robust foundation in digital literacy and technical skills. Immerse yourself in coding, data analysis, and the fundamentals of artificial intelligence. However, do not simply delegate your critical thinking to AI systems. Instead, use AI as an aid for data gathering and pattern recognition, and then engage deeply with the results through your own analysis. Get involved in hackathons, maker spaces, and Fab Labs, where hands-on

TABLE 18.2 Scenario 1: The AI-augmented global workforce: Embracing Human+ transformation.

Stakeholder	Core Strategies
Students	Digital literacy + ethical foundations
Parents	Balance STEM with humanities education
Mid-Career	Position as technical-strategic bridge
Industrial	Master advanced systems operation
Educators	Design human–AI integrated curricula

experimentation and collaborative problem-solving are the norms. Supplement your technical education with courses in ethics, philosophy, and communication to develop mediation skills and socio-technical finesse. This balanced skill set will prepare you for roles where you guide and critically assess AI outputs. For Scenario 1, see Chapter 4 on the challenges of Human+.

For parents, begin by supporting your children's exploration of STEM fields by encouraging them to participate in coding clubs, robotics competitions, and online AI courses. At the same time, foster an appreciation for the humanities and ethical reflection by discussing the social and environmental impacts of technology. Ensure that their education integrates both technical prowess and a humanistic perspective, cultivating an innate interoperability mindset that bridges the gap between advanced technologies and human needs.

For mid-career professionals, embrace lifelong learning to remain competitive. Assess which elements of your current role might be automated and pursue upskilling in AI, digital transformation, and advanced analytics. Attend professional workshops and industry conferences that focus on human–AI collaboration. Use AI tools to produce preliminary analyses or data visualizations, but always refine these outputs with your own critical insights. This approach will help you maintain cognitive control over decision-making processes. Further, develop skills in megascale operations and R&D hacks to manage large-scale projects, and position yourself as an Interoperability Catalyst by bridging technical and strategic departments within your organization.

For industrial workers on the factory floor, embrace the integration of smart robotics and digital monitoring systems. Seek out employer-sponsored training that focuses on the operation and maintenance of these advanced tools. Build maker skills through hands-on workshops, and cultivate eco-awareness as industries pivot toward sustainable production practices. By acquiring an interoperability mindset, you can effectively navigate the interface between human operators and AI-driven systems, thereby ensuring that you remain indispensable in an evolving manufacturing landscape.

For educators (whether in High School or College), you must prepare students for an AI-augmented world by integrating human–AI collaboration into curricula. At the high school level, include modules on digital literacy that go beyond basic computer skills to cover introductory coding, data analysis, and ethical considerations in technology. Encourage project-based learning that involves using AI tools for research while emphasizing critical reflection. At the college level, design interdisciplinary courses that combine technical subjects with courses in ethics, systems thinking, and human-centered design. Foster maker spaces and innovation labs where students can experiment with emerging technologies and develop hands-on skills. Emphasize the emerging role of the Interoperability Catalyst, preparing students to break down silos and facilitate integration across diverse systems. Collaborate with industry partners to ensure that curriculum content remains cutting-edge and relevant to real-world applications.

Fragmentation Amid Geopolitical Uncertainty: Navigating a Divided World

In contrast to the seamless integration envisioned in the AI-augmented scenario, another plausible future is one characterized by geopolitical tensions and protectionist policies. Here, the global economy fractures into regional clusters, each governed by distinct political, regulatory, and cultural norms. In this scenario, the smooth flow of talent, capital, and technology is disrupted, requiring a nuanced and flexible skill set to navigate complex, localized environments. In a fragmented world, the ability to mediate between global trends and regional realities becomes crucial.

Certain jobs—especially those reliant on standardized global processes, such as central supply chain management or roles within multinational conglomerates—might shrink or transform. Instead, there will be a heightened demand for professionals who possess deep knowledge of local market dynamics, regulatory environments, and cultural subtleties, as well as the ability to bridge regional divides.

Equipping Regional Pioneers

For students, you should prepare to thrive in a complex, regionally diverse world by building a versatile skill set. In addition to developing digital and technical proficiencies, immerse yourself in the study of international relations, cultural diversity, and local economic histories. Learn multiple languages to enhance your ability to navigate different cultural contexts. Engage in exchange programs, community projects, and Model United Nations simulations that sharpen your mediation skills and socio-technical finesse. This broad educational experience will equip you to understand and mediate the tensions between global innovation and local practice.

For parents, you should encourage your children to cultivate both a global perspective and a deep understanding of their local context. Support their participation in international programs, language courses, and cultural exchange initiatives. Discuss current events and geopolitical developments at home to build their awareness of the complex forces shaping our world. By fostering a balanced educational approach, you help your children develop an innate interoperability mindset that will be essential in bridging global trends with regional needs.

For mid-career professionals, I'd recommend to expand your expertise beyond narrow specializations to navigate a fragmented economic landscape. Enroll in executive education programs focusing on international business strategy, regulatory compliance, and geopolitical risk management. Develop robust mediation skills by engaging in cross-border projects and building networks with professionals from diverse regions. This broad perspective will help you serve as an Interoperability Catalyst, aligning global strategies with regional execution. Understanding local market dynamics will be key to adapting your organization's approach in a world of increasingly segmented economies.

For industrial workers, keep in mind that local adaptability is crucial in regions affected by geopolitical fragmentation. Take advantage of community-based training programs that emphasize both technical skills and local regulatory knowledge. Engage in workshops that merge eco-awareness with maker skills to adapt to regional shifts in production practices and sustainability

TABLE 18.3 Scenario 2: The fragmented workforce: Navigating regional economic divisions.

Stakeholder	Core Strategies
Students	Multi-language + regional expertise
Parents	Foster global-local understanding
Mid-Career	Develop cross-border capabilities
Industrial	Adapt to localized requirements
Educators	Incorporate geopolitical context

standards. Participate in local professional groups to learn strategies for navigating regulatory changes and integrating technological advancements in a localized context. This dual focus will enhance your resilience and ensure that you remain a vital part of your community's economic fabric. For Scenario 2, see Chapter 15 on workforce risks and Chapter 16 on mastering gigascale.

For educators (whether in High School or College), you must prepare students to excel in a world marked by regional disparities and localized governance. At the high school level, incorporate curricula that explore geopolitical history, cultural studies, and regional economics alongside digital literacy and technology courses. Use project-based learning to simulate real-world scenarios where students must navigate complex sociopolitical landscapes. At the college level, offer interdisciplinary courses that combine international relations, regional studies, and technical training, emphasizing mediation skills and socio-technical finesse. Establish partnerships with local organizations and governments to provide students with practical experiences and internships that reinforce their understanding of regional dynamics. Encourage educators to stay informed about global trends and to integrate current geopolitical developments into their teaching, ensuring that students can apply a global perspective to local challenges.

A Sustainable and Equitable Work Ecosystem: Leading the Green Revolution

The third scenario envisions a future where sustainability and social equity are not peripheral but central to work. In this narrative, environmental stewardship and social justice drive business strategies and workforce development. Here, success hinges on integrating eco-awareness, maker skills, and systems thinking with the core competencies of human–AI collaboration and interoperability. The emergence of roles like the Eco-Strategist—professionals who design and implement strategies that integrate environmental considerations into every facet of operations—illustrates the shift toward a greener, more equitable economy.

Traditional roles in industries with high environmental impacts, such as fossil fuel extraction and conventional manufacturing, are likely to diminish. Meanwhile, new opportunities will arise in green technologies, renewable energy, sustainable urban planning, and related fields. Organizations will increasingly value professionals who can manage megascale operations, navigate complex risk landscapes, and implement innovative R&D hacks that drive systemic change (Table 18.4).

TABLE 18.4 Scenario 3: The sustainable workforce: Prioritizing ecological transition.

Stakeholder	Core Strategies
Students	Environmental + technical integration
Parents	Nurture eco-awareness + ethics
Mid-Career	Lead sustainable transformation
Industrial	Master green production methods
Educators	Embed sustainability in curriculum

For Scenario 3, see Chapter 8 on the Eco-Strategist role.

Cultivating Green Leaders for the Future

For students, if you aspire to be a pioneer in a sustainable work ecosystem, pursue interdisciplinary programs that merge environmental science, digital technology, and ethics. Engage in internships and projects focused on renewable energy, sustainable urban planning, or social entrepreneurship. Build your maker skills by participating in design challenges and hackathons aimed at solving environmental problems. Simultaneously, refine your systems thinking to understand the long-term impacts of decisions and to manage large-scale sustainability projects. Use AI as a tool to simulate environmental impacts and optimize green solutions, but always ensure that your critical analysis guides these efforts.

For parents, try to support your children's passion for sustainability by encouraging participation in environmental clubs, community clean-ups, and local green initiatives. Advocate for school programs that integrate eco-awareness and systems thinking into the curriculum. Discuss the importance of balancing economic growth with ecological preservation and promote activities that develop both technical and ethical perspectives on sustainability. This holistic approach will empower your children to become future leaders in the green revolution.

For mid-career professionals, keep in mind that transitioning to a sustainable work ecosystem is an opportunity to redefine your career trajectory. Seek advanced training in sustainable business practices, renewable energy innovations, and green technology. Develop an entrepreneurial mindset that values long-term impact and ethical leadership. Enhance your capabilities in megascale operations and risk management to lead large-scale sustainability projects. Engage with professional networks dedicated to corporate social responsibility and consider roles that allow you to act as an Eco-Strategist, integrating environmental principles into core business strategies. In doing so, you will position yourself as a leader in the global shift toward sustainability while maintaining your strategic edge.

For industrial workers, as manufacturing processes evolve toward eco-friendly practices, it is essential to update your skills accordingly. Pursue training in sustainable production techniques and environmental compliance. Develop maker skills that allow you to innovate on the factory floor, and adopt an interoperability mindset that facilitates the integration of new sustainable technologies with traditional practices. Strengthen your resilience through targeted training in risk aptitude and psycho-resilience, ensuring that you can adapt to rapid technological and regulatory changes. Participation in local community initiatives will also reinforce your role as a key contributor to a greener economy.

For educators (whether in High School or College), you would do well to champion sustainability as a core element of the curriculum. At the high school level, integrate environmental science and ethics into technology courses, and develop project-based learning modules that challenge students to devise sustainable solutions for real-world problems. At the college level, design interdisciplinary courses that blend sustainability, digital technology, and business strategy. Encourage students to engage in community-based projects that address local environmental challenges, and facilitate internships with organizations focused on green innovation. Additionally, foster maker spaces and innovation labs that allow students to experiment with sustainable technologies and systems thinking. By preparing students to think holistically about ecological and social impacts, you help shape future leaders who can drive systemic change in a sustainable work ecosystem.

The Role of Wild Cards: Adapting to Uncertainty

While these three scenarios provide structured visions of the future of work, the landscape remains inherently unpredictable. Wild cards—unexpected breakthroughs or disruptions—could dramatically alter these trajectories. For example, a sudden breakthrough in AI and robotics might accelerate the transition to a Human+ workforce, demanding an immediate boost in skills such as risk aptitude, megascale operations, and R&D hacks. In such a case, mid-career professionals and industrial workers must rapidly update their expertise while reinforcing their interoperability mindset.

Alternatively, major geopolitical shifts could intensify fragmentation, with protectionist policies or regional conflicts leading to deeper local divisions. In this context, a heightened focus on regional studies, mediation skills, and cultural mobility becomes even more crucial. Students and professionals alike should embrace diversity, learn multiple languages, and build networks with local experts to navigate a more insular economic landscape.

Environmental catastrophes also serve as potent wild cards. Such events may catalyze the shift toward a sustainable work ecosystem by forcing rapid innovation in green technologies, or they might cause short-term disruptions that overwhelm existing systems. In either event, all groups should continuously refine their eco-awareness and systems thinking skills while bolstering psycho-resilience and socio-technical finesse. This dual approach enables rapid crisis response while maintaining long-term strategic focus.

Finally, significant cybersecurity breaches or other technological disruptions could undermine trust in digital systems, impacting the AI-augmented workforce most acutely. In these turbulent times, strengthening digital risk management and maintaining a vigilant interoperability mindset are essential. Whether you are a mid-career professional, industrial worker, or educator, staying updated on the latest security protocols and ensuring that AI tools augment—rather than replace—critical human judgment will be crucial to sustaining progress.

Conclusion: Resetting for a Human+ Future

The future of work is multifaceted and dynamic, shaped by the interplay of technological innovation, geopolitical shifts, and the imperative for sustainability. In the three scenarios explored—the AI-Augmented Global Workforce, fragmentation amid geopolitical uncertainty, and a Sustainable and Equitable Work Ecosystem—success will be built on two core skills: the ability to engage in seamless human–AI collaboration and the capacity to integrate diverse systems through an innate interoperability mindset. These foundations, when complemented by 11 critical skills—from eco-awareness and maker skills to mediation, megascale operations, AI tool management, and systems thinking—will empower us to lead in an era of Human+.

For students, the journey involves immersing yourself in interdisciplinary learning, harnessing digital tools to augment your creativity, and developing the soft skills that will enable you to navigate both global and local landscapes. For parents, your guidance in nurturing both technical and humanistic values is indispensable—help your children build a balanced skill set that prepares them for an ever-evolving world. Mid-career professionals must commit to life-long learning, updating their expertise to serve as Interoperability Catalysts and innovative leaders. Industrial workers should seize training opportunities that enable you to thrive alongside emerging technologies, contributing to a sustainable and resilient production environment.

Educators, both at the high school and college levels, play a critical role in shaping this future. By integrating cutting-edge technological literacy with ethical, environmental, and socio-cultural insights, you are preparing the next generation to be both creative innovators and responsible global citizens. Your efforts in building interdisciplinary curricula, fostering maker spaces, and establishing industry partnerships will ensure that your students are ready to lead in the Human+ era.

Wild cards and unforeseen events will undoubtedly challenge our expectations, but by developing these core and complementary skills, we can transform uncertainty into opportunity. As we step into a future where technology augments our natural capabilities—where Human+ is not just a vision but a lived reality—we have the chance to redefine what it means to work, to lead, and to thrive. Embrace the reset, invest in continuous learning, and become part of the generation that bridges the gap between human potential and technological innovation. The roadmap is clear: a future of work that is dynamic, inclusive, and truly transformative awaits.

CONCLUSION

Creating the *Platinum Workforce*

When we look back at the twenty-first century, what will we remember most? This conclusion must be read in light of the journey taken: Part I set out the cascading disruptions, Part II assembled the skills architecture, and Part III applied those skills to risk and foresight. Wars and catastrophes will certainly leave their mark. But just as enduring may be the unprecedented transformations in work, knowledge, and human agency. In this book, I've argued that *skills*—not just jobs—are the essential scaffolding of society's ability to adapt. The rise of AI, environmental volatility, and social upheaval demand a radically more resilient, strategic, and human-centric response to change.

In Section I, we captured the cascading changes shaking the foundations of labor and value. From the erosion of stable employment models to the employer's growing preference for machines over humans, these early chapters called for an urgent reevaluation of work's meaning and structure. In Section II, we mapped a new skill architecture, one no longer organized around tasks or credentials, but around agility, augmentation, and systems-level insight. From the Human+ collaborator to the AI Agent orchestrator, we envisioned a workforce that learns how to think, adapt, mediate, and build across evolving interfaces. Finally, in Section III, we examined how to scale these competencies. We explored how to manage skills like infrastructure, teach them through cognitive scaffolding, and ultimately design governance systems for a future of continuous, high-stakes learning and interdependence (Figure C.1).

This is the terrain from which the *platinum workforce* must emerge. The metaphor matters. Platinum evokes durability, rarity, catalytic properties, and value. These are not adjectives we have typically assigned to the labor force. And yet—across history—civilizations have achieved greatness through the mobilization of sophisticated, skilled populations. From the artisans of imperial China and the cathedral builders of medieval Europe to the engineers of

FIGURE C.1 Taxonomy of twenty-first-century workforce skills.

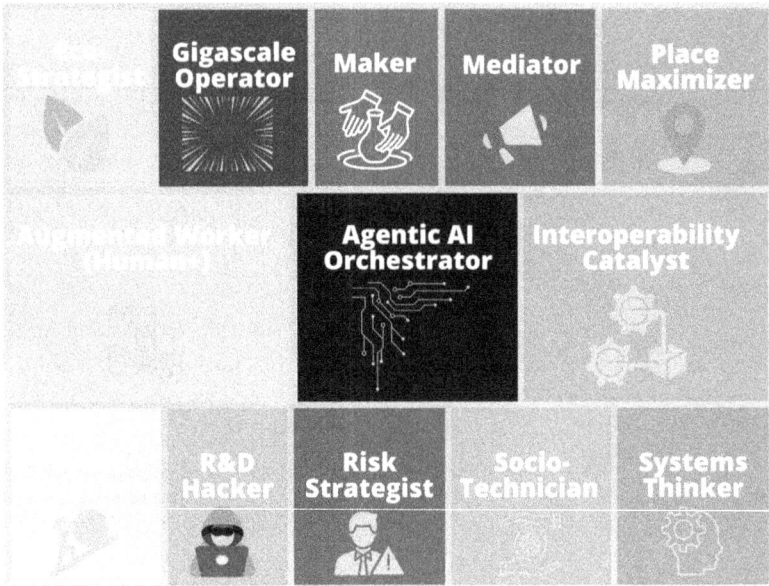

the Apollo program and the programmers of the internet age, history's triumphs have always depended on aligned, capable, future-facing people.

But this time, something is different. The feat that now lies ahead is not merely one of technical construction or intellectual discovery. It is one of strategic coordination across polycrisis: environmental, geopolitical, technological, and moral. The challenge is not just to *solve problems*, but to design an adaptive global workforce that can shift—from infrastructure rebuilding to emergency response, from AI alignment to pandemic mitigation—on a dime. This is why the *platinum workforce* is not an elite—it is an egalitarian platform for survival and regeneration.

One of the most urgent developments shaping this need is the rise of agentic AI—systems that reason, act, and learn independently across workflows. These are no longer just tools; they are autonomous collaborators. Future work will demand the ability to design, monitor, and orchestrate fleets of intelligent agents. Prompting is dead. Orchestration lives. And this shift requires new literacies: the ability to create cognitive feedback loops, persist agent memory, define system roles, and govern behavior across distributed ecosystems of human and machine actors. *Agent managers* will be the new operators—hybrid roles that blend engineering, strategy, and ethical discernment. And that leads us back to the core idea: Skills are being rewritten. What once sat on the technical margins—AI literacy, systems thinking, psychological resilience, and interoperability—is now foundational. It is not enough to know things. We must know how to think in loops: plan > act > evaluate > refine. We must move beyond content mastery toward *cognitive design*—where humans build the scaffolding for insight, discovery, and action.

This is what the *platinum workforce* must embody. It must be flexible, collaborative, and ready to redeploy toward global needs—not just personal ambitions. It must internalize the moats of the future: proprietary data, elegant interfaces, and last-mile integration of human–AI workflows. It must center *judgment*, not just output; *narrative coherence*, not just information; and *discernment*, not just decision trees. And here's the reality: we are, for the first time in history, on the brink of being able to educate every human on the planet to a similar level of conceptual sophistication. Mobile platforms, AI tutors, and real-time feedback systems offer an infrastructure for planetary learning. What's missing is not the tech. It's the vision—the willingness to reframe schools, reimagine institutions, and rebuild the interface between learning and labor.

That is why I wrote this book. After two years researching existential risk and scanning countless mitigation strategies, I concluded that skills—not tech, not ideology, not geopolitics—are the *critical ingredient* in society's agile response to change. Yet skills are still debated in terms of employability, not survivability. The Platinum Workforce's ambitious and *civilization-enhancing skills* are not abstract. They are real. And they matter.

The *platinum workforce* can be thought of as an antidote to the downsides of humanity's quest for "progress" through uncontrolled economic growth. It offers a different kind of prestige than platinum—not in wealth, but in wisdom; not in extraction, but in durability. The number and scope of problems gathering on the horizon will give humanity its greatest challenge yet—and its greatest opportunity.

What began in Part I as a taxonomy of disruption and cascading change, and in Part II as a skills architecture for the workforce, has here, in Part III, been tested against risk, resilience, and foresight. This continuity shows that the platinum workforce is at once a skills system, a paradigm, and a societal blueprint.

For readers seeking clarity on the key terms and concepts that anchor this book, a short glossary follows. It serves as a reference guide to the skills, roles, and paradigms that frame the platinum workforce.

To my children, who will be entering the workforce in the next 5 to 15 years, I say: we can do this. You can do this.

GLOSSARY

AI (Artificial) Intelligence	Computer systems that perform tasks typically requiring human intelligence. Large-scale infrastructure or industrial projects, typically costing $1 billion or more, flanked by an emerging category, Gigaprojects ($20B+).
AI Agent	An autonomous software entity that performs tasks, manages workflows, or interacts with humans and machines to achieve goals.
AI Orchestrator	A system or role coordinating multiple AI agents and human workers to deliver complex outcomes.
Agentic AI	AI systems designed with the capacity to act independently and make decisions in pursuit of defined objectives.
Augmented Intelligence	AI that enhances human decision-making and performance rather than replacing human input.
Cascading Risks	Interconnected disruptions where one failure amplifies others across systems.
Digital Twin	A real-time digital replica of a physical object, system, or process used for monitoring, analysis, and optimization.
Eco-Awareness	The skill of recognizing, understanding, and acting on the ecological impacts of decisions and behaviors.

Eco-Strategist	A formal role that institutionalizes eco-awareness within organizations by embedding ecological intelligence into strategy and governance.
Flow	A state of deep focus and immersion where skill and challenge are balanced.
Foresight	Systematic exploration of possible futures to inform strategy and decisions.
Human+	Enhancement of human capabilities through technology integration; both a paradigm and a skillset.
Human –Machine Resource Management (HMRM)	Discipline aligning human and AI resources for organizational effectiveness.
Interoperability	The ability of systems to work together and exchange information seamlessly.
Megaprojects	Large-scale infrastructure or industrial projects, typically costing $1 billion or more.
Platinum Workforce	A resilient, adaptive workforce combining human skills with AI augmentation.
Polycrisis	Multiple interconnected global crises occurring simultaneously.
Reskilling / Upskilling	Training workers in new or advanced skills to adapt to changing technologies.
RPA (Robotic Process Automation)	Software robots automating repetitive, rules-based tasks.
Skills Taxonomy	Classification of competencies (e.g., Human+, systems thinking, eco-awareness) used to assess workforce capabilities.
Socio-Technical	An approach integrating social and technical factors in system design.
STEM	Science, Technology, Engineering, Mathematics.
Synthetic Biology	Engineering biological systems for useful purposes.
Systems Thinking	A holistic approach that views organizations and problems as interconnected systems.
T-shaped Worker	An individual with deep expertise in one domain and broad competence across others.

INDEX